Taxation, Responsiveness and Accountability in Sub-Saharan Africa

It is increasingly argued that bargaining between citizens and governments over tax collection can provide a foundation for the development of responsive and accountable governance in developing countries. However, while intuitively attractive, surprisingly little research has captured the reality and complexity of this relationship in practice. This book provides the most complete treatment of the connections between taxation and accountability in developing countries, providing both new evidence and an invaluable starting point for future research. Drawing on cross-country econometric evidence and detailed case studies from Ghana, Kenya and Ethiopia, Wilson Prichard shows that reliance on taxation has, in fact, increased responsiveness and accountability by expanding the political power wielded by taxpayers. Critically, however, processes of tax bargaining have been highly varied, frequently long term and contextually contingent. Capturing this diversity provides novel insight into politics in developing countries and how tax reform can be designed to encourage broader governance gains.

WILSON PRICHARD is an assistant professor in the Department of Political Science and Munk School of Global Affairs at the University of Toronto, Research Fellow at the Institute of Development Studies, United Kingdom, and Research Director of the International Centre for Tax and Development. He works closely with national governments, civil society groups and international organizations on strategies to strengthen tax reform and encourage state-society bargaining over taxation.

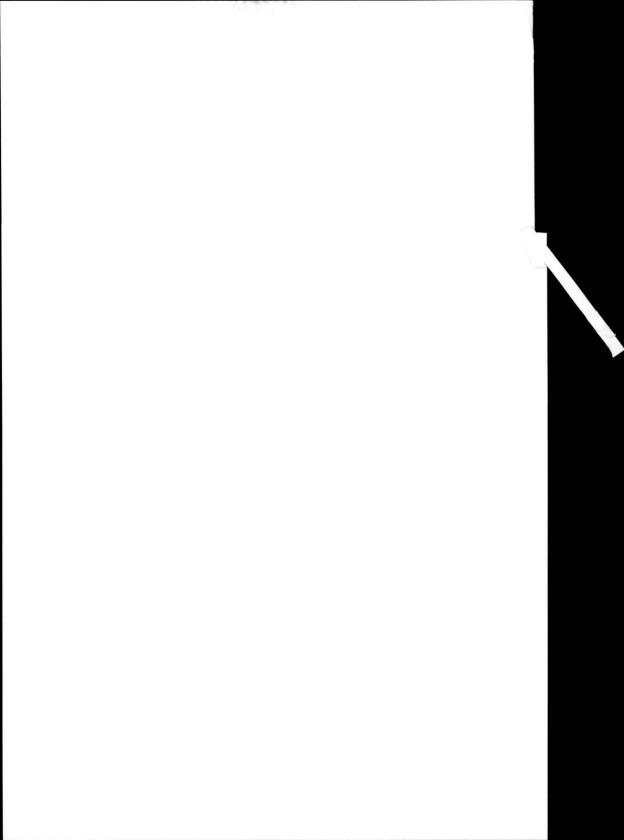

Taxation, Responsiveness and Accountability in Sub-Saharan Africa

The Dynamics of Tax Bargaining

Wilson Prichard
University of Toronto

CAMBRIDGE
UNIVERSITY PRESS

University Printing House, Cambridge CB2 8BS, United Kingdom

Cambridge University Press is part of the University of Cambridge.

It furthers the University's mission by disseminating knowledge in the pursuit of education, learning and research at the highest international levels of excellence.

www.cambridge.org
Information on this title: www.cambridge.org/9781107110861

© Wilson Prichard 2015

This publication is in copyright. Subject to statutory exception and to the provisions of relevant collective licensing agreements, no reproduction of any part may take place without the written permission of Cambridge University Press.

First published 2015

A catalogue record for this publication is available from the British Library

Library of Congress Cataloguing in Publication data
Prichard, Wilson, author.
Taxation, responsiveness, and accountability in Sub-Saharan Africa : the dynamics of tax bargaining / Wilson Prichard.
    pages cm
Includes bibliographical references and index.
1. Taxation – Ghana. 2. Taxation – Kenya. 3. Taxation – Ethiopia. 4. Public administration – Ghana. 5. Public administration – Kenya. 6. Public administration – Ethiopia. I. Title.
HJ3021P75   2015
336.200967 – dc23   2015027738

ISBN 978-1-107-11086-1 Hardback

Cambridge University Press has no responsibility for the persistence or accuracy of URLs for external or third-party internet websites referred to in this publication, and does not guarantee that any content on such websites is, or will remain, accurate or appropriate.

Contents

List of figures		*page* vii
List of tables		viii
List of abbreviations		ix

1 Introduction: taxation, responsiveness and accountability in developing countries — 1
  1.1 Linking taxation, responsiveness and accountability — 4
  1.2 The extent and limits of cross-country econometric evidence — 8
  1.3 The importance of detailed country-level research — 24
  1.4 The argument of the book — 28
  1.5 Revenue, tax bargaining and the politics of development — 31
  1.6 Research strategy and methodology — 35
  1.7 Structure of the book — 43
  Statistical appendix — 43

2 Linking taxation, responsiveness and accountability: theoretical model and research strategy — 48
  2.1 The lessons of history: diverse pathways linking taxation and political change — 49
  2.2 A model of tax bargaining — 54
  2.3 Narrowing the focus and defining specific outcomes — 62
  2.4 Contextual factors affecting tax bargaining — 68
  2.5 Incorporating context and strategic interaction in the model — 77
  2.6 Conclusions — 81

3 Taxation, responsiveness and accountability in Ghana, 1981–2008 — 83
  3.1 The political economy of taxation in Ghana, 1981–2008 — 84
  3.2 Evidence of tax bargaining — 97
  3.3 The role of contextual factors — 111
  3.4 Conclusions — 116
  Appendix — 117

4 Direct and indirect tax bargaining in Kenya, 1963–2008 — 119
  4.1 The political economy of taxation in Kenya — 120
  4.2 Taxation, responsiveness and accountability in Kenya — 137
  4.3 Explaining patterns of tax bargaining — 146

	4.4	Conclusions	157
		Appendix	158

5 **The quiet politics of taxation in Ethiopia, 1974–2008**   160
    5.1 The Derg and the end of the feudal state, 1974–1991   162
    5.2 Liberalization and decentralization under the EPRDF,
        1991–2008   169
    5.3 The dynamics of regional government taxation   185
    5.4 Taxation, responsiveness and accountability in contemporary
        Ethiopia   189
    5.5 Explaining outcomes: political, economic and social barriers to
        tax bargaining   199
    5.6 Conclusions   208
        Appendix   210

6 **Understanding tax bargaining: complexity and contingency**   212
    6.1 Taxation, responsiveness and accountability: reviewing the
        evidence   212
    6.2 Causal processes and outcomes   217
    6.3 Contextual factors and tax bargaining   223
    6.4 Conclusions   246

7 **Looking forward: broader messages, policy lessons and directions for further research**   248
    7.1 A broader and more nuanced understanding of tax bargaining   249
    7.2 From broad claims to specific policy implications   251
    7.3 Limitations and future research   261

Key interviews   267
References   272
Index   293

Figures

1.1 Relationship between tax reliance and democracy using
    country averages, 1990–2010 *page* 12
1.2 Relationship between total tax revenue and democracy using
    country averages, 1990–2010 13
1.3 Relationship between total non-tax revenue and democracy
    using country averages, 1990–2010 14
2.1 Taxation and the expansion of responsiveness and
    accountability 62
2.2 Strategic interaction and tax bargaining 79
3.1 Ghana: total revenue by component, 1982–2008 117
3.2 Ghana: direct tax revenue by component, 1982–2008 117
3.3 Ghana: indirect tax revenue by component, 1982–2008 118
3.4 Ghana: trade tax revenues by component, 1982–2008 118
3.5 Ghana: expenditure by category, 1982–2008 118
4.1 Kenya: composition of government revenue, 1971–2008 158
4.2 Kenya: government expenditure and revenue, 1971–2008 159
5.1 Ethiopia: composition of revenue, 1949–2010 210
5.2 Ethiopia: expenditure and revenue, 1949–2010 210
5.3 Ethiopia: composition of regional tax revenue, 1996–2007 211

Tables

1.1 Impact of composition of government revenue on
    continuous measures of democracy *page* 16
1.2 Impact of composition of government revenue on likelihood
    of regime transitions 18
1.3 Likelihood of transitions to democracy 20
1.4 Effect of tax reliance, total tax and non-tax revenue on
    polity, using different lags 22
1.5 Effect of tax reliance, total tax and non-tax revenue on
    regime, using random effects logit model and different lags 23
1.6 Key characteristics of the case study countries 38
2.1 Contextual factors shaping the potential for tax bargaining 71
3.1 Ghana: the role of contextual factors 112
4.1 Kenya: the role of contextual factors 147
5.1 Ethiopia: the role of contextual factors 201
6.1 Summary of key episodes of tax bargaining 216

Abbreviations

AGI	Association of Ghanaian Industries
ATAF	African Tax Administration Forum
CDFs	Constituency Development Funds
CEPAL	Comisión Económica para América Latina y el Caribe
CEPS	Customs, Excise and Preventive Services
CGD	Centre for Governance and Development
CJA	Committee for Joint Action
CMB	Cocoa Marketing Board
COMESA	Common Market for Eastern and Southern Africa
CVC	Citizens' Vetting Committees
EPLF	Eritrean People's Liberation Front
EPRDF	Ethiopian People's Revolutionary Democratic Front
EPRP	Ethiopian People's Revolutionary Party
ERP	Economic Recovery Program
ETR	Electronic Tax Registers
GDP	Gross Domestic Product
GET	Ghana Education Trust
GFS	Government Finance Statistics
GMM	Generalized method of moments
GPRTU	Ghana Private Road Transport Union
GPT	Graduated Personal Tax
GUTA	Ghana Union of Traders Association
HIPC	Highly Indebted Poor Countries
ICRG	International Country Risk Guide
ICTD	International Centre for Tax and Development
GRD	Government Revenue Database
IFIs	International financial institutions
IMF	International Monetary Fund
IRS	Internal Revenue Service
IT	Information Technology
KARA	Kenya Alliance of Resident Associations
KEPSA	Kenya Private Sector Alliance

List of abbreviations

KLDA	Karen and Langata District Association
KRA	Kenya Revenue Authority
LTU	Large Taxpayers Unit
MPs	Members of Parliament
NARC	National Rainbow Coalition
NDC	National Democratic Congress
NHIL	National Health Insurance Levy
NHIS	National Health Insurance Scheme
NISCOF	Nairobi Informal Sector Confederation
NPP	National Patriotic Party
NRL	National Reconstruction Levy
NRS	National Revenue Secretariat
NTA	National Taxpayers' Association
ODA	Official Development Assistance
OECD	Organisation for Economic Cooperation and Development
OLS	Ordinary least squares
PA	Peasant associations
PNDC	Provisional National Defence Council
RML	Road Maintenance Levy
SMEs	Small and medium enterprises
SOEs	State-owned enterprises
SSA	Sub-Saharan Africa
TMP	Tax Modernization Program
TPLF	Tigray People's Liberation Front
UBA	United Business Association
VAT	Value-added tax
WB	World Bank
WCDI	We Can Do It
WGI	Worldwide Governance Indicators
YES	Youth Employment Scheme

1 Introduction
Taxation, responsiveness and accountability in developing countries

Scholars have long argued that bargaining between citizens and governments over the collection of tax revenue can provide a foundation for the development of responsive and accountable governance. Taxation lies at the foundation of the relationships between governments and their citizens, and governments seeking expanded tax revenue are likely to face demands from taxpayers for reciprocal service provision and expanded accountability in exchange for tax payments. This intuition is reflected in well-known accounts capturing the role of tax bargaining in the emergence of representative political institutions in early modern Europe, and in the well-known American revolutionary slogan "no taxation without representation."

However, our understanding of these relationships in contemporary developing countries has remained surprisingly limited, despite growing scholarly and public attention. Research has provided growing but still fragmented evidence, while offering little insight into either the specific causal pathways underpinning these relationships or the conditions under which bargaining over taxation is most likely to yield broader governance gains. This book seeks to fill this empirical gap through a detailed investigation of the links between taxation, responsiveness and accountability in three countries in sub-Saharan Africa: Ghana, Kenya and Ethiopia. The book presents detailed evidence that bargaining over taxation has played an important role in spurring expanded responsiveness and accountability in all three countries. However, contrary to any simple image of relatively explicit and predictable bargaining over taxation, the book stresses that these connections have been both complex and contingent. The links between taxation, responsiveness and accountability have been frequently indirect, long-term and difficult to observe, while the emergence of positive connections has hinged on specific features of tax systems and of the broader political and economic environment.

The positive potential of tax bargaining is reflected nowhere more clearly than experiences in Ghana in the mid-1990s. The government of President Jerry Rawlings had come to power through a military coup in

1981, before winning elections in 1992 that were boycotted by the opposition. Throughout that period large-scale public protests and opposition remained almost entirely absent, owing to the repressive strength of the state and the weakness of the fragmented political opposition. This began to change decisively in 1995 when the government, facing growing fiscal deficits, moved to introduce a new value-added tax on goods and services. The government quickly, and unexpectedly, found itself confronted by nationwide protests that brought tens of thousands of people into the streets for the first time in more than a decade. Crucially, while opposition to the tax initially spurred these protests, they quickly came to encompass broader demands for political liberalization, while playing a crucial role in unifying a previously fragmented opposition. Ultimately, these protests helped to catalyse a significant political transformation, reflected in more open national elections and an increasingly inclusive approach to policymaking. Reflecting on these events, senior political leaders recall the protests as having been a pivotal moment in accelerating political change,[1] while those involved in the protests argue that it was "the first time they [the government] felt like they could lose power"[2] and was evidence that in Ghana, "taxes have always provided a focal point for public mobilization. Have provided momentum for the resistance."[3]

This experience is exemplary of the kind of explicit tax bargaining evoked by existing accounts, and speaks to the potential for conflicts over taxation to spur broader governance gains. However, this example provides only an incomplete picture of the more complex and contingent connections that have linked taxation, responsiveness and accountability. Consistent with popular narratives, tax bargaining has in some cases involved relatively explicit government concessions in response to short-term public mobilization or threats of non-compliance. However, in most cases the connections between taxation, responsiveness and accountability have been comparatively implicit, indirect and long-term. Rather than involving explicit government concessions, these connections have been grounded in the role of conflicts over taxation in undermining the longer-term fiscal positions of unpopular governments and strengthening long-term political engagement and mobilization amongst taxpayers.

In some cases popular resistance to taxation has not led to explicit bargaining or compromise, but has instead undermined the fiscal

---

[1] Personal interviews on 21 March 2008 with Former Minister in PNDC and NDC governments, and on 10 April 2008 with former Deputy Minister of Finance and senior official in PNDC and NDC governments.
[2] Personal interview on 17 March 2008 with senior leader, Committee for Joint Action.
[3] Ibid.

foundations of the state and helped to precipitate changes in government over the medium or long term. This was the case, for example, in Kenya in the late 1990s, where public resistance to taxation failed to prompt immediate government concessions. Instead, persistent and politically motivated tax evasion progressively undermined the fiscal position of the increasingly unpopular government. By starving the government of revenue, this tax resistance helped to precipitate a political transition in 2002, as the incumbent government was removed from power. In turn, the new government brought meaningful improvements in accountability, while explicitly linking improved tax collection to the expansion of popular social programs. While the threat of tax resistance thus shaped the expansion of accountability, this relationship did not reflect explicit bargaining between taxpayers and the government. Instead, it reflected unresolved conflict over taxation, and the ability of taxpayers to use tax resistance as a strategy for undermining an unpopular government.

In other cases conflict over taxation has helped to fuel longer-term political engagement and the strengthening of civil society, including the coalescing of more constructive political engagement by business associations. One such example comes from Ethiopia, where the expansion of business taxes at the regional level led local business associations to become increasingly engaged with government. Despite significant continuing constraints on democracy, the result was an expanded role for businesses in overseeing tax collection as well as the creation of new forums for consultation between the regional government and taxpayers. An alternative example comes from Kenya, where conflicts over the introduction of electronic tax registers to strengthen tax compliance prompted the mobilization and strengthening of the United Business Association (UBA) to represent medium-sized firms. While business protests failed to secure immediate government concessions, they established the UBA as an important new political actor, with longer-term implications for engagement between the state and business. None of these examples fit a simple image of explicit and immediate tax bargaining, but they are all essential to a full understanding of the links between taxation, responsiveness and accountability.

Unsurprisingly, the particular forms that tax bargaining has taken, and the particular outcomes that have emerged, have been heavily dependent on the specific features of tax systems and tax reforms, and on the broader political and economic environment. More simply, the experiences explored in this book make clear that while conflicts over taxation *can* emerge as an important spur to broader governance gains, these connections are far from guaranteed. Specifically, this book argues that relatively explicit forms of tax bargaining have been more likely when governments have faced significant revenue pressure, when taxpayers have enjoyed significant capacity for both collective action and tax resistance, when institutions have existed to facilitate bargaining between taxpayers and governments and when taxes have been comparatively politically salient. Shedding light on the contexts in which constructive tax bargaining is most likely serves not only to provide a more complete understanding of the issue; it also points towards practical strategies for strengthening links between taxation, responsiveness and accountability at the country level.

With these broad messages in mind, this introductory chapter proceeds as follows. It begins by providing a more detailed review of existing arguments linking taxation, responsiveness and accountability, the growing prominence of these ideas within contemporary development debates and key remaining questions. This is followed by an extended discussion of existing cross-country econometric evidence and the presentation of new econometric results. While the core focus of this book is on country-level *qualitative* evidence of tax bargaining, these new econometric results are a critical starting point for the analysis to follow, and reflect the prominent role of cross-country econometric findings in shaping existing understanding of the relationship between taxation, responsiveness and accountability. Having thus reviewed the cross-country econometric evidence, the remainder of this introductory chapter is committed to reviewing existing country-level evidence, summarizing the core focus, arguments and goals of the book, highlighting connections to broader currents in the study of politics in developing countries and describing the overall research strategy.

1.1 Linking taxation, responsiveness and accountability

Arguments linking taxation, responsiveness and accountability are both intuitive and elegant in their simplicity. On the one hand, a government that is forced to collect tax revenue from citizens will face incentives to be responsive and accountable to those taxpayers in order to encourage "quasi-voluntary" tax compliance and minimize conflicts over taxation (Bates and Lien 1985; Levi 1988). On the other hand, citizens who are forced to pay taxes will have a greater interest in how their money is spent, and thus be more likely to actively demand public services and expanded accountability from governments. The incentives generated by the need for taxation may thus lead to explicit and implicit "tax bargaining" between citizens and governments, as increased tax collection is exchanged for greater responsiveness and accountability. These processes of bargaining may, in turn, provide the foundation for the

1.1 Linking taxation, responsiveness and accountability

construction of durable "fiscal social contracts" (Moore 2004, 2008). While contemporary accounts have frequently focused narrowly on the expansion of democracy, historical and contemporary research suggests that tax bargains may prompt a much broader range of government concessions, which are here captured by the broader concepts of responsiveness and accountability. Following common usage, "responsiveness" is used here to refer broadly to the substance of government action, while the term "accountability" focuses on the institutionalized processes that shape government action and state-society relationships.[4]

The attractiveness of arguments linking taxation, responsiveness and accountability lies largely in two key elements. First, they draw on a long academic tradition highlighting the historical centrality of taxation to state-building and the expansion of political accountability in early modern Europe in particular (Levi 1988; Brewer 1989; Schumpeter 1991 [1918]; Tilly 1992; Ertman 1997; Daunton 2001). Studies in this tradition suggest that the need for states to expand taxation, largely in response to the escalating costs of warfare, forced them also to expand accountability in order to secure the support and tax compliance of wealthy taxpayers. It is this basic historical narrative that provides the foundation for much of the contemporary interest in the potential connections between taxation, responsiveness and accountability in developing countries. Second, this argument dovetails with increasing interest in the so-called political resource curse – the possibility that access to non-tax revenue may be an important cause of weak governance in states dependent on natural resources or foreign aid. While this is a diverse literature, many accounts in this tradition have attributed poor governance in resource-dependent states specifically to the reduced need to raise taxes from, and thus bargain with, citizens (Beblawi and Luciani 1987; Ross 2001).

Growing interest in the potential centrality of taxation to the emergence and expansion of political responsiveness and accountability is reflected in the appearance of this argument in many prominent recent works about the broader politics of developing countries. In an early example, Huntington (1993: 65) wrote of access to oil revenues, "because they reduce or eliminate the need for taxation, they also reduce the need for the government to solicit the acquiescence of the public to taxation. The lower the level of taxation, the less reason for publics to demand representation." Paul Collier (2009: 126), who has emerged as one of the best-known voices in the development field, has written more recently that access to natural resource wealth "enable[s] the government to

---

[4] These definitions, and the decision to adopt this focus, are discussed in much greater detail in Chapter 2.

function without taxing the incomes of citizens, which gradually detaches it from what citizens want." In similar fashion, Larry Diamond (2010: 98), a leading scholar of democratization, has argued of oil-rich states that "most are so awash in cash that they do not need to tax their own citizens. And that is part of the problem – they fail to develop the organic expectations of accountability that emerge when states make citizens pay taxes." Writing of the potential dangers of dependence on foreign aid, Moss, Pettersson and van de Walle (2006: 14) have written that "large aid flows can result in a reduction in governmental accountability because governing elites no longer need to ensure the support of their publics and the assent of their legislatures when they do not need to raise revenues from the local economy."

However, while the potential connections between taxation, responsiveness and accountability have become increasingly widely accepted, empirical research into these connections in contemporary developing countries has remained surprisingly limited. This is substantively important, as there are compelling reasons to believe that tax bargaining may be more limited, complex and contingent than is sometimes assumed. Recent arguments have continued to rely heavily on historical evidence from early modern Europe in particular (Tilly 1992). Yet historical evidence is far from constituting proof that similar processes are likely in the vastly different context of contemporary developing countries (Moore 1998, 2004, 2008). Amongst other considerations, these historical connections emerged during a period in which increasingly costly wars were the primary focus of government spending. In this context, warfare provided a uniquely powerful stimulus to revenue raising and a shared external threat able to catalyse collective action and bargaining between citizens and governments. By contrast, interstate warfare has become comparatively uncommon in the contemporary developing world, thus largely eliminating the historically predominant stimulus to overcoming daunting barriers to collective action and tax bargaining. At the same time, access to a range of non-tax revenue sources, including from natural resources, foreign assistance and foreign credit markets, has reduced the need for governments to bargain with citizens over taxation in order to respond to short-term crises (Centeno 1997, 2002; Herbst 2000). There are equally questions about why citizen demands for responsiveness and accountability should require the additional spur provided by taxation. In a period of expanded formal democracy, shouldn't we expect citizens to be willing and able to aggressively demand improved governance even in the absence of taxation (Herb 2005: 299)? Finally, historical narratives raise important questions about *who* is, in fact, likely to be able to participate in processes of tax bargaining, as tax bargaining in early

1.1 Linking taxation, responsiveness and accountability

modern Europe was generally confined to a small economic elite (Levi 1988; Gehlbach 2008).

Beyond historical differences, there are a variety of social, economic, political and historical reasons to expect that tax bargaining of the kind observed historically may, in fact, be relatively unlikely in contemporary low-income countries. At a minimum, these factors suggest that tax bargaining is likely to be both more diverse and more contingent than is often implied. While governments *may* choose to bargain with citizens over taxation, historically states have relied overwhelmingly on coercion to enforce tax compliance amongst populations lacking the ability to resist. Consistent with this fact, Moore (2008: 51) has pointed towards a range of reasons why positive connections between taxation and broader governance gains might be comparatively rare in low-income countries. He has proposed that tax bargaining is most likely when (a) governments have long time horizons, limited access to non-tax revenues and pressing revenue needs; (b) citizens enjoy "many of the conditions conducive to collective action," including shared interests and an understanding of the tax system; and (c) the state is sufficiently well established and effective to provide incentives for citizens to engage with government. Conversely, he suggests that coercive forms of taxation are particularly likely at the local government level and, more generally, where alternative revenue sources are plentiful, incomes are limited, tax systems are complex and poorly regulated, and the state is weak and poorly institutionalized (Moore 2008: 44). Perhaps most broadly, tax bargaining appears to be less likely where there is very limited trust in the state, as tax evasion, avoidance and resistance may then be more attractive to citizens than the search for reciprocity around expanded taxation (Fjeldstad and Semboja 2001; Juul 2006).

Critically, these expected barriers to tax bargaining are all characteristic of low-income states in sub-Saharan Africa and elsewhere. Countries in sub-Saharan Africa are disproportionately poor and agrarian, which may be expected, amongst others things, to inhibit effective collective action around taxation. They tend to be home to relatively fragmented tax systems, characterized by a range of formal and informal incentives and exemptions, which are likely to further undermine collective action and coherent tax bargaining (Klemm 2009).[5] Low-income countries

---

[5] While this concern holds at all levels of government, it may be particularly acute at the local government level in sub-Saharan Africa. The potential for tax bargaining presumes that citizens have strong incentives to bargain with an integral state, but the reality in many African nations is very different. For one, tax collection, particularly at the local level, is often fragmented, with multiple government bodies, and sometimes non-governmental entities as well, involved in collecting taxes and levies from citizens (Iversen et al. 2006;

frequently enjoy access to significant levels of non-tax revenue, either from natural resources or foreign aid, which may make governments less willing to engage in bargaining with citizens (Centeno 1997, 2002). Finally, and most broadly, trust in government is frequently very limited, as are institutionalized channels for interaction between citizens and the state, thus raising the likelihood that taxation will be characterized by coercion and resistance rather than more constructive forms of bargaining.[6] This possibility that low-income countries may pose particular barriers to tax bargaining is, in turn, reflected in a handful of case studies at the local government level, primarily in sub-Saharan Africa, which have explicitly highlighted the conspicuous *absence* of obvious links between taxation, responsiveness and accountability. Consistent with theory, these studies have, in broad terms, attributed these patterns to historical legacies, the weakness of local governments, entrenched patterns of patronage politics and stark barriers to effective citizen mobilization to demand reciprocity from governments (Fjeldstad 2001; Fjeldstad and Semboja 2001; Juul 2006; Bernstein and Lü 2008; Fjeldstad and Therkildsen 2008). While these authors do not deny the potential for tax bargaining, they have sought to highlight the likely diversity and context-specificity of positive outcomes.

1.2 The extent and limits of cross-country econometric evidence

There are thus important reasons both to treat with caution simplistic claims about the connections between taxation, responsiveness and

---

Fjeldstad, Katera and Ngalewa 2009). In such circumstances citizens may lack both the ability and the inclination to bargain constructively with the state around the use of tax revenue. There is also evidence that, again particularly at the local level, citizens frequently contribute more to community projects and organizations than they pay in taxes. This suggests that rather than bargaining with the state over taxation, citizens often choose to circumvent it by supporting community self-help projects, religious organizations and similar efforts (Chazan 1988; Barkan and Chege 1989; Guyer 1992).

[6] A lack of trust in the state in relation to tax issues may be reinforced by the history of taxation in sub-Saharan Africa, which has been characterized by conflict and illegitimacy (Young 1986; Mamdani 1996). The "modern" tax systems that remain in place today were introduced to a significant degree during the colonial period, in a process that was both externally driven and highly coercive. As much as raising revenue, colonial taxation was about "the recognition of allegiance and . . . inculcation of habits of work" (Pim 1948: 232, quoted in Guyer 1992: 43), and thus not surprisingly was met with hostility and derision amongst the local population. This led to periodic tax revolts and, in some cases, to tax resistance becoming intertwined with broader independence movements (Simensen 1974; Nyangira 1987; Guyer 1992; Bush and Maltby 2004). While poorly documented, there is evidence that this history has continued to shape perceptions of taxation, particularly at the local level, where poll taxes, the hallmark of colonial taxation, have been a lightning rod for controversy (Guyer 1992; Fjeldstad and Therkildsen 2008).

accountability, as well as to seek a more nuanced understanding of the nature of these connections and the contexts in which they are most likely in contemporary developing countries. However, despite strong a priori reasons to seek a nuanced and context-specific understanding of these processes at the country level, research in this area has continued to be dominated by cross-country econometric studies seeking to capture a more general relationship between the sources of government revenue and levels of democracy. Cross-country econometric results are thus a strategic starting point for framing the qualitative analysis presented in the remainder of this book.

The section to follow correspondingly presents a relatively extended discussion of what cross-country econometric results can, and cannot, reveal about the relationship between taxation, responsiveness and accountability. It begins by considering the key messages from existing cross-country research, but suggests that this research has been plagued by substantial data, methodological and conceptual problems. This is followed by the presentation of a set of new econometric results. The new results are clearly *consistent* with the existence of a positive relationship between taxation, responsiveness and accountability. However, the results are insufficient to establish decisively the existence of a *causal* relationship, while they can, in any case, offer only a partial and limited picture of the likely complexity of the relationship. This conclusion, in turn, provides the background for the key contribution of this book, which is taken up in the next section: the presentation of more detailed country-level evidence.

1.2.1   Existing cross-country evidence

The most influential work seeking to link taxation to broader improvements in governance is that of Ross (2004), who reported evidence that countries that are more reliant on tax revenue, as a share of total government revenue, are more likely to be democratic. This result has been echoed by subsequent studies (Mahon 2004; Andersen and Ross 2014), including one study reporting a positive and significant association between absolute levels of taxation, as a share of GDP, and democratization (Baskaran and Bigsten 2013). It is important to note that these studies – and all of the results to follow – focus exclusively on measures of democracy and accountability, owing to the availability of appropriate cross-country measures, but do not focus on responsiveness, owing to the absence of similarly effective measures of the concept for cross-country econometric research.

Alongside this comparatively limited set of studies linking taxation, democracy and accountability lies a much broader body of research presenting evidence of a negative relationship between non-renewable natural resource wealth, most notably from oil, and the quality of governance – widely labelled the political resource curse (Ross 2001; Wantchekon 2002; Jensen and Wantchekon 2004; Aslaksen 2010; Tsui 2010; Ramsay 2011; Ross 2012, 2014; Andersen and Aslaksen 2013; Andersen and Ross 2014; Wiens et al. 2014). While these latter studies have not focused specifically on taxation, the negative association between natural resource wealth and the quality of governance has frequently been attributed, at least in part, to the comparative absence of taxation, and tax bargaining, in resource rich states (Ross 2001).

Collectively these studies have offered evidence that cross-country patterns are minimally consistent with the existence of a positive relationship between taxation and accountability. However, several recent studies have questioned the robustness of this finding. Most notably, Haber and Menaldo (2011) employ a much longer time series, and a new set of econometric methods, and find no significant relationship between either natural resource wealth or tax reliance and the extent of democracy. In a similar vein, Morrison (2009, 2014) argues that non-tax revenue does not lead to autocracy, but simply encourages regime stability, while arguing that tax reliance does not promote democracy, but simply makes political transitions of all kinds more likely.

However, all of these studies have been plagued by substantial concerns related to data quality, model specification, and robustness to the use of alternative econometric methods, thus calling existing findings significantly into question. Most simply, existing studies have generally relied on highly problematic government revenue data from the IMF's *Government Finance Statistics (GFS)*.[7] While the GFS was the best available international source at the time of most existing research, it includes a huge range of (non-random) missing data, as well as data which are analytically problematic owing to the inconsistent treatment of

---

[7] In fact, most studies of the political resource curse do not rely on government revenue data at all, but instead focus on the relationship between total resource income – that is, the total value of natural resource production – and democracy. This is true despite the fact that dominant theories of the political resource curse explicitly focus on the relationship between the sources of government revenue and governance outcomes. It appears likely that continued reliance on measures of resource income has been, at least in part, an implicit acknowledgement of the weakness of cross-country government revenue data. While resource revenue and resource income are, of course, closely related, the latter is at best a highly imperfect proxy for the former, thus calling the precision of the tests into question (Prichard, Salardi and Segal 2014).

natural resource revenues, and increasingly well-documented concerns with underlying GDP series (Jerven 2013a, 2013b, 2013c; Prichard, Cobham and Goodall 2014). In addition, existing studies have generally failed to disentangle the distinct causal impacts of reliance on tax revenue and non-tax revenue, respectively. That is, most studies have focused on the relationship between *tax reliance* – defined as the share of tax revenue in total government revenue – and democracy. However, the aggregate value of tax reliance reflects levels of both tax revenue and non-tax revenue. It is thus ambiguous whether a positive relationship between tax reliance and democracy reflects the existence of governance-enhancing tax bargaining, or is driven by alternative mechanisms through which resource wealth may undermine democracy.[8] Finally, recent results have appeared to be highly sensitive to the use of alternative econometric methods, but most studies have failed to test an inclusive battery of methods, thus raising concerns about the robustness of particular results.

The core messages from existing cross-country econometric research are ultimately threefold. First, the strong majority of existing studies are consistent with the existence of a positive relationship between taxation and accountability. Second, while they are *consistent* with a relationship between taxation and accountability, cross-country studies have yet to convincingly isolate the impact of taxation on governance outcomes, as distinct from the better-established negative impact of natural resource wealth. And third, all of these results should be treated with significant caution owing to concerns about data quality, model specification and robustness.

1.2.2 New estimates of the cross-country relationship

Against this background, I have worked with colleagues to produce new, and significantly more robust, cross-country econometric evidence linking the composition of government revenue to governance outcomes. The results are reported at length in Prichard, Salardi and Segal (2014), while they are summarized here, in order to set the stage for the case study evidence that comprises the core contribution of this book. At the core of the results is a simple intuition: to produce more reliable findings, it is necessary to rely on higher-quality data. The results correspondingly are the first to draw on the newly created International Centre for Tax and Development Government Revenue Dataset (ICTD GRD), which

---

[8] The most notable exception to this pattern is Morrison (2009, 2014), although his results are plagued instead by serious problems of data quality.

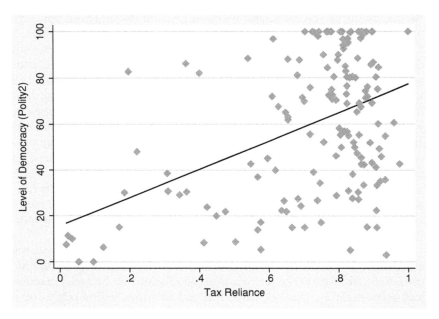

Figure 1.1 Relationship between tax reliance and democracy using country averages, 1990–2010.

was created specifically with this research question in mind, and offers dramatically improved data coverage and accuracy relative to earlier studies, including a more consistent approach to recording natural resource revenues (Prichard, Cobham and Goodall 2014).[9] In doing so it mirrors a growing recognition that social science research has too often privileged methodological innovation over careful attention to data quality – with potentially serious consequences for research (Herrera and Kapur 2007).

With the new data in hand, it is useful to begin with a descriptive look at the relationship between government revenue and democracy. Figure 1.1 presents the relationship between *tax reliance* – defined as

---

[9] Following a series of recent, but less complete, initiatives, the dataset is constructed by meticulously combining data from multiple international sources, including compiling and drawing on data from all available IMF Article IV reports. These alternative sources fill gaps in the data, allow for comparison across sources to root out errors, and make it possible to draw on appropriate sources (most often IMF Article IV reports) in order deal consistently with natural resource revenues. Unlike several other initiatives of this kind, the data has also been made publicly available in order to invite scrutiny or replication by other researchers.

1.2 The extent and limits of cross-country econometric evidence   13

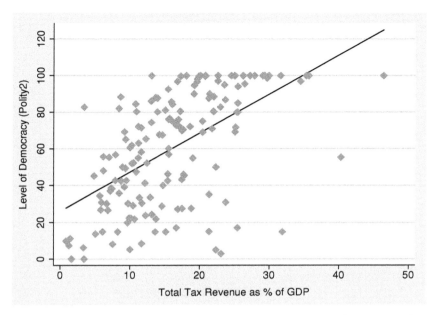

Figure 1.2 Relationship between total tax revenue and democracy using country averages, 1990–2010.

the share of tax revenue in total government revenue – and democracy, as measured by the Polity IV dataset. Critically, using the new ICTD GRD ensures that this tax revenue figure is *exclusive* of revenues from the extraction of non-renewable natural resources, and thus closely reflects the theoretical argument of interest.[10] Figures 1.2 and 1.3 then divide tax reliance into its component parts by looking at the simple correlations between democracy and, in turn, *total tax revenue* as a share of GDP and *total non-tax revenue* as a share of GDP, where the latter includes all natural resource revenues. Dividing tax reliance into its component

[10] Other international datasets vary in whether natural resource revenues are recorded as tax revenue or non-tax revenue. Revenues collected from private resource firms are generally divided between corporate taxes (recorded as taxes) and royalties and other related payments (generally recorded as non-tax revenue), although even this categorization is not always strictly adhered to. However, this does not match the analytical distinction of interest, which is between non-resource taxes collected from a broader base of firms and citizens (what Moore [1998] calls "earned income") and revenues from natural resources and other more captive sources ("unearned income"). Unlike earlier sources, the ICTD GRD adheres strictly to this distinction by reallocating taxes from natural resource firms as non-tax revenue (Prichard, Cobham and Goodall 2014).

14   Introduction

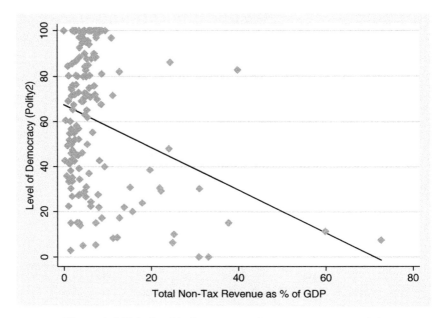

Figure 1.3 Relationship between total non-tax revenue and democracy using country averages, 1990–2010.

parts is intended to shed light on whether it is increases in tax revenue, or decreases in non-tax revenue, that are most strongly associated with expanded democracy.

The core message from the tables is clear: Greater tax collection is strongly correlated with higher levels of democracy, while higher levels of non-tax revenue are strongly correlated with lower levels of democracy. Of course, this is a merely descriptive relationship, whereas we are interested in ascertaining whether taxation has a *causal* impact on levels of democracy.

To do so, we re-test the dominant econometric approaches used previously in the literature using the new ICTD data. The core results draw on data for up to 155 countries over the period between 1990 and 2010, as it is only during this period that available government revenue data is relatively complete and reliable. Following the literature, the dependent variable is democracy, measured as either a continuous variable (*Democracy*, based on the Polity IV dataset) or as a binary variable (*Regime*, based on Cheibub et al. 2010) depending on the particular econometric model. All of the core results also include standard controls for log

1.2 The extent and limits of cross-country econometric evidence 15

GDP, population size, the occurrence of civil war and regional democratic diffusion, along with time dummies in order to account for any time trends in the data.[11]

Results are reported for five alternative econometric methods drawn from the recent literature, in order to guard against the results being driven by specific methodological choices. This is particularly important amidst growing recognition that the findings of cross-country econometric studies of complex political relationships can be highly sensitive to methodological choices (e.g., Acemoglu, Johnson, Robinson and Yared 2008). The first three methods estimate the relationship between the revenue variables and the continuous measure of democracy. They are: the System-GMM version of the Generalized Method of Moments estimator developed by Arellano and Bond (Blundell and Bond 1998; Roodman 2006), the Common Correlated Effects version of the Mean Group (CCE-MG) estimator developed by Pesaran and Smith (1995), and the Error Correction Mechanism estimator favoured by Haber and Menaldo (2011).

However, recent literature has suggested that a more appropriate strategy may be to focus not on continuous measures of democracy, but on the likelihood of transitions to or from democracy (Andersen and Ross 2014; Wiens et al. 2014). This approach is attractive in part because it captures the possibility that resource wealth may in many cases not have resulted in a *decline* in democracy, but may have reduced the likelihood of initially autocratic countries *transitioning to* democracy.[12] Equally important, it allows us to consider the possibility that the political impacts of tax and non-tax revenue may differ between autocracies and democracies. Following this intuition, we thus test both fixed and random effects logit models, which focus attention on the likelihood of transitions between autocracy and democracy.[13] Additional details about each of the

---

[11] In order to match earlier results in the literature, the logit regressions drop the controls for population size and democratic diffusion, and include a control for growth per capita. Results are, in any case, robust to alternative sets of controls.

[12] Most resource-dependent states were relatively autocratic at the point of discovering large mineral deposits, making this an empirically significant concern (Wiens et al. 2014)

[13] We would normally prefer to rely on fixed effects estimates, which control most effectively for unobserved country heterogeneity. However, the inclusion of fixed effects results in dropping every country that did not undergo a regime transition from 1990 to 2010 – a group that includes most countries, and almost all major resource producers. Following Wiens et al. (2014), reliance on random effects is a second-best option to account for unobserved country heterogeneity as far as possible while retaining necessary country coverage. However, owing to the imperfection of this option, we also report results from the simple fixed effects model.

Table 1.1 *Impact of composition of government revenue on continuous measures of democracy*

	(1) Sys-GMM two-step b/se	(2) Sys-GMM two-step b/se	(3) CCE-MG w/o trend b/se	(4) CCE-MG w/o trend b/se	(5) ECM b/se	(6) ECM b/se
L.Democracy	0.8671***	0.8624***			−0.2806***	−0.2800***
	(0.0353)	(0.0278)			(0.0269)	(0.0268)
L.Tax Reliance	15.8768***		20.6028***		5.5581	
	(5.2605)		(7.6264)		(4.5820)	
L.Total Tax Revenue		−25.5627*		51.7679		35.4939***
		(15.2234)		(35.1532)		(11.9656)
L.Total Non-Tax Revenue		−29.7871***		−155.2035**		−3.1885
		(10.1836)		(66.4175)		(4.9855)
L.Log GDP	−1.7376	−2.5850	5.5947	4.7162		
	(1.5148)	(1.6874)	(8.3597)	(10.6713)		
L.Population	−0.0000	−0.0000	0.0000	−0.0000		
	(0.0000)	(0.0000)	(0.0000)	(0.0000)		
L.Civil_War	−1.3181	−1.7057	−0.1046	−0.5235		
	(1.4771)	(1.3935)	(0.4150)	(0.3874)		
L.Regional_ Democratic_ Diffusion	0.0755	0.1562***				
	(0.0501)	(0.0503)				
Implied long-term effects						
L.Tax Reliance	119.4643***				10.3429	
L.Total Non-Tax Revenue		−216.476***				−36.0118***
AR(1)	0.000	0.000				
AR(2)	0.693	0.731				
Hansen	0.521	0.259				
N	2536	2536	2634	2604	2539	2539
N_g	152.000	152.000	149.000	144.000	153.000	153.000

Notes: All regression results based on the two-step system-GMM procedure. Windmeijer standard errors in parentheses: * $p<0.10$, ** $p<0.05$, *** $p<0.01$. The p-values reported for the Hansen statistic are for the null hypothesis that instruments are valid. The values reported for AR(2) are p-values for tests of second order autocorrelation. Implied long-term effect calculated using the formula $\beta/(1 - \omega)$, where ω is the coefficient on the lagged dependent variable, and β is the coefficient on the revenue variable of interest. Long-term effects in Columns (1)–(5) are for *Tax Reliance*, while for columns (6)–(10) they are for *Total Non-Tax Revenue*.
Source: ICTD GRD (2014).

individual models are provided in the Statistical Appendix to this chapter, while what follows focuses on the overall pattern of results.

Table 1.1 reports the core results of the Sys-GMM, CCE-MG and ECM regressions, which estimate the short- and long-term relationships between the revenue variables and democracy. For each model the first column reports the relationship between *tax reliance* and *democracy*, while the second column reports results when *tax reliance* is disaggregated into

1.2 The extent and limits of cross-country econometric evidence 17

total tax revenue and *total non-tax revenue*, respectively. For the Sys-GMM and ECM results, the coefficients on the revenue terms capture the short-term effect, while the long-term effects are reported towards the bottom of the table.[14] The CCE-MG results focus exclusively on the long-term effects, captured by the coefficients on the revenue terms.

Table 1.2 then reports the results for the logit regressions, which estimate the effect of the revenue variables on the likelihood of transitions between autocracy and democracy. Both models include interaction terms between the independent variables and the binary democracy variable, in order to explore whether tax and non-tax revenue may have distinct effects in autocracies and democracies. Thus, the coefficients on the revenue variables capture the impact of those revenue variables on democracy *in existing autocracies* only. In turn, the coefficients on the interaction terms tell us whether those effects are different in existing democracies, with the total impact of the revenue variables *in existing democracies* reported near the bottom of the table.

For the purposes of this book, the key messages from these tables are threefold. First, there is strong and relatively consistent support for the contention that countries that are more reliant on (non-resource) tax revenue are more likely to be democratic. While there is significant variation in the magnitude of the effects, the coefficient on the tax reliance variable is positive and strongly significant in three of the five models, and is positive and near significant in the remaining two models. This variation across the models is a reflection of the increasingly recognized sensitivity of many cross-country econometric results in political science to econometric choices, and speaks to the importance of implementing a wide range of tests. Despite this variation, the broad finding is reasonably robust. First and foremost, despite variation in magnitude, the overall direction of the results is consistent across a range of highly diverse estimators. Meanwhile, the pattern of results is also robust to a variety of additional checks, including employing alternative control variables, limiting the sample to particular regions and subsets of countries and employing alternative measures of democracy and accountability as dependent variables (see Prichard, Salardi and Segal 2014).

The second key message is that there is similarly strong and relatively consistent support for the contention that non-tax revenue, primarily in the form of natural resource wealth, has a negative impact on democracy. The coefficient on non-tax revenue is negative and significant in

---

[14] Following Aslaksen (2010) the long-term effect is calculated as $\beta/(1-\delta)$, where δ is the coefficient on the lagged dependent variable and β is the coefficient on the revenue variable of interest.

Table 1.2 *Impact of composition of government revenue on likelihood of regime transitions*

	(1) Logit – random effects b/se	(2) Logit – random effects b/se	(3) Logit – fixed effects b/se	(4) Logit – fixed effects b/se
L.Regime	−5.2888	−0.6607	4.3906	4.9988
	(3.5544)	(2.8037)	(5.0130)	(3.8021)
L.Tax Reliance	1.5100		7.6642**	
	(1.0490)		(3.3890)	
L.Regime x Tax Reliance	1.9235		−0.2264	
	(1.8691)		(2.3673)	
L.Total Tax Revenue		−6.2755*		21.6904
		(3.7480)		(15.8069)
L.Total Non-Tax Revenue		−12.5968**		−15.0584
		(5.3654)		(10.0924)
L.Regime x Total Tax Revenue		16.7894**		−4.5262
		(8.1804)		(9.6103)
L.Regime x Total Non-Tax Revenue		8.6665		2.0054
		(7.4713)		(8.0799)
L.Log GDP	−0.2379	0.1238	0.9682	0.9285
	(0.2263)	(0.2608)	(1.8678)	(1.9143)
L.Population				
L.Civil_War	−1.0092	−1.1202	−0.8119	−0.7654
	(0.7729)	(0.7740)	(1.0971)	(1.1020)
L.Regional_Democratic_Diffusion				
L.Growth Per Capita	−0.0333	−0.0336	0.0173	0.0061
	(0.0303)	(0.0295)	(0.0389)	(0.0420)
L.Regime x Log GDP	1.5121***	0.7510*	0.0445	−0.0090
	(0.3810)	(0.4431)	(0.5593)	(0.5763)
L.Regime x Population				
L.Regime x Civil_War	0.2652	0.3397	−0.4830	−0.4226
	(1.1874)	(1.1855)	(1.3719)	(1.3703)
L.Regime x Regional_Democratic_Diffusion				
L.Regime x Growth Per Capita	0.0917	0.0911	0.0759	0.0797
	(0.0681)	(0.0685)	(0.0848)	(0.0853)
Aggregate effects in democracies				
L.Tax Reliance ($\beta 1 + \beta 2$)	3.4334**		7.4378*	
	(1.5399)		(3.8090)	
L.Total Tax Revenue ($\beta 1 + \beta 3$)		10.5138		17.1641
		(7.2802)		(16.4619)
L.Total Non-Tax Revenue ($\beta 2 + \beta 4$)		−3.9303		−13.0529
		(5.1777)		(8.7285)

(*cont.*)

1.2 The extent and limits of cross-country econometric evidence

Table 1.2 *(cont.)*

	(1) Logit – random effects b/se	(2) Logit – random effects b/se	(3) Logit – fixed effects b/se	(4) Logit – fixed effects b/se
Random effects model descriptors			458	458
	0.0021	0.0015	28.000	28.000
	1.31e-06	6.61e-07		
N	2305	2305		
N_g	157.000	157.000		

Notes: * p<0.10, ** p<0.05, *** p<0.01. '$\beta 1 + \beta 2$' captures the joint significance of the *Tax Reliance* and *Regime x Tax Reliance* variables, and thus captures the impact of *Tax Reliance* on *Regime* in democracies (e.g., when *Regime* = 1). '$\beta 1 + \beta 3$' similarly captures the joint significance of *Total Tax Revenue* and *Regime x Total Tax Revenue*, while '$\beta 2 + \beta 4$' captures the joint significance of *Total Non-Tax Revenue* and *Regime x Total Non-Tax Revenue*.
Source: ICTD GRD (2014).

four of the five specifications, and is negative and near significant in the remaining specification, while it is similarly robust to the variety of additional checks noted earlier.[15] Whereas Morrison argues that non-tax revenue has a stabilizing rather than antidemocratic effect, the logit results here, which rely on much improved data, do not support this conclusion. Instead, we find that non-tax revenue reduces the likelihood of transitions to democracy, while it has no significant impact in existing democracies (although the coefficient is negative, which would imply, if anything, an antidemocratic effect). This is consistent with a more widely made argument: that the antidemocratic effects of natural resource wealth are likely to be moderated by stronger countervailing institutions in existing democracies (Mehlum et al. 2006).

Notably, the magnitudes of the positive effect of tax reliance, and the negative effect of non-tax revenue, are very substantial. Taken collectively, the estimated magnitudes in the Sys-GMM and CCE-MG models indicate that a shift from a highly tax-reliant state (e.g., Senegal, with tax reliance around 0.9) to a highly resource-dependent state (e.g., Nigeria, with tax reliance around 0.2) reduces the expected level of democracy from that of an OECD country (Polity score of 10, on a scale of −10 to 10, in 2010) to that of a highly undemocratic country like Kazakhstan

---

[15] The coefficient on non-tax revenue is only significant over the long term in the ECM estimates, but the long-term estimate is the value of greatest in interest.

20   Introduction

Table 1.3 *Likelihood of transitions to democracy*

	Level of tax reliance (tax revenue share of total government revenue)				
	0.2	0.4	0.6	0.75	0.9
Pr(Democracy) at *t*	0.0114	0.0155	0.0211	0.0265	0.0333
95% confidence interval (upper)	0.0247	0.0280	0.0321	0.0387	0.0524
95% confidence interval (lower)	−0.0019	0.0031	0.0101	0.0143	0.0142

	Level of non-tax revenue as % of GDP				
	2%	5%	10%	20%	30%
Pr(Democracy) at *t*	0.0422	0.0292	0.0157	0.0044	0.0012
95% confidence interval (upper)	0.0652	0.0425	0.0266	0.0128	0.0046
95% confidence interval (lower)	0.0192	0.0159	0.0047	−0.0029	−0.0021

Notes: Likelihood of transitions to democracy at different values of non-tax revenue and tax reliance. Calculated based on columns 1 and 2 of table 1.2, using *margins* command in Stata, with Regime = 0, Civil_War = 0 and other variables set to their mean values excluding OECD countries. The mean level of *lgdp* is 7.89 (equivalent to per capita income of $2,670), the mean level of *Growth Per Capita* is 2.51 and the mean level of *Total Tax Revenue* is 0.136 (13.6% of GDP).
Source: ICTD GRD (2014).

(Polity score −6 in 2010). In similar fashion, the logit results suggest that reduced tax reliance substantially reduces the likelihood of transitions from autocracy to democracy, as reported in Table 1.3. Using the same comparison as presented earlier, a country with high tax reliance is about three times more likely to transition to democracy in a given year, while the likelihood of a transition to democracy shrinks close to zero at extremely high levels of non-tax revenue.

These first two findings are undoubtedly consistent with the existence of democracy-enhancing processes of tax bargaining, which could explain higher levels of democracy where tax reliance is greater. However, there remains significant ambiguity: while higher levels of democracy where tax reliance is higher *may* reflect the democratizing effects of tax bargaining, it may equally reflect a range of other causal processes through which access to significant non-tax revenue may undermine democracy. These include, amongst others, the potential for non-tax revenue

1.2 The extent and limits of cross-country econometric evidence 21

to drive expanded patronage and repression (Ross 2001, 2004; Smith 2004), increased corruption (Kolstad and Wiig 2009), the deterioration of state institutions (Ross 2001; Acemoglu and Robinson 2006) or higher levels of conflict (Collier and Hoeffler 1998, 2004; Fearon and Laitin 2003; Snyder and Bhavnani 2005; Humphreys 2005; Collier et al. 2009).[16]

In an effort to isolate the causal significance of taxation, all of these results report the independent impact of levels of taxation, as a share of GDP, on democracy (*Total Tax Revenue*). However, the results are striking primarily for their ambiguity. In the baseline results the coefficients on total tax revenue vary widely across estimation methods, from positive and statistically significant to negative and significant. Morrison (2009, 2014) offers one possible explanation: taxation may have a destabilizing effect rather than a democratizing effect. This would imply a positive impact on the likelihood of democratization in existing autocracies (a positive coefficient on *Total Tax Revenue* in Table 1.2), and an increase in the likelihood of transitions to autocracy in existing democracies (a negative coefficient on $\beta 1 + \beta 3$ in Table 1.2). However, the logit results here do not fit this explanation. An alternative possibility is that the relationship between taxation and democracy occurs over the relatively long term, and thus is not captured effectively by the baseline model, which looks for the political consequences of taxation a single year after any change in tax collection.[17] Tables 1.4 and 1.5 correspondingly report results when the time horizon for these effects is extended to three and five years, respectively, in the Sys-GMM and random effects logit models. As expected, the coefficients on total tax collection become more positive as we allow the impact of tax collection to occur over multiple years (as does the already positive association between tax reliance and democracy). However, while always positive, the coefficients on total tax collection remain statistically insignificant.

What, then, can we conclude about the relationship between taxation, responsiveness and accountability? On one hand, the results are entirely *consistent* with the existence of such a relationship. Contrary to some recent studies, there is relatively clear evidence that countries that are more reliant on tax revenue as a share of total revenue are more likely to be democratic. This offers a critical foundation and starting point for the remaining evidence presented in this book. On the other hand,

---

[16] Ross (2014) provides a recent overview of these different possibilities, and of evidence in this area more generally.
[17] More formally, and as described in the Appendix, the explanatory variables are lagged by a single year in the baseline model, while we then extend the length of these lags to three and five years, respectively.

Table 1.4 *Effect of tax reliance, total tax and non-tax revenue on polity, using different lags*

	(1) Sys-GMM two-step b/se $\lambda = 1$	(2) Sys-GMM two-step b/se $\lambda = 3$	(3) Sys-GMM two-step b/se $\lambda = 5$	(4) Sys-GMM two-step b/se $\lambda = 1$	(5) Sys-GMM two-step b/se $\lambda = 3$	(6) Sys-GMM two-step b/se $\lambda = 5$
Lλ.Democracy	0.8741*** (0.0359)	0.5991*** (0.0811)	0.5008*** (0.0915)	0.8612*** (0.0280)	0.5904*** (0.0768)	0.4316*** (0.1088)
Lλ.Tax Reliance	18.0684*** (5.3422)	19.4390** (7.9695)	23.8694** (10.0033)			
Lλ.Total Tax Revenue				−11.7086 (15.5717)	7.0397 (31.2309)	22.2667 (39.0345)
Lλ.Total Non-Tax Revenue				−26.0380*** (8.3181)	−39.0786** (17.1580)	−35.7187 (32.7934)
Lλ.Log GDP	−0.8896 (1.2806)	0.6934 (2.0321)	−1.6613 (2.4600)	−1.6612 (1.3640)	0.0153 (1.9998)	−0.5000 (2.6180)
AR(1)	0.000	0.150	0.316	0.000	0.208	0.436
AR(2)	0.648	0.470	0.390	0.650	0.420	0.285
Hansen	0.376	0.228	0.374	0.291	0.181	0.054
N	2579	2308	2024	2579	2308	2024
N_g	155.000	155.000	152.000	155.000	155.000	152.000

Notes: Columns (1), (4) use lags t-1; columns (2), (5) use lags t-3; columns (3), (6) use lags t-5. All regression results based on the two-step system-GMM procedure. Windmeijer standard errors in parentheses: * $p<0.10$, ** $p<0.05$, *** $p<0.01$. The p-values reported for the Hansen statistic are for the null hypothesis that instruments are valid. The values reported for AR(2) are p-values for tests of second order autocorrelation.
Source: ICTD GRD (2014).

Table 1.5 *Effect of tax reliance, total tax and non-tax revenue on regime, using random effects logit model and different lags*

	(1) Logit b/se $\lambda=1$	(2) Logit b/se $\lambda=3$	(3) Logit b/se $\lambda=5$	(4) Logit b/se $\lambda=1$	(5) Logit b/se $\lambda=3$	(6) Logit b/se $\lambda=5$
L.Regime	−5.2888 (3.5544)	−18.1924*** (3.9408)	−25.7939*** (4.7138)	−0.6607 (2.8037)	−12.5082*** (3.2157)	−20.0787*** (3.9071)
L.Tax Reliance	1.5100 (1.0490)	4.4561*** (1.6442)	7.2327*** (2.0780)			
L.Regime x Tax Reliance	1.9235 (1.8691)	2.7075 (1.9330)	3.6250 (2.2226)			
L.Total Tax Revenue				−6.2755* (3.7480)	−2.3642 (5.0183)	7.8482 (6.7844)
L.Total Non-Tax Revenue				−12.5968** (5.3654)	−16.4260*** (5.7189)	−20.2697*** (6.9277)
L.Regime x Total Tax Revenue				16.7894** (8.1804)	12.3545 (8.1421)	3.7831 (9.8485)
L.Regime x Total Non-Tax Revenue				8.6665 (7.4713)	3.1397 (6.4659)	−2.0186 (6.9634)
Aggregate effects in democracies						
L.Tax Reliance ($\beta 1 + \beta 2$)	3.4334*** (1.5399)	7.1636*** (2.1194)	10.8576*** (2.4668)			
L.Total Tax Revenue ($\beta 1 + \beta 3$)				10.5138 (7.2802)	9.9903 (7.6084)	11.6313 (9.1243)
L.Total Non-Tax Revenue ($\beta 2 + \beta 4$)				−3.9303 (5.1777)	−13.2862** (5.7665)	−22.2882*** (6.8447)
Random effects model descriptors						
σ_v	0.0021	2.373	3.584	0.0015	2.1104	3.5227
ρ	1.31e-06	0.6312	0.7961	6.61e-07	0.5752	0.7904
N	2305	2025	1730	2305	2025	1730
N_g	157.000	156.000	152.000	157.000	156.000	152.000

Notes: Columns (1), (4) use lags t-1; columns (2), (5) use lags t-3; columns (3), (6) use lags t-5. All regressions include a standard set of control variables, which are excluded in order to conserve space: *Log GDP*, *Civil War* and *Growth Per Capita*. * p<0.10, ** p<0.05, *** p<0.01. $\beta 1 + \beta 2$ captures the joint significance of the *Tax Reliance* and *Regime x Tax Reliance* variables, and thus captures the impact of *Tax Reliance* on *Regime* in democracies (e.g., when *Regime* = 1). $\beta 1 + \beta 3$ similarly captures the joint significance of *Total Tax Revenue* and *Regime x Total Tax Revenue*, while $\beta 1 + \beta 3$ captures the joint significance of *Total Non-Tax Revenue* and *Regime x Total Non-Tax Revenue*.
Source: ICTD GRD (2014).

cross-country econometric tests are clearly not *sufficient* to establish the specific causal role of *tax bargaining* in driving this broader relationship between tax reliance and democracy. It may be tempting to interpret the absence of an unambiguous statistical relationship between total tax collection and democracy as evidence of the absence of a relationship in practice. However, the absence of clear statistical results may equally reflect the comparative complexity and contingency of the causal processes of interest, and the associated difficulty of capturing them using relatively crude cross-country econometric tools. The latter seems intuitively possible: as has already been noted, and will be described in greater detail in Chapter 2, the causal processes that are expected to link taxation, responsiveness and accountability are highly varied, complex and frequently long term. Greater, and more diverse, evidence is clearly needed in order to draw stronger conclusions, and it is to this task that we now turn.

1.3 The importance of detailed country-level research

Presented with supportive but ultimately inconclusive econometric evidence, the research challenge lies in adopting complementary, country-level research methods that are better placed to confirm (or not) the existence of the specific causal processes of interest, and, as importantly, to shed light on the potential diversity of those processes and the contextual factors shaping their emergence in individual cases. However, while there is a clear need for such research, in practice such studies have remained relatively infrequent and comparatively limited in scope and ambition. They consequently offer valuable initial insights but few definitive answers.

One source of evidence has been behavioural and survey evidence confirming the tendency of tax compliance decisions to be shaped by trust in government and satisfaction with government performance (Alm, Sanchez and de Juan 1995; Bosco and Mittone 1997; Scholz and Lubell 1998; Bergman 2002, 2003; Cummings et al. 2005; Levi and Sacks 2005; Torgler 2005; Berenson 2006; Ali, Fjeldstad and Sjursen 2014; Bodea and LeBas 2014). More ambitiously, recent studies have presented evidence that tax payments can spur expanded citizen engagement. Paler (2013: 707) has presented evidence from controlled revenue and information experiments in Indonesia that "citizens have greater incentives to take action when government depends on their taxes rather than on windfalls." More recently, and in a similar vein, Martin (2014: 3) has argued, based on a lab-in-the-field experiment in Uganda, that "taxed citizens have a lower tolerance for poor performance and corruption,

1.3 The importance of detailed country-level research

and are more likely to punish nonaccountable leaders." Broms (2014) likewise provides evidence, based on the Afrobarometer surveys, that taxation increases "political interest." Collectively, these studies provide a very important behavioural foundation for theories of tax bargaining, but they fall short of providing empirical evidence that conflicts over taxation have driven *actual* governance changes. While we have increasingly clear evidence that attitudes towards compliance improve in response to greater governmental accountability, governments may nonetheless continue to turn to coercion to collect taxes rather than making concessions designed to increase compliance. Likewise, while recent studies provide evidence that paying taxes leads taxpayers to feel a stronger willingness and desire to hold governments to account, such willingness is only a first step towards the costly and challenging process of effective political mobilization.[18]

Recognizing the value, but also the limits, of behavioural research and controlled field experiments, alternative evidence has come from a small but growing body of country-level research, including a handful of qualitative case studies, as well as econometric studies drawing on subnational revenue data and survey results. A first group of country-level studies has linked the absence of taxation to poor governance in resource-dependent states. Chaudhry (1997) provides the most compelling account as she looks at the impact of the expansion of non-tax revenue on the state in Saudi Arabia (oil revenue) and Yemen (remittances). She provides significant evidence that reduced taxation contributed to the broader decay of public administration and, consequently, the overall responsiveness of government. Crystal (1990) arrives at similar conclusions in her case studies of Kuwait and Qatar, where she argues that the merchant classes relinquished some of their political claims after the discovery of oil and the elimination of taxation. In an African context, Guyer (1992) notes the connection between expanded oil revenues and the broad weakening of local taxation and local government in Nigeria, although without providing a systematic body of empirical evidence. McGuirk (2013) looks at the same question at the national level in Nigeria and presents evidence, using data drawn from initial rounds of the Afrobarometer survey, that oil wealth has induced weaker tax enforcement, which has, in turn, weakened popular demands for democracy.

---

[18] Indeed, Paler (2013: 707) explains in her study that while the simulated tax payment increased *willingness* to monitor the budget and take political action, "the tax treatment did not cause more political participation as measured both by turnout in the postcard campaign and in the survey, however. It is likely that the effect of the tax treatment was too weak to elevate the perceived benefits of taking action above the costs."

A parallel group of studies have sought, instead, to explore the potentially positive connections between taxation and government performance. Drawing on subnational data, Hoffman and Gibson (2005) find evidence in a study of local governments in Tanzania and Zambia that a higher share of local revenue is allocated to programme budgets, as opposed to salaries, where reliance on local tax revenue (as opposed to aid and transfers) is higher. However, their study faces major challenges in establishing causality, while there are various questions about the measurement of the concepts of interest. Gervasoni (2010) finds stronger indicators of democratic practice in regions of Argentina in which the level of reliance on subnational taxation, as opposed to central government fiscal transfers, is higher. However, he does not specifically identify reduced taxation as the cause of reduced accountability. Finally, Gadenne (2014) finds evidence that municipalities in Brazil that have expanded tax collection have also experienced comparatively larger improvements in key measures of governance than have municipalities more reliant on central government transfers, although it has, again, been comparatively difficult to establish unambiguously that changes in taxation have been the cause of broader governance gains.[19]

Looking to qualitative research, Bräutigam (2008b) provides evidence that conflict over taxation played an important role in the institutionalization of greater domestic control over politics in Mauritius during the period of British colonial rule. Herbst (2000) argues that the absence of broad-based direct taxation in sub-Saharan Africa, owing particularly to the absence of interstate conflict, has undermined broader processes of state-building, but he provides little in the way of specific causal evidence. In a more contemporary setting, Brand (1992) argues that a sharp reduction in foreign aid and remittances forced the Jordanian government to increase taxes, which, in turn, became a catalyst for political liberalization. In the most ambitious work in the tradition, Easter (2008, 2012) compares Poland and Russia after the fall of the Soviet Union and argues that the heavier reliance of the Polish state on comparatively broad-based income taxes contributed to expanded bargaining with citizens and the emergence of more accountable and rules-based governance. Eubank (2012) argues that in Somaliland the absence of foreign aid forced the nascent government into conflict with rival groups over major sources of

---

[19] Kasara and Suryanarayan (2014) provide cross-country evidence that the rich are more likely to vote where government tax capacity is higher, consistent with the mobilizing potential of taxation. However, their study does not focus on the governance *outcomes* resulting from expanded political engagement by elites in response to greater taxation, and thus leaves open the question of whether taxation results in expanded responsiveness and accountability.

1.3 The importance of detailed country-level research

tax revenue, and that this contributed to a democratic bargain between the government and its rivals. Finally, several authors have suggested a connection between taxation and governance in Chile, where an inclusive fiscal pact, detailing the outlines of tax and expenditure policy, was central to the establishment of a broader democratic bargain during the transition from autocratic rule at the beginning of the 1990s (Boylan 1996; Weyland 1997; Bergman 2002, 2003).[20]

Taken together, there thus exists a meaningful body of research suggesting that taxation can be an important catalyst for the expansion of responsiveness and accountability. However, country-level evidence remains incomplete. While consistent with broad claims about taxation, responsiveness and accountability, subnational econometric evidence has been plagued by methodological challenges and its limited ability to confidently establish causality. Meanwhile, existing country-level case studies have offered important illustrative evidence of connections between taxation, responsiveness and accountability, but have remained fragmented and incompletely theorized. There has yet to be an extended, systematic and comparative study of these relationships at the country level.[21] Underlying all of this research, meanwhile, has been a continued focus on broad and general propositions linking taxation, responsiveness and accountability, thus downplaying the likely diversity and contingency of these processes. We continue to know very little about the potentially multiple causal processes through which connections between taxation, responsiveness and accountability may be manifested in practice in contemporary developing countries. Research has similarly offered few

---

[20] Several additional studies have highlighted the extent to which tax collection in developing countries has been intimately connected to the broader alignment of elite political and economic interests. Thus, for example, Lieberman (2002) presents a detailed account of the connections between the nature of the political community and levels of tax compliance and collection in Brazil and South Africa. Specifically, he argues that income taxation has been higher in South Africa because economic and political elites were unified behind a broader state-building project, and were thus willing to pay for it through taxation. Schneider (2012) presents similar evidence that tax collection in Central America has tended to reflect the broader characteristics of ruling coalitions and associated state-building projects. Slater (2010) identifies taxation as an essential component of broader state-building projects in Southeast Asia and suggests that increased taxation emerged as a result of greater cohesion amongst competing elite groups when confronted with threats to their positions. While these studies do not focus explicitly on tax bargaining, they are again consistent with such processes. Effective taxation has emerged from the construction of more inclusive elite coalitions, with key groups of elites consenting to expanded taxation when their interests have been aligned with those of the state.

[21] The most ambitious existing study is the work of Kiren Chaudhry (1989, 1997), noted earlier. However, her approach is focused on capturing the negative implications of a rapid increase in external revenue, rather than on the potential for positive governance dynamics to emerge as a result of greater reliance on taxation.

empirical insights into the contextual factors that may shape how and where such connections emerge. These oversights are of particular concern given that historical research has explicitly stressed the diversity and contingency of processes of tax bargaining.

1.4 The argument of the book

Research in this area thus begins from an unusual starting point. On one hand, the central proposition that the need for taxation may be a catalyst for broader governance gains is, in many respects, widely accepted. On the other hand, detailed empirical evidence of this relationship in contemporary developing countries remains surprisingly limited. While existing evidence provides a strong indication that taxation has in some cases been a catalyst for broader governance gains, it provides few insights into the specific causal processes through which these connections have been manifested or into the contexts in which such connections are most likely. These limitations of existing research motivate the focus of this book, which makes three broad contributions.

First, it provides the most complete evidence to date of the existence of causal connections between taxation, responsiveness and accountability in contemporary developing countries. The econometric evidence presented earlier provides a necessary starting point, as it establishes that cross-country data is minimally consistent with the broader claims of this book. However, it proves impossible to establish conclusively, using cross-country econometric methods alone, that the broader relationship between tax reliance and accountability is driven by tax bargaining. This suggests both the likely complexity and contingency of any underlying relationship as well as the need for case study evidence to reinforce and extend the econometric results. This sets the stage for the case studies presented in the remainder of this book, which offer detailed country-level evidence of the existence of the causal relationships of interest in Ghana, Kenya and Ethiopia. While neither the quantitative nor the qualitative evidence is perfectly suited to proving the existence of the relationship of interest beyond dispute, the combination of the two types of evidence provides the strongest foundation to date for such claims.

The second contribution of the book lies in moving beyond broad and abstract claims by drawing on the case studies to capture the diversity of specific causal processes linking taxation, responsiveness and accountability. Specifically, it argues that it is useful to distinguish three distinct but closely related types of causal processes: *direct tax bargaining, tax resistance and changes in government* and *strengthened political capabilities of taxpayers*. The most straightforward are cases of relatively explicit bargaining – *direct tax bargaining* – in which governments have provided expanded

1.4 The argument of the book

services or accountability in an effort to respond explicitly to taxpayer demands and encourage tax compliance. Somewhat different are cases, collectively termed *indirect tax bargaining*, in which conflicts over taxation have shaped political outcomes in more long-term, implicit and indirect ways. These cases are more easily overlooked both because they are difficult to observe and because they do not conform to a simple narrative in which tax revenue is exchanged directly for government concessions. In some cases, termed *tax resistance and changes in government*, popular resistance to taxation has failed to prompt immediate concessions, but has served to weaken the fiscal position of unpopular governments. In this way tax resistance has increased the likelihood of changes in government and contributed to generating long-term incentives for subsequent tax and governance reform. Alternatively, conflicts over taxation have sometimes prompted popular engagement and mobilization that have similarly failed to secure immediate concessions. However, this short-term mobilization has often provided the foundation for *strengthening civil society organizations and the political capabilities of taxpayers*, including business associations, taxpayers' associations and broader-based groups pursuing governance reform. By acting as a catalyst for long-term collective action and political engagement, conflicts over taxation have thus shaped subsequent political outcomes in important, albeit indirect, ways. The critical insight underlying these processes of indirect bargaining is that even where governments have refused to grant immediate concessions in response to taxpayer demands, conflicts over taxation have nonetheless frequently had longer-term governance implications.

These diverse processes are unified by the fact that they have turned on the potential for conflicts over taxation to spur collective action by citizens and to incentivize concessions by governments seeking to expand revenue collection. However, they go beyond existing accounts in providing a richer and more varied picture of the multiple ways in which conflicts over taxation may alter political incentives and state-society relations. Whereas there has been an often-implicit tendency to equate "tax bargaining" with relatively explicit processes of exchange, this book brings indirect and implicit forms of tax bargaining to the fore.[22] These alternative

---

[22] The importance of such indirect and implicit processes is suggested quite clearly in the historical accounts presented by Tilly (1992: 98–99), who highlights the fact that "tax bargaining" was often reflected in repeated processes of conflict rather than in explicit processes of exchange. He writes: "What we in blithe retrospect call 'state formation' included the setting of ruthless tax farmers against poor peasants and farmers, the forced sale for taxes of animals that would have paid for dowries, the imprisoning of local leaders as hostages to the local community's payment of overdue taxes, the hanging of others who dared to protest, the loosing of brutal soldiers on a hapless civilian population, the conscription of young men who were the parents' main hope for comfort in old age, the forced purchase of tainted salt, the elevation of already arrogant local property

processes follow a common logic, but they are easily overlooked by a narrow focus on the explicit, short-term, and readily observable political consequences of taxation. In capturing this diversity, the account here is consistent with the diversity of historical experiences, described in detail in Chapter 2, and with the expectation that processes of tax bargaining may vary significantly in response to contextual differences.

The final contribution of this book correspondingly lies in highlighting that tax bargaining has been far from universal or guaranteed, and has, instead, been powerfully shaped by differing contexts within and across countries. For every case in which expanded taxation has generated meaningful tax bargaining, there are corresponding cases in which expanded taxation has been met with little response from citizens or has been imposed entirely coercively by governments. This is consistent with the simple fact that taxation is, even at the best of times, a fundamentally coercive act. As Ross (2004: 234) has noted, "Many people dislike paying taxes, and some will cause trouble when governments raise them. But democracy is only one possible outcome of these conflicts. Historically, people have borne crushingly high tax rates with few rebellions; when they do revolt, they have often been met with intensified repression, not democratic concessions." The existence of episodes of *taxation without bargaining* is thus unsurprising. The more important goal of this book is to understand why positive outcomes have emerged in some cases and not in others, and, further, why tax bargaining has taken different forms in different contexts.

While there is evidence of both direct and indirect tax bargaining in each of the three case study countries, the extent and character of these processes varies significantly. Whereas direct tax bargaining has been particularly common in Ghana, indirect tax bargaining has predominated in Kenya. Meanwhile, tax bargaining of all kinds has been comparatively limited in Ethiopia in recent decades. While these outcomes are idiosyncratic, and embedded in broader processes of political change, the analysis highlights five factors that have been critical in shaping divergent outcomes. First is the *revenue pressure* facing governments, as tax bargaining has been more likely where governments have faced urgent revenue needs and lacked access to alternative revenue sources. Second is the *scope for tax resistance* through evasion and avoidance, with increased scope for resistance offering taxpayers greater political leverage in making demands

---

holders into officers of the state, and the imposition of religious conformity in the name of public order and morality." He continues: "[Y]ou may object to using the word 'bargain' for the sending in of troops to crush a tax rebellion or capture a reluctant taxpayer. Nonetheless, the frequent use of exemplary punishment indicates that the authorities were negotiating with the bulk of the population" (1992: 101).

on governments or prompting broader political change. Third is a set of factors shaping *taxpayer capacity for collective action*, with the role of elite groups proving particularly pivotal in shaping the potential for effective bargaining by taxpayers. Fourth is the *nature of political institutions*, with more inclusive and open political institutions offering greater scope for more direct forms of tax bargaining between taxpayers and governments. And fifth is the *political salience of taxation*, as taxpayers have been more likely to become politically mobilized where taxes and tax reform have been comparatively "visible" and broadly felt. Collectively, attention to these factors offers a more complete account of the links between taxation, responsiveness and accountability, as well as a starting point for identifying policy options for fostering broader governance gains in low-income countries. These somewhat more speculative policy implications are addressed in detail in the final chapter of the book.

This is an ambitious research agenda, and as such it is important to stress that this research is in many respects exploratory. The causal connections linking taxation, responsiveness and accountability are likely to be complex and varied, and embedded in broader processes of political change. These process are correspondingly inherently difficult to observe and study. As such, this book does not claim to capture every way in which taxation may shape broader political outcomes. It focuses instead on a set of comparatively concrete and observable processes, which can offer specific insights while speaking to the likelihood of more subtle behavioural changes. It likewise does not claim to capture every way in which contextual factors may shape these processes, nor does it aspire to present a highly deterministic model of these relationships, which inevitably form part of broader, and unpredictable, processes of bargaining and political contestation. Instead, it seeks to present an encompassing framework for studying the connections between taxation, responsiveness and accountability, while presenting concrete empirical evidence of specific manifestations of these processes in contemporary developing countries. This research thus aims to provide important new academic and policy insights at a relatively broad level, while equally providing a foundation for subsequent research that can further interrogate key propositions being advanced here.

1.5 Revenue, tax bargaining and the politics of development

While this book aims to provide new insights into the specific relationship between taxation, responsiveness and accountability, it is also informed by, and contributes to, a broader resurgence in academic and policy interest in the connections between the composition of government revenue, institutional development, and a wider range of development outcomes. It is correspondingly useful to briefly chart the growth of interest in these broader questions, in order to situate more fully the intellectual approach and contribution of this book.

As has already been noted, resurgent interest in questions linking government revenue and broader development outcomes has been spurred by widespread attention to the potential developmental costs of heavy reliance on non-tax sources of revenue, primarily from non-renewable natural resources. Building on early case study evidence from the Middle East and Africa, research into the so-called resource curse has provided clear evidence that differences in the sources of government revenue can have important implications for broader patterns of state-building, accountability and economic growth (Mahdavy 1970; Beblawi and Luciani 1987; Chaudhry 1997; van de Walle 1998; Guyer 1992; Yates 1996; Karl 1997; Collier and Hoeffler 1998, 2004; Ross 2001, 2012; Smith 2007). Parts of the resource curse literature have focused specifically on the role of taxation, with Luciani (1990: 75), for example, having argued in one of the earliest works on the subject that unlike a resource-dependent state, a state dependent on taxation "must give credibility to the notion that it represents the common good." However, this literature has equally advanced evidence that changes in the composition of government revenue may have significantly broader implications in shaping patterns of state-building, economic growth and conflict (Collier and Hoeffler 1998, 2004; Humphreys 2005; Ross 2009; Torvik 2009; van der Ploeg 2011). While research into the resource curse has often struggled to unpack the role of specific causal processes underlying these diverse relationships[23] – including an inability to isolate the particular role of tax bargaining – it has left little doubt that differences in the sources of government revenue are likely to have much broader development implications.

This recognition has contributed to a broader resurgence of interest in much older ideas associated with the subfield of fiscal sociology. In

---

[23] Humphreys (2005) offered an early effort to explicitly distinguish alternative causal explanations, although focusing more narrowly on the observed connection between resource revenues and civil conflict. However, he highlighted the difficulty of this task, writing that "[e]conometric tests of the effects of natural resources on conflicts, including those presented here, continue to suffer from severe problems of data, model specification and in particular a sensitivity of coefficient estimates to variations in model specification. In this article, I have found evidence to support some mechanisms and reported the lack of support for others, but I have not constructed sufficient tests to distinguish between all the mechanism identified." Ross (2009) has pursued a similar strategy in relation to the connections between tax reliance and accountability, but that work remains unpublished, apparently owing to similar methodological constraints.

1.5 Revenue, tax bargaining and the politics of development

1918, Joseph Schumpeter (1991 [1918]: 101), a pioneer in the field, captured the now oft-quoted idea that "public finances are one of the best starting points for an investigation of society, especially although not exclusively of its political life." Central to his approach was the belief that understanding the ways governments were funded was fundamental to understanding the way society was organized and governed. He recognized that states and governments that relied on their citizens for revenue through taxation were likely to rule very differently, and to face very different political pressures, than those that relied on independent resources to finance their activities.[24]

This basic insight has been borne out by numerous accounts of state formation in early modern Europe (Tilly 1975, 1992; Brewer 1989; Ertman 1997; Daunton 2001). Some of these accounts have highlighted the importance of the need to expand tax collection in shaping the responsiveness and accountability of governments, and this research has directly inspired this book (Levi 1988; North and Weingast 1989; Tilly 1992). However, historical accounts have equally captured the broader importance of taxation to economic growth and the building of state capacity.[25] Collecting taxes required the development of a complex and intrusive bureaucratic apparatus, and in many cases this became the leading edge of bureaucratic modernization and the strengthening of central states (Brewer 1989; Tilly 1992; Chaudhry 1997; Bräutigam 2008a; Prichard and Leonard 2010).[26] The need for taxation likewise strengthened incentives for governments to create conditions conducive to economic growth, based on a common interest in promoting the prosperity of taxpayers in order to maximize levels of tax revenue. As Bates (2001: 69) has written, "governments pursued policies that promoted the development of the economy not because they wanted to but because they had to, the better to secure the resources with which to fight."[27] While this book

---

[24] Equally central to the evolution of scholarship in this field was the work of Rudolf Goldscheid. Unfortunately, little of that work has been translated into English, although it is summarized in Schumpeter (1991 [1918]) and (Moore 2001: 399–400).

[25] These processes have elsewhere been termed "state apparatus processes," "common interest processes" and "responsiveness and accountability processes," respectively (Prichard 2010).

[26] This possibility has been well documented in early modern Europe (Brewer 1989; Tilly 1992), while a growing body of research has also pointed to the importance of taxation to the development of broader administrative capacity in contemporary developing countries (Chaudhry 1997; Bräutigam 2008a; Prichard and Leonard 2010).

[27] While such processes are inherently difficult to observe, Gehlbach (2008) has provided evidence from the former Soviet Union that governments have invested heavily in promoting the success of those industries most likely to contribute tax revenue to the state. The experience of fiscal decentralization in China in encouraging subnational governments to vigorously promote economic growth is also consistent with this argument

is narrowly about the relationship between taxation, responsiveness and accountability, it also reflects the broader conviction that differences in the sources of government revenue are likely to have significantly broader implications for development outcomes.

However, despite the centrality of taxation to broader processes of state-building and political change in early modern Europe, questions about taxation have historically figured much less prominently in the study of politics in the developing world (Moore 1998). This has begun to change, with the incorporation of differences in the composition of government revenue as a key variable in broader theories of political and institutional change (Bates 2001; Doner, Ritchie and Slater 2005; Besley and Persson 2011). Studies in this tradition have generally understood institutional development and change as the outcome of processes of bargaining and contestation both between political and economic elites and between state and society more broadly (Doner, Ritchie and Slater 2005; Acemoglu and Robinson 2006; North, Wallis and Weingast 2009; Slater 2010; Besley and Persson 2011).[28] They have, in turn, identified the composition of government revenue as a critical factor in shaping the incentives and bargaining power of competing groups within these contests.[29]

Besley and Persson (2011), for example, identify four "fundamental determinants"[30] of political incentives to invest in state capacity and more effective institutions: the presence or absence of war, ethnic homogeneity, the pre-existence of effective political institutions and *the extent to*

(Bahl 1998; Lin and Liu 2000), while economic models have noted the related possibility that governments might give priority to economic activities that are more readily taxable (Auriol and Warlters 2005).

[28] Within this research tradition institutions are dynamic: existing institutions structure contestation and bargaining between competing groups, but equally change in response to shifting interests and alignments of power (Hall and Taylor 1996). More developmental institutions may, for example, be adopted by elites in order to respond to broader societal demands (Acemoglu and Robinson 2006), or may emerge as a means to manage conflict and rents amongst competing elite groups (North, Wallis and Weingast 2009).

[29] Such bargaining between state and society is often implicitly conceptualized as pitting a broad-based citizenry against a state controlled by elites. However, while this is often a useful simplification, tax bargaining is often likely to centre on large taxpayers, who account for the bulk of tax revenues, and thus potentially pit elites who control the state against economic elites that wish to avoid taxation. Consistent with this view, several recent works highlight the extent to which developing cohesion amongst elite groups has been central to constructing more effective tax regimes in the developing world (Lieberman 2002; Slater 2010; Schneider 2012).

[30] They adopt the term "fundamental determinants" based on the observation that "almost all dimensions of state development and effectiveness are positively correlated" (2011: 13), thus suggesting that they are grounded in a core set of factors that tend to shape the incentives for state elites to invest in strengthening state capacity and developing effective institutions.

which political elites are able to rely on non-tax sources of revenue rather than on taxing their own citizens.[31] In similar fashion, Doner, Ritchie and Slater (2005: 327) argue that the success of the East Asian developmental states was the result of the coexistence of "restive popular sectors... extreme geopolitical insecurity and *severe resource constraints*" [emphasis added]. They argue that the absence of alternative sources of revenue forced the political leadership to expand taxation and thus shaped their incentives to invest in the state, promote economic growth, and build more effective institutions. In a similar vein, Bates (2001) identifies the need to raise revenue as a key incentive for African leaders to invest in promoting economic growth, whereas Slater (2010) identifies the need for expanded revenue as having been a central motivation for elite investments in state capacity in Southeast Asia. While these works have addressed questions of government revenue and development outcomes at only a very broad level, they reflect important initial efforts to incorporate questions about the composition of government revenue centrally within broader discussions of institutional development and political change.

While this book seeks narrowly to address the questions of whether and how tax bargaining has contributed to the expansion of responsiveness and accountability in developing countries, it is equally inspired by, and seeks to contribute to, these broader research currents. Conceptually, it similarly situates processes of tax bargaining within the context of broader processes of contestation between state and society. In doing so, it seeks to move the discussion of tax bargaining closer to the centre of broader discussions of politics in developing countries, and thus to contribute to debates about the foundations of state-building and institutional change.

1.6 Research strategy and methodology

While the goals of this research are ultimately relatively straightforward, confidently capturing processes linking taxation, responsiveness and accountability implies significant methodological challenges. The causal processes of interest are likely to be diverse, contingent and – in many cases – both long-term and relatively implicit. The implication is

---

[31] They also refer more explicitly to the specific research tradition into which this book falls: "An important research strand in political science and political sociology stresses that legitimate political institutions, which give citizens a true say in how the money is spent, might be a necessary quid pro quo for them to go along with increased collection of taxes. It is argued that such "fiscal contracts" may explain the historical joint building of tax capacity and representative political institutions in many developed countries (see, for example, Levi, 1988), and that a similar mechanism could potentially be operating in developing countries today (see, for example, the contributions in Bräutigam, Fjeldstad and Moore 2008)."

that the causal impact of taxation may be difficult to observe and to isolate from broader processes of political contestation and change. These methodological challenges help to explain the relative absence of existing case study research in this area, and point towards the importance of developing a clear strategy for capturing processes that are difficult to observe. With this challenge in mind, it is useful to conclude this introductory chapter with a more detailed discussion of the research strategy and methodology.

At a broad level, the research seeks to combine quantitative and qualitative research findings in the spirit of Lieberman's (2005) model of "nested-analysis," which calls for cross-country econometric results to provide the starting point for the analysis and drive subsequent case selection. The econometric results reported already provide significant support for the existence of a causal relationship between tax reliance and accountability. However, they are inconclusive about the specific role of tax bargaining in shaping this relationship, and they are unable to offer insight into the details of underlying causal processes or the contextual factors that are likely to shape particular outcomes.

These limitations of the econometric results set the stage for a "model-building" approach to case selection. This has implied the purposeful selection of cases that stand to enhance our understanding of the specific causal processes and contextual factors underpinning the broader hypothesized relationship. While this strategy cannot confirm that the causal processes of interest exist in all cases, it can buttress generally supportive econometric evidence and minimally confirm that such processes are common in a wide variety of cases. More importantly, this strategy offers the greatest potential for offering new insights into the diversity and contingency of processes of tax bargaining, which remains the most glaring limitation of existing research.

In practice, this has meant selecting states that are relatively highly dependent on taxes for their incomes, and where there have been significant changes in tax collection over time. This book is focused on understanding the *potentially positive governance benefits of dependence on taxation*, and it is only where taxation is substantial that tax bargaining in any form seems likely. Meanwhile, periods of change in tax policy or administration are more likely to offer analytical leverage by bringing tax bargaining into the political foreground.[32] With these requirements in

[32] Critically, this does not amount to picking only "successful cases," as cases were not chosen on the basis of any pre-existing evidence of tax bargaining. It is simply an instance of choosing cases that are analytically tractable given the methodology being employed. In the absence of significant taxation, there is simply little potential for studying the practical manifestations of tax bargaining. While low-tax and resource-dependent states

1.6 Research strategy and methodology

mind, Ghana, Kenya and Ethiopia have been selected for in-depth study. All three of these countries collect significant taxation by the standards of low-income countries, with Kenya and Ghana both generally held to be amongst the top tax collectors in the region.[33] All three have equally experienced significant changes in tax revenue over time.

In addition to comparatively high and variable levels of tax collection, the three cases also capture significant variation in key political and economic variables, as detailed in Table 1.6. This variation is important in order to capture the expected diversity of the causal processes of interest, to increase the external validity of the findings and to shed light on the importance of different contextual factors in shaping outcomes. Economically, Kenya has long been amongst sub-Saharan Africa's most successful non-resource economies, while Ghana has experienced rapid and sustained growth since the early 1980s. By contrast, Ethiopia is amongst the world's lowest-income countries, with a particularly weak private sector, despite very rapid growth over the past two decades. Politically, Kenya has been amongst the region's most politically stable countries, although its democracy has been highly flawed; whereas Ethiopia has remained highly autocratic throughout its history, despite some brief steps towards greater political openness from 1991 to 2005. Ghana again presents the greatest variation, as it remained under military rule throughout much of the 1970s and 1980s, but has since emerged as arguably sub-Saharan Africa's most successful democracy. The three countries also vary significantly in their levels of aid dependence. This is of interest in part because of the importance of foreign aid and external pressure in shaping tax policy and administration (Fjeldstad and Moore 2008). Equally, there is a significant, although contested, literature arguing that access to foreign aid may reduce tax collection and the potential for tax bargaining in ways analogous to the resource curse (Moore 1998; Moss, Pettersson and van de Walle 2006; Prichard, Brun and Morrissey 2012). Finally, Ethiopia

---

are undoubtedly interesting, they are particularly unlikely to shed light on the character of the connections between taxation, responsiveness and accountability.

[33] At the time of conducting this research in 2008, Ghana reported a tax to GDP ratio greater than 20%, thus placing it amongst the most successful tax collectors in the developing world. However, revised GDP estimates produced in 2010 resulted in a 60% increase in nominal GDP, and a correspondingly dramatic decline in the tax ratio, to around 14% of GDP. This figure is officially about average amongst sub-Saharan Africa countries, but this comparison is biased by the likelihood that GDP remains underestimated in many other African nations (Jerven and Duncan 2012). The overriding message is that precise comparison of tax ratios across countries can be extremely misleading owing to inconsistencies in the calculation of GDP. As a consequence, the focus here has been on selecting countries above an implicit minimum threshold of tax collection, which have also experienced variable collection trends over time.

Table 1.6 *Key characteristics of the case study countries*

	Ghana	Kenya	Ethiopia
Tax Revenue (% GDP, 2008)	13.9[34]	18.8	9.6
Level of Tax Collection	Amongst stronger tax collectors in SSA since the mid-1990s	Consistently amongst top SSA performers since independence	Average performance given very limited tax base
Historic Trends in Tax Collection	Experienced unusually consistent and large increases in tax revenue beginning in mid-1980s following economic crisis.	Substantial revenue gains in early 1990s, followed by revenue decline later in the decade and renewed gains after 2002.	Consistent gains after 1991 end of civil war and Marxist rule, while revenue declined sharply after flawed 2005 elections.
GDP per capita (2008, US$)	1,226	794	335
GDP capita PPP (2008, US$)	1,499	1,564	884
Historic Economic Performance	Dramatic economic decline beginning in 1970s, followed by relatively continuous economic growth since the mid-1980s, when it was the first SSA state to implement structural adjustment.	Amongst SSA's most successful non-resource economies since independence, despite economic stagnation throughout much of the 1990s and early 2000s.	Amongst lowest-income countries in the world, although with high growth rates over the past decade. Weak private sector owing largely to state-controlled economic system from 1974 to 1991, along with continued high levels of state involvement.
Democracy (2008, Freedom House)[35]	1 (Free)	4 (Partially Free)	5 (Partially Free)
Historic Political Openness	Repeated military coups throughout 1970s, culminating in establishment of the PNDC military regime from 1983 to 1992. Formal transitions to democracy in 1992, with electoral alternation in power in 2000 and 2008.	Nominally democratic since independence, but elections during the 1980s and 1990s were highly flawed. Relatively open and successful elections in 2002, followed by contested elections at the end of 2007.	Highly autocratic under Imperial rule until 1974, and then under Marxist rule until 1991. Slow opening of democratic competition until 2005 elections, which were marked by fraud and repression. Political repression has continued since 2005.
Aid % of GDP (2008)	4.6	4.5	12.5
Historic Aid Reliance	Has received consistently high levels of aid, often greater than 10% of GDP, since mid-1980s introduction of structural adjustment. Aid has declined to around 5% of GDP since 2006 owing in part to rising incomes and the discovery of oil.	Received relatively high levels of aid during the Cold War period, but aid levels have remained low by regional standards, at between 5% and 10% of GDP since the early 1990s amidst somewhat strained donor relations.	Amongst SSA's most heavily aid-dependent countries since 1991, with aid averaging well higher than 10% of GDP, and approaching 20% in 2002–2003. Modest decline in aid after flawed elections in 2005.

[34] See the previous footnote describing the 2010 re-estimation of GDP, and its impact on the implied tax ratio.

[35] The Freedom House database ranks countries from 1 (Free) to 7 (Not Free) with respect to political rights and civil liberties. The rankings reported here are for political rights.

1.6 Research strategy and methodology

never experienced full-blown colonial rule, and thus presents a unique historical context.

With the case study countries thus selected, the more daunting challenge has been the development of a research strategy to capture implicit, long-term and difficult-to-observe causal processes through case study research. The first step has been the development of a detailed analytical model that highlights specific processes and outcomes of interest. The model expands on earlier models developed by Bates and Lien (1985) and Levi (1988) and explicitly identifies multiple alternative causal processes through which the need for taxation may contribute to the broader expansion of responsiveness and accountability, while highlighting a set of contextual factors that are expected to shape particular outcomes. The model, presented in Chapter 2, provides a framework for making sense of complex case study evidence and for assessing the overall quality of that evidence.

With the analytical model in place, the case studies follow a process tracing methodology, and are centred on the construction of detailed analytical narratives of taxation and political change over several decades in each country, thus mirroring the approach adopted in seminal work linking taxation and state-building in early modern Europe (Tilly 1992). This approach holds the potential to capture a diversity of outcomes, to take account of the importance of political and economic context, and to accommodate the likelihood that some processes of tax bargaining are likely to play out over multiple years or even longer. More broadly, it accounts for the path dependency of taxation and the consequent importance of historical context (Levi 1988; Lieberman 2002; Mahon 2004; Bird and Zolt 2005; Torgler 2005).

Owing to the relative absence of existing research dealing with the political economy of taxation in sub-Saharan Africa, the construction of detailed narratives has relied heavily on primary research conducted during eleven months of continuous field research over the course of 2008, and during subsequent trips to Kenya and Ghana in 2009. The most important component of the research has been more than 120 formal interviews with key stakeholders, drawn primarily from amongst former and current politicians, civil servants and leading members of civil society. These interviews have been complemented by the collection of documentary evidence and official tax data not available outside of the individual countries, and by a wide range of more informal discussions with senior tax officials from across sub-Saharan Africa in subsequent years. The interviews have targeted those best placed to comment on the politics surrounding taxation, including Ministers of Finance, parliamentarians, directors of tax agencies and the leaders of civil society bodies, while long-serving members of the civil service were frequently of particular importance in reconstructing the historical record and in identifying key developments and political controversies.

Throughout these interviews the goal was to allow stakeholders to identify key events and recount them in their own terms in order to develop narratives that closely reflect the experiences of the key stakeholders involved. In particular, the interviewees have been central to identifying for each case study a subset of key *tax episodes*, centred on particularly important changes in, or debates over, levels of tax collection, tax policy or tax administration. These tax episodes ground the case study analysis, and can be usefully thought of as a subset of interconnected observations, thus expanding the number of "cases" from three countries to a much larger number of tax episodes. A standard three-country comparison may offer too few degrees of freedom to disentangle the roles of a wide range of potentially important contextual factors shaping particular outcomes. By contrast, a focus on individual tax episodes makes it possible not only to compare outcomes across countries, but also to compare outcomes within countries at different moments in time – and thus, under often very different contextual conditions. Thus, for example, patterns of tax bargaining in Ghana can be compared to those in Kenya and Ethiopia, but equally it is possible to explore how patterns of tax bargaining in Ghana have differed before and after democratization in the mid-1990s. Indeed, this latter comparison is in many ways more compelling, as a range of country specific variables are kept relatively constant, alongside variation in political institutions.

It is around these interconnected tax episodes that the analysis traces the complex political interactions and outcomes that are the practical manifestation of the abstract idea of tax bargaining. Moore (2007: 16) has written: "Any realistic understanding of these processes [of tax bargaining] requires that we go beyond the initial reactions to taxation of each type of actor, and take into account the ways in which they then interact, whether conflictually, cooperatively, or in more complex ways." As such, for each tax episode the analysis attempts to answer four initial questions. What were the technical details of the change in, or debates over, tax collection, policy, or administration? What political economy factors explain the timing and details of these changes or debates? How did taxpayers and/or government actors react to the change or debate? What subsequent interactions occurred between taxpayers and government, and what were the outcomes?

Having constructed these analytical narratives, the analysis then turns to assessing whether these narratives constitute significant evidence of the existence of a causal relationship between taxation, responsiveness

1.6 Research strategy and methodology

and accountability. This sequencing is important. By presenting detailed narratives of the development of individual tax systems first, and only subsequently asking whether those narratives constitute evidence of tax bargaining, the goal has been to allow the conclusions to emerge directly from the empirical evidence. There is a clear risk in a study of this kind of focusing exclusively on episodes that conform to received theory, or of distorting the evidence to fit a particular set of theoretical expectations. The structure adopted here is, therefore, a strategy to avoid bias in selecting cases and writing the account, as well as a means to invite in-depth scrutiny of the empirical evidence by readers. While this structure necessarily implies a degree of repetition in the presentation of the case study evidence, the benefits for the reliability of the conclusions seem to far outweigh those costs.

While the concrete details of the narratives provide initial insight in the relationship between taxation, responsiveness and accountability, the conclusions rest primarily on *causal process observations* (Collier, Brady and Seawright 2004; Bennett and Elman 2006; Brady, Collier and Seawright 2006); that is, in this case, on statements by stakeholders themselves about the motivations behind particular actions and outcomes. Ultimately, the vast majority of the causal claims in the case studies are based on explicit statements by public officials and stakeholders explaining that their actions were motivated by tax concerns and that outcomes can be reasonably understood in those terms. This is reflected in detailed references to individual interviews through the case study chapters, while conclusions based on interview evidence have been included in the text only where they could be verified with multiple respondents or with reference to alternative sources.[36]

This reliance on causal process observations is motivated by the fact that tax bargaining is likely to be frequently implicit, and may thus be extremely difficult to observe. Moore (2008: 38) captures this challenge clearly when he asks, "To the extent that revenue bargaining is indirect, taking the form of strategic interaction and mutual behaviour adjustment, rather than public haggling and agreements, how do we know it is taking place? Like some other types of political action, this one is not always easily observable." In simpler terms, various types of political action may be motivated by tax concerns, without this being readily apparent to an outside observer. It is by constructing detailed historical narratives, framed by a careful analytical model and supported by specific

---

[36] The references in the footnotes refer to the "primary" sources of particular information, but are not exhaustive of those who in formal or informal discussions confirmed the reliability of particular information.

statements from key stakeholders themselves, that this study is able to make confident assertions about causality despite the complexity of the political processes in question. As explained in the next chapter, the goal is not to capture *every* way in which taxation may shape political engagement, but to capture a subset of specific manifestations of tax bargaining. These are, in turn, expected to also be indicative of a range of more subtle ways in which taxation may shape the behaviour and bargaining power of citizens and governments.

Of course, there are inherent risks of bias when relying so heavily on interview evidence, and thus a final note is warranted about measures taken to guard against these risks. Recognizing that perspectives may vary across different actors and that political actors may have an interest in recounting particular versions of events, every effort has been made to interview actors from different perspectives and political parties. The potential sensitivity of these issues has required promises of anonymity, but an anonymized list of those interviewed is included at the end of the book to provide a clearer indication of the sources of the interview evidence. A broader but subtler risk lies in the possibility of unconsciously imposing theoretical expectations on the content of interviews. This may happen in two primary ways: (1) the interviewer may ask leading questions, which encourage theoretically "attractive" responses; or (2) the researcher may interpret interview responses in a way consistent with theory, but inconsistent with the intentions of the respondent. Efforts have been made to guard against these risks in three main ways. First, the research was presented to respondents as investigating the "political dynamics surrounding taxation and tax reform," to avoid inadvertently encouraging respondents to present evidence of tax bargaining where it may not exist.[37] Second, within each interview respondents were initially asked to identify key tax episodes and their politics in their own words, before any more specific questions were posed. These initial responses, interrupted only for clarification, frequently took longer than a half hour, and marked an effort to secure an unvarnished account of events, as understood by individual respondents. Third, whenever possible the particular focus of the research on tax bargaining was explained to respondents towards the end of the interview, in order to ask respondents more precise variants of the question "Do you think that it is accurate to interpret government/taxpayer/civil society actions as being

---

[37] This presentation of the research project was not in any sense misleading, as it precisely described the goal of each interview, which was to understand key tax episodes and the politics surrounding them. It was, however, an important simplification if the interview evidence was to be reliable.

representative of a process of tax bargaining?" This acted as an important check that respondents themselves felt that events could reasonably be interpreted in the ways reported in this book. While there are inescapable questions of reliability in relation to interview evidence, every effort has been made to ensure that the evidence reported here is as complete, accurate and reliable as possible.

1.7 Structure of the book

This introduction has set out the broad argument, research agenda and intellectual approach of this book. Stated most simply, this book aims to provide new insights into the connections between taxation, responsiveness and accountability, with an emphasis on understanding the diversity and contingency of these relationships in contemporary developing countries. Simply identifying the need for such research is straightforward – and, indeed, the need for such research is widely recognized. The greater challenge lies in developing an operational research agenda that can credibly capture the causal processes of interest and translate a complex empirical reality into a manageable set of key messages. Chapter 2 is correspondingly focused on laying out this detailed research framework. This involves the development of a detailed causal model and the presentation of specific operational indicators against which to assess the extent and character of connections between taxation, responsiveness and accountability. The chapter concludes with the identification of a set of contextual factors that are expected to shape particular outcomes and the incorporation of these contextual factors into a dynamic model that seeks to account for divergent outcomes across cases.

Having laid out the research strategy in detail, Chapters 3, 4 and 5 comprise the empirical core of the book, presenting the case study evidence from Ghana, Kenya and Ethiopia. Following these case studies, Chapter 6 draws the evidence together, proposing broader conclusions about the specific causal processes linking taxation, responsiveness and accountability, and about the contextual factors that have shaped the likelihood and character of those processes. Finally, Chapter 7 moves beyond the core empirical findings in order to explore possible policy implications and directions for further research.

Statistical appendix

In an effort to ensure the robustness of the econometric findings, we implement five distinct econometric estimation models, the details of which are summarized here and described in greater detail in Prichard, Salardi and Segal (2014).

The analysis begins from a relatively standard dynamic specification:

$$Democracy_{i,t} = \delta Democracy_{i,t-1} + \beta_1 Tax\_rel_{i,t-1} + X'_{i,t-1}\gamma + \alpha_i \\ + \lambda_t + e_{i,t} \quad [1]$$

where $Democracy_{i,t}$ is the measure of accountability for country i in period t. On the right-hand side of equation [1], we include a lagged value of the dependent variable both to model the persistence of democracy over time and to account for potential mean reverting dynamics. Tax_rel_i is the key independent variable in the first set of tests, while we subsequently disaggregate it into its component parts – tax revenue as a share of GDP (*tottax*) and non-tax revenue as a share of GDP (*totnotax*), as follows:

$$Democracy_{i,t} = \delta Democracy_{i,t-1} + \beta_1 tottax_{i,t-1} + \beta_2 totnontax_{i,t-1} \\ + X'_{i,t-1}\gamma + \alpha_i + \lambda_t + e_{i,t} \quad [2]$$

In both [1] and [2] the right-hand side variables are lagged by a single year to capture the temporal dimension of the relationship. The estimated parameter β_1 captures the impact of tax reliance on *Democracy*. The vector $X'_{i,t}$ includes our time-varying control variables. Country-fixed effects, α_i, are included to account for unobserved country-specific factors, and time dummies, λ_t, are included to control for time-varying shocks across countries.

Following Ross (2004) and a series of subsequent studies, the inclusion of the lagged dependent and independent variables on the right-hand side of the equation is an effort in part to control for the possibility of endogeneity – that is, the fact that while higher taxation may spur the expansion of democracy, it is equally possible that democracy might contribute to higher taxation. However, this is an imperfect approach to addressing the potential for endogeneity, while the inclusion of lagged dependent variables alongside fixed effects can bias the results (Nickell 1981).

As such, the core analysis begins by implementing the System-GMM estimation method introduced by Blundell and Bond (1998). The System-GMM estimator employs both first differences and lagged levels of the explanatory variables as instruments, and has been widely adopted when considering dynamic processes with fixed effects where there are potentially endogenous regressors and idiosyncratic disturbances. By using lagged levels of the variables as instruments, the System-GMM estimator preserves information on cross-country differences that is lost when only the first differenced equation is estimated, and is therefore more efficient than the closely related Difference-GMM estimator (Aslaksen 2010).

While System-GMM has been widely adopted in similar studies, it has been criticized for being a "black box," while its comparative advantage is with large-N but small-T datasets. By contrast, we employ up to twenty-one years of data from 1990–2010, thus suggesting the potential value of alternative panel data methods.

One such option is the Common Correlated Effects-Mean Group (CCE-MG) estimator, which has been developed to deal specifically with such macro panels (Pesaran and Smith 1995). The key advantage of the CCE-MG estimator is that it addresses both parameter heterogeneity and cross-section dependence, with the former making it more flexible in addressing the potential diversity of the relationships of interest across countries. The downside of the CCE-MG is that it does not model dynamics, and thus cannot account for potential reverse causation leading from democracy to taxation. It is thus complementary with the Sys-GMM results, as each option addresses potential weaknesses of the other.

An alternative option, favoured by Haber and Menaldo (2011), is to move away from explicitly panel data methods in favour of methods that emphasize the time series dimension of the data, and they correspondingly employ Error Correction Mechanism (ECM) regressions. ECM regressions provide estimates of both the short-term and long-term effects of the explanatory variables, using the *change* in *Democracy* as the dependent variable, denoted:

$$\Delta_n Democracy_t = Democracy_t - Democracy_{t-n}.$$

This gives the following specification:

$$\Delta_n Democracy_{i,t} = \alpha Democracy_{i,t-n} + \beta \Delta Revenue_{i,t-n} \\ + \gamma (Democracy_{i,t-n} - \delta Revenue_{i,t-n}) \\ + X'_{i,t-n}\rho + u_{i,t} \qquad [3]$$

The ECM model suffers from several notable drawbacks, however. First, it does not allow for heterogeneous coefficients or cross-section dependence, as with the CCE-MG. Second, Andersen and Ross (2014) have criticized it for focusing exclusively on the year-on-year change in the variables of interest. They argue that this may be problematic if the relationship between the composition of government revenue and democracy is reflected not in relatively contemporaneous changes in the dependent and independent variables, but, instead, in the longer-term levels of those variables (see also Ross 2014). The potential advantages of ECM are amplified for Haber and Menaldo (2011), owing to the dramatically longer length of their time series data, but – given our shorter time series – these methods are best understood as a robustness check for our results.

Finally, all of the Sys-GMM, CCE-MG and ECM estimators are potentially limited by their reliance on continuous measures of democracy, as several studies have argued instead for a focus on the likelihood of *transitions* between autocracy and democracy, as described in the main text. To address this possibility, we adopt a dynamic logit model drawn from Wiens et al. (2014), which captures the impact of the composition of government revenue on the likelihood that a country will transition between democracy and autocracy. Using *Tax_rel* as the independent variable:

$$\Pr(\text{Regime}_{i,t}) = \Lambda[\delta \text{Regime}_{i,t-1} + \beta_1 \text{Tax\_rel}_{i,t-1} + \beta_2 \text{Regime} \\ \times \text{Tax\_rel}_{i,t-1} + \beta_3 X'_{i,t-1} + \beta_4 \text{Regime}_{i,t-1} \\ \times X'_{i,t-1} + \lambda_t + \Delta_{i,t}] \qquad [4]$$

Using *tottax* and *totnontax*:

$$\Pr(\text{Regime}_{i,t}) = \Lambda[\delta \text{Regime}_{i,t-1} + \beta_1 \text{tottax}_{i,t-1} + \beta_2 \text{Regime} \\ \times \text{tottax}_{i,t-1} + \beta_3 \text{totnontax}_{i,t-1} + \beta_4 \text{Regime} \\ \times \text{totnontax}_{i,t-1} + \beta_5 X'_{i,t-1} + \beta_6 \text{Regime}_{i,t-1} \\ \times X'_{i,t-1} + \lambda_t + \Delta_{i,t}] \qquad [5]$$

The inclusion of the interaction terms between lagged *Regime* and each of the variables on the right-hand side of the equation allows us to identify whether the revenue variables have distinct impacts in democracies and autocracies. The total effect of the revenue variables in democracies is the sum of the coefficients on the revenue term alone and on the relevant interaction term.

Accounting for unobserved country heterogeneity is more complicated when focusing on regime transitions, as the inclusion of fixed effects results in dropping every country that did not undergo a regime transition from 1990 to 2010 – a group that includes most countries and almost all major resource producers. Wiens et al. (2014) seek to address this problem by adopting a random-effects specification to account for unobserved country heterogeneity as far as possible while retaining necessary country coverage, which is the best available option, although it is imperfect. We correspondingly also report results using a standard fixed-effects model for robustness, while recognizing the risks associated with the loss of a large share of the sample.[38]

[38] We employ a Hausman (1978) test of the validity of the random effects specification. It returns a negative value, which is generally interpreted as evidence that a random-effects specification can be used (Hausman and McFadden 1984), but may potentially be misleading, which prompts our reporting the fixed effects results as well (Vijverberg 2011).

2 Linking taxation, responsiveness and accountability
Theoretical model and research strategy

The central contribution of this book lies in presenting detailed case studies of the politics of taxation, which provide new insights into how and when connections between taxation, responsiveness and accountability have emerged in practice. However, moving from broad propositions about taxation and governance to detailed empirical research at the country level confronts two closely related challenges. First, existing models have focused on broad causal arguments, while saying much less about the specific ways in which bargaining over taxation may play out in practice in contemporary developing countries. Second, there are good reasons to believe that these processes may be frequently difficult to observe, owing to the fact that bargaining over taxation is likely to be frequently "indirect, taking the form of strategic interaction and mutual behaviour adjustment, rather than public haggling and agreements" (Moore 2008: 38).

This chapter is aimed at translating the existing body of theoretical and historical literature into a more specific set of propositions for empirical investigation through extended case study research. This involves defining and operationalizing key concepts and outcomes of interest in order to construct a model linking taxation, responsiveness and accountability through three clearly defined causal processes. This, in turn, provides the foundation for developing a more dynamic model. This dynamic model seeks to capture the importance of strategic bargaining between taxpayers and governments and to highlight the role of contextual factors in shaping bargaining processes and outcomes. The goal is not to capture every possible process through which taxation may shape levels of responsiveness and accountability. Instead, the focus is on translating a comparatively broad, difficult-to-observe, research question into a set of clearly defined and observable empirical possibilities to guide the case study analysis.

With these goals in mind, this chapter is organized in five parts. It begins by revisiting the key lessons that can be drawn from historical experience, as they provide the foundation for the model to follow. The second section develops the basic model, capturing the causal mechanisms and processes that are expected to link taxation to broader changes in responsiveness and accountability. The third section presents a subset of specific operational outcomes of interest, in order to establish a clear standard against which to assess the case study evidence. The fourth section turns to the role of context and highlights five sets of factors that are likely to shape the character and extent of tax bargaining. Finally, the fifth section incorporates these contextual factors into a dynamic model of tax bargaining, which captures the likely diversity and contingency of connections between taxation, responsiveness and accountability.

2.1 The lessons of history: diverse pathways linking taxation and political change

Seminal models of tax bargaining developed by Bates and Lien (1985) and Levi (1988) are the most common starting point for discussion of the connections between taxation, responsiveness and accountability. In their model, Bates and Lien (1985) propose that when taxpayers are mobile, and thus able to evade taxation, governments will have incentives to make concessions to those taxpayers to secure their tax compliance. Levi (1988) takes this basic logic a step further, arguing that the ability of a government to collect tax revenue from citizens depends on three factors: coercion, ideology and, crucially, quasi-voluntary compliance. Quasi-voluntary compliance captures the idea that citizens will be more likely to comply with taxation when the government is perceived to be responsive and accountable, and when other citizens comply as well. Within this framework, governments have incentives to become more responsive and accountable to taxpayers so as to increase quasi-voluntary compliance. This may occur through broad-based concessions to the majority of taxpayers, or may be dominated by elite interests, as governments focus on delivering more modest "side-payments" to the most important larger taxpayers.

While these models derive much of their power from their ability to simplify a more complex reality, Moore (2008) has argued for the need to dig more deeply into the likely complexity and diversity of processes of tax bargaining in contemporary developing countries. He follows earlier models in proposing that tax bargaining refers to "the exchange of tax revenues (for the state) for institutionalized influence over public policy (for citizens)," but then goes on to propose that "bargaining ranges from (a) direct and explicit haggling and agreement to (b) indirect strategic interaction and mutual behaviour adjustment without direct negotiation." He thus highlights what is relatively implicit in earlier models:

while "tax bargaining" is a usefully broad concept, specific instances of tax bargaining are likely to be extremely varied and relatively more complex than the term "bargaining" may evoke. This suggests the value of further exploring the multiple and relatively distinct processes that may underpin the broader concept of tax bargaining in contemporary developing countries, although without entirely abandoning the obvious benefits of parsimony and simplification.

The diverse historical experiences captured in the work of Charles Tilly (1992) are a valuable starting point for understanding this likely complexity. In simplified form, Tilly argues that in early modern Europe the rising costs of warfare forced states to extract an increasingly heavy tax burden from taxpayers, with significant consequences for the character of states and of political power. Most famously, he argues that in England the need for taxation led to conflicts between taxpayers and the monarchy, eventually resulting in tax bargains that granted taxpayers greater representation and legal protection in exchange for higher taxes. However, while the comparatively straightforward example of tax bargaining in England has become the starting point for much contemporary discussion,[1] Tilly's model is significantly more diverse and expansive, and this diversity holds important additional lessons.

While European states faced a common need to expand revenue collection, Tilly argues that differences in the characteristics of individual states led to different revenue-raising strategies and divergent outcomes. He particularly highlights the importance of differences in the extent to which states were characterized by two elements: capital and coercion. Capital-intensive states were home to powerful commercial classes that controlled access to significant and mobile economic resources, while coercion-intensive states were largely agrarian and lacked a large commercial class of significant influence or wealth. This difference was at the root of profoundly different responses to the need for revenue.

In capital-intensive states, the primary challenge was to gain access to the mobile economic resources controlled by capitalists. This was achieved by ceding institutionalized political power to capitalists in exchange for their willingness to contribute tax revenue. Such bargaining was necessary because capitalists were otherwise able to resist taxation by force or, more simply, through tax evasion facilitated by the mobility and

---

[1] While the English case has attracted significant attention in discussion of Tilly's work, the role of taxation in the evolution of the English state has also been particularly widely studied elsewhere (for example, Brewer 1989; North and Weingast 1989; Ertman 1997; Daunton 2001).

2.1 The lessons of history

secrecy of their assets. The tax bargains that resulted fragmented political power and limited the impetus for the construction of powerful central states. This was exemplified by the city-states of Italy, where councils of merchants and capitalists governed and the central state remained weak.

By contrast, states where capital was weak tended to turn towards coercion to extract a small surplus from the rural poor. These states generally relied on bargains between central states and the landowning elite, according to which the central state granted land and power to elites in exchange for the ability to extract tax revenue from a peasantry that was both immobile and weak. This system of revenue mobilization was coercive and unequal but nonetheless gave rise to powerful central bureaucracies capable of extracting significant revenue. This model extended throughout much of Eastern Europe and Scandinavia, and was exemplified by experiences in Russia, where an increasingly powerful central state gradually extended its coercive power over the landed nobility and the subjugated peasantry.

The most successful and inclusive tax bargains, as in the English case, occurred where the relative power of capitalists and of coercive states was most balanced. The strength of capitalists provided strong incentives for the state to reach a revenue-enhancing compromise, while states were strong enough to establish themselves as the central political actors. However, even such cases of relatively successful and inclusive tax bargains come with important caveats. Most obviously, the extension of responsiveness and accountability was not initially universal, but was restricted to a limited group of elites and large taxpayers. Equally important, there were important differences in the particular pathways leading from taxation to the expansions of responsiveness. This can be seen in a comparison between the English and French cases addressed by Tilly, while the experience of the American Revolution, which gave rise to the oft-quoted revolutionary slogan "no taxation without representation," offers a third meaningfully distinct pathway.

The experience of seventeenth-century England epitomizes the ideal of relatively explicit tax bargaining, as it involved a comparatively explicit exchange of tax compliance for the expansion of accountability. By the beginning of the seventeenth century, Britain had established a relatively independent court system to defend the rule of law and a parliament with legal control over taxation. Yet, despite the legal status of Parliament and the courts, the ambitions of the monarchy and the escalating costs of war led successive kings to defy both Parliament and the courts by resorting to unilateral revenue-raising strategies, which included new customs charges, forced loans, the sale of monopolies, property seizures and the sale of peerages (North and Weingast 1989; Tilly 1992). Over time, these abuses by the Crown contributed to growing anger amongst taxpayers and Parliamentarians and ultimately, to civil war, which began in 1642 and eventually resulted in the overthrow of the monarchy. The decision to reinstall the monarchy in 1660 was taken only on the condition that it "confirmed the power of Parliament within the British state, especially when it came to revenues and expenditures" (Tilly 1992: 157).

Despite this apparent agreement, it was not long before conflicts between Parliament and the monarchy re-emerged, thus contributing to a second overthrow of the Crown in 1688, dubbed the Glorious Revolution. That same year, Parliament elected to offer the Crown to the future King William and Queen Mary, but did so only after another institutional revolution, which strengthened the position of Parliament and the courts and shifted the locus of effective power away from the monarchy. This represented a classic tax bargain, as taxpayers agreed to accept increased tax collection in exchange for the institutionalized expansion of governmental accountability. This tax bargain figured centrally in the flourishing of the British state, as it facilitated an increase in the level and stability of tax revenue, a correspondingly increased capacity to borrow abroad, and the construction of a more sophisticated bureaucratic apparatus (Brewer 1989; Tilly 1992).

A century later in France, the need for tax revenue to meet the escalating costs of warfare and debt repayment similarly sparked a period of political conflict that ended with the establishment of a more capable, responsive and accountable government. However, this outcome lacked the relatively explicit tax bargaining of the English case, instead emerging from revolution and an extended period of political upheaval. By the second half of the eighteenth century, the escalating costs of war had led the French state to the brink of bankruptcy. At the time France relied on an inefficient feudal tax system in which the clergy and nobility largely avoided taxation, while the greatest burden fell on agricultural producers and a growing bourgeoisie. Efforts to increase the share of revenue collected by the central state proved both ineffective and unpopular, and led to increasing conflict between the state and taxpayers. By 1789, the fiscal situation had become sufficiently desperate that the king was compelled to summon the Estates General, comprised of the clergy, the nobility and the more broadly representative Third Estate, in order to debate a new fiscal regime. This meeting failed to yield a tax bargain in which increased revenue was exchanged for greater accountability. Instead, the summoning of the Estates General, which was prompted by fiscal crisis and had not occurred since 1614, catalysed the coalescing of a much wider array of grievances amongst the members of the Third Estate, who had soon declared themselves the new National Assembly.

The initial phase of the French Revolution lasted until Napoleon seized power in 1799 and yielded two new constitutions during a complex period of political upheaval and conflict. By the end of the process, the feudal system of rural relations had been largely eliminated and replaced by a powerful and centralized bureaucratic state, with a much-expanded role for the emerging bourgeoisie. Moreover, while the revolutionary government was overthrown after only a decade, it nonetheless introduced the tradition of republican government and contributed to the long-term expansion of accountability. Thus, the Revolution, which was precipitated by a fiscal crisis, gave rise to dramatic political changes. However, the path from tax conflict to political change did not rely on bargaining in the relatively explicit sense of English experience. Instead, it was persistent and unresolved resistance to taxation that precipitated a national crisis and generated pressure for dramatic change through a long, complex and often violent process (Tilly 1992).

A final, and again dramatically different, example relates to the role of taxation in the genesis of the American Revolution. Throughout the latter half of the eighteenth century there had been a debate in the American colony over whether the British Parliament had the right to impose taxes, with the Americans and their allies arguing that under British law only their own representatives could tax them. During the 1760s, this objection led to the repeal of various taxes, including the stamp tax, but the British maintained a tax on tea. This was both a symbolic assertion of power and a means to raise very modest revenue to pay the salaries of various colonial officials, in an effort to reaffirm their loyalty to Britain. In 1773 the issue came to a head when the British government passed the Tea Act, aimed at strengthening the legal standing of the tax on tea. This prompted the so-called Boston Tea Party during which protesters not only refused to allow a shipload of taxed tea to be unloaded, but also destroyed it by throwing it overboard. While this episode had relatively little practical impact on government revenue, it became a symbolic flashpoint for the independence movement, as it highlighted questions about the autonomy and rights of the colony and became a catalyst for popular mobilization. It thus contributed to spurring the onset of the American Revolutionary War that began in 1775 and culminated in the achievement of formal independence in 1783 (Morgan and Morgan 1953; Bailyn 1967; Adams 1998).

Once again, conflict over taxation was an essential component of the eventual expansion of responsive and accountable government, but in a manner unlike that which prevailed in either England or France. The process in Britain, while not without conflict, relied on a relatively explicit tax bargain between taxpayers and the government in the face of a fiscal crisis, while the process in France saw resistance to taxation precipitate a fiscal crisis which, in turn, opened the door to dramatic and tumultuous political changes. By contrast, the tax conflict that helped spark the American Revolution involved neither explicit tax bargaining nor a fiscal crisis. Instead, it revealed the ability of debates about taxation, even when relatively insignificant in simple revenue terms, to catalyse political action around broader political grievances. Meanwhile, all of these examples stand in sharp contrast to experiences elsewhere in Europe, where states either profited through continued and often brutal coercion or, in many other cases, were wiped off the map as a result of their failure to raise revenue effectively.

The overarching message that emerges from even this relatively superficial exploration of historical cases is that the relationship between taxation, responsiveness and accountability is unlikely to be simple and linear. Instead, any relationship is likely to be conditional on contextual factors, and to operate, where it does exist, through multiple causal processes, ranging from explicit tax bargaining to much more indirect processes of political contestation and mobilization. This basic insight frames the model to follow. It ultimately posits three distinct causal processes linking taxation, responsiveness and accountability, and these three processes roughly mirror the differing experiences of Britain, France and the United States. Importantly, the model and the case studies to follow do not insist on a linear relationship, but instead emphasize contingency and the contextual factors that may shape outcomes.

2.2 A model of tax bargaining

Against this backdrop, the remainder of this chapter is devoted to developing a detailed model of tax bargaining, moving progressively from the relatively general and abstract to a more focused operationalization of the variables of interest. This section begins by laying out the core elements of the model, which are presented in two parts. The first part summarizes the broad mechanisms that are likely to link taxation to the expansion of responsiveness and accountability. The second part moves from these broad mechanisms to the identification of three specific causal processes through which taxation may contribute to broader political change in practice. The use of the terms "mechanisms" and "processes" here builds loosely on McAdam, Tarrow, and Tilly (2001: 24–27): mechanisms are defined as specific actions or events that may result from a particular cause across a variety of contexts, while processes are defined as particular sequences of events through which these mechanisms combine with other contextual factors to produce particular outcomes.[2]

2.2.1 Causal mechanisms: tax resistance and collective action

Rather than treating tax bargaining as a relatively distinct political process, the model developed here situates tax bargaining within the context of broader theories of political contestation and change. Specifically, it is inspired by simple models of politics in which political outcomes are understood largely as the result of contestation and conflict between citizens and governing elites, with expanded responsiveness and accountability resulting when citizens are able to wield sufficient political power to demand concessions from governments (e.g., Acemoglu and Robinson 2006; Gervasoni 2010). Approached through this lens, the need for taxation can be understood as contributing to the expansion of responsiveness and accountability by increasing taxpayers' bargaining power vis-à-vis governments and the state (Moore 2007: 14–15). Put another way, the need for taxation is expected to strengthen the ability of citizens to make demands on governments, while simultaneously strengthening the incentives for governments to make concessions to taxpayers. This reflects two related mechanisms: (1) the potential for tax resistance; and (2) the role of taxation in spurring public engagement and collective action.

The importance of the *potential for tax resistance* emerges from the possibility that governments may choose to make concessions to taxpayers in order to enhance quasi-voluntary tax compliance (Bates and Lien 1985, Levi 1988). In turn, the greater the willingness and ability of taxpayers to resist taxation, the greater will be the incentives for governments to

---

[2] There is no universally accepted usage of the terms "mechanism" and "process" in the social sciences (Hedstrom and Ylikosky 2010). McAdam, Tarrow, and Tilly (2001: 24) define mechanisms as "a delimited class of events that alter relations amongst specified sets of elements in identical or closely similar ways over a variety of situations," while they define processes as "regular sequences of such mechanisms that produce similar (generally more complex and contingent) transformations of those elements." These definitions are somewhat more general than those used here, reflecting their goal of presenting tools for analysing a wider variety of social and political phenomena. They make clear that processes and mechanisms exist on a continuum, while the assignment of particular events to either category is somewhat "arbitrary." More important is the goal underlying the uses of these concepts, which Tilly (2007: 2) describes as "reducing complex episodes to their component mechanisms and processes." This commonality of approach is similarly reflected in their definition of the research agenda, which is equally reflected here: "identifying contentious episodes or families of contentious episodes having some problematic feature; locating processes within them that constitute or produce the problematic feature; searching out the crucial causal mechanisms within those processes" (McAdam, Tarrow, and Tilly 2001: 29).

make concessions in order to reduce resistance and improve compliance (Bates and Lien 1985). In a contemporary setting, the ability to resist taxation may encompass a wide range of possibilities, including taxpayers who are able to escape detection, engage in collusion or use political influence to avoid enforcement; taxpayers who wield the collective threat of political mobilization against taxation; taxpayers who are able to easily disguise their wealth and profits, including through the use of offshore financial centres; or highly mobile multinational firms wielding the threat of relocation in seeking tax and governance concessions (Moore 2008).

While the potential for tax resistance may thus contribute to the expansion of responsiveness and accountability, it is important to reinforce that this does not imply that all interests will be equally represented in such processes of tax bargaining. Levi (1988) has argued that governments are likely, to the extent possible, to make *targeted* concessions to large taxpayers who have greater potential for tax resistance, rather than more broadly based concessions. Large taxpayers offer the largest potential revenue gains, while encouraging quasi-voluntary compliance is most important where the potential for resistance and evasion is high. By contrast, government incentives to make concessions to taxpayers that contribute only very small amounts of revenue, or who have very little scope for resistance or evasion, are likely to be much weaker. The logic of tax bargaining driven by the threat of tax resistance thus frequently predicts narrow tax bargains with economic elites, rather than broad and inclusive outcomes.[3] Of course, in many cases the demands of larger taxpayers may overlap at least to some extent with those of smaller taxpayers, ensuring that elite-driven bargains entail broader gains, but this is not necessarily the case.[4]

An alternative causal mechanism lies in the possibility that taxation may encourage *public engagement and collective action*, as taxpayers demand government concessions in exchange for tax revenue. This possibility stems from the simple idea that "people take more interest in what they

---

[3] This is consistent with the logic developed by Timmons (2005), who specifically proposes that governments will provide benefits in proportion to the share of taxes paid by different groups, and consequently suggests that taxes paid primarily by economic elites will result in stronger property rights protection, while broader-based taxes will prompt investments in public services.

[4] Hassan and Prichard (2013) capture this tension in an exploration of the nature of bargaining around the character of the tax system in Bangladesh. They find that bargaining has been elite-driven, and dominated by informal networks linking large business taxpayers, senior tax administrators and political elites. The resulting bargain has been a tax system that produces little revenue and is home to high levels of corruption, but which has also provided predictability and competitiveness to important economic sectors, which have contributed to consistently high economic growth. The bargain has thus served the interests of elites, while creating both benefits and costs to society more broadly.

2.2 A model of tax bargaining

have to pay for and are hence more likely to be interested in ensuring that they get value for their contributions" (Bird and Vaillancourt 1998: 10–11).[5] Taxpayers may mobilize *against* a given tax if they feel that they are not likely to get value in return, while the experience of being taxed may also lead groups of taxpayers to become politically organized in order to make *positive demands* for greater responsiveness and accountability. While the mobilization of collective resistance to taxation may prompt quite specific concessions from government, it is the potential for taxation to act as a broader and more ubiquitous spur to collective action and political organization that is most provocative.

Of course, collective action is inherently challenging and is likely to frequently fall short of the mass political mobilization that the term tax bargaining sometimes evokes. The experience of taxation may prompt relatively modest but broad-based increases in political engagement, manifested not in mass protests, but in the gradual strengthening of civil society and of demands for responsiveness and accountability (Paler 2013). Alternatively, the political engagement spurred by taxation may take the form of more focused, behind-the-scenes organizing by elite groups, reflecting the comparative ease of collective action amongst relatively small and comparatively homogenous groups (Olson 1965). Such processes may be comparatively subtle and more difficult to observe, but they are an important component of constructing an inclusive model of tax bargaining.

2.2.2   Causal processes: tax bargaining, tax resistance and political capabilities

Notwithstanding differences of emphasis, these two mechanisms, centred on tax resistance and public engagement, are both relatively uncontroversial and broadly accepted. The literature is less clear about how these mechanisms may translate into specific causal processes linking taxation, responsiveness and accountability. That is, the particular sequences of events that may link taxation to greater responsiveness and accountability in practice are comparatively poorly understood. Drawing again on Moore's (2008: 37) terminology, tax bargaining may be relatively direct and explicit, but may equally rely on more subtle "indirect strategic interaction and mutual behaviour adjustment" amongst taxpayers and

---

[5] This same sentiment has been captured, for example, by Huntington (1993: 65), when he writes that the "lower the level of taxation, the less reason for the public to demand representation," while Paler (2013) provides detailed micro-level experimental evidence from Indonesia that supports this behavioural proposition.

governments. In simpler terms, some cases may resemble the historical experience in England, where there was a relatively explicit exchange of tax compliance for political reform. However, other cases equally may resemble France, where tax resistance precipitated fiscal crisis and political upheaval, or the United States, where grievances around taxation fed into broader demands for political reform.

Consistent with this diversity of historical experiences, what follows identifies three specific causal processes of interest: *direct tax bargaining*, *tax resistance and changes in government* and *strengthened political capabilities of taxpayers*. Following Moore (2008: 37), *direct tax bargaining* is taken to refer to the exchange of tax revenues (for the state) for expanded responsiveness and accountability (for citizens). While direct tax bargaining may not take the form of explicit negotiation between taxpayers and governments, it is expected to involve a clearly discernible element of exchange, with governments making certain concessions specifically to increase tax compliance and/or curtail tax-related public mobilization.

By contrast, the remaining causal processes lack an immediate and explicit element of exchange between taxpayers and governments, but capture often-overlooked ways in which taxpayer responses to taxation may nonetheless contribute to longer-term political changes. The first, *tax resistance and changes in government*, captures situations in which taxpayers aggressively and successfully resist taxation, thus undermining the fiscal position of governments and contributing to changes in government and subsequent reform. The second, *strengthened political capabilities of taxpayers*, captures cases in which increased taxation leads to collective action that *does not* lead to immediate government concessions, but *does* contribute to reform over the longer-term by catalysing sustained political engagement and organization amongst taxpayers. For convenience, the term *indirect tax bargaining* is frequently employed to refer collectively to these latter two processes. This reflects the fact that *they rely on the same causal logic as direct tax bargaining*, as taxation expands the effective political power of taxpayers by expanding opportunities for tax resistance and collective action. Indeed, the level of conceptual overlap makes it possible to understand processes of indirect tax bargaining simply as longer-term and less linear manifestations of direct tax bargaining. However, despite this conceptual overlap, there is significant value in highlighting these additional processes explicitly. Indirect tax bargaining may in practice be difficult to identify, as the links between taxation and governance outcomes are long term and intertwined with broader processes of political change. They are thus easily overlooked, and highlighting them explicitly makes it possible to provide a fuller account of the relationships of interest.

Direct tax bargaining

Direct tax bargaining most closely resembles the idealized image of tax bargaining from early modern Europe, as governments make relatively explicit concessions to taxpayers in order to secure increased tax compliance and reduce public opposition prompted by tax-related concerns. In practice, direct tax bargaining is likely to proceed in one of two ways. First, taxpayers may respond to new or existing taxation through collective action or tax resistance, prompting *subsequent* concessions from governments seeking to restore political order and/or tax compliance. Second, the threat of collective action or tax resistance by taxpayers may lead governments to make *pre-emptive concessions* to taxpayers in order to prevent future conflict over taxation.

The latter processes do not fit the classic image of mass protest and subsequent government concessions, but may nonetheless be an important manifestation of the broader logic of arguments linking taxation, responsiveness and accountability. In both cases, it is the reality or threat of conflict over taxation that drives change, but the second of these two highlights the subtlety sometimes needed in identifying instances of tax bargaining. As Timmons (2005: 545) has previously argued, "the fiscal contract is agnostic about the order of play: either the state or citizens could move first." In practice, however, processes of pre-emptive bargaining have been implicitly overlooked by much research, and most notably by cross-country econometric studies, which are built frequently on the implicit or explicit assumption that if there is a causal relationship "a change in the independent variables (taxes) should precede a change in the dependent variable (regime type)"(Ross 2004: 238). Critically, if direct tax bargaining frequently involves pre-emptive government concessions, this would undermine the effectiveness of many existing econometric tests – and help to explain the ambiguity of econometric results linking total tax collection and democracy, as reported in Chapter 1.[6]

Tax resistance and changes in government

Somewhat more complex is the possibility that tax resistance may contribute to the expansion of responsiveness and accountability by weakening the fiscal position of the government and, in turn, precipitating longer-term changes in government. Direct tax bargaining is dependent on governments making explicit concessions to taxpayers in response to the emergence of tax resistance and collective action. However, in reality,

---

[6] There is no obviously superior econometric alternative, which explains the decision to employ these same potentially flawed tests in Chapter 1 – and to now highlight potential reasons for the ambiguous results of those tests.

such straightforward outcomes are likely to be infrequent. Governments confronted by tax resistance and public mobilization frequently turn to repression rather than compromise. Meanwhile, citizens confronted with unpopular taxation often face severe barriers to collective action and are thus likely to have little recourse other than tax resistance through avoidance and evasion. In some cases such tax resistance alone may lead to government concessions; however, in many cases tax resistance will not prompt explicit concessions from government, but will instead simply result in reduced levels of tax revenue reaching the government.

Although such a low-revenue stalemate does not fit the classic image of tax bargaining, it may nonetheless contribute indirectly to the emergence of responsive and accountable governance. In stylized fashion, resistance to taxation has the potential to weaken the fiscal base of an incumbent government. This fiscal contraction may, in turn, undermine the ability of the government to secure political support, and thus increase the likelihood of a change in government. Finally, this series of events may provide positive incentives for an incoming government to make governing concessions in order to improve tax collection in the future. In these cases, any governance reforms that are ultimately undertaken by an incoming government do not result from an easily observable or proximate process of bargaining. Instead, they are the result, at least in part, of an extended period of unresolved conflict over taxation, and resultant fiscal crisis. Notably, such processes would, again, fail to be captured by many existing econometric tests, as in these cases tax revenue is expected to decline initially, sparking increases in accountability which, in turn, precede subsequent increases in revenue collection.

Although this process may initially appear convoluted, it is in fact highly consistent with historical experience. In France, longstanding and unresolved conflicts over taxation contributed to the declining fiscal position of the monarchy. This fiscal pressure ultimately prompted the summoning of the Estates General in 1789 and the subsequent outbreak of the French Revolution. Even in seventeenth century England, which is generally held up as an exemplar of direct tax bargaining, the strengthening of Parliament and the rule of law came at the end of decades of armed conflict and tax resistance, as taxpayers sought to limit the fiscal capacity of the monarchy. More generally, while the image of the reformist government responding to citizen demands is attractive in the abstract, historical experience suggests that major governance changes often occur only through changes in government. Indeed, contemporary patterns of taxation and tax reform appear to be at least broadly consistent with this view: Bates (2008) notes that many unpopular governments in Africa over the past three decades were hampered by declining capacity for revenue collection, while many authors have noted the counterpoint that new regimes have frequently been particularly successful in pursuing tax reform (Ascher 1989; Bates 1989). In a recent research contribution, for example, Soliman (2011) traces the crisis of the since-deposed Mubarak regime in Egypt in large part to a continuous fiscal crisis rooted in repeated failures to increase revenue collection.

At a micro level, this argument also follows the spirit of James C. Scott's (1987) work on the "weapons of the weak." He recounts the experience of poorly organized taxpayers at the village level in Malaysia who consciously resisted the payment of anything more than a small part of the official tax burden as a consistent form of protest against what they viewed as unfair incursion by the regime. In so doing, they subtly weakened the capacity and legitimacy of the government, while building ties of resistance within the community. He writes:

> Although this activity cannot be deemed a form of collective action or a social movement, its result is comparable and it has the added advantage of denying the state an easily discernable target. There is no organization to be banned, no conspiratorial leaders to roundup or buy off, no protestors to haul before the courts – only the general non-compliance of thousands of peasants who, without much fuss, are tearing down the edifice of the official zakat brick by brick (Scott 1987: 431).

Strengthened political capabilities of taxpayers

The final causal process explored here focuses on the long-term impact of taxation on the *political capabilities of taxpayers*, which Whitehead and Gray-Molina (2003: 32) define as "the institutional and organizational resources as well as the collective ideas available for effective political action." The prediction that the need for taxation may contribute to the expansion of responsiveness and accountability rests to a significant degree on the possibility that taxation may lead citizens to make increased demands on government. However, while taxation may encourage public engagement, achieving politically effective collective action is both challenging and potentially risky. Taxpayers may fail to coordinate effective collective action despite widespread public anger, or may succeed but then find their demands rebuffed by the government.

However, even where taxpayers are unable to successfully demand specific concessions from governments in the short-term, taxation may enhance the political capabilities of taxpayers in the long term. Taxation may alter norms and public expectations of government,[7] cultivate

---

[7] There is an extended body of research arguing that norms and expectations are essential to shaping levels of political engagement and accountability, as they prescribe the

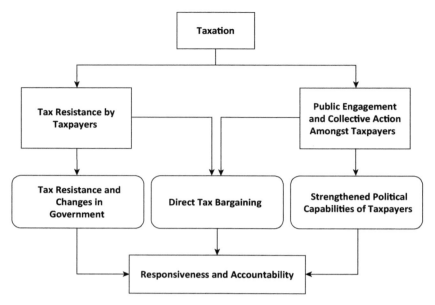

Figure 2.1 Taxation and the expansion of responsiveness and accountability.

a stronger sense of ownership over government activities (Bird and Vaillancourt 1998; Juul 2006), encourage more active day-to-day involvement in political processes, or catalyse the strengthening of civil society and long-term political mobilization. The American experience noted earlier is exemplary of this possibility: conflict over the British tax on tea, which culminated in the Boston Tea Party, did not result in significant immediate governing concessions by the British government. Instead, it provided a rallying point for resistance to British rule, thus fuelling longer-term political mobilization and resistance, and eventually coming to be remembered as a pivotal moment in the broader push towards independence.

2.3 Narrowing the focus and defining specific outcomes

The model developed so far provides a broad framework for analysing the causal processes linking taxation, responsiveness and accountability; the core elements of the model are summarized in Figure 2.1. Within

demands that citizens believe that they can, and should, make on government (e.g., Chazan 1983; Goetz and Jenkins 2005; Grant and Keohane 2005; Newell and Wheeler 2006; Moehler 2008).

2.3 Narrowing the focus and defining specific outcomes 63

this basic model, efforts by the government to raise tax revenue may prompt taxpayers to engage in either tax resistance or collective action to demand reciprocal concessions. These two causal mechanisms may, in turn, prompt three alternative causal processes leading to gains in responsiveness and accountability: direct tax bargaining, tax resistance and changes in government, or strengthened political capabilities of taxpayers. However, while this basic model provides a starting point for analysis, the research challenge is not only conceptual, it is also practical, as these causal processes may frequently be very difficult to identify in practice. With this challenge in mind, the next step in developing the research strategy lies in more precisely defining and operationalizing the specific processes and outcomes of interest.

The difficulty of observing tax bargaining in practice can be captured through two simple illustrations, which inform the approach adopted here. As a first example, it is likely to be difficult to observe the long-term impact of taxation on taxpayers' expectations and levels of political engagement. Some forms of political engagement, such as mass protest, are easy to observe. However, if the experience of paying taxes subtly shifts expectations and levels of engagement over several years, or even decades, those changes will be difficult or impossible to observe using a case study approach.[8] A second example deals with the difficulty of identifying the motives of decision makers. In some cases, tax considerations are likely to be central to explaining government actions, and thus are easy to identify. However, it is equally possible that tax considerations may consistently function at the margin of decision-making, thus appearing politically insignificant in isolation despite a potentially significant aggregate impact across multiple decisions over time.

These challenges of observation make it particularly important to define clear and observable indicators against which to measure the presence or absence of the three causal processes proposed by the model. However, in focusing on comparatively observable processes and outcomes, such a strategy ignores less observable, but still potentially important, processes through which taxation may influence the responsiveness and accountability of governments. The implication is that clear and observable examples of the three causal processes are likely to also be

---

[8] As noted already, studies elsewhere have sought to capture such behavioural changes using survey and experimental evidence. Both McGuirk (2013) and Kasara and Suryanarayan (2014) use survey evidence to illustrate differences in engagement around elections in response to variation in the tax burden, although they note inevitable challenges related to data, measurement and establishing causation. Meanwhile, Paler (2013) and Martin (2014) illustrate similar changes in public engagement in response to taxation in controlled field experiments in Indonesia and Uganda.

indicative of the existence of the more subtle behavioural changes predicted by the model. That is, *the actual importance of taxation in shaping political outcomes likely exceeds that which can be observed effectively using the case study methodology that is the focus here.*

2.3.1 Defining the dependent variables: responsiveness and accountability

Given the importance of defining clear outcomes, the starting point lies in providing more precise definitions of responsiveness and accountability, as the breadth of the concepts makes clear definitions essential (Lindberg 2009). Of the two terms, responsiveness is the more straightforward, and is here taken to refer broadly to the substance of government action. Manin, Przeworski and Stokes (1999: 9) propose simply that "[a] government is 'responsive' if it adopts policies that are signalled as preferred by citizens." Thus, responsiveness captures the range of concrete actions that governments may take in order to respond to the interests and preferences of citizens, which may be expressed in both explicit and implicit ways.

Accountability is taken here to refer broadly to *institutionalized processes* that shape government action and state-society relationships. Schedler (1999: 14) provides a relatively standard and widely accepted definition of accountability: "The notion of political accountability carries two basic connotations: answerability, the obligation of public officials to inform about and to explain what they are doing; and enforcement, the capacity of accounting agencies to impose sanctions on power-holders who have violated their public duties." Institutions of accountability are thus those formal and informal sets of rules that provide for the dual requirements of answerability and sanction. Accountability relationships may be of three broad types: vertical-upward, vertical-downward or horizontal (Lindberg 2009). This research is essentially concerned with vertical-downward accountability, which focuses on the ability of citizens to hold politicians and the state to account, and on the ability of parliaments to hold the executive to account.

Of course, there is also a need to look beyond formal rules to consider differences in the extent of accountability in practice. To what extent, and in what degree of detail, are agents compelled to explain and justify their actions? Are principals able to sanction the failure to provide a justification, or also the content of the actions taken? How powerful and effective are the sanctions that are available to principals (Lindberg 2009: 28–29)? Even for nominally similar formal institutions, the answers to these questions are likely to vary over time and across cases. Understanding the extent and character of accountability in practice demands attention to

2.3 Narrowing the focus and defining specific outcomes

questions of power and to the coexistence of formal and informal institutions. Formal institutions of accountability may have limited meaning if those who are nominally empowered to demand accountability lack the power to demand actual accountability in practice. In similar fashion, *formal institutions* of accountability, defined by the law, may be relatively ineffective where they are inconsistent with *informal institutions*, which lack legal definition but may nonetheless reflect important and normalized relationships and modes of decision-making (Helmke and Levitsky 2004; Grant and Keohane 2005: 31). By the same token, changes in informal institutions may sometimes imply major changes in effective accountability, even where formal rules remain unchanged. Attention to these nuances is thus an important aspect of interpreting the case study evidence.

Framing the concept of accountability in terms of processes and institutions creates a clear distinction with responsiveness, which is concerned with the substance of government action. This should not, however, obscure the fact that the two concepts are very closely related. Responsiveness may frequently be a precursor to the creation of institutions of accountability, insofar as short-term responsiveness creates pressure for the institutionalization of that behaviour. This reflects the fact that the primary purpose of institutions of accountability is frequently to guarantee that governments will be responsive. Lindberg (2009: 36) writes: "The sought after effect [of accountability] is to make agents be responsive to the wishes and interests of the principals." But, he continues, "responsiveness ... should not be understood as integral to accountability itself" (2009: 37).

Appreciating the interconnectedness of these concepts is critical, as it helps to explain the decision to treat both as potential outcomes of interest. As was noted in the Introduction, many studies within this academic tradition have focused specifically on the potential connections between taxation and representation (e.g., Ross 2004), but there is no compelling theoretical reason for such a narrow focus. Herb (2003) has argued particularly forcefully that the specific historical connection between taxation and representation reflected particular institutional features of early modern European states. Meanwhile, alternative studies have increasingly focused on a broader set of potential outcomes, including the rule of law, property rights, the extent of corruption, and the provision of public services (North and Weingast 1989; Fjeldstad and Semboja 2001; Timmons 2005; Baskaran and Bigsten 2013). This broader focus is consistent with a simple bargaining logic, which demands that governments make reciprocal concessions to taxpayers in exchange for taxation, but does not specify what types of concessions may be prioritized by either set of actors. With the breadth of potential outcomes in mind, we now turn to providing greater detail about the specific outcomes that would constitute evidence of each of the three causal processes of interest.

2.3.2 Direct tax bargaining

In cases of direct tax bargaining, it should be possible to observe (a) government efforts to tax, (b) taxpayer responses, and (c) their interaction and subsequent outcomes. The outcomes of interest are responsiveness and accountability, but in an empirical setting it is useful to focus on a subset of more specific and observable outcomes that fall within these broad concepts: improved provision of public services, changes in tax policy and administration, and broad expansions of accountability.

Improved provision of public services

A focus on public services follows the work of Fjeldstad and Semboja (2001), Timmons (2005) and others who have argued that popular demands are often aimed narrowly at the provision of public services (responsiveness), rather than at the more fundamental reform of institutions of accountability. This reflects the fact that public services including health, education, water and electricity are highly visible and amongst the most basic necessities for the majority of citizens in developing countries. These outcomes can be further distinguished by the extent to which improvements in public service provision are persistent and institutionalized. At one end of this spectrum lie cases in which governments provide one-time improvements in the provision of public services, but in which these gains are neither institutionalized nor sustained over time. At the opposite end of the spectrum are cases in which governments not only increase the quality of public services, but also institutionalize those changes, through such things as oversight committees, boards of directors or legislation to enforce funding commitments. These latter cases constitute not only the expansion of responsiveness, but also a broader element of accountability.

Changes in tax policy and administration

An alternative possibility is that a government seeking to secure acceptance of taxation may reform the tax system itself by increasing transparency, equity and consultation in tax policy and administration. This might entail simple improvements in administrative performance or changes in the distribution of the tax burden, both of which are broadly consistent with the concept of responsiveness. Alternatively, the government may expand institutionalized accountability around taxation through, for example, the elimination of discretionary tax policies, increased transparency, or the creation of dedicated tax tribunals, consultative bodies or oversight committees. While such changes are relatively narrow in their scope, they are nonetheless potentially significant. First, more equitable and transparent tax policy and administration may have large revenue and welfare implications by increasing public revenue and reducing the burden on existing taxpayers. Second, improvements in the performance of tax administration may become a catalyst for broader administrative gains across government (Chaudhry 1997; Bräutigam 2008a; Prichard and Leonard 2010). Finally, and perhaps most importantly, greater consultation and transparency around taxation may expand public access to information on public spending and enhance expectations of reciprocity, thus encouraging long-term public engagement and broader demands on government.

Broad expansions of accountability

Finally, the government may institute broad-based expansions of political accountability to improve acceptance of, and compliance with, taxation. These outcomes most closely mirror the outcomes that emerge from the historical literature on this topic, as they represent fundamental changes in the broad rules of the game. It is useful to distinguish specific categories of outcomes, all of which may be more or less formal or informal: (1) *the creation of new institutions of accountability*; (2) *the strengthening of existing institutions of accountability*; and (3) the *strengthening of the rule of law and of property rights*, which, while they are not institutions of accountability as such, restrict the arbitrary power of government and are likely to provide a valuable foundation for future accountability (North and Weingast 1989; Bräutigam 2002; Mahon 2005).

2.3.3   Tax resistance and changes in government

Processes of tax resistance that contribute to changes in government are more methodologically complex, as – in these cases – tax resistance is not expected to contribute to a single visible outcome. Instead, tax resistance is understood as a factor contributing to much larger processes of political change. The challenge is thus to establish reasonable criteria for asserting that taxation has, in fact, played such a role. This minimally means acknowledging both that tax resistance is not sufficient to ensure political change and that political change does not necessarily imply the expansion of responsiveness and accountability. As such, any causal claim should ideally rest on evidence that (a) tax resistance contributed to a change in government, (b) the change in government brought important improvements in governance, and (c) fiscal issues were a meaningful priority for the new government. In practice, outcomes are likely to fall into three categories. First are cases in which tax resistance leads to a reduced revenue stalemate, but there is no change in government. Second are cases in which tax resistance contributes to a change in government, but where the new government does not expand responsiveness or accountability. Third are cases in which tax resistance contributes to a change in government, the new government is more responsive and accountable, and tax compliance subsequently improves. Outcomes that fall within this final category would offer the strongest evidence that tax resistance has, in fact, been an important indirect catalyst for expanded responsiveness and accountability.

2.3.4 Strengthened political capabilities of taxpayers

Finally, the challenge of observing the causal processes of interest is most acute in relation to the impact of taxation on the political capabilities of taxpayers. While the impact of taxation on norms, expectations and political engagement is likely to be an important part of the causal story – and has been captured at the micro level by recent studies (McGuirk 2013; Paler 2013; Martin 2014) – these individual level preferences and behaviours are difficult to observe in a case study setting. As such, this research is focused on two related, but much more concrete, ways in which taxation may strengthen the political capabilities of taxpayers. First, taxation may lead to the strengthening of civil society organizations or other relevant forms of political organization. Second, collective action in response to taxation may open up new spaces for political engagement, including the legitimization of new forms of political action and mobilization. These processes may not yield direct tax bargains in the short term, but in the long term they are likely to contribute to diverse processes of political contestation and potentially broader expansions of responsiveness and accountability.

2.4 Contextual factors affecting tax bargaining

The preceding discussion provides a picture of the multiple ways in which conflicts over taxation may shape the expansion of responsiveness and accountability, while also translating comparatively broad concepts into a set of more specific and observable outcomes of interest. To complete the model, these alternative causal processes need to be placed in broader context. Whereas the discussion so far has identified

2.4 Contextual factors affecting tax bargaining

multiple possible causal processes, we equally need a framework for thinking about why specific outcomes may emerge in any individual case. That is, we need to understand why in some contexts taxpayers may respond to taxation through collective action, while in others reliance on quieter forms of tax resistance will be more likely. Why in some contexts governments will be strongly inclined to bargain with taxpayers, while in others they are likely to rely heavily on coercion. The goal is not, it should again be emphasized, to present a highly deterministic model: processes of tax bargaining are expected to be embedded within broader processes of political contestation and change, and thus subject to significant uncertainty. The goal is instead to highlight broad factors that are, on average, likely to drive distinctive patterns over time and across diverse contexts.

In seeking to identify relevant contextual factors it is useful to again turn to historical accounts of tax bargaining, in which contextual factors play a prominent role. This is most explicit in Tilly's (1992) account of taxation and state-building in early modern Europe. In his model, it is the balance between coercion and capital in individual states that is essential to determining whether the need for taxation results in consensual tax bargaining or the expansion of coercion, while he also focuses attention on the importance of factors shaping the capacity for collective action amongst taxpayers. Looking to similar historical cases, Levi (1988) draws particular attention to the importance of political institutions in facilitating tax bargaining and shaping outcomes. Moore (2008: 51) highlights similar issues, including the importance of government time horizons, access to non-tax revenue, factors conducive to collective action, economic structure and the level of institutionalization of the state. Finally, a long tradition in political science has highlighted the possibility that different tax types may produce divergent incentives and outcomes (Martin and Gabay 2007).

Given the extent to which the outcomes of tax bargaining are likely to be intertwined with broader political processes, the range of potentially important contextual variables is enormous. As such, a core analytical challenge lies in simplifying this comparatively complex reality within a manageable analytical framework. To do so, the analysis is organized around a set of five *structural factors* that are expected to shape the extent and character of tax bargaining through relatively distinct pathways. These *structural factors* are, in turn, expected to be shaped by a wide range of more specific and idiosyncratic *contextual variables* within individual cases.

Thus, for example, the extent of *taxpayer capacity for collective action* is a *structural factor* expected to shape the nature of tax bargaining by influencing the ability of taxpayers to become collectively mobilized and to make effective demands on government. This *structural factor* is, in turn, expected to be shaped by a wide range of more case-specific *contextual variables*, including the extent of political openness or repression, the strength of elite leadership and business associations, the unity of taxpayer interests, the strength of pre-existing civil society and the nature of expectations.

Table 2.1 captures the five structural factors that are the focus here, summarizes the pathway through which each is expected to shape the extent and character of tax bargaining and provides an illustrative list of more specific contextual variables that are expected to shape these structural factors in individual cases. Notably, some contextual variables appear in the table more than once, with the strength of business elites, for example, shaping both taxpayer capacity for collective action, and the scope for tax resistance. This overlap points to the potential for individual variables to shape tax bargaining through multiple pathways.

The appeal of this focus on structural factors is twofold. First, relying on categories tied explicitly to the political logic of tax bargaining allows the role of contextual factors to be incorporated explicitly within the broader model. That is, there is a clear and explicit link between each structural factor and the mechanisms and causal processes defined so far. Second, it provides a relatively parsimonious and portable framework that can accommodate the particular features of individual cases. A focus on more specific contextual variables, in the absence of this broader framework, would result in the potentially limitless proliferation of relevant variables in response to the idiosyncratic features of individual cases. By contrast, a focus on these structural factors captures the intuition that a large and diverse set of contextual variables nonetheless are likely to shape tax bargaining in a relatively standard set of. With this overarching framework in mind, the following sections describe each structural factor in greater detail.

2.4.1 Revenue pressure facing governments

The importance of the level of *revenue pressure* facing governments is straightforward: governments facing the most urgent revenue needs (*revenue pressure*) are intuitively most likely to be willing to bargain with, and make concessions to, taxpayers, owing to the absence of alternatives. The most obvious determinant of the level of revenue pressure facing governments is, in turn, *access to non-tax revenue*. Between two countries

2.4 Contextual factors affecting tax bargaining

Table 2.1 *Contextual factors shaping the potential for tax bargaining*

Structural factor	Pathway of impact on tax bargaining	Relevant contextual variables
Revenue pressure facing government	Increases incentives for governments to bargain and compromise	• Foreign aid • Natural resource wealth • Fiscal crises • External shocks
The potential and scope for tax resistance	Shapes the fiscal power wielded by taxpayers, and their ability to create fiscal incentives for government concessions	• Strength and autonomy of the private sector • Extent of reliance on direct taxes • Effectiveness of tax administration • Politicization of tax policy and collection
Taxpayer capacity for collective action	Shapes the ability of taxpayers to become collectively mobilized and make effective demands on government	• Extent of political openness or repression • Strength of elite leadership • Strength of business associations • Unity of taxpayer interests • Strength of pre-existing civil society • The nature of expectations
Institutions for bargaining	Shapes the feasibility of more direct forms of tax bargaining	• Effectiveness of parliamentary processes • Effectiveness of forums for engaging with taxpayers • Informal institutions shaping trust and bargaining
The political salience of taxation	Increases the likelihood that particular groups of taxpayers will engage in tax resistance or collective action	• Incidence and visibility of different taxes • The visibility of the tax reform process • The role of the media and elites in publicizing tax issues • Historical legacies • Specific events raising the profile of specific taxes

that levy the same taxes and *differ only in their level of additional non-tax revenue*, governments with greater access to non-tax revenue are less likely to face acute revenue pressure, owing to a larger overall resource envelope. Consequently, they are likely to be more willing to forego additional revenue rather than making concessions to taxpayers, while they may equally be less vulnerable to tax-related collective action owing to their capacity for repression and their ability to dispense public services and patronage (Ross 2004).

While access to non-tax revenue thus shapes the revenue pressure faced by governments *on average*, the revenue pressure felt by governments, and their consequent willingness to bargain, is also likely to be highly idiosyncratic. The onset of a fiscal crisis, driven by internal or external factors, can sharply and unexpectedly increase the revenue pressure faced by governments. Similarly, two governments facing an economic downturn and declining revenue may face sharply different levels of revenue pressure if they differ in their ability either to borrow or to reduce expenditure. In this vein, Centeno (2002) has emphasized the importance of the ability to borrow as one reason why the costs of warfare historically in Latin America did not necessitate processes of state-building similar to those that emerged in early modern Europe. A further possibility is that different elite state-building projects may vary in the extent to which they require public revenue and investment, thus creating variation in the extent to which state elites are under pressure to expand revenue collection (Schneider 2012). As such, the willingness of elites to bargain over taxation is likely to be dependent on the variety of factors that shape the urgency of revenue needs.

Finally, recent years have witnessed contentious debates about the impact of foreign aid on the potential for tax bargaining. A significant literature has argued that foreign aid may reduce incentives for domestic tax collection, thus directly reducing opportunities and incentives for tax bargaining (e.g., Bräutigam and Knack 2004; Gupta et al. 2004; Moss, Pettersson and van de Walle 2006; Benedek et al. 2012; Eubank 2012). At a minimum, this literature captures a concern that access to foreign aid may reduce the revenue pressure facing governments, much like other sources of non-tax revenue (Moore 1998). However, more recent research has provided mounting evidence that, while access to foreign aid may reduce tax effort in some cases, it equally may support expanded collection – and thus expanded opportunities for tax bargaining – owing to the sometimes positive revenue impacts of conditionality, technical assistance and expanded public spending (Collier 2006; Gupta 2007; Brun, Chambas and Guerineau 2008; Clist and Morrissey 2011; Prichard, Brun and Morrissey 2012; Morrissey, Prichard and Torrance 2014). This is reflected, for example, in evidence that donors have often played an important role in pushing for, and supporting, major tax reform initiatives (Mahon 2004; Sanchez 2006; Bird 2008; Fjeldstad and Moore 2008; Keen 2011). Ultimately, there is thus

2.4.2 The potential and scope for tax resistance

The potential and scope for tax resistance captures the extent to which taxpayers enjoy political leverage by virtue of their ability to constrain the fiscal capacity of the state through evasion or avoidance. This reflects the role of capitalists in historical accounts of tax bargaining, as it was the threat of reduced tax revenue posed by the secrecy and mobility of their assets that was a critical source of leverage in bargaining with governments (Tilly 1992). As noted earlier, processes of tax bargaining have historically been elite-driven, in large part because of the disproportionate share of elite tax payments in total government revenue and the multiple channels available to elites seeking to engage in tax avoidance or evasion (Levi 1988; Gehlbach 2008).[9]

Features of the tax system itself may also frequently be important to understanding the scope for tax resistance by different groups. Where tax administration is comparatively weak, or prone to corruption and politicization, this may facilitate efforts by taxpayers to reduce their tax burdens as a form of protest. Similarly, where the policy process is subject to high levels of discretion and politicization, as with the existence of extensive tax incentives and exemptions, this may open space for tax resistance. Finally, the scope for evasion and avoidance is not expected to be equal across tax types or taxpayer groups. Taxes collected at the border are comparatively straightforward to enforce, while domestic sales taxes and income taxes often offer greater scope for evasion. Within these latter categories, there is likely to be additional variation with, for example, income taxes deducted at sources much harder to avoid than self-declared taxes paid by the self-employed. As such, the leverage wielded by taxpayers in any individual conflict over taxation will be shaped by which taxes

---

[9] Existing research, while limited by data availability, has highlighted the extent to which larger firms often pay lower tax rates than mid-sized firms owing to greater scope for reducing tax liabilities. This is potentially attributable to their ability to access political networks, to engage in collusion with tax officials, or to access international opportunities for profit shifting, frequently through tax havens (Gauthier and Reinikka 2006; Palan, Murphy and Chavagneux 2010). In a similar vein, a broad literature looking at economic globalization has noted the bargaining power enjoyed by highly mobile multinational firms seeking tax and other incentives from host governments (Keen and Simone 2004). Finally, at the individual level, it has long been recognized that self-employed professionals, including consultants and lawyers, are frequently amongst the hardest groups to tax in low-income countries, owing to the difficulty of tracking their incomes (Bird and Zolt 2005).

they pay and by the character of tax policy and administration (Gordon and Li 2009).

2.4.3 Taxpayer capacity for collective action

The importance of *taxpayer capacity for collective action* again emerges most explicitly from Tilly's (1992: 101) account, where he writes that general unhappiness with taxation was likely to become "mass rebellion chiefly when (1) the state's demands and actions offended citizens' standards of justice or attacked their primary collective identities, (2) the people touched by offensive state actions were already connected by durable social ties, (3) ordinary people had powerful allies inside or outside the state, and (4) the state's recent actions or interactions revealed that it was vulnerable to attack." Moore (2008) similarly highlights the importance of these factors in facilitating tax bargaining, given the centrality of collective political action to making demands on governments.

The range of factors relevant to shaping taxpayer capacity for collective action around taxation is, of course, enormous and context-specific. It is, however, worth highlighting several elements that have gained particular attention in the literature. The first and most intuitive variable is the *extent of political openness*. Comparatively open political environments are expected to create greater opportunities for citizens to engage in collective action. By contrast, repressive governments leave few spaces for taxpayers, citizens and civil society to engage in overt and confrontational forms of collective action. Where there is less political space for citizens to engage in collective action, we may thus expect taxpayers to rely more heavily on quieter forms of tax resistance as forms of protest and bargaining.

The second is the possibility that *the strength, organization and interests of the private sector and elite groups* may be particularly critical to the potential for effective collective action by taxpayers. In Tilly's (1992) accounts of taxation and state-building in early modern Europe, the strength of the private sector is *the* decisive determinant of whether the need for taxation leads to the expansion of responsiveness and accountability or simply to the intensification of coercion. This largely reflects the fact that elite groups controlled a significant share of potential state revenue and were comparatively mobile, as discussed previously. However, it also reflects the fact that a more powerful and independent private sector and middle class is likely to enjoy a range of political resources valuable to efforts to bargain with government, including an ability to mobilize broader political constituencies (Moore 1966; Acemoglu and Robinson 2006; Gervasoni 2010).

2.4 Contextual factors affecting tax bargaining

While elite groups are thus expected to figure prominently in processes of tax bargaining, the potential for broader based popular engagement with tax issues is also likely to depend substantially on the *nature of existing civil society groups*. This not only reflects the importance of existing organizations and social ties in facilitating collective action, but also the fact that many taxes may be relatively invisible to, or poorly understood by, large parts of the population (Martin and Gabay 2007). Civil society organizations may thus play an important role in highlighting tax payments and unifying disparate and poorly defined grievances. The success of these efforts is, in turn, likely to depend in important ways on the nature of *existing expectations*. In particular, the potential for collective action is likely to be shaped by perceptions about whether tax demands are reasonable and fair, and by the extent to which taxpayers have developed expectations of reciprocity around taxation.[10]

2.4.4 Institutions for tax bargaining

Equally important is the *existence of institutions to facilitate bargaining between taxpayers and governments*. The most prominent expression of this idea comes from Levi (1988), who has highlighted the potential for *representative and inclusive institutions* to reduce transaction costs and thus facilitate less confrontational forms of bargaining, as taxpayers are able to engage with the state through formal channels. The intuition is straightforward: where existing institutions offer few spaces for dialogue between taxpayers and governments, tax bargaining is likely to be comparatively confrontational, indirect and long-term. By contrast, formal institutions that allow taxpayer representatives to engage with governments are likely to facilitate more direct forms of bargaining based on compromise.

While political institutions may shape the potential for more direct forms of tax bargaining, they are also likely to shape the content of those bargains. Particular political institutions are likely to empower particular types of interests, while disempowering others. This notion draws on the well-known "polity approach" associated with Skocpol (1992: 41),

---

[10] Research on tax compliance has consistently highlighted the importance of perceptions of fairness as key determinants of tax compliance (summarized in Fjeldstad, Schulz-Herzenberg, and Sjursen 2012). The importance of expectations has also been increasingly noted, including some suggestions that expectations of reciprocity may be weak in developing countries. Recent research has provided evidence that expectations of reciprocity are, in fact, frequent even amongst low-income taxpayers (e.g., Fjeldstad and Semboja 2001; Fjeldstad, Schulz-Herzenberg, and Sjursen 2012). However, it remains plausible that the extent of expectations of reciprocity may vary across countries or population groups.

which "understands political activities, where carried on by politicians or by social groups, as conditioned by the institutional configuration of governments." Thus, for example, institutions may create specific spaces for interaction between governments and business interests, thus offering them additional bargaining options.

A somewhat less intuitive role for political institutions lies in their potential to shape the *time horizons of political leaders*, and their consequent incentives to bargain around taxation. As Levi (1999: 115) has written, "secure and relatively powerful rulers will [enter into broad tax bargains, while] insecure rulers will grant exemptions to those whose alliance is necessary to protect power." The intuition is that a ruler who is secure in power will have incentives to arrive at compromises that are costly in the short term, but yield revenue benefits over the long term. By contrast, insecure rulers will have few incentives to make revenue-enhancing compromises that are only likely to benefit their successors. More uncertain is what types of political institutions are likely to generate these long time horizons. Democracy may lead to shorter time horizons by increasing the frequency of changes in political leadership, but may also extend political time horizons by offering assurance of the opportunity to return to power in the future (Olson 1993).

Alongside the role of formal institutions, there is emerging evidence that informal institutions linking taxpayers, tax administrators and political elites may play a similarly important role in facilitating bargaining processes (Hassan and Prichard 2013). The role of informal institutions appears to speak more broadly to the importance of trust in shaping the potential for tax bargaining. This is intuitively unsurprising: tax bargaining requires that taxpayers trust governments to follow through on promised concessions, while it requires that governments trust taxpayers to comply with future taxes. In practice, existing research has suggested that in low-income countries citizens may frequently have so little trust in government that they simply prefer to resist or avoid taxation, rather than bargaining more constructively with the state (Fjeldstad and Semboja 2001).

2.4.5 *The political salience of taxation*

Finally, existing research suggests that the potential for tax bargaining is likely to be shaped by the *incidence and political salience of taxation*. While taxation is frequently treated as a single variable in discussions of tax bargaining, in practice aggregate government tax revenue is composed of an array of taxes with vastly different characteristics. These differences have already been noted as important determinants of the scope for tax resistance. Meanwhile, different taxes vary in their incidence and political salience, with potentially equally important implications.

Most obviously, different taxes affect different groups of taxpayers, and are correspondingly likely to drive diverse patterns of tax bargaining that reflect the priorities of affected groups (Timmons 2005). For example, a comparatively small share of the population in most developing countries pays direct income taxes, and bargaining around income taxes is thus likely to be driven by those groups. By contrast, consumption taxes have a much broader incidence, and are therefore more likely to prompt broad-based political engagement.

An alternative set of predictions emerges from a long research tradition proposing that income and other direct taxes are comparatively likely to spark political mobilization because they are more "visible" to taxpayers than indirect taxes on consumption and trade. This argument rests on the fact that income taxes are paid directly by taxpayers to the government, whereas indirect taxes are collected by intermediaries (e.g., shop owners, importers) and often hidden within the final price of goods. More recently, however, Martin and Gabay (2007) have argued that the simple distinction between direct and indirect taxes may be too simplistic, arguing instead that the contextually defined "political salience" of particular taxes is more relevant as a predictor of public protest and engagement. Thus, for example, where indirect taxes have been the subject of prominent public debate or media coverage, they may prove to be more politically salient – and thus more "visible" – than direct income taxes.

2.5   Incorporating context and strategic interaction in the model

As noted previously, a primary advantage of an analytical focus on these structural factors is that it is then possible to incorporate them explicitly into the basic causal model developed earlier in this chapter. Doing so produces a more dynamic model in which specific outcomes emerge from particular strategic choices by key stakeholders, which are in turn shaped by broader contextual factors. This reflects Moore's (2007: 16) observation, noted earlier, that "any realistic understanding of these processes requires that we go beyond the initial reactions to taxation of each type of actor, and take into account the ways in which they then interact, whether conflictually, cooperatively, or in more complex ways." Accordingly, what follows assumes two groups of actors – taxpayers and governments – and spells out the stylized decisions faced by each group, and the outcomes that result. The broad logic of this more sophisticated model is laid out in Figure 2.2, which highlights the simplified decisions available to each set of actors at each stage of the model, as well as the structural factors that are expected to influence these decisions.

The model begins with a government seeking to expand tax collection to finance its activities. The government is immediately confronted with the first "decision-point" in the model, which is reflected in the top "level" of Figure 2.2 and is summarized in point (1) of the same figure. One option is to pre-emptively bargain with taxpayers, offering commitments and concessions in exchange for popular acceptance of, and compliance with, expanded taxation. Alternatively, the government may seek to coercively impose new taxes, or strengthen enforcement of existing taxes, without making any reciprocal commitments to taxpayers. The choice made by the government is likely to be shaped by a variety of features of the broader context, including the urgency of government revenue needs, expectations about the ability and willingness of taxpayers to engage in tax resistance or collective action, and the ability of existing institutions to lower the costs of bargaining and facilitate pre-emptive agreement.

If the government opts to expand taxation coercively, without making pre-emptive concessions to taxpayers, then taxpayers may respond in one of three broad ways – summarized in point (2) of Figure 2.2. First, they may simply accept taxes without overt complaint, resulting in a case of expanded taxation without tax bargaining. Second, taxpayers may engage in tax resistance through evasion and avoidance, as a way of undermining government revenue-raising efforts and/or as a strategy for prompting government concessions. Third, they may seek to engage in collective action and public mobilization aimed at demanding that the government make reciprocal concessions to taxpayers or else repeal the tax. The course of action adopted by taxpayers is again likely to be shaped by context. Important factors include the scope for resistance through evasion and avoidance, the capacity of affected taxpayers to engage in effective collective action and the incidence and political salience of the particular taxes in question.

Confronted by taxpayer resistance or collective action, the model returns to governments, as they are forced to decide how to respond – with this decision summarized in point (3) of Figure 2.2. The government is presented with two main choices: it may compromise by offering reciprocal concessions to taxpayers or it may refuse to bargain with taxpayers and attempt to expand taxation through coercion. Where governments opt to compromise, as with the Ghanaian example summarized at the outset of this book, the result is an example of *direct tax bargaining*, with the government offering specific concessions in response

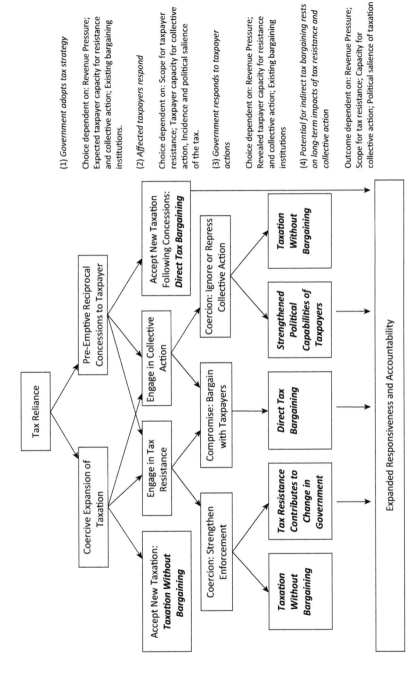

Figure 2.2 Strategic interaction and tax bargaining.

to taxpayer demands. The alternative is that the government refuses to compromise, choosing instead to ignore or repress collective action and to tolerate any loss of revenue resulting from tax resistance. The way in which governments manage this decision is likely to reflect broadly the same contextual factors shaping the earlier decision about whether or not to pursue pre-emptive bargaining with taxpayers. The critical difference at this stage is that the capacity of taxpayers to engage in resistance and collective action will have been revealed, with bargaining facilitated by greater certainty about the relative power wielded by competing groups (e.g., Fearon 1995).

The final uncertainty that is addressed by the model relates to the longterm political consequences when governments consistently refuse to compromise in response to taxpayer resistance and collective action. This final stage is summarized in point (4) of Figure 2.2. One possibility is that conflict over taxation may simply fail to spur any meaningful bargaining or political change, as taxpayer resistance and collective action simply fade into history after a failure to achieve short-term gains. However, the model developed here suggests that, in many cases, these processes of unresolved conflict may nonetheless generate indirect pressure for political reform over the longer-term, despite the absence of short-term compromise.

Where citizens are engaged in tax resistance, and the government refuses to make concessions, this may result in reduced tax revenue. This may, in turn, weaken the fiscal position of the government, increasing the likelihood of a change in government and of subsequent reform (*tax resistance and changes in government*). Whether or not this occurs is likely to depend – to an important degree – on the scope for tax evasion and avoidance, and on the extent to which that additional revenue is pivotal to the political prospects of the government (*revenue pressure*). Similarly, political engagement and collective action by taxpayers, even where unrequited in the short-term, may contribute to *strengthening the political capabilities of taxpayers* in the long-term. This outcome is likely to be dependent on the capacity of civil society actors to transform short-term political mobilization into long-term collective action, and on the extent to which tax debates remain politically salient over the longer-term.

Ultimately, this model is attractive because it captures the potential diversity and complexity of the links between taxation, responsiveness and accountability. Whereas most contemporary discussion has focused implicitly or explicitly on direct tax bargaining, the model here captures multiple alternative pathways, emerging from differences in (a) government efforts to impose taxation, (b) taxpayer responses, and (c) the interaction between those two groups. This focus on repeated interaction allows alternative outcomes to emerge as a result of different strategic choices by taxpayers and governments, shaped by broader contextual factors.

A final note about the model is that it focuses on capturing alternative causal processes rather than on predicting specific types of outcomes. This is not an omission, but reflects the fact that there is no compelling reason to expect particular causal processes to lead to distinctive outcomes within the broad universe captured by the concepts of responsiveness and accountability. Instead, the specific concessions made by governments are likely to reflect the relative power wielded by different groups, idiosyncratic features of taxpayer demands and the particularities of government strategies.

2.6   Conclusions

Drawing on a careful reading of historical evidence, and building on earlier models, this chapter has presented the elements of a dynamic model of tax bargaining. The model proposes that the need for taxation can contribute to the expansion of responsiveness and accountability by increasing the bargaining power of taxpayers vis-à-vis the government. The need for taxation may increase the relative bargaining power of taxpayers through the potential for *tax resistance* and by *encouraging political engagement and collective action*. These may, in turn, give rise to three causal processes linking taxation, responsiveness and accountability: direct tax bargaining, tax resistance and changes in government, and strengthened political capabilities of taxpayers. Which of these specific outcomes, if any, emerges in practice is expected to be shaped to an important degree by a core set of contextual factors: the level of revenue pressure facing governments, the scope and potential for tax resistance, factors affecting taxpayer capacity for collective action, the existence of institutions that facilitate bargaining, and the incidence and political salience of taxation.

This model serves not only to clarify the causal logic linking taxation, responsiveness and accountability, but is also an integral part of the broader research strategy. These processes are likely to be difficult to observe, as they are expected to be frequently long-term and intertwined with broader political processes. The model developed here thus provides the foundation for trying to make sense of a messier empirical reality. However, there remains a need for care and nuance in evaluating the case study evidence that follows.

On the one hand, even if tax bargaining is significant to long-term political outcomes, there are still likely to be many cases in which episodes of increased taxation yield little or no evidence of direct or indirect tax bargaining. In even the best circumstances taxation remains a fundamentally coercive act. It is often only with a longer-term view that conflicts over taxation may come to be seen as part of larger processes of bargaining and political transformation. The question is thus not whether there will be episodes of *taxation without bargaining*, but whether those episodes will be so frequent, or so lacking in any evidence of public engagement and mobilization, as to outweigh competing evidence of a positive relationship between taxation, responsiveness and accountability. More simply, the question is whether evidence of tax bargaining is sufficiently strong to meaningfully enhance standard accounts of political contestation and change in developing countries.

On the other hand, precisely because processes of tax bargaining are expected to be difficult to observe, case study evidence is likely to underestimate the full political importance of tax bargaining. That is, if the case studies reveal readily observable tax bargaining, there is every reason to believe that additional, harder to observe processes are also operating below the surface. The case studies to follow are correspondingly an effort to capture comparatively visible examples of tax bargaining, but, in so doing, to also shed light on the existence of the broader causal mechanisms and processes described in this chapter. In turn, this reliance on case study evidence will allow for new insights into the diversity of the causal processes of interest, and into the contextual factors shaping outcomes both within and across countries. With this in mind, the chapters that follow present in-depth empirical evidence from case studies of Ghana, Kenya and Ethiopia.

3 Taxation, responsiveness and accountability in Ghana, 1981–2008

The case studies in this book rest on a simple premise: if taxation is an important contributor to expanded responsiveness and accountability, then it should be possible to observe the role of processes of direct and indirect tax bargaining in shaping governance outcomes. While taxation may also shape political dynamics in more subtle and unobservable ways, it is difficult to sustain the claim that taxation is of central importance to broader responsiveness and accountability if issues around taxation have not at least occasionally prompted discernible changes in political behaviour consistent with the model of tax bargaining developed here.

With this in mind, the presentation of the empirical evidence begins with the case of Ghana since 1981, when it began to transition from a period of comparatively unstable military rule. As described briefly in the opening chapter, Ghana has been home to repeated examples of direct tax bargaining in which the government has made relatively explicit concessions to taxpayers in response to the reality or threat of popular mobilization and tax resistance. Amongst the three cases examined in this book, it thus provides the most compelling and clear-cut evidence of the role of tax bargaining in contributing to increased responsiveness and accountability. It therefore offers a useful starting point for the analysis, while subsequent case study chapters add nuance by shedding light on the sources of variation in patterns of tax bargaining across countries.

However, even in Ghana the story has not been uniform, as the extent and character of tax bargaining has varied over time and across tax episodes, thus offering initial lessons about the role of contextual factors in shaping outcomes. Most notably, the case highlights the importance of *taxpayer capacity for collective action* and the existence of *institutions for tax bargaining* in shaping outcomes. During the 1980s tax bargaining was essentially non-existent, owing to a combination of a repressive government, weak civil society and divided elites. As new political space opened, civil society grew stronger, opposition elites became more unified, and tax bargaining became more common and meaningful from the 1990s onward. Meanwhile, the creation of new democratic and consultative institutions – that is, *institutions for tax bargaining* – from 1996 onwards saw tax bargaining shift away from highly confrontational protests towards more institutionalized forms of bargaining.

To capture these political dynamics as completely and transparently as possible, this and the two subsequent chapters begin with the presentation of a historical narrative of the political economy of taxation, with a focus on the analysis of particular tax episodes – that is, moments of significant tax reform, changes in tax collection or political debates about taxation. The narrative account is accompanied by detailed revenue figures in the appendix to the chapter. Following the presentation of the historical narratives, the remainder of each chapter is devoted to analysing the evidence that emerges from these narratives. This involves, first, assessing the extent to which the narratives provide persuasive evidence of alternative forms of tax bargaining; and, second, assessing the role of particular contextual factors in shaping specific outcomes.

3.1 The political economy of taxation in Ghana, 1981–2008

In 1981, the Ghanaian state and economy were deeply in crisis. The preceding five years in particular had been defined by rapid economic decline, rampant rent-seeking and the atrophying of the state. The democratically elected government of Hilla Limann had replaced a string of military governments in 1979, but had been unable to slow the downward trend. Government revenues had fallen to below 4 per cent of GDP, which was not nearly sufficient to sustain a well-functioning government, and reflected the state of economic and political collapse (Chazan 1983).

This changed dramatically when military officers led by Flight Lieutenant Jerry Rawlings took power on December 31, 1981 under the banner of the Provisional National Defence Council (PNDC). Rawlings had already gained a reputation for ruthlessly attacking the perceived corruption of previous regimes during a short-lived seizure of power in 1979. This ruthlessness, coupled with the simple weakness of other forces within society, allowed the new regime to establish unquestioned dominance relatively quickly, ushering in what historian Adu Boahen (1997: 135–136) has called the period of the "Culture of Silence." While the government arrived under the banner of populist revolution, the regime ultimately used its political dominance to implement an IMF- and World Bank-sponsored structural adjustment programme, known as the Economic Recovery Program (ERP). The vestiges of the early ideology nonetheless remained in evidence, particularly in several early measures that took aim at the purportedly ill-gotten gains of the political and economic elite.

3.1 The political economy of taxation in Ghana, 1981–2008

The second Rawlings coup represented a major break in the economic and political history of the country, and thus provides a sensible starting point for the analysis presented here (Chazan 1983; Herbst 1993; Nugent 1995). What follows divides subsequent Ghanaian history into several periods, each of which exhibits particular political dynamics surrounding taxation. The Appendix to this chapter provides a detailed view of the evolution of tax collection and expenditure over the entire period.[1]

3.1.1 The imperative of revenue generation, 1983–1986

By 1983 the new regime had consolidated power and initiated the ERP. This entailed major economic reform, including efforts to rapidly increase government revenue. Academic writing on tax reform during the period tends to focus on major institutional reforms undertaken in 1985–1986. These reforms fundamentally reorganized the institutional structure for tax collection, creating the National Revenue Secretariat (NRS) to oversee the Internal Revenue Service (IRS) and the Customs, Excise and Preventive Services (CEPS). Each agency was granted increased independence from the Ministry of Finance in a pioneering example of a semi-autonomous revenue authority (Terkper 1998, Osei and Quartey 2005).

While these administrative reforms set the stage for long-term improvements in taxation, however, the most dramatic increases in revenue occurred *prior* to these reforms, as the PNDC moved to address its crippling fiscal weakness and more than doubled tax collection between 1982 and 1986, from less than 4 per cent to more than 10 per cent of GDP. Part of the revenue improvement was attributable to the ERP, which, thanks to the rapid depreciation of the exchange rate, led to increased exports and imports, with corresponding increases in import duties, export taxes, excise taxes and sales taxes. However, it was only taxes on exports that consistently met or exceeded budgeted expectations, while other indirect taxes lagged behind budgetary targets.[2]

---

[1] The tax revenue share of GDP in individual years is sensitive to the choice of GDP series, as Ghana finalized an updating of GDP estimates in 2010, resulting in a very large upward revision of earlier GDP figures. This exercise also resulted in modest changes in the overall trend during the 1980s in particular, with the tax share of GDP declining during the second half of the 1980s using the new data, whereas earlier data had suggested that collection was somewhat more stable during this period. The narrative presented here relies on the updated GDP data, but is broadly consistent with both sets of data. The sensitivity of specific figures to data choices is more broadly reflective of the need to treat the data with some caution.

[2] Based on review of budgetary documents in the parliamentary archives.

The impressive performance of export taxes, which were levied almost entirely on cocoa production, thus warrants special attention. From 1955 to 1975, cocoa provided the strong majority of Ghanaian export earnings and an average of greater than 13 per cent of national GDP. Cocoa production was also heavily taxed through a combination of export taxes and below-market prices paid by the Cocoa Marketing Board (CMB), which had monopoly control over official cocoa exports. While the data is imperfect, Frimpong-Ansah (1991) estimates that from 1958 to 1980 cocoa taxation averaged almost 40 per cent of the export price and accounted for 32.95 per cent of total government revenues, which is broadly consistent with estimates found elsewhere (Stryker et al. 1990; Bulir 1998).

These high levels of revenue collection masked the progressive decline of the sector. Producer prices during the 1960s and early 1970s were below those that prevailed prior to independence, owing to lower world prices, continued high levels of taxation, and an increasingly inefficient CMB. Lower prices led to a gradual decline in production, owing to lower levels of harvesting and reduced tree planting and upkeep. When world and producer prices plummeted after 1976, smuggling increased, harvesting declined, and official production fell to less than 300,000 tons, as compared to 450,000 tons in the 1960s. While small farmers were relatively poorly organized politically, reduced production and increased smuggling were effective forms of everyday resistance (Chazan 1983; Scott 1985; Herbst 1993; Widner 1993).

Even as decline set in, the government continued to extract a large revenue surplus, but this revenue stream dried up at the end of the decade. The growing economic crisis included the dramatic overvaluation of the exchange rate, and this depressed the real value of cocoa exports, such that neither producers nor the government was able to profit. Ultimately, mismanagement, short-sighted revenue goals, and major exchange rate imbalances eroded an essential economic sector, and dramatically undermined the fiscal solvency of the government (Stryker et al. 1990; Frimpong-Ansah 1991; McMillan 2001).

Given this history, it is little surprise that cocoa played an important part in the fiscal recovery. With the devaluation of the currency, exports resumed and export taxes averaged 3 per cent of GDP, and accounted for more than 25 per cent of total government tax revenue during the period between 1985 and 1987. Further supporting the recovery was an increase in prices paid to producers, as the producer share of world prices was increased during the period between 1983 and 1985, while these higher prices for producers were then sustained by a brief recovery of world prices. While the government continued to extract significant revenue from the cocoa sector, its early policy stance nonetheless broke

3.1 The political economy of taxation in Ghana, 1981–2008   87

the pattern of unsustainable exploitation in favour of long-term improvements in production. In doing so, the PNDC resisted the urban bias of the past, adopted a longer-term view and sought to gain the support of rural constituents (Stryker et al. 1990; Martin 1993; McMillan 2001).

Alongside export taxation, the most unexpected source of increased revenue was a dramatic increase in corporate and personal taxation. This is attributable to the Citizens' Vetting Committees (CVCs), which – reflecting the ideological radicalism of the early Rawlings years – identified citizens of conspicuous wealth who were suspected of tax evasion. Where that wealth could not be accounted for and/or taxes had not been paid, the CVCs enforced tax compliance in a somewhat ad hoc and extralegal manner, collecting not only annual taxes, but also substantial tax arrears, which accounted for the dramatic surge in revenue from 1983 to 1985. While many elites resent the events of this period and the methods employed to pursue these revenues, there is no question about the short-term effectiveness of the strategy.[3]

Ultimately, the virtual collapse of government revenue in the early 1980s created a desperate need to expand the fiscal capacity of the state. This was matched by the ideological commitment of the government to bringing elites back into the tax net and reviving some notion of a "social contract" (Nugent 1995). Lurking in the background were the IMF and World Bank, both of them influential advocates of tax reform and increased tax collection.[4] The rapid pace of reform bred major discontent amongst elites, but witnessed very little overt public opposition, owing to the entrenched position of the government and its popularity in many circles. In the words of one senior political official, "the fear of the Lord was put in [taxpayers],"[5] while senior tax officials stress that taxpayers "were rushing to the offices to pay their taxes."[6] Thus, the expansion of tax revenue resulted from a combination of expediency, ideology and outside pressure, all implemented effectively by government decree.[7]

---

[3] Personal interview on 21 March 2008 with former minister in PNDC and NDC governments.
[4] Personal Interview on 10 April 2008 with former Deputy Minister of Finance and senior official in PNDC and NDC governments.
[5] Personal interview on 21 March 2008 with former minister in PNDC and NDC governments.
[6] Personal interview on 10 March 2008 with Deputy Commissioner, Internal Revenue Service.
[7] Those who led the reform during this period are explicit in explaining that the same methods would have been impossible under a democratic government, explaining that, under a military regime "you can take liberties with certain things," while "there were a lot of things that [we] could not do today." Personal interview on 21 March 2008 with former minister in PNDC and NDC governments.

3.1.2 Rationalization and consolidation, 1987–1991

Total tax collection reached a high of 10.2 per cent of GDP in 1986, while the following years witnessed gradually declining tax revenue amidst important changes in the composition of that revenue.[8] During this period, the shares of export taxes and corporate taxes declined rapidly, and were progressively replaced by sales taxes, import duties and fuel taxes. These changes were facilitated by major improvements in administrative capacity resulting from the administrative reforms of 1985–1986 (Terkper 1998).

The rapid decline in export taxation followed a fall in world cocoa prices. In the face of falling world prices, the government maintained real producer prices at a relatively constant level, thus sacrificing government revenue in favour of the long-term rehabilitation of the sector. This decision broke with the short-term revenue focus that had characterized earlier regimes and marked a major transfer of benefits to rural constituents (Herbst 1993; Martin 1993). Politically, the decision to maintain cocoa prices reflected both external pressure and the political interests of the regime. Externally, the World Bank in particular favoured reduced export taxation to spur cocoa production. Internally, President Jerry Rawlings had an ideological commitment to supporting rural areas and to maintaining producer prices. More generally, there appears to have been a desire to build a rural political constituency for the PNDC, which ran counter to the longstanding urban bias of parties in Ghana and much of sub-Saharan Africa (Bates 1981; Herbst 1993; Martin 1993).[9]

The rapid decline in corporate taxation had a more technical origin, but also reflected the ideological evolution of the regime. The dramatic increase in corporate tax collection had been reliant on both improved enforcement and the collection of substantial tax arrears. The revenue from arrears could only provide a temporary revenue increase before being exhausted. Two other factors were also at play. First, with revenue stabilized, the government, under pressure from the IMF and World Bank, wished to reduce the tax burden in order to promote private sector growth. Second, as the revolutionary fervour of the populace abated, the

---

[8] As noted in an earlier footnote, earlier GDP estimates indicated that tax collection remained relatively constant as a share of GDP during this period. By contrast, updated GDP figures show a modest decline in tax collection.

[9] Personal interview on 10 April 2008 with former Deputy Minister of Finance and senior official in PNDC and NDC governments.

government was compelled to relax the aggressiveness of the sometimes extra-legal pursuit of large taxpayers.[10]

As export and corporate taxation declined, the government struggled to raise new revenue, but remained opportunistic in seeking ways to strengthen still relatively low tax revenues. This was most apparent in the case of government-controlled petroleum prices, which experienced a very sharp rise in late 1990 in response to world price increases caused by the Gulf War. When world fuel prices declined in early 1991, the government chose to maintain increased domestic prices, thus increasing the share of taxes in the pump price of gasoline from 16.5 per cent in early 1990 to 47.8 per cent by mid-1991. The Gulf War had justified the original price increase, and thus obscured the subsequent imposition of additional taxation from public view. This ensured that public opposition was modest, leading one key policymaker to view the increase in petroleum taxes as "opportunistic," "a windfall," and "a God send" amidst challenges raising revenue from other sources.[11]

The most troubling development of the period in the realm of taxation was the reversal of some earlier administrative reforms in 1991. The creation of the NRS in 1985 had given it significant independence from the Ministry of Finance, had allowed for improved conditions of work within the tax agencies, and had included the creation of the post of Minister of Revenue. The revenue gains that resulted from more skilled staff and greater political focus were undeniable, but the new structure also bred jealousies. At the highest level, the Minister of Finance felt that his authority was being undermined, while within the bureaucracy, complaints were emerging about special treatment being afforded to the revenue agencies. These tensions appear to have contributed to declining revenue collection in 1989 and 1990, while the Minister of Finance moved to abolish the NRS and bring the tax agencies back under Ministerial control in 1991. This decision reduced overall political attention to tax collection, and undermined bureaucratic morale, thus setting the stage for a further decline in tax revenue the following year.

---

[10] Personal interviews on 21 March 2008 with former minister in PNDC and NDC governments, and on 10 April 2008 with former Deputy Minister of Finance and senior official in PNDC and NDC governments. This sentiment was echoed by senior tax officials, one of whom captured this development poetically, ascribing it to the fact that "the temple of the revolution had worn down," while more and more heavily taxed businesses had closed their doors or found a way to hide from the authorities. Personal interview on 10 March 2008 with Deputy Commissioner, Internal Revenue Service.

[11] Personal interview on 2 April 2008 with director of leading Ghanaian economic policy think tank and former senior member of PNDC Economic Management Team.

This episode demonstrated both the difficulties inherent in major administrative reform and the threat to the effectiveness of tax collection posed by growing political tensions at the highest level.[12]

3.1.3 Elections, public spending and popular opposition, 1992–1996

Overt political conflict was very rare under the military regime, but that changed when an increasingly assertive domestic opposition and growing international pressure persuaded the PNDC government to hold elections late in 1992. The political temperature subsequently rose even further when Jerry Rawlings was declared victorious in the Presidential elections as head of the newly named National Democratic Congress (NDC), while the opposition National Patriotic Party (NPP) responded with accusation of electoral fraud and a boycott of parliament. While many observers believe that NPP claims of fraud may have been overblown, the boycott nonetheless created an extended political standoff, while democratization opened the door to more open political conflict (Nugent 1999; Osei 2000).

Tax issues played an important role throughout the period following the 1992 elections as a result of the emergence of a major fiscal deficit during the election year. The fiscal deficit reflected three factors. First was a continued decline in tax revenue during the election year, which was driven by upheaval caused by the abolition of the NRS and government reluctance to enforce taxation aggressively in the face of mounting popular resistance.[13] Second was a dramatic increase in public spending in response to repeated strikes by labour unions, who exploited their election year leverage to successfully demand increased wages and improved benefits.[14] Third, the looming fiscal crisis generated by increased spending and declining revenue was exacerbated when the IMF and World Bank interpreted the concessions as discretionary and reckless pre-election spending, and cancelled aid disbursements in protest.[15] As soon as the elections were over, the government was thus confronted with the urgent need to raise new revenue.

As the government sought out new tax revenue, the first conflict emerged in 1993 when the government attempted to further increase

---

[12] Personal interviews on 21 March 2008 with former minister in PNDC and NDC governments, on 21 April 2008 with former Commissioner, Internal Revenue Service, and on 16 April 2008 with former Commissioner, Internal Revenue Service.
[13] Ibid.
[14] Personal interview on 2 April 2008 with director of leading Ghanaian economic policy think tank and former senior member of PNDC Economic Management Team.
[15] Ibid.

3.1 The political economy of taxation in Ghana, 1981–2008

petroleum prices. Petroleum price increases were by far the most administratively simple way to quickly increase revenue, but were also highly politically salient. The first increase took effect in January 1993, days before the inauguration of the new parliament and constitution. While the increase met some public outcry, the decision to introduce the price increases before inaugurating the new parliament ensured that opposition remained fragmented. The government proposed a second price increase to parliament in the spring, assuming that the NDC-dominated parliament would accept it without protest. In the words of one key policymaker at the time, "[w]e were in for a shock," as the increase was rejected by parliament. With this the party leadership "realized that the whole relationship had changed," and the executive would no longer be able to make policy by decree.[16]

This conflict over petroleum taxation paled in comparison to the protests that greeted the introduction of a value-added tax (VAT) at a rate of 17.5 per cent to replace the existing system of sales taxes in 1995. The introduction of the new VAT was undertaken on relatively short notice, owing to major fiscal concerns as well as additional pressure from the IMF.[17] It resulted in arguably the most dramatic public protests of the era, and in the ultimate repeal of the tax, despite its centrality to the government agenda (Ninsin 2007). The scale of the protests was attributable in part to the fact that the tax was introduced relatively suddenly, at a high rate, and with limited public consultation, but also reflected the strength of broader public grievances (Osei 2000).[18]

Much of the leadership of the protests came from the opposition NPP, but the scale of the protests was largely unexpected, as was the need for the government to repeal the new tax to restore order. It was, in the words of one leading participant, "a sobering moment for the government."[19] As important as the repeal of the tax itself, the protests came to encompass broader demands for democratization, reduced

---

[16] Personal interview on 10 April 2008 with former Deputy Minister of Finance and senior official in PNDC and NDC governments.

[17] Personal interviews on 10 April 2008 with former Deputy Minister of Finance and senior official in PNDC and NDC governments, on 18 January 2008 with former leader of Tax Reform Program and senior official in Ministry of Finance, on 2 April 2008 with director of leading Ghanaian economic policy think tank and former senior member of PNDC Economic Management Team, on 20 April 2008 with Former Deputy Minister of Finance, and on 27 February 2008 with senior official, VAT Service.

[18] Personal interviews on 10 April 2008 with former Deputy Minister of Finance and senior official in PNDC and NDC governments, on 2 April 2008 with director of leading Ghanaian economic policy think tank and former senior member of PNDC Economic Management Team, and on 17 March 2008 with senior leader of Committee for Joint Action.

[19] Personal interview on 17 March 2008 with senior leader of Committee for Joint Action.

corruption and improved public services,[20] and prompted the government to adopt a fundamentally more open governing style thereafter.[21] The protests also figured prominently in the resignation of long-serving Minister of Finance Kwesi Botchwey, thus highlighting the depth of the political conflict (Terkper 1998; Assibey-Mensah 1999; Osei 2000).[22]

3.1.4 Open elections, increased harmony and modest revenue growth, 1997–2000

The NDC won a second popular mandate at the end of 1996 in an election that was accepted by the opposition and prompted their entry into parliament. This ushered in a period of greater political harmony, as structured parliamentary debate facilitated bargaining and the NDC adopted a relatively more inclusive governing style. Nonetheless, while the NDC government continued to achieve some revenue gains, increasing public unhappiness prevented it from expanding revenue sufficiently to fully close the fiscal gap.

The VAT was reintroduced in parliament in 1998 and was smoothly implemented in early 1999. The reintroduction of the tax resulted from internal commitment and growing pressure from the IMF, while its smooth implementation reflected both policy changes and changes in the political context. First, although the government had agreed with the IMF to subsequently raise the rate to 15 per cent, the initial rate was only 10 per cent, which was below the 15 per cent of the existing sales tax that it was replacing. Second, a major programme of public outreach and education was carried out, thus reducing public misunderstanding of the tax and, critically, clarifying the relatively limited expected impact on prices. Finally, the entry of opposition political parties into parliament increased the scope for structured debate and created a shared interest in fiscal stability, both of which reduced the likelihood that the formal opposition would again join in organizing street demonstrations (Osei 2000).[23]

In accordance with its earlier plan, the NDC government proposed a 2.5 per cent increase in the VAT the following year. This prompted public outcry, and the government responded by announcing that the

---

[20] Ibid.
[21] Personal interviews on 21 March 2008 with former minister in PNDC and NDC governments and on 10 April 2008 with former Deputy Minister of Finance and senior official in PNDC and NDC governments.
[22] Personal interview on 10 April 2008 with former Deputy Minister of Finance and senior official in PNDC and NDC governments.
[23] Ibid., and interview on 20 April 2008 with Former Deputy Minister of Finance.

new funds would be earmarked for a Ghana Education Trust (GET) Fund. The fund was to be used primarily for educational infrastructure and scholarships, with a focus on tertiary education. While the Ghana National Union of Students had long been mobilizing in favour of increased tertiary funding, there is ample evidence that the decision to create the GET Fund was first and foremost a politically motivated means to secure passage of the increase in the VAT rate (Prichard 2009).[24]

Despite significant revenue gains associated with the VAT, the overall fiscal position of the NDC government remained weak. Faced with a persistent fiscal deficit, and constrained by huge debt repayment costs, the government found itself unable to further increase tax revenue. Senior officials report that while there was a desire to increase taxation, they could not mobilize the necessary political support to do so in the face of growing public opposition. This was most apparent in the slow erosion of petroleum taxation to the point that the government was subsidizing fuel prices by the end of the decade. As the world price of fuel rose in the late 1990s, the government judged that, owing to persistent political opposition, it could not afford to increase domestic prices. This political stalemate left the government fiscally crippled as it moved towards the 2000 elections.[25]

Although it attracted less public attention, the faltering political position of the government appears to have similarly forestalled reforms in tax administration. During the 1990s, several administrative reform programs remained on hold despite protests from the IFIs. These included: the functional integration of the IRS and CEPS (and eventually the VAT Service as well), the creation of a Large Taxpayers Unit (LTU), and the computerization of the IRS. The government repeatedly expressed a commitment to move ahead with these initiatives in order to improve its fiscal position, but major progress did not occur until after a change in power in the 2000 elections.

The lack of progress appears to have had multiple causes, beginning with resistance within the Ministry of Finance to the prospect of a more autonomous revenue agency. There equally appears to have been some tension between the different tax agencies, as their functional integration would have reduced the control and autonomy exercised by senior officials in any individual agency. Similarly, there was bureaucratic resistance to the creation of an LTU owing to the revenue losses that would be

---

[24] Ibid., and interviews on 27 February 2008 with senior official, VAT Service, on 25 March 2008 with director of leading advocacy NGO, and on 26 March 2008 with senior budget expert, NGO advocacy initiative.

[25] Personal interview on 21 March 2008 with former minister in PNDC and NDC governments.

suffered by individual offices. Many tax administrators further resisted, and even undermined, computerization efforts out of a concern that their limited computer skills would put their jobs in jeopardy (Bird and Zolt 2007). Finally, any effort at tax reform, particularly as it related to income taxation, was bound to encounter staunch opposition from the economic elite, who were amongst the greatest beneficiaries of weak tax enforcement (Ascher 1989). The computerization of the IRS, in particular, threatened to dramatically improve transparency surrounding the economic activities of taxpayers, with risks to those who preferred to have their activities remain secret (Fjeldstad 2005: 11–12).[26]

While the challenges inherent in administrative reform warrant much further discussion, these issues are not the focus here. The relevant point for this research is that administrative reform in the tax agencies held the potential to generate important revenue gains, but also faced entrenched opposition on many fronts. Consequently, any reform effort would require significant political capital, and in the late 1990s the increasingly unpopular NDC government was unable to generate the necessary support.

3.1.5 A new government and expanded public revenue, 2001–2008

At the end of 2000, the NPP was voted into office and it immediately enjoyed significant goodwill, even amongst its opponents, owing to its promise of increased political openness (Amponsah 2007; Frempong 2007). This goodwill provided the government with much greater freedom than its predecessor in implementing its policy agenda.[27] Central to this agenda was a programme to restore fiscal balance in the wake of the large deficits of previous years. Two immediate measures were particularly noteworthy: (1) accession to the Highly Indebted Poor Countries (HIPC) initiative for debt relief, which was accompanied by a large increase in petroleum prices and petroleum taxes; and (2) the introduction of the National Reconstruction Levy (NRL).

Ghana had first been offered access to the HIPC initiative for debt relief in 1999, but the NDC government did not accede to the

---

[26] Personal interviews on 9 September 2008 with program officer, PUFMARP Project, World Bank; on 16 April 2008 with former Commissioner, Internal Revenue Service; on 13 March 2008 with senior official, Research Planning and Monitoring, Revenue Agencies Governing Board; and on 14 March 2008 with professor, University of Ghana and former auditor, Internal Revenue Service.

[27] Personal interviews on 21 March 2008 with former minister in PNDC and NDC governments, on 20 April 2008 with former Deputy Minister of Finance, and on 27 February 2008 with senior official, Bank of Ghana.

3.1 The political economy of taxation in Ghana, 1981–2008

agreement. This partly reflected an unwillingness to accept the stigma that President Rawlings associated with admitting the need for debt relief, given uncertainty about the magnitude of the immediate benefits.[28] More important though, was the fact that increasing petroleum prices was a central condition of HIPC, and the government considered this to be politically impossible prior to the election.[29] By contrast, the new NPP government quickly joined HIPC and implemented large petroleum price increases in 2001 and 2003. In fact, not only did the government increase petroleum prices, which implied proportional increases in tax revenue, it also simultaneously increased the share of taxation in the total price. Unlike the harsh reception that would have met such action by the NDC, the government faced limited popular opposition. This reflected a combination of the goodwill enjoyed by the new government, and the ability to blame the stigma of HIPC, and the hardship of new prices, on the NDC.[30] The decision to simultaneously increase petroleum taxation demonstrated the potential for disguising new taxes within apparently inevitable price increases mandated by the IMF.

In 2004, the HIPC conditions called for the government to increase prices again, but a temporary waiver was granted by the IMF in recognition of the political difficulty posed by price increases in the run up to the election. The government thus went ahead with the promised increase in petroleum prices in 2005, after winning the 2004 elections.[31] However, the new round of price increases nonetheless involved a decrease in the share of taxation in the total price, owing to faster increases in global prices. Having exhausted some of the goodwill that had greeted it in 2001, the NPP was unable to keep price increases in line with increasing global prices,[32] thus again highlighting both the political salience of petroleum prices and the close relationship between the ability to raise revenue and the broader political popularity of government.

---

[28] Personal interviews on 21 March 2008 with former minister in PNDC and NDC governments, on 10 April 2008 with former Deputy Minister of Finance and senior official in PNDC and NDC governments, and on 20 April 2008 with former Deputy Minister of Finance.

[29] Personal interviews on 21 March 2008 with former minister in PNDC and NDC governments, on 16 April 2008 with senior official, Bank of Ghana, and on 20 April 2008 with former Deputy Minister of Finance.

[30] Personal interviews on 27 February 2008 with senior official, Bank of Ghana, on 20 April 2008 with former Deputy Minister of Finance, on 21 March 2008 with former minister in PNDC and NDC governments, and on 10 March 2008 with senior official, Tax Policy Unit, Ministry of Finance and Economic Planning.

[31] Personal interviews on 16 April 2008 with senior official, Bank of Ghana, and on 10 March 2008 with senior official, Ghana National Petroleum Authority.

[32] Personal interviews on 10 April 2008 with director of leading civil society advocacy network and on 20 April 2008 with former Deputy Minister of Finance.

In addition to these measures related to HIPC, the government introduced the NRL in 2001 as a 2.5 per cent surcharge tax on corporate profits, with a special rate of 15 per cent for financial institutions. The tax was initially meant to last for three years, although it was ultimately renewed in 2004 before being removed in 2007. Surprisingly, the tax was subject to relatively muted opposition from the business community. This reflected the strategic mobilization of public opinion in favour of the tax, but also the increasingly conciliatory relationship between government and business.[33] While the NDC had improved the business climate during its tenure, business confidence increased dramatically after the election of the NPP, while the new government also expanded consultation (Amponsah 2007). The NPP also managed to play shrewd politics when it extended the NRL in 2004, co-opting significant opposition by promising that 25 per cent of the levy would be used to create a venture capital fund.[34]

Having stabilized the fiscal situation, the government undertook two major additional revenue measures. The first was the introduction of the National Health Insurance Levy (NHIL), which amounted to a 2.5 per cent increase in the VAT rate, and was earmarked to fund a new National Health Insurance Scheme (NHIS). The new government was adamant that the new tax be separately quoted as the NHIL, and not be called VAT, owing to very vocal opposition to the VAT from 1994 to 2000. It is also widely believed that, as in the case of the GET Fund, the primary government objective was to increase revenue, while the decision to earmark funds for the NHIS was a concession to political necessity.[35]

The second important revenue measure was the introduction of a Communications Tax, which was primarily a tax on mobile phone calls. The tax was first proposed quickly in 2007 as the government encountered mounting revenue needs and was met by a significant public backlash. This prompted the government to seek a political strategy to ease its

---

[33] Personal interviews on 26 March 2008 with senior budget expert, NGO advocacy initiative, on 28 February 2008 with senior official, Private Enterprise Foundation, and on 27 March 2008 with senior official, Ghana National Chamber of Commerce and Industry.

[34] Personal interviews on 28 February 2008 with senior official, Private Enterprise Foundation, and on 15 April 2008 with Opposition Member of Parliament and Member of Parliamentary Finance Committee.

[35] Personal interviews on 15 April 2008 with Opposition Member of Parliament and Member of Parliamentary Finance Committee, on 26 March 2008 with senior budget expert, NGO advocacy initiative, on 15 April 2008 with senior budget official, Ministry of Finance and Economic Planning, and on 25 March 2008 with director of leading advocacy NGO.

passage.[36] The government initially claimed that the tax was meant to offset customs losses from mobile phone smuggling, but this rationale was quickly abandoned when the public realized that the expected revenue far exceeded any plausible losses from smuggling.[37] The government subsequently announced that the tax revenue would be earmarked to fund the Youth Employment Scheme (YES). This was a largely political strategy by political leaders who "wanted this money immediately" and proved to be politically effective.[38] However, it was also deeply disingenuous, as the Act itself only actually earmarked 20 per cent of the revenue for youth employment, with no dedicated line item in the budget or oversight committee.[39] This highlights the scope for deception in building public support for earmarking, along with the weakness of parliament, which failed to draw attention to the discrepancy. While this parliamentary failure may reflect the simple weakness of the opposition, it also highlights the extent to which the NDC saw the merits of increased government revenue given its hopes of regaining power in upcoming elections.

3.2 Evidence of tax bargaining

Having presented this detailed historical narrative, the first analytical challenge lies in assessing whether these developments constitute evidence of the existence of the hypothesized causal processes linking taxation, responsiveness and accountability. In some cases this only requires explicitly summarizing connections that are relatively self-evident in the preceding historical narrative. In other cases, additional information about the motives, perceptions and activities of political actors allows us to add nuance to the overview provided so far. On balance, the Ghanaian case presents extensive evidence of tax bargaining, but specific outcomes have been diverse. What follows captures the diversity of these outcomes under four distinct categories, which mirror those introduced in the model in Chapter 2: taxation without bargaining, direct tax

---

[36] Personal interview on 14 April 2008 with government MP and member of Parliamentary Finance Committee.
[37] Personal interview on 15 April 2008 with Opposition Member of Parliament and Member of Parliamentary Finance Committee.
[38] Personal interview on 14 April 2008 with government MP and member of Parliamentary Finance Committee.
[39] Personal interview on 15 April 2008 with Opposition Member of Parliament and Member of Parliamentary Finance Committee. Even senior officials working on the YES were surprised to discover upon passage of the bill that so little revenue was actually earmarked for the YES, as they had expected most or all of the new revenue to flow to them. Personal interview on 17 April 2008 with senior official, Youth Employment Scheme, Ministry of Manpower, Youth, and Employment.

bargaining, taxation as a driver of strengthened political capabilities of taxpayers, and tax resistance as a contributor to changes in government.

3.2.1 Repression, coercion and the absence of tax bargaining

The first lesson that can be drawn from the Ghanaian narrative is that sufficiently coercive governments can, for a time at least, push through major new taxation without prompting effective citizen demands for responsiveness or accountability. Research on structural adjustment in Ghana has focused on the extent to which the government was sufficiently well entrenched to be able to undertake reforms with minimal political opposition (Herbst 1993; Martin 1993). Taxation was no different. During the 1980s, the government undertook major reforms of tax policy and administration, and dramatically increased tax collection, but leading government officials make clear in interviews that they had little concern for any potential political consequences.[40]

While the overall picture during the period was one of coercion, rather than tax bargaining, several caveats are warranted – and these caveats serve to reinforce key messages from the initial model. First, this state of affairs was temporary. By the end of the decade the repressive power of the state was diminishing, while taxpayers had gradually become more organized. One result was the emergence of scattered tax protests,[41] while, as tellingly, revenue generation had begun to decline amidst falling administrative morale and declining compliance.[42] Second, part of the absence of taxpayer mobilization is explained by the fact that a significant share of Ghanaians held a positive of view of the reforms, despite the overall increase in collection.[43] Increases in income taxation clearly targeted an unpopular and elite minority, while renewed cocoa tax collection was a reflection of improved prices and production following the devaluation of the currency. Finally, there is a sense amongst some observers that aggressive taxation may have quietly fuelled levels of political

---

[40] Personal interviews on 21 March 2008 with former minister in PNDC and NDC governments, on 10 April 2008 with former Deputy Minister of Finance and senior official in PNDC and NDC governments, and on 25 March 2008 with senior NDC and government official.
[41] Personal interviews on 10 April 2008 with former Deputy Minister of Finance and senior official in PNDC and NDC governments, on 18 March 2008 with senior official, Ghana Union of Traders Association, and on 17 March 2008 with senior leader of Committee for Joint Action.
[42] Personal interviews on 21 March 2008 with former minister in PNDC and NDC governments and on 10 April 2008 with former Deputy Minister of Finance and senior official in PNDC and NDC governments.
[43] Ibid.

3.2 Evidence of tax bargaining

engagement and mobilization, both at the grassroots level and within the ranks of the organized political opposition.[44] At a minimum, the aggressive taxation of elite incomes became the subject of future political attacks by the opposition, suggesting that, while taxation during the period was achieved coercively, it was not entirely without longer-term political consequences.

3.2.2 Direct tax bargaining: protests, earmarking and compromise

While the expansion of taxation in the 1980s was driven by coercion, there is significant evidence that tax bargaining was an important contributor to the process of democratization in the first half of the 1990s, and to the further expansion of responsiveness and accountability thereafter. While these political processes undoubtedly had multiple and complex roots, the goal here is to highlight the important contribution of relatively direct forms of tax bargaining. The analysis focuses on three distinct parts of this story: (1) tax protests and democratization in the early 1990s; (2) tax earmarking and government responsiveness during the next decade; (3) and the particular case of tax bargaining around informal sector taxation.

Tax protests and government accountability

As Ghana slowly emerged from a period in which political opposition was sharply controlled, various anti-tax mobilizations, particularly by traders, were amongst the first signs of political agitation in the late 1980s. A senior PNDC official explained that "the first time I felt political pressure was from the women who were going to Nigeria and bringing back plastic goods."[45] When the government tried to crack down through the collection of customs taxes, the traders organized to resist. Likewise, the Ghana Union of Traders Association (GUTA) was formed as part of mass protests responding to new municipal market taxes introduced in 1989.[46] While these early examples were ultimately repressed, they are evidence of the role played by tax protests in opening space for political opposition.

More significant was the political conflict that surrounded efforts to increase petroleum prices in 1993. Although the PNDC government had

---

[44] Personal interviews on 21 March 2008 with former minister in PNDC and NDC governments and on 28 February 2008 with senior official, Private Enterprise Foundation.
[45] Personal interview on 10 April 2008 with former Deputy Minister of Finance and senior official in PNDC and NDC governments.
[46] Personal interviews on 10 April 2008 with former Deputy Minister of Finance and senior official in PNDC and NDC governments and on 18 March 2008 with senior official, Ghana Union of Traders Association.

been able to implement price increases by decree earlier in the year, the second fuel price increase in 1993 was rejected by the NDC-controlled parliament. In acting against its own executive, the NDC parliament was responding to public outcry against the first fuel price increase, which had led the budget to be dubbed the "killer budget." While the government did not make immediate concessions during the parliamentary debate over the proposed price increases, party officials make clear that the emergence of public and parliamentary opposition forced the leadership to rethink their highly centralized approach to decision-making. The debate thus changed the informal rules of decision-making and accountability.[47]

A very similar, but more dramatic, process played out two years later with the repeal of the newly introduced VAT amidst mass public demonstrations that left several people dead. The protests, known as *Kume Preko*, were loosely organized by the Alliance for Change, which comprised civil society leaders as well as prominent members of the opposition NPP and other political parties. The involvement of the formal political opposition was pivotal and resulted from the fact that they had boycotted parliament and thus were compelled to engage in mass politics rather than parliamentary debate. While the protests were initially a response to the VAT, they quickly came to encompass a much broader range of grievances against the government, including demands for political liberalization. The eventual government decision to repeal the VAT was of major consequence, as it was both profoundly embarrassing and significantly undermined its fiscal and economic objectives.[48]

In the long term, what was most noteworthy about the protests was that they significantly advanced the process of democratization. For the opposition, the protests were a watershed, as – unlike during the elections – they were able to present a fully unified front. This greater unity carried over to subsequent elections and was a sine qua non of political success (Frempong 2007). More importantly, the protests made clear that the government could not continue to govern without opening the political process and inviting deliberation. Amongst other factors, the prominent role of opposition political parties in organizing the protests made clear to the government that it was better off with these groups

---

[47] Personal interview on 10 April 2008 with former Deputy Minister of Finance and senior official in PNDC and NDC governments.
[48] Personal interviews on 17 March 2008 with senior leader of Committee for Joint Action, on 10 April 2008 with former Deputy Minister of Finance and senior official in PNDC and NDC governments, and on 18 January 2008 with former leader of Tax Reform Program and senior official in Ministry of Finance.

in parliament than in the streets.[49] If the government wished to pursue its policy agenda successfully, it became clear that parliament would be an important institution for facilitating bargaining and dialogue (Osei 2000).

Thus, there is little doubt that conflict over taxation was a catalyst for significant changes in the informal institutions of accountability, as the role of parliament and the inclusiveness of the ruling NDC expanded meaningfully in the aftermath of the protests. A more nuanced lesson is that while taxation was a catalyst for the protests, the protests were not simply about the tax. Instead, taxation was the spark that unleashed much broader grievances. Finally, although the VAT was a broad-based tax, and the protests attracted a diversity of taxpayers, elite involvement was absolutely central to what transpired. Whether or not the protests would have enjoyed the same success in the absence of leading politicians is very much open to question (Ninsin 2007).

Tax earmarking and responsiveness
The failed implementation of the VAT resulted in a significant expansion of accountability, but this outcome was largely implicit and was achieved through very public political conflict. By contrast, subsequent government efforts to expand taxation were characterized by relatively explicit, pre-emptive, forms of tax bargaining that ensured the smooth implementation of reform. Unlike the broad changes in accountability that resulted from the original VAT protests, these later tax bargains, which relied on earmarking tax revenues for popular programs, were focused on more narrow improvements in the responsiveness of government.

The most dramatic examples of such tax bargaining were the earmarking of successive increases in the VAT rate to the GET Fund in 2000 and the NHIS in 2003. In both cases, the preponderance of evidence indicates that the ultimate decision to earmark funds was a purely political strategy to reduce public opposition to tax increases. This is not to imply that the earmarked activities were not legitimate, and justified, government priorities. It is simply that the decision to explicitly earmark the funds, and create dedicated oversight bodies, would not have occurred if not for public resistance to the prospect of additional taxation.[50] This

---

[49] Personal interviews on 10 April 2008 with former Deputy Minister of Finance and senior official in PNDC and NDC governments, on 21 March 2008 with former minister in PNDC and NDC governments, and on 17 March 2008 with senior leader of Committee for Joint Action.
[50] Personal interviews on 27 February 2008 with senior official, VAT Service, on 10 April 2008 with former Deputy Minister of Finance and senior official in PNDC and NDC governments, on 15 April 2008 with senior budget official, Ministry of Finance and

marks the process of earmarking as a clear example of tax bargaining leading to the expansion of government responsiveness.

While the evidence of tax bargaining is clear, the more challenging, and more important, question is whether that bargaining resulted in genuinely improved outcomes. Put another way, the fact that the government created the appearance of responding to popular demands is not sufficient evidence that this commitment was carried out in practice. Untangling the actual impact of earmarking requires consideration of four related issues: the actual content of the legal commitment, the impact on the budget process, the risk of fungibility, and the quality of oversight.

The first risk is that the government may announce that funds are being earmarked for a particular purpose but fail to follow through on that promise in practice. This was the case for the Communications Tax, as the public was led to believe that revenues would be earmarked for the Youth Employment Scheme, but in practice only a small share of revenue was allocated to that programme. Worse still, even the 20 per cent allocated to youth employment was defined so vaguely in the law as to call into question the reliability of the earmarking. Yet, despite the overt deception practised by the government, the public remained overwhelmingly unaware of the discrepancy. In this case, tax bargaining was, to a significant degree, a mere "gimmick" for easing the passage of legislation.[51]

The second concern is that the practice of earmarking can be a mixed blessing, as it is politically useful and can ensure certain types of spending, but also reduces budgetary flexibility and, potentially, the overall quality of the budgeting process (McCleary 1991). The earmarking of tax revenue has been widely supported in the case of Road Funds, owing to the chronic failure of governments to invest in road maintenance, but "best practice" has generally been to discourage earmarking in other areas because of the impact on budget flexibility (Gwilliam and Shalizi 1999). While resolving this debate is beyond the scope of this research, it is possible that responsiveness through earmarking has hidden costs.

The third risk is that earmarked funds may be fungible. In such cases, total funding for earmarked activities might increase by far less than the amount of the earmark, as existing funds are shifted elsewhere in the budget. While this is a risk in principle, it has so far not been borne out

Economic Planning, on 26 March 2008 with senior budget expert, NGO advocacy initiative, and on 25 March 2008 with director of leading advocacy NGO.

[51] Personal interviews on 15 April 2008 with Opposition Member of Parliament and Member of Parliamentary Finance Committee, on 17 April 2008 with senior official, Youth Employment Scheme, Ministry of Manpower, Youth, and Employment, and on 15 April 2008 with senior budget official, Ministry of Finance and Economic Planning.

3.2 Evidence of tax bargaining

in practice in Ghana.[52] Overall levels of health and education funding expanded significantly more than the amount of the new revenues earmarked for the GET fund and NHIL, respectively. Two concerns persist nonetheless. First, some officials believe that the share of spending on health outside of the NHIS may begin to decline in subsequent years, which would be consistent with the use of earmarked funds to substitute for general budgetary funding.[53] Over time, this relationship inevitably becomes more difficult to monitor. Second, there is evidence that the earmarked funds have not been used exclusively for their prescribed purposes within the health and education budgets.[54] Most notably, both programs, and particularly the GET Fund, should have led to increased non-wage expenditures. Yet, in practice, the share of non-wage spending in the core health and education budgets fell during the years following the introduction of the new taxes (Lawson et al. 2007). Regardless of the justification for this choice, it indicates some degree of fungibility in the use of funds.

Finally, all of these issues point to the broader reality that the long-term impact of earmarking will be dependent largely on the extent to which earmarking strengthens the quality of internal and external oversight. In the absence of effective monitoring, deception by the government, fungibility, corruption and waste are all made more likely. The impact of earmarking in Ghana on the quality of oversight remains somewhat ambiguous and under-researched. Both the GET Fund and NHIS are managed by appointed Boards of Directors, and audited by the Auditor General, rather than being subject to the standard oversight mechanisms of the Ministry of Finance. The merit of this decision is a much larger research question, but it is not a given that the new structures will be more effective, particularly given the costs of more fragmented monitoring of the budget as a whole (Gwilliam and Shalizi 1999). Perhaps more tellingly, little attention seems to have been paid to this question by either internal or external actors, despite rapid escalation in the share of tax revenue subject to earmarking.[55]

---

[52] Interviews with budget staff make this potential fungibility clear, although they also make clear that in practice the earmarks reduced budgetary discretion, as there was pressure to increase spending in prescribed areas. Personal interview on 15 April 2008 with senior budget official, Ministry of Finance and Economic Planning.
[53] Personal interviews on 15 April 2008 with senior budget official, Ministry of Finance and Economic Planning and on 23 April 2008 with international advisor to Ministry of Health.
[54] Personal interviews on 26 March 2008 with senior budget expert, NGO advocacy initiative and on 10 April 2008 with director, leading civil society advocacy network.
[55] Personal interviews on 10 April 2008 with former Deputy Minister of Finance and senior official in PNDC and NDC governments, on 15 April 2008 with senior budget

A more interesting possibility is that earmarking may improve external oversight by making spending more transparent or by generating greater public attention and interest. While these factors are difficult to evaluate, civil society and opposition leaders generally feel that modest oversight benefits exist, but remain limited because of the lack of available information.[56] For example, a public backlash forced the government to return revenues to the GET Fund after the government had initially appropriated tax revenues that were collected after the passage of the law but before the Fund was operational.[57] On the other hand, the GET Fund has been beset by detailed accusations that funds are being used beyond the originally prescribed purposes, and that it has suffered from significant corruption.[58] It is thus difficult to assess fully the extent of the gains in responsiveness resulting from tax earmarking. However, the balance of evidence seems to suggest some benefits in terms of the overall quality of spending, consistent with the potential governance benefits of bargaining over taxation.

Accountability and co-optation in informal sector taxation

Recent government efforts to expand taxation of the informal sector have also prompted relatively explicit tax bargaining, although with mixed results. The government push to improve taxation of the informal sector has been motivated by a combination of internal commitment from tax administrators, international pressure and pressure from the major business associations. The role of business is particularly interesting, as it reflects an apparent tax bargain in its own right: formal sector businesses report that they have been willing to expand their own tax compliance on the condition that the government simultaneously endeavours to expand the tax base.[59]

While the government has undertaken many measures to expand taxation of small and medium enterprises (SMEs) in the informal sector, this analysis focuses on two measures in particular: taxes on public transport operators and the introduction of a Flat Rate VAT Scheme for small retailers. In the early 1990s, government efforts to expand informal sector taxation initially focused on public transport operators – that is, the

---

official, Ministry of Finance and Economic Planning, and on 11 April 2008 with official, IMF.

[56] Personal interviews on 20 April 2008 with Former Deputy Minister of Finance, on 25 March 2008 with director of leading advocacy NGO, and on 10 April 2008 with director, leading civil society advocacy network.
[57] Personal interview on 25 March 2008 with director of leading advocacy NGO.
[58] Personal interview on 10 April 2008 with director, leading civil society advocacy network and on 26 March 2008 with senior budget expert, NGO advocacy initiative.
[59] Personal interview on 28 February 2008 with senior official, Private Enterprise Foundation.

3.2 Evidence of tax bargaining

operators of privately owned buses responsible for the majority of urban transport – using what has been called "associational taxation" (Joshi and Ayee 2008). The government agreed with the Ghana Private Road Transport Union (GPRTU) leadership that the union would collect taxes itself from its members and then remit the revenue to government. The goal was to make compliance as simple as possible, with taxes collected on a daily or weekly basis to accommodate the difficulties that operators faced in paying large lump sum taxes. In exchange for tax compliance, the GPRTU membership expected to be relatively protected from the arbitrary assessment of penalties by the police and tax officials. While this tax arrangement was one of the first of its kind, over time the model was extended to many other sectors. This agreement was facilitated by the fact that the leadership of the GPRTU and the NDC government were close allies (Joshi and Ayee 2008).

In the short term the arrangement was a mutually beneficial tax bargain, but the relationship soured over time. The government became frustrated with the union leadership as revenues failed to expand at the expected rate and checks and balances were progressively eroded. Meanwhile, the union membership became increasingly disenchanted owing to a feeling that the union leadership was pocketing much of the tax revenue that was being collected. In 2003, the agreement with the GPRTU was replaced by a Vehicle Income Tax, which mandated that every commercial operator would prominently display a tax sticker purchased from the tax authorities on a quarterly basis. The new scheme immediately yielded significantly more revenue, while also being more popular with much of the membership of the GPRTU.

Thus, the system of associational taxation provides a mixed picture as a form of tax bargaining. On one hand, public transport operators were successfully brought into the tax net, and – in exchange – appear to have been spared certain forms of police harassment. While these gains are relatively narrow, they are nonetheless indicative of a more responsive government. On the other hand, while the original scheme was apparently well intentioned, it evolved into a more cynically corporatist relationship. Even as collection efficiency declined, the NDC gained the support of the union leadership by allowing them to retain part of the collection, while the union leadership remained in the good graces of government by offering legitimacy to the tax. Meanwhile, it was individual operators who were forced to pay higher taxes for smaller benefits. It was only after the exit of the NDC that the tax system was regularized.[60]

---

[60] Personal interviews on 3 March 2008 with Assistant Deputy Commissioner, Internal Revenue Service and on 20 March 2008 with senior official international NGO working on informal sector taxation in Accra. These sentiments are widely echoed by

The second prominent effort to tax SMEs has been the introduction of the Flat Rate VAT Scheme by the NPP government, and it has resulted in a similarly complex relationship between the government and GUTA. The new tax aimed to improve compliance amongst small retailers by replacing the more complex accounting requirements of the standard VAT with a flat 3 per cent tax on turnover. The government would benefit from additional revenue, while traders would face reduced harassment, simpler accounting requirements, and greater legitimacy. To ease acceptance of the new tax, the government sought an endorsement from GUTA, and this did, indeed, facilitate implementation.[61]

To some extent, GUTA entered into partnership with the VAT Service to create a legitimate tax bargain, with benefits for both the government and taxpayers.[62] Yet there are suggestions in many quarters that the GUTA leadership was also willing to endorse a higher tax burden on its members in order to secure narrow personal benefits. For one, the GUTA leadership were larger traders, and thus had an interest in bringing smaller traders into the tax net in order to improve their own competitive position in a dynamic common to many countries (Goldsmith 2002). Equally, it is widely believed that the GUTA leadership were willing to cooperate with the government to further their own political ambitions or, even more cynically, to improve their access to government contracts.[63] While these claims cannot be verified, there is a strong sense that co-optation was as much a part of the introduction of the Flat Rate Scheme as was improved government responsiveness. Thus, again, we see evidence of meaningful benefits flowing from tax bargaining, but are also reminded of the complexity of these processes.

3.2.3 Taxes, civil society and public engagement

The analysis so far has considered relatively clear-cut examples of direct tax bargaining, or its conspicuous absence. Yet, taxation may also encourage the expansion of responsiveness and accountability indirectly by

---

public transport operators themselves, and by researchers who have looked at these arrangements.
[61] Personal interviews on 27 February 2008 with senior official, VAT Service and on 18 March 2008 with senior official, Ghana Union of Traders Association.
[62] Personal interview on 18 March 2008 with senior official, Ghana Union of Traders Association.
[63] Personal interviews on 15 April 2008 with Opposition Member of Parliament and Member of Parliamentary Finance Committee, on 27 February 2008 with senior official, VAT Service, and on 20 March 2008 with senior official international NGO working on informal sector taxation in Accra.

catalysing longer-term processes of political organizing within society, thus expanding the ability of taxpayers to exercise oversight and make demands on government. While these processes are similar to processes of direct tax bargaining, they are distinct in that they do not involve an immediately observable quid pro quo, but are instead likely to encourage increased public engagement, and reform, over time. There is significant evidence that taxation has, indeed, encouraged the strengthening of civil society in Ghana, and the analysis is usefully divided into two components: broad-based advocacy groups and business associations.

Taxation and the Committee for Joint Action
The prototypical example of taxation catalysing new civil society organizations is the creation of the Alliance for Change in response to the introduction of the VAT in 1995. While the anti-VAT protests yielded relatively immediate gains in the accountability of the government, they also contributed to longer-term processes of political organizing and engagement. At the level of the formal political opposition, the period of cooperation as part of the Alliance for Change provided the foundation for more unified efforts by the opposition in the 1996 and 2000 elections (Frempong 2007). Equally important, the experience of 1995 was a precursor to the coalescing of civil society grievances in response to new taxation in subsequent years.

At the centre of these efforts has been the Committee for Joint Action (CJA), a loose association of civil society actors often working in partnership with opposition parties in parliament. The CJA has been a prominent voice of discontent with government policy, and has been most notable for its ability to coordinate mass public mobilization. Building on the early pro-democracy movement and the VAT protests, it has demanded policies including political liberalization, anti-corruption efforts, expanded public spending and reduced taxes.

The political prominence of the CJA has ebbed and flowed over time, with its moments of strength consistently a response to high taxes. Of particular salience have been highly visible and contentious conflicts over petroleum prices (and the petroleum taxes embedded in those prices), consistent with the politicization of petroleum prices in other countries as well (Gupta and Mahler 1995; Esfahani 2001). Petroleum price increases in 1998 vaulted the CJA to prominence as an heir to the fragmented Alliance for Change, and made the CJA a major factor in the inability of the government to implement subsequent price increases. The CJA faded from prominence amidst the goodwill welcoming the new NPP government to power in 2001, but a second round of petroleum price increases in 2002–2003 catalysed renewed activism. This pattern was repeated at the end of 2007, as the CJA led mass demonstrations in the north that were reputed to be the largest since the VAT protests of 1995. The backdrop was, again, high petroleum prices, although the demands of protesters were much broader. In the words of a CJA leader: "Taxes have always provided a focal point for public mobilization. Have provided momentum for the resistance."[64]

Taxation and business associations

Taxation has likewise played an important role in the expansion of the political activism of business associations. The Association of Ghana Industries (AGI) had existed since independence, but only re-emerged as an important political player after 1999. While this has been facilitated by political liberalization, the immediate catalyst for AGI's revival was the need to respond to the VAT. Whereas sales tax had been collected after production, the VAT was collected on inputs at the point of import, only to be subsequently refunded after the final sale. This meant that a share of the firms' working capital remained tied up in what were effectively advance tax payments. The AGI lobbied for tax compliant firms to be exempted from the upfront payment of taxes on inputs, on the assumption that full taxes would be paid after production and sale. This effort was ultimately successful and the increased staffing and political assertiveness of the AGI has persisted far beyond the initial advocacy campaign.[65]

Other business associations offer similar, although more modest, lessons. For example, the major business associations in Ghana came together to form an umbrella organization, the Private Enterprise Foundation, in 1994, just as the VAT was initially emerging as a major political issue facing business.[66] Similarly, the GUTA was initially formed as a response to new market taxes being imposed by the Accra Metropolitan Authority, and coalesced around a series of major protests beginning in 1989.[67]

The remaining question is what implications stronger business associations are likely to have for broader political developments. Business

---

[64] Personal interview on 17 March 2008 with senior leader of Committee for Joint Action. The broader role of the CJA described here is confirmed universally by respondents from within government and civil society.

[65] Personal interview on 18 March 2008 with senior official, Associations of Ghana Industries.

[66] Personal interview on 28 February 2008 with senior official, Private Enterprise Foundation.

[67] Personal interviews on 18 March 2008 with senior official, Ghana Union of Traders Association and on 10 April 2008 with former Deputy Minister of Finance and senior official in PNDC and NDC governments.

3.2 Evidence of tax bargaining

associations may have relatively narrow interests that differ from those of citizens in general. Thus, while some researchers view business associations as potentially important contributors to improved governance, others see them primarily as rent-seeking organizations (Olson 1965; Goldsmith 2002; Handley 2008). This is a larger question than can be addressed here, but the prevailing view in Ghana is that, while business associations may seek certain special benefits, greater organization of the business community has, on the whole, contributed to their being more active in pushing for the expansion of responsiveness and accountability. AGI has emerged as a prominent voice pushing for more open political processes and for greater macroeconomic stability, while GUTA has remained an important voice for retail traders.[68]

3.2.4 Tax resistance, changes in government and reform

Finally, it is clear that in Ghana the revenue-raising ability of successive governments has been shaped by public perceptions of their performance, and that this, in turn, has had important implications for their political prospects. Consistent with the model developed in Chapter 2, the Ghanaian case provides significant evidence that the ability of taxpayers to resist taxation by unpopular governments can contribute to the expansion of responsiveness and accountability by increasing the likelihood of a change in government and by providing incentives for incoming governments to adopt a reformist agenda. While this is a particularly indirect form of tax bargaining, it is nonetheless potentially very significant.

This possibility is illustrated most clearly by the period following the 1996 elections, during which the NDC government experienced a progressively deepening fiscal crisis, and was unable to raise the revenues necessary to close the gap owing to its growing unpopularity. While the government was successful in re-introducing the VAT, and in raising the rate, it was crippled by its inability to raise petroleum prices or to undertake desired administrative reforms. Former members of the government are adamant that their inability to raise additional tax revenue was the result of relentless popular opposition to such measures. In this way, the wavering popularity of the NDC government exacerbated the fiscal crisis, which, in turn, further eroded the ability of the government to supply public services or implement popular public policies. While the NDC may have lost the elections in 2000 in any event, there is little doubt that their revenue difficulties rendered this outcome significantly more likely,

---

[68] This sentiment that business associations have become more engaged and constructive was near universal amongst those interviewed.

and thus made tax resistance an important means by which taxpayers indirectly encouraged reform.[69]

Of course, the simple fact that taxation gave taxpayers and the opposition an additional lever through which to hasten the removal of the incumbent government does not necessarily imply that tax resistance made the expansion of responsiveness and accountability more likely. Drawing such a causal connection rests on the strength of three additional considerations: (1) is there evidence that the new government was significantly more responsive and accountable than its predecessor? (2) is there evidence that the greater responsiveness and accountability of the new government resulted in a greater ability to raise revenue? and (3) is there evidence that the incoming government behaved more responsively and accountably at least in part owing to the need to increase tax collection? In Ghana, there is strong evidence for at least the first two conditions, and some evidence for the third.

The arrival of the new NPP government unquestionably brought with it the expansion of political freedom and the strengthening of formal institutions of accountability. At a macro level, the Freedom House index of political and civil liberties registered one-point improvements (on a seven-point scale) in both measures by 2004. At a micro level, one of the first actions of the new government was to abolish the Criminal Libel Act, which restricted press freedom, while consultation with civil society was expanded and business confidence increased significantly.[70] While the NDC government had made large strides in these areas, it is clear that the transfer of power further changed the tone of politics.

Even more evident is that the political goodwill engendered by these measures eased the passage of revenue measures that would have been impossible under the NDC, most notably fuel price increases, the NRL and the NHIL. It is widely accepted that the new government enjoyed a revenue dividend as a result of the goodwill accompanying its political openness.[71] There is also a general sentiment that the speed with which

---

[69] Personal interviews on 21 March 2008 with former minister in PNDC and NDC governments, on 10 April 2008 with former Deputy Minister of Finance and senior official in PNDC and NDC governments, and on 20 April 2008 with Former Deputy Minister of Finance.

[70] Personal interviews on 28 February 2008 with senior official, Private Enterprise Foundation, on 18 March 2008 with senior official, Associations of Ghana Industries, and on 27 March 2008 with senior official, Ghana National Chamber of Commerce and Industry.

[71] Personal interviews on 27 February 2008 with senior official, Bank of Ghana, on 20 April 2008 with Former Deputy Minister of Finance, on 21 March 2008 with former minister in PNDC and NDC governments, and on 10 March 2008 with senior official, Tax Policy Unit, Ministry of Finance and Economic Planning.

the NPP government expanded the inclusiveness of policy consultation, particularly with the private sector, partly reflected the revenue pressures it faced.[72] While it is difficult to conclusively claim that expanded government engagement was motivated *primarily* by tax concerns, there is little doubt that the need to raise revenue acted as a catalyst for expanded responsiveness and accountability.

3.3 The role of contextual factors

Experience in Ghana thus presents significant, but also highly varied, evidence of tax bargaining between citizens and governments. The remaining challenge is thus to assess what these instances of tax bargaining reveal about the role of contextual factors in shaping divergent patterns of tax bargaining. What follows provides an initial assessment by drawing on differences in tax bargaining across tax episodes over time, as well as on insights offered explicitly by key political actors. These preliminary messages are followed by stronger conclusions in Chapter 6, when it is possible to draw on comparative experiences across the case study countries. The core messages from what follows are summarized in Table 3.1, which mirrors Table 2.1 from the previous chapter.

3.3.1 *Taxpayer capacity for collective action*

The most prominent message that emerges from the case study surrounds the importance of taxpayer capacity for collective action and the central roles of three contextual variables in shaping this potential: the effectiveness of government repression, the position of existing civil society organizations and the unity of elites in responding to taxation. During the 1980s, the PNDC military government was firmly entrenched in power, and was able to thoroughly limit the scope for taxpayer protests, despite the rapid expansion of tax collection. This was aided by the weakness of both established civil society and elite resistance. Decades of political instability and economic decline had fragmented and eroded the political strength of civil society, which was only gradually rebuilt over the course of the decade (Boahen 1989; Herbst 1993).[73] Meanwhile, the new regime successfully targeted elite groups that were relatively unpopular following two decades of decline, thus fragmenting and limiting their

---

[72] Personal interviews on 28 February 2008 with senior official, Private Enterprise Foundation, on 18 March 2008 with senior official, Associations of Ghana Industries, and on 27 March 2008 with senior official, Ghana National Chamber of Commerce and Industry.
[73] Personal interview on 17 March 2008 with senior leader of Committee for Joint Action.

Table 3.1 *Ghana: the role of contextual factors*

Structural factor	Relevant contextual variables	Impact
Taxpayer capacity for collective action	• Government repression under the PNDC • Strength of civil society organizations • Unity and strength of elite leaders within the opposition	• Sharply reduced scope for collective action and tax bargaining in 1980s, amidst repression, weak civil society and fragmented elite • Large-scale popular action in the 1990s as repression declines, civil society grows stronger and opposition elites become more unified
Institutions for bargaining	• Establishment of democracy and strengthening of parliament • Creation of new consultative forums with business associations	• Emergence of less conflictual forms of direct tax bargaining from 1996 onward, both through parliament and with business associations
The potential and scope for tax resistance	• Aggressive (sometimes extra-legal) tax enforcement in 1980s, and normalization thereafter • Waning focus on administrative reform in the late 1980s and late 1990s facilitated tax avoidance and evasion • Introduction of democracy offered scope for popular resistance to tax policy changes	• Reduced scope for tax resistance during 1980s, limiting tax bargaining • Threat of tax resistance from late1990s onwards contributed to the earmarking of taxes for popular social programs. • Effective resistance to increased taxes, particularly from petroleum, in lead up to elections in 2000 contributes to change in government
Revenue pressure facing government	• Post-election fiscal crisis from 1992 to 1996, including threats of reduced aid from donors • Growing fiscal deficits in late 1990s	• Pressured government to introduce 1995 VAT, and to subsequently bargain with the opposition • Increased the efficacy of tax resistance in contributing to eventual change in government in 2000 elections
The political salience of taxation	• Elite leadership in responding to, and politicizing, the VAT • Earmarking of VAT increases	• VAT became highly politicized catalyst for public engagement, including subsequent earmarking • Modestly increased popular oversight of earmarked taxes

potential to lead popular mobilization in response to taxation (Nugent 1995).

The importance of these variables is revealed by the surge in direct tax bargaining in the 1990s, first in response to increased fuel prices, and most dramatically in the emergence of the *Kume Preko* protests. Put simply, the context had changed sufficiently by the 1990s to allow profoundly new popular responses to taxation. Most obviously, the repressive capacity and intent of the government was sharply diminished, amidst a transition to formal democracy in 1992. This was accompanied by a parallel, and related, expansion of organized civil society groups, which would provide the foundation for the emergence of larger scale protests. Finally, and perhaps most importantly, state action against opposition elites began to decline, opening space for the re-emergence of the formal political opposition and a growing role for business associations. The formal political opposition eventually played a critical role in leading the *Kume Preko* protests, and in spearheading the earmarking of increases in the VAT rate in subsequent years, while business associations began to play a regular role in negotiating tax changes with the government (Osei 2000; Ninsin 2007).[74]

Finally, similar lessons emerge from smaller-scale negotiations between informal sector operators and the state during the same period. During the 1980s, informal sector operators remained relatively silent in the face of a unified and autocratic state owing to the absence of collective actors to represent them. However, as state repression declined, new organizations emerged to represent these small-scale operators and began to engage more actively with the government, with the GPRTU and GUTA both figuring prominently in negotiating new informal sector tax regimes. However, here again the role of elites in shaping collective action emerges prominently, with the GPRTU and GUTA leaderships widely felt to have profited disproportionately from their cooperation with state elites.[75]

3.3.2 Institutions for tax bargaining

The second major message from Ghanaian experience surrounds the role of institutions in shaping the form and content of tax bargaining, as the

---

[74] Ibid., and interviews on 10 April 2008 with former Deputy Minister of Finance and senior official in PNDC and NDC governments and on 28 February 2008 with senior official, Private Enterprise Foundation.
[75] Personal interviews on 15 April 2008 with Opposition Member of Parliament and Member of Parliamentary Finance Committee and on 20 March 2008 with senior official, international NGO working on informal sector taxation in Accra.

creation of more inclusive bargaining institutions drove the emergence of more direct, formal and consensual forms of tax bargaining around the VAT over time.

When the VAT was first introduced in 1995, the opposition was boycotting parliament, while policymaking remained driven by the executive, thus leaving the opposition largely excluded from discussions of the new tax. They therefore responded with large-scale, and highly confrontational, street demonstrations. Opposition leaders, lacking other channels for engagement, had little choice but to turn to large-scale public mobilization in order to be heard, and one of the defining features of the *Kume Preko* protests was the presence of opposition politicians in leadership roles (Osei 2000).[76]

One of the core outcomes of those protests was the strengthening of parliamentary democracy, and the creation of broader forums for consultation around tax matters. This was reflected in more cooperative forms of tax bargaining in subsequent years. The peaceful reintroduction of the VAT involved extensive consultation with the parliamentary opposition, which had been brought into parliament through more open elections in 1996. Subsequent increases in the VAT rate were then earmarked for particular, and popular, social programs, as the growing role of parliament allowed for these compromises to be negotiated peacefully, and prior to implementation.

3.3.3 Additional factors

Beyond these core messages, experiences in Ghana offer hints about additional factors shaping tax bargaining outcomes. These elements are thus introduced here, but find fuller expression in the subsequent case studies of Kenya and Ethiopia.

The importance of the political salience of taxation is particularly clear-cut, with tax bargaining and protests in Ghana having revolved primarily around highly salient petroleum taxes and the uniquely politicized VAT. The CJA has been the leading civil society organization seeking to use taxation as a platform for broader public mobilization, and its leaders make clear that changes in fuel prices and taxes, which are particularly visible to the public, have historically offered the greatest mobilizing potential. Similarly, repeated rounds of bargaining around the VAT have reflected its unique political salience, as it has remained highly

---

[76] Personal interviews on 17 March 2008 with senior leader of Committee for Joint Action and on 10 April 2008 with former Deputy Minister of Finance and senior official in PNDC and NDC governments.

3.3 The role of contextual factors

politically visible, even to relatively marginalized populations, following the initial *Kume Preko* protests.[77] This experience with the VAT is particularly interesting, as it reveals that the political salience of a tax derives not only from inherent features of particular tax types, but from the role of politicians, elite groups and the media in giving particular taxes political prominence – that is, in taking tax disputes to a broader audience, which may otherwise be only weakly aware of major national taxes.[78]

The importance of the potential for tax resistance can be seen in its role in shaping both the initial move towards elections in 1992, and the first democratic electoral transition in 2000. In the first half of the 1980s, aggressive tax enforcement made tax resistance exceptionally difficult, and tax collection correspondingly rose rapidly. However, by the latter half of the decade political and administrative focus was waning, and government leaders at the time cite sporadic anti-tax protests and stagnating tax collection as amongst the first signs that governance changes were needed.[79] A decade later, the arrival of political liberalization created space for mobilization against tax increases on a scale that had not previously been possible. In turn, this tax resistance played an important role in preventing the government from raising additional revenue prior to the 2000 elections, thus contributing to its electoral defeat.

Finally, the role of revenue pressure lies further in the background, but is nonetheless apparent, in shaping both the willingness of the government to bargain over the VAT, and the political effectiveness of tax resistance prior to the 2000 elections. Bargaining over the VAT occurred against the backdrop of significant fiscal deficits and substantial pressure from donors to increase domestic revenue collection. Both of these factors left the government little option other than to pursue new taxes – and to accept the compromises that this might require. Senior officials in the government are particularly clear about the fact that donor pressure played an important role in pushing them to introduce the VAT more quickly and at a higher rate than they would have liked,[80] thus

---

[77] Personal interviews on 15 April 2008 with Opposition Member of Parliament and Member of Parliamentary Finance Committee, on 14 April 2008 with government MP and member of Parliamentary Finance Committee, and on 20 April 2008 with Former Deputy Minister of Finance.
[78] Personal interview on 27 February 2008 with leading political journalist.
[79] Personal interviews on 10 April 2008 with former Deputy Minister of Finance and senior official in PNDC and NDC governments and on 10 March 2008 with Deputy Commissioner, Internal Revenue Service.
[80] Personal interviews on 21 March 2008 with former minister in PNDC and NDC governments, on 10 April 2008 with former Deputy Minister of Finance and senior official in PNDC and NDC governments, and on 20 April 2008 with former Deputy Minister of Finance.

prompting the conflicts and bargaining to follow. Meanwhile, it was large fiscal deficits in the late 1990s that made mounting tax resistance so effective in undermining the electoral prospects of the NDC government, as this revenue pressure ensured that tax resistance would entail concrete constraints on the ability of the government to pursue its policy and political agendas.

3.4 Conclusions

The evidence presented here leaves little doubt that in Ghana since 1981 both direct and indirect forms of tax bargaining have contributed to the expansion of responsiveness and accountability. Beginning in the late 1980s, conflict over taxation was an important catalyst for the gradual expansion of accountability, and, eventually, for the strengthening of democratic institutions. Following the arrival of full-blown parliamentary politics in 1996, Ghana witnessed a series of relatively explicit tax bargains in which the government exchanged greater responsiveness for tax compliance. These included both broad bargains surrounding increases in the VAT rate, and more narrow bargains around informal sector taxation. During this period, the drive for additional taxation likewise spurred the strengthening of civil society. Finally, government reliance on taxation gave citizens additional leverage in precipitating a change of government in 2000, with positive consequences for the subsequent expansion of responsiveness and accountability.

While highlighting the importance of tax bargaining, the case study evidence also speaks to the fact that the likelihood of tax bargaining, and the nature of that bargaining, has been shaped by context. The military government faced remarkably little opposition to major tax reforms in the 1980s, highlighting the extent to which highly repressive governments can prevent tax bargaining, at least for a time. In the same vein, the expansion of democracy throughout the 1990s not only opened new space for tax bargaining, but also shaped the character of that bargaining, as it became increasingly explicit and comparatively consensual. Finally, several of the episodes of tax bargaining point towards the important role played by elites not only in leading bargaining processes, but in organizing protests and shaping the political salience of taxation.

The emerging lesson is that tax bargaining has been an important contributor to the expansion of responsiveness and accountability, but that tax bargaining is a more complex process than has often been implied by earlier work. Not only is it clear that the term tax bargaining encompasses a diverse set of causal processes, both implicit and explicit, but it is also clear that particular outcomes are shaped in important ways by contextual factors. These broad messages are developed further in the two case studies to follow.

Appendix

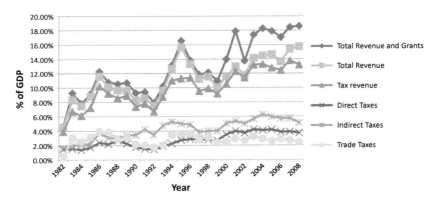

Figure 3.1 Ghana: total revenue by component, 1982–2008.

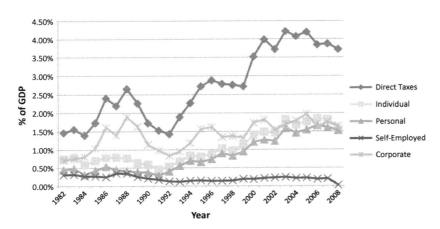

Figure 3.2 Ghana: direct tax revenue by component, 1982–2008.

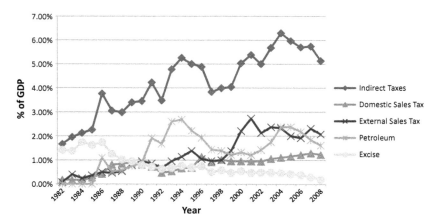

Figure 3.3 Ghana: indirect tax revenue by component, 1982–2008.

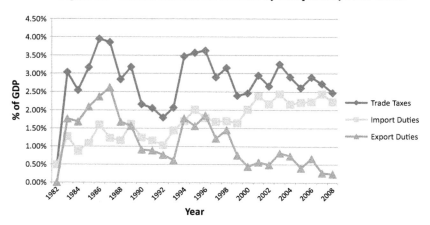

Figure 3.4 Ghana: trade tax revenues by component, 1982–2008.

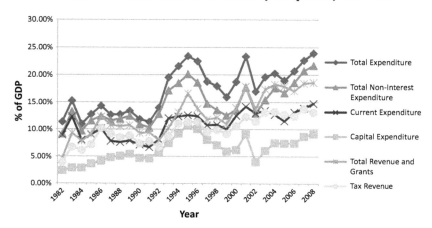

Figure 3.5 Ghana: expenditure by category, 1982–2008.

4 Direct and indirect tax bargaining in Kenya, 1963–2008

Tax bargaining in Ghana occurred against the backdrop of dramatic changes in taxation and economic performance, while Kenya has experienced remarkable stability by comparison. Kenya has long been regarded as one of sub-Saharan Africa's success stories, owing to a history of consistent economic growth and political stability. Despite periods of autocratic rule and economic stagnation under President Moi during the 1980s and 1990s, Kenya still can claim that, in contrast to almost every country in the region, it has experienced neither wholesale economic collapse nor military rule. This has been reflected in tax collection, which has consistently been amongst the highest in the region since independence. Despite this stability, Kenya has nonetheless struggled with high levels of corruption and deep ethnic and racial divisions, the latter the product in large part of having been a British settler colony until independence. These unique features of the Kenyan case make it a valuable context in which to study the dynamics of tax bargaining.

The analysis once again begins with a detailed historical narrative of the political economy of taxation, with detailed revenue figures again provided in the appendix to the chapter. This is followed by a discussion of the implications of that narrative for our understanding of tax bargaining. As with the previous chapter, the discussion focuses first on assessing the extent and character of tax bargaining, followed by an examination of the contextual factors that have shaped particular outcomes. What emerges is that governance-enhancing tax bargaining has been somewhat less prominent in Kenya than in Ghana, with cases of direct tax bargaining proving particularly uncommon. However, there is evidence that, despite the relative absence of direct tax bargaining, indirect forms of tax bargaining have nonetheless played an important role in the expansion of responsiveness and accountability.

This pattern is intuitively somewhat surprising, as theory would seem to predict more extensive and direct experiences of tax bargaining in Kenya, given the combination of a strong private sector and relative political openness and stability. In practice, however, the relative absence of direct tax bargaining appears attributable most notably to the weakness of taxpayer capacity for collective action. To some extent this reflects government repression, but it has equally been driven by two more case specific variables: the success of the government in limiting the political salience of tax debates, and the fragmentation of taxpayer interests along both economic and ethnic lines. The role of these and other contextual factors is discussed in greater detail towards the end of the chapter.

4.1 The political economy of taxation in Kenya

Despite the economic and political stability that has prevailed throughout most of Kenya's history, the country presents a complex political economy setting. Politics is often carried out behind closed doors, and has been shaped by complex patronage networks, ethnic and racial divisions, powerful special interests and a sometimes very influential bureaucratic elite (Throup and Hornsby 1998). The complexity of this political environment warrants detailed consideration, but the constraints of space dictate a narrow focus here on the fiscal evolution of the state. The tax narrative that is presented here integrates broader reflections on the political economy of the country where necessary, although these are invariably simplified caricatures of a more complex reality. What follows consequently aims not at providing a perfectly nuanced account, but, instead, at highlighting those issues that tell us most about the relationship between taxation, responsiveness and accountability.

4.1.1 Independence and revenue growth, 1963–1973

During the colonial period, Kenya was a British settler colony and also became home to a large Asian population. The presence of the privileged white settler population contributed to the development of a more sophisticated political and economic base than in other colonies in the region, but also led to more extensive exploitation, inequality and conflict. Within the realm of taxation, the White and Asian populations were subject to income taxes, excise taxes and import duties, whereas the African population was primarily subjected to a poll tax, which evolved into the Graduated Personal Tax (GPT) late in the colonial period (Waris 2008). While resistance to colonial rule had broader foundations, it is worth noting that the poll tax was a source of significant political mobilization, with, for example, one of the early political associations in Western Kenya being the North Kavirondo Taxpayers Association (Nyangira 1987).

Independence brought little change to the formal structure of taxation. Africans with significant incomes joined Whites and Asians in being subject to income taxation, while the remaining population continued to be subject to the collection of GPT by local governments until its abolition in 1974. The abolition of the GPT appears to have been largely a response to its historical association with colonial rule and exploitation, though its abolition also served to increase the dependence of local governments on the central government.[1]

The period witnessed a progressive rise in tax revenues as a share of GDP, reflecting gradual improvement in administration and continuous economic growth in the country. By the beginning of the 1970s, tax revenue had already reached almost 15 per cent of GDP, while income taxation, at greater than 5 per cent of GDP, had attained a level that was not meaningfully surpassed until the 1990s. In the context of significant revenue growth and broad fiscal balance, there was limited political attention to taxation, and little pressure for change (Muriithi and Moyi 2003).

The revenue gains of the period prompted virtually no public opposition, which is attributable to three factors. First, President Kenyatta, as the champion of independence, initially enjoyed overwhelming authority and goodwill. Second, those Africans who became subject to the income tax were a very small minority, and in the context of tremendous improvements in their overall situation, were not inclined to protest against government tax measures. Third, and most importantly, because most of the private sector remained under the control of Europeans and Asians, the African population, having gained political power, had strong incentives to ensure effective income taxation as a means of redistribution.[2]

4.1.2 *Uncertainty, administrative decay and new taxes, 1973–1978*

The period from 1973 to 1978 brought much greater uncertainty, owing to major external economic shocks and the deteriorating health of President Kenyatta (Throup and Hornsby 1998). The first major event was the OPEC oil crisis, which led to a sharp increase in world oil prices and, subsequently, a major foreign exchange shortage and a growing, although still manageable, fiscal deficit. In response to the growing fiscal deficit, an internal constituency for expanded taxation emerged, bolstered by

---

[1] Personal interview on 19 August 2008 with former Permanent Secretary, Ministry of Finance.
[2] Personal interviews on 20 August 2008 with former Permanent Secretary Ministry of Finance and on 15 September 2008 with former Commissioner, VAT, KRA.

similar demands from the IMF, from whom the government was seeking additional foreign exchange.[3]

In 1974 the government introduced a sales tax on most goods. The tax immediately led to large revenue gains, as goods and services taxation increased from 3.5 per cent of GDP in 1973–1974 to 5.9 per cent in 1975–1976. Despite the relatively broad incidence of the tax, it saw limited popular resistance. This is largely attributable to the factors that facilitated the expansion of income taxation: the overwhelming political authority of President Kenyatta and the continuing assumption that the tax would be borne primarily by Europeans and Asians. A senior official put it bluntly: "Sales tax was seen to be paid by Indians and Europeans... you could find a Minister saying '*we* are not supposed to be paying that tax.'"[4] Two other factors also played a role. First, the sales tax was an indirect tax, and was often levied several levels removed from the point of sale, thus reducing the visibility of the tax to consumers.[5] Second, the government exempted "essential commodities" from taxation, selling the tax as a tax on luxury goods, and thus reinforcing the image that it would be borne by Whites and Asians (Karingi and Wanjala 2005; Moyi and Ronge 2006).[6]

While the new tax was leading to significant revenue growth, income taxes were stagnant and trade taxes falling, as earlier improvements in administrative effectiveness slowed. Several of those interviewed attribute this weaker-than-expected revenue performance to Kenyatta's flagging health and popularity. By the mid-1970s, Kenyatta's declining health weakened his attention to policy and administration, which permitted poorer performance and the expansion of official corruption (Leonard 1991: 283). Meanwhile, the assassination J.M. Kariuki in 1975, on the heels of the assassination of Tom Mboya in 1969, saw the previously unassailable popularity of Kenyatta's government begin to decline (Throup and Hornsby 1998). This reduction in legitimacy, and in government professionalism at the highest levels, contributed to increased collusion between administration officials and taxpayers for purposes of tax evasion.[7]

---

[3] Personal interview on 19 August 2008 with Former Permanent Secretary, Ministry of Finance.

[4] Personal interview on 15 September 2008 with former Commissioner, VAT, KRA.

[5] In the words of one observer, "the public were not even supposed to know how these taxes work." Personal interview on 15 September 2008 with former Commissioner, VAT, KRA and on 8 August 2008 with former Director of Tax Policy, Ministry of Finance.

[6] Personal interviews on 15 September 2008 with former Commissioner, VAT, KRA and on 20 August 2008 with former Permanent Secretary, Ministry of Finance.

[7] Personal interviews on 8 August 2008 with former Director of Tax Policy, Ministry of Finance and on 19 August 2008 with former Permanent Secretary, Ministry of Finance.

In 1977–1978 there was a major surge in tax revenue, as trade taxes, sales taxes, and, to a lesser extent, income taxes, increased in response to a major coffee boom that had begun in 1976. This served to disguise the declining performance of the central government, and eased the foreign exchange and fiscal crises of earlier years. The death of President Kenyatta came in 1978, at the height of the coffee boom, and after a period of intense political manoeuvring, Daniel Arap Moi assumed the Presidency.[8]

4.1.3 Political transition and stabilization, 1979–1982

The rise of President Moi had two dramatic implications for politics in Kenya. First, unlike Kenyatta, Moi was initially relatively weak politically, and was forced to rely heavily on Mwai Kibaki, his Minister of Finance and Vice-President, and Charles Njonjo, the Attorney General, to secure his position. Second, whereas Kenyatta had been a member of the demographically and economically dominant Kikuyu ethnic group, Moi was a member of the smaller and more economically marginalized Kalenjin group. He was consequently committed to redistributing economic resources towards the less developed areas of the country, and particularly the Kalenjin areas of the Rift Valley. This necessitated the dismantling of Kenyatta's elaborate patronage network, and the creation of a political environment more firmly centred on himself and his allies (Barkan and Chege 1989; Leonard 1991; Throup and Hornsby 1998).

Given his relative political vulnerability and the positive fiscal impact of the coffee boom, it is not surprising that Moi did not pursue any major taxation initiatives during his early years in office. However, despite the absence of new tax policy initiatives, tax collection was significantly stronger in the wake of the coffee boom than had been the case before it. In particular, there was a sharp and sustained increase in the collection of goods and services taxes in 1980–1981. These improvements resulted from Moi's dismantling of the networks of patronage and corruption that had emerged under Kenyatta. Quoting Leonard (1991: 283): "The dangerous narrowing of the interests pursued in the late Kenyatta years was partly reversed when Daniel Arap Moi became President. This correction of the ship of state was reinforced by cabinet ministers such as Njonjo, Kibaki and later, Vice-President Saitoti, who tended to think of policy in terms that were broader than immediate personal interest." While similar networks of patronage and corruption eventually grew up around

---

[8] Personal interview on 19 August 2008 with former Permanent Secretary, Ministry of Finance.

Moi, the early years of transition were a period of relatively effective administration.[9]

The only major tax event during the period was the reduction of the capital gains tax in 1981, a precursor to its suspension in 1985. The capital gains tax had initially been introduced in 1975 as Minister of Finance Mwai Kibaki responded to growing demands for equity and redistribution by seeking to tax the earnings of the wealthy. The tax was popular with the public but faced very vocal opposition from Members of Parliament (MPs) and other elites who had to bear the weight of the new tax. While Kenyatta's backing had been enough to force the tax through parliament, his death opened the door for MPs to renew their demands for repeal. The reduction in the tax, and its subsequent repeal, were the predictable outcome of Kibaki's declining political influence and Moi's need to secure political allies. That said, the fact that the tax was repealed despite broad popular support, and not long after the introduction of a broad-based sales tax, was an early indicator of the ability and willingness of elites to manipulate tax policy to their benefit.

4.1.4 Political and economic decline, 1982–1990

The coffee boom of the late 1970s had given rise to large increases in expenditure, and the inability of the government to rein in this spending gave rise to subsequent fiscal deficits. In response, leading technocrats in the Ministry of Finance, who were given significant independent authority, proposed a phased process of economic liberalization, along with efforts to continue to strengthen the administration of taxation in order to further increase revenue. The spirit of reform was thus in the air amidst the broadly positive developments of Moi's early years in office (Leonard 1991).

The situation changed somewhat in August 1982, when a coup attempt against President Moi put plans for reform on hold as he moved to consolidate his power (Throup and Hornsby 1998).[10] While Kenyatta had monopolized decision-making power at the national level, he had generally allowed local elections and politics to be carried out comparatively unimpeded. By contrast, the elections of 1983 saw a level of electoral fraud and intimidation not previously seen in Kenya, and by 1988 elections had lost virtually all legitimacy (Throup and Hornsby 1998).

---

[9] Personal interview on 8 August 2008 with former Director of Tax Policy, Ministry of Finance.
[10] Personal interview on 22 August 2008 with former senior official and current Advisor to Central Bank of Kenya.

However, despite this move against the political opposition, economic decision-making retained significant rationality during the first half of the 1980s, with slow economic growth largely reflecting political uncertainty and external developments. Moi appointed George Saitoti, a talented mathematician and well-respected academic, as Finance Minister in 1983, and gave Saitoti and his team of leading civil servants, led by Philip Ndegwa, Harris Mule and Simeon Nyachae, significant latitude (Leonard 1991). While corruption and other forms of public sector manipulation were becoming more widespread, it was clear to those involved that Moi saw it as being in his interest to put broad economic management in capable hands (Leonard 1991). The ambitious liberalization agenda of those reformers was summarized in Sessional Paper #1 of 1986, *Economic Policy for Renewed Growth*.[11] With tax revenue already high by regional standards, the President overwhelmingly concerned with consolidating power, and aid flows helping to close the fiscal gap, no significant new taxes were introduced during the 1980s (O'Brien and Ryan 2001). Instead, the tax reform agenda focused on administrative improvements, reducing income and corporate tax rates, and rationalizing import, excise and sales tax rates.

However, despite initial enthusiasm for economic reform broadly, and for tax administration reform specifically, progress slowed markedly after 1986. The leading bureaucrats behind the reform programme had all been forced into retirement by 1987, owing to a combination of age and high-level political manoeuvring, while Minister Saitoti's attention was diverted elsewhere when he was named Vice-President in 1988. While commitment to reform did not vanish, the absence of these reform leaders sapped the reform programme of its dynamism and leadership.[12] Thus, despite an apparently genuine commitment to reform and administrative improvements in many quarters, overall revenue generation declined slightly during the decade from 18.2 per cent of GDP in 1981–1982 to 16.4 per cent in 1990–1991. While taxes on goods and services experienced a slight improvement, income tax collection fell, and taxes on international trade experienced a prolonged and significant decline.

Those involved attribute the modest fall in collection to four factors. First was the growth slowdown, as both income and trade taxes tend to be higher during periods of rapid growth. Second, taxation became

---

[11] Personal interviews on 19 August 2008 with former Permanent Secretary, Ministry of Finance and on 22 August 2008 with former senior official and current Advisor to Central Bank of Kenya.
[12] Ibid.

increasingly politicized, as parastatals increasingly failed to remit sales tax revenues to the tax agencies and according to a senior tax official, "[Moi's] allies were not paying tax because they were protected... it was very hard to collect tax from the big people."[13] Third, the popularity and legitimacy of the regime were declining, and, as in the late Kenyatta period, this contributed to declining tax compliance and administrative probity.[14] Finally, the overall policymaking environment remained extremely hierarchical, which reduced the level of initiative within the tax administration.[15]

4.1.5 Political conflict and the VAT, 1990–1992

After a decade of relative inaction, the 1989 Budget Speech announced that a VAT would be implemented the following year. This announcement was remarkable both for its timing and because of the subsequent manner in which the tax was introduced. The timing was surprising in that the announcement came just as opposition to Moi's government was becoming more politically assertive, and implementation consequently occurred during a period of high political tensions. The political repression that accompanied the 1988 elections had finally spurred the fracturing of Moi's political coalition, while the end of the Cold War led aid donors to become increasingly assertive about the need for political liberalization. These forces culminated in a period of intense political conflict and demands for democratization, with elections eventually being held in 1992 (Throup and Hornsby 1998).

The decision to implement the VAT during this period largely reflected technocratic concerns, as the tax reform agenda had been plotted earlier, while fiscal pressure, as well as external pressure from the IMF, was slowly mounting.[16] However, delay was still an option. There is consequently a widespread belief that the government made a political decision that it would be best able to weather the political storm if it had greater resources at its disposal. One official explained that once it became clear that elections were going to occur, the government decided that "elections were not won, they were bought," and that additional revenue was therefore a necessity.[17] This view is supported by the fact that increases

---

[13] Personal interview on 15 September 2008 with former Commissioner, VAT, KRA.
[14] Personal interviews on 15 September 2008 with former Commissioner, VAT, KRA and on 8 August 2008 with Former Director of Tax Policy, Ministry of Finance.
[15] Ibid.
[16] Personal interviews on 20 August 2008 with former Permanent Secretary, Ministry of Finance and on 22 July 2008 with former Advisor to Ministry of Finance and KRA.
[17] Personal interview on 22 July 2008 with former Advisor to Ministry of Finance and KRA.

4.1 The political economy of taxation in Kenya

in tax revenues in 1991–1992 and 1992–1993 were further accompanied by a surge in non-tax revenue.[18]

As interesting as the motivation for the tax was the gradualist approach to implementation that was adopted. Across sub-Saharan Africa, VATs have generally been implemented with a single standard rate between 10 per cent and 20 per cent, along with a well-defined set of exemptions, which is consistent with IMF and World Bank advice. By dramatic contrast, the Kenyan government introduced the VAT with *fifteen* rates, ranging from 0 to 150 per cent, which broadly reflected the structure of the sales tax that preceded it (Muriithi and Moyi 2003; Karingi and Wanjala 2005).

While concerns about administrative capacity played some role in this decision, it appears to have been overwhelmingly driven by politics. By gradually moving away from the multiple rates that existed under the sales tax regime, the government could simultaneously accommodate powerful, but narrow, special interests and obscure the impact of the changes from public view.[19] Such gradualism was an established characteristic of economic reform in Kenya, and officials are transparent about the fact that it was a means to reduce opposition.[20] And indeed, the government had achieved a more conventional rate structure by 1997, just as it had planned (Karingi and Wanjala 2005). Of course, the ability of the government to adopt this gradualist approach reflected the fact that it was not in a state of fiscal crisis and was, consequently, not entirely beholden to the IFIs and their preference for rapid reform.[21]

Ultimately, the political strategy adopted by the government was highly successful, as revenues increased in subsequent years, while the tax prompted very little public opposition despite the tense political environment. On top of the basic effectiveness of gradualism as a reform strategy, the government won business support by simultaneously reforming the hugely inefficient system of sales tax refunds.[22] Meanwhile, the government secured public approval, as it had with the sales tax in 1974, by exempting "essential commodities" from taxation and initially selling the

---

[18] Unfortunately, a detailed breakdown of the sources of this revenue is unavailable from government or external sources.

[19] Personal interviews on 15 September 2008 with former Commissioner, VAT, KRA, on 8 August 2008 with former Director of Tax Policy, Ministry of Finance, and on 20 August 2008 with former Permanent Secretary, Ministry of Finance.

[20] Personal interviews on 22 August 2008 with former senior official and current Advisor to Central Bank of Kenya, on 20 August 2008 with former Permanent Secretary, Ministry of Finance, and on 22 July 2008 with former Advisor to Ministry of Finance and KRA.

[21] Personal interview on 20 August 2008 with former Permanent Secretary, Ministry of Finance.

[22] Personal interview on 15 September 2009 with former Commissioner, VAT, KRA.

VAT as a luxury tax. The importance of this strategy was apparent when the government attempted to apply the VAT to restaurants after the elections. They immediately encountered public condemnation on the basis that food should not be taxed; this forced the government to rescind the VAT on restaurants, which it subsequently replaced with a 5 per cent tax on turnover. This was evidence that if the VAT had not been sold to the public effectively, there likely would have been resistance. Interestingly, a 5 per cent turnover tax on restaurants is, in fact, roughly equal in magnitude to a 15 per cent VAT, but the government was able to take advantage of the lack of public understanding to sell the former as a tax reduction.[23]

4.1.6 Elections, economic crisis and reform, 1993–1997

At the end of 1992, national elections returned Moi to power thanks to the combination of a divided opposition and the shrewd use of vote buying and intimidation by the government (Throup and Hornsby 1998). The years that followed witnessed renewed economic growth, rapid economic liberalization and major improvements in tax revenue, which increased from 17.4 per cent of GDP in 1992–1993 to 20.5 per cent in 1995–1996.

Both the acceleration of liberalization and tax reform flowed from a major economic crisis that emerged after the election. The government had engaged in substantial pre-election spending, and thus opened up a large fiscal deficit. The government was not able to turn to donors as it had in the past, because they had become more aggressive in their demands for political liberalization with the end of the Cold War, and as a result had largely cut off aid in 1991. The resulting fiscal imbalances became a full-blown crisis when the government uncovered the Goldenberg Scandal,[24] which had allowed theft from the Central Bank on a sufficient scale to destabilize the entire economy, sending inflation skyrocketing, decimating foreign reserves and leading to major depreciation and very high interest rates (O'Brien and Ryan 2001; Legovini 2002).

The government was consequently forced to turn to the IMF for emergency support, and this accelerated the reform process at the Ministry of Finance, which was now led by an energetic and influential new Finance

---

[23] Ibid.
[24] Orchestrated by Kenyan businessman Kamlesh Pattni in cooperation with the government, the Goldenberg Scandal saw the perpetrators receive enormous export refunds for fictitious exports of diamonds and gold.

4.1 The political economy of taxation in Kenya

Minister, Musalia Mudavadi (Morton 1998).[25] The reform programme centred on devaluation and the rapid liberalization of exchange and interest rates, and included an accelerated process of tax reform (O'Brien and Ryan 2001; Legovini 2002). The rationalization of tax rates and tariffs had begun in 1986. Reform accelerated with the beginning of the donor supported Tax Modernization Program (TMP) in 1990, but the TMP only gained full political priority after the elections and in response to the fiscal crisis.[26]

The post-1993 reforms focused on administration and prompted a dramatic improvement in income tax collection, which was further aided by a tax amnesty granted in 1994. The period witnessed, amongst other things, the introduction of income tax self-assessment, strengthened audit capacity, improvements in customs processes, and the progressive rationalization of VAT rates. These changes were followed in 1994–1995 by the creation of the Kenya Revenue Authority (KRA), which brought all of the tax agencies under one roof and provided greater decision-making autonomy from the Ministry of Finance, greater flexibility with respect to hiring and salary scales and stable funding through a revenue retention scheme (Glenday 1996). While the large revenue gains of the period were partially a consequence of renewed economic growth, real improvement was evident in expanded compliance by parastatals, a sustained improvement in the collection of trade taxes and improved income tax compliance.[27]

Despite the large increase in tax collection, the reforms experienced very little popular opposition, which is attributable to three major factors. First, the reforms were primarily administrative and did not involve introducing new taxes. As a result, the changes were less immediately visible, and – more importantly – they provided a weak basis for public opposition, as they were aimed broadly at improving equity in the application of the law.[28] Second, while elites and the business community might have been expected to vigorously oppose improved collection behind closed doors, their concerns were muted by the fact that the administrative changes continued to be accompanied by rate reductions. Furthermore, large businesses had long sought the expansion of the tax

---

[25] Personal interviews on 22 August 2008 with former senior official and current Advisor to Central Bank of Kenya and on 19 August 2008 with former Permanent Secretary, Ministry of Finance.

[26] Personal interviews on 22 July 2008 with former Advisor to Ministry of Finance and KRA and on 8 August 2008 with former Director of Tax Policy, Ministry of Finance.

[27] Personal interview on 22 July 2008 with former Advisor to Ministry of Finance and KRA.

[28] In the words of one leader of the reform effort, "People didn't even realize it has actually happened." Ibid.

net to medium-sized firms in order to increase competitive parity, and appear to have viewed this as an important benefit of the reform program. Finally, the elections, for all of their limitations, had provided the government with some renewed popular legitimacy. Several administrators are adamant that this improved taxpayers' compliance and that it contributed to improvements in the performance of the tax administration.[29]

Finally, it is worth highlighting the expansion of fuel taxes, which, while small in absolute revenue terms, were indicative of the broader absence of political conflict around taxation. Beginning in 1994, the government introduced a new fuel tax, the Road Maintenance Levy (RML), increased fuel prices through deregulation, and introduced an additional fuel tax earmarked for rural electrification (Wasike 2001). All of these changes had a reasonably broad-based and visible impact, but yet prompted little public response beyond the protests of public transport operators.

This can partly be explained by the effective framing of the new taxes by government: the RML reduced reliance on an unpopular and inefficient system of tolls, while road maintenance and rural electrification were both popular initiatives. The government further justified the RML by arguing that poor roads were dramatically increasing the costs of vehicle upkeep, and whether or not this was true, "the public swallowed the explanation wholesale."[30] The other factor was that public transport operators, who attempted to lead resistance to the tax, were so unpopular with the public that their campaigning generated little public support.[31] Thus, while the earmarking of the tax provided a degree of responsiveness to public preferences, the overall level of political engagement around taxation remained very low.

4.1.7 Instability and upheaval, 1998–2002

President Moi was returned to power at the end of 1997 in elections that were contested by a divided opposition and were again marred by vote buying, intimidation and sporadic violence. More troubling, however, was that 1997 marked a transition from economic growth and stability to economic stagnation and uncertainty. Economic crisis began to set in through a combination of runaway pre-election spending, a sudden and

---

[29] Personal interview on 8 August 2008 with Former Director of Tax Policy, Ministry of Finance.
[30] Personal interviews on 8 October 2008 with former Minister of Energy in Kibaki government and on 20 August 2008 with senior policy researcher on tax issues, Kenya Institute for Public Policy Research and Analysis.
[31] Ibid., and interview in September 2008 with Former matatu conductor and taxi company owner.

4.1 The political economy of taxation in Kenya

significant impasse with donors, and a series of negative external shocks to the economy (Legovini 2002). Growing political conflict and instability quickly reinforced the initial economic crisis. From 1998–2002 Kenya experienced four Ministers of Finance, beginning with Simeon Nyachae, while the civil service experienced major personnel changes, particularly in its upper ranks (Southall 1999). This political and administrative upheaval had roots in, amongst other things, an intensified form of winner-take-all politics, the fracturing of existing patronage networks, uncertainty around succession to Moi, and an antagonistic relationship with donors. While a more detailed explanation of the crisis is of significant interest, it is beyond the scope of this particular account (Southall 1999).

Developments in the revenue sphere reflected the state of decline and uncertainty. Tax revenue experienced a dramatic fall, from 20.5 per cent of GDP in 1995–1996 to 15.7 per cent in 2001–2002. A significant part of this fall in revenue was attributable to technical factors. First, the economic crisis implied declining corporate profits, and thus lower corporate income tax collection. Second, the reduction of tariffs under the Common Market for Eastern and Southern Africa (COMESA) treaty led to a gradual decline in import duties (Cheeseman and Griffiths 2006). This decline accelerated at the end of the decade amidst increasing problems with goods being reimported into Kenya from other COMESA countries, and corresponding pressure for reduced tariffs for other importers. Third, and more generally, the government was reluctant to increase tax rates during a time of severe economic recession.[32]

Despite these technical issues, it is widely believed that declining revenue was also the result of the prevailing administrative and political turmoil, and the sheer scale of the revenue losses supports this claim. While the government remained committed to tax collection, and the administrative apparatus remained very sophisticated by regional standards, there is a belief amongst many senior officials that staff turnover and disillusionment with the broader political context led to declining performance. High levels of staff turnover led to a loss of competence and institutional memory, but equally had a sharply negative impact on morale. Meanwhile, the declining legitimacy and popularity of the government led to some decline in commitment to probity within the tax administration.[33]

---

[32] Personal interviews on 22 July 2008 with former Advisor to Ministry of Finance and KRA and on 8 August 2008 with former Director of Tax Policy, Ministry of Finance.

[33] Personal interviews on 8 August 2008 with former Director of Tax Policy, Ministry of Finance, on 15 September 2008 with former Commissioner, VAT, KRA, on 26 September 2008 with former Commissioner, Domestic Tax Department, KRA, and

The declining legitimacy and popularity of the government equally appears to have prompted declining tax compliance. In fact, several senior officials of mixed political orientation argue confidently that it was an informal "opposition strategy" to seek to actively undermine the fiscal position of the government.[34] "Those who were not allies of Moi became more difficult to tax" owing to a willingness to "do almost anything to stifle the government," and a feeling that "we don't want to give them the money to beat us."[35] The impact of popular opposition to taxation carried over to the inability of the government to introduce new taxation. This was exemplified by a government attempt to introduce new taxes in 1998. The government proposed the introduction of taxes on low-interest loans that financial institutions were providing to their employees as a tax-free benefit. This was a relatively modest tax proposal affecting a tiny segment of the population, but became a significant factor, along with a proposal to revoke pay increases for teachers, in launching a nationwide strike. The strike came to focus on broader issues of official corruption and mismanagement, and while it was ultimately broken up by force, it did lead the government to back down on the new tax proposal (Southall 1999).[36]

The one exception to the inability of the government to secure new revenue was the introduction of a 5 per cent excise tax on mobile phone use in 2002. The tax was attractive to the government owing to its administrative simplicity and guaranteed revenue impact. It is of interest to this research because it reveals that even at times of high political tension, the government was able to pass new taxation if it was sufficiently strategic, as only the service providers themselves presented significant opposition to the tax. One reason for this muted public response was that the timing was highly effective, as the tax was introduced early on in the history of mobile telephony, when use remained less common and when consumers remained focused on the enormous benefits relative to the use of landlines. In addition, the new revenue was officially earmarked for microfinance initiatives, rural electrification and HIV/AIDS programs, all of which were popular with the public and, as importantly, parliament. Yet, while the earmarking strategy was effective for selling the tax,

---

on 8 September 2008 with senior official, Fiscal and Monetary Affairs Department, Ministry of Finance.
[34] Personal interviews on 15 September 2008 with former Commissioner, VAT, KRA, on 8 August 2008 with former Director of Tax Policy, Ministry of Finance, and on 20 August 2008 with Tax Officer, Domestic Tax Department, KRA.
[35] Personal interview on 15 September 2008 with former Commissioner, VAT, KRA.
[36] Personal interview on 20 August 2008 with senior policy researcher on tax issues, Kenya Institute for Public Policy Research and Analysis.

there is great uncertainty about whether all of the resources were ever, in fact, used for those purposes.[37]

4.1.8 Political liberalization and economic recovery, 2003–2007

The elections at the end of 2002 brought President Mwai Kibaki to power as the leader of a unified national opposition under the banner of the National Rainbow Coalition (NARC). The new government ushered in a period of unprecedented, if still very imperfect, political openness, with the Freedom House indicators of political and civil liberties jumping by three and two points respectively between 2001 and 2003. These changes, coupled with improved external economic conditions and renewed dialogue with donors, facilitated a major economic recovery. While fissures in the ruling coalition emerged dramatically in 2005, progress during the first three years under the new government was notable.

These gains were reflected in exceptional improvements in tax revenue collection, which expanded from 15.7 per cent of GDP in 2001–2002 to 21.8 per cent of GDP in 2004–2005. The period did not witness any major tax policy changes, and the major revenue gains are thus attributable to the economic recovery and to improved collection of existing taxes. Improved compliance was attributable in large part to significant administrative reforms, which were the product of high-level political commitment. These reforms included the functional integration of the various tax departments within the KRA, a new cross-cutting staff training programme, the increasing use of computers, and a dramatic new emphasis on Results Based Management and the attainment of revenue targets.[38] These administrative reforms were coupled with an informal understanding that the new government was significantly less willing than its predecessor to countenance tax evasion by its allies (Moyi and Ronge 2006).

Political commitment to these reforms appears to reflect four factors. First, the government was confronted with a significant fiscal deficit. Second, this fiscal deficit made the government relatively beholden to donors, and the government was eager to reduce this reliance given a long history of antagonism. Third, the government had made large

---

[37] Ibid., and interviews on 15 September 2008 with Former Commissioner, VAT, KRA, and on 8 September 2008 with senior official, Fiscal and Monetary Affairs Department, Ministry of Finance.

[38] Personal interviews on 20 August 2008 with Tax Officer, Domestic Tax Department, KRA, on 24 September 2008 with senior official, IT Division, KRA, and on 18 August 2008 with senior official, Research, Monitoring and Planning, KRA.

spending promises during the elections, most notably to provide free primary education. These commitments all required additional revenue. Finally, many of those close to the process attribute it to the fact that Kibaki was a technocrat committed to effective management, whereas Moi's more populist instincts had made taxation less of a priority.[39]

Equally important to revenue gains was the public goodwill that greeted the new government, as this increased the willingness of taxpayers to comply and improved morale within the tax administration.[40] In fact, increases in public revenue often appeared to be as much a source of public pride as of popular anger, regularly appearing prominently in the major newspapers and in speeches by politicians. Public interest in revenue collection is widely noted by those within the tax administration, and is reflected in the fact that the huge revenue gains during the period elicited very little public resistance. A tax officer explained that "the biggest thing is that there is renewed goodwill towards the government... this has made it much easier to extract revenue from taxpayers."[41] Tax officials likewise explain that when disagreements emerged within the ruling coalition in 2005, tax compliance simultaneously declined; this was reflected in reduced levels of tax collection in 2004–2005 and 2005–2006.[42]

Not only did the NARC government benefit from public goodwill, it sought to explicitly connect its popular initiatives with the drive for increased tax revenue. This was true of the provision of free primary education, and was likewise true of the creation of Constituency Development Funds (CDFs), which were introduced in 2003, and which earmarked 2.5 per cent of total ordinary revenues for local development projects under the leadership of local MPs. Despite concerns about the mismanagement of the CDFs, they achieved significant public notoriety and popularity and were an obvious way to ensure the support of MPs for revenue measures (Kimenyi 2005).[43] Particularly interesting was a government effort to link tax compliance to the more amorphous goal

---

[39] Personal interviews on 15 September 2008 with former Commissioner, VAT, KRA, on 18 September 2008 with senior leader, Kenya Private Sector Association, on 24 September 2008 with senior official, IT Division, KRA, and on 18 August 2008 with senior official, Research, Monitoring and Planning, KRA.
[40] There is a widespread belief that some of the administrative and policy reforms implemented from 2003 to 2005 could not have been implemented under the Moi government owing to both administrative and popular resistance. Personal interview on 8 September 2008 with senior official, Fiscal and Monetary Affairs Department, Ministry of Finance.
[41] Personal interview on 20 August 2008 with Tax Officer, Domestic Tax Department, KRA.
[42] Ibid.
[43] Personal interviews on 29 August 2008 with two senior civil society leaders working on budget monitoring, on 30 August 2008 with researcher working on politics surrounding CDFs, and on 22 September 2008 with Senior Donor Official.

4.1 The political economy of taxation in Kenya

of achieving aid independence, as reflected in the KRA slogan *"Tulipe Ushuru, Tujitegemee"* – roughly, "paying tax is earning independence." While the practical impact of aid independence on citizen welfare is difficult to assess, it is clear that the call for aid independence achieved public resonance, and thus aided tax collection.[44]

Aside from this general story, various tax episodes with smaller revenue implications provide useful insights into the politics of taxation during the period. Most of these cases point to the weakness of public resistance to taxation, and the relative absence of direct tax bargaining. In July 2003, the government increased the excise tax on mobile phone usage from 5 per cent to 10 per cent, but – as was the case in 2002 – public opposition was largely restricted to the mobile operators themselves (GSM Association 2007).[45] The 2006 Budget Speech included an almost 50 per cent increase in the RML, but resistance was again muted because of genuine public interest in road maintenance and the inability of transport operators to mobilize public support. The only major hurdle to passing the new tax was parliamentary approval, which was achieved through an earlier decision to decentralize part of the funds for use in the upkeep of local roads.[46] Similarly, a Turnover Tax, which imposed a 3 per cent tax on the turnover of small and informal sector firms, was passed in parliament in 2007, and introduced in early 2008, apparently in response to demands from larger firms for greater equity in taxation. While the implementation was slowed by an apparent lack of enthusiasm at the KRA, which had long viewed the costs of collection as excessively high, the passage of the bill was never subject to significant or effective organized resistance.[47]

A government decision to require the use of Electronic Tax Registers (ETRs) in all VAT registered shops was the only tax episode that spurred significant public opposition, but nonetheless yielded little in the way of direct tax bargaining. The ETRs were expected to reduce the scope for tax evasion by firms by creating an inalterable record of every transaction. The drawback was that compliance costs for firms were meaningful, including purchase and maintenance of ETRs, additional bookkeeping requirements, and difficulty in dealing with refunds. These

---

[44] Personal interview on 8 October 2008 with former Minister of Energy in Kibaki Government and on 18 September 2008 with senior leader, Kenya Private Sector Association.
[45] Personal interview on 20 August 2008 with senior policy researcher on tax issues, Kenya Institute for Public Policy Research and Analysis.
[46] Ibid.
[47] Personal interview on 8 September 2008 with senior official, Fiscal and Monetary Affairs Department, Ministry of Finance, on 15 September 2008 with former Commissioner, VAT, KRA, on 28 August 2008 with senior leader, United Business Association, and on 18 September 2008 with senior leader, Kenya Private Sector Association.

concerns, along with a general desire to avoid tighter tax enforcement, led traders, under the umbrella of the newly formed United Business Association (UBA), to engage in large-scale protests in Nairobi, Mombasa and Kisumu, and to bring lawsuits against the government.

Yet, despite substantial resistance, the government offered neither concessions nor compromise, as it retained popular support outside of the protesters. This was largely attributable to the political goodwill that continued to sustain the government, as there is a widespread belief that the same reform could never have succeeded under the Moi government.[48] The inability of the UBA to garner public support was further exacerbated by the fact that members quickly came to be labelled tax evaders, which in turn, was facilitated by popular perceptions of the protesters as a "group of Asians" (despite having an African chairman). Thus, as had been the case in the 1960s and 1970s, the implementation of new taxes was facilitated by the perception that the weight of taxation would be borne by the economically privileged minority.[49]

While most of the population thus remained relatively unable, or unwilling, to mobilize against taxation or to engage in tax bargaining, events from 2006 onwards provided further evidence of the power exercised by elites. The 2006 Budget Speech announced two tax measures that would specifically target elites: the taxation of the very large non-salary benefits enjoyed by MPs and the reintroduction of the capital gains tax, which had been suspended in 1985. These two measures, and particularly the tax on MPs, enjoyed overwhelming public support, but were nonetheless rejected by parliament.[50] Voters vowed that they would punish the intransigent MPs at the ballot box, and there was indeed enormous turnover of MPs in the 2007 elections. There was thus some expectation that when the taxation of MP benefits was reintroduced in the 2008 Budget Speech, MPs would be forced to accept the measure.[51]

---

[48] Personal interviews on 8 September 2008 with senior official, Fiscal and Monetary Affairs Department, Ministry of Finance, on 15 September 2008 with former Commissioner, VAT, KRA, on 20 August 2008 with Tax Officer, Domestic Tax Department, KRA, and on 20 August 2008 with senior researcher on tax issues, Institute for Economic Affairs.

[49] Personal interviews on 15 September 2008 with former Commissioner, VAT, KRA, on 28 August 2008 with senior leader, United Business Association, and on 28 August 2008 with official, United Business Association.

[50] Ibrahim Mathwane, "Kenya: Why MPs Shot Down Capital Gains Tax," *East African*, November 28, 2006.

[51] Personal interviews on 20 August 2008 with senior policy researcher on tax issues, Kenya Institute for Public Policy Research and Analysis, on 20 August 2008 with senior researcher on tax issues, Institute for Economic Affairs, and on 11 September 2008 with senior policy researcher on petroleum prices and taxation, Kenya Institute for Public Policy Research and Analysis.

Yet, in spite of public outrage, MPs again rejected the measure,[52] while the reintroduction of the capital gains tax was not even proposed.[53]

4.1.9 Political crisis and the elections of 2007

The elections at the end of 2007 resulted in accusations of electoral fraud and the outbreak of widespread violence along ethnic, regional and political lines. With both sides initially refusing to make concessions, the violence continued unabated for more than a month, killing at least a thousand people and displacing more than half a million. The violence and political uncertainty prompted a growing economic crisis as businesses shut down, tourism ground to a halt and investment ceased.

While taxation did not figure prominently in the political conflict, the course of the conflict sheds light on the impact of tax reliance on broader political outcomes. The crisis saw the business community emerge as a powerful voice in favour of a settlement, and as the crisis wore on, business leaders used the threat of refusing to pay taxes to prod the political leadership towards a resolution.[54] While those involved cannot say with certainty how large a role this threat played, there is a general sense that pressure from the business community was important.[55] More generally, it is clear that the economic costs of political stalemate, including the potentially crippling impact on government revenue, increased the urgency with which political leaders sought a resolution.

4.2 Taxation, responsiveness and accountability in Kenya

On the surface, Kenya would seem to present an ideal context for relatively extensive and direct tax bargaining, owing to a combination of a strong private sector and relative political openness and stability. However, the history of tax reform presented so far presents a significantly more complex story. Tax reform itself has been characterized not by a set of discrete, well-defined changes, but by often-gradual reform, which has been accompanied by significant ups and downs in collection performance over time. Meanwhile, public mobilization in response to taxation

---

[52] BBC News, "Kenya Team to Probe MPs Tax Plan," December 2 2008.
[53] A capital gains tax was eventually introduced in 2014, although still only at a rate of 5%, which is far below the rate in neighbouring countries. Reuters Africa, "Kenya's President Approves 5 pct capital gains tax," 15 September 2014.
[54] Personal interview in September 2008 with prominent business leader and KAM and KEPSA member.
[55] Ibid., and interview on 18 September 2008 with senior leader, Kenya Private Sector Association.

has been comparatively infrequent, while the government has appeared frequently unwilling to compromise with taxpayers. Against this background, this section seeks to assess the extent and character of tax bargaining. It focuses first on the relative absence of direct tax bargaining, before highlighting significant evidence of more indirect forms of tax bargaining. This is then followed by a discussion of the contextual factors that can explain this somewhat unexpected pattern.

4.2.1 The absence of direct tax bargaining

The most striking feature of the politics of taxation in Kenya has been the relative absence of significant public conflict over taxation, and even less evidence of direct tax bargaining between taxpayers and governments. One very well placed policymaker put it plainly, explaining that "I have always been very surprised that Kenyans don't take more [political] interest in tax issues, but they simply do not."[56]

There has been an absence of meaningful public engagement during several periods of significant tax reform. From 1993–1996, total levels of tax collection, especially of income and corporate taxes, increased dramatically. While increasing collection was partly the result of strong economic growth, it is widely accepted that tax enforcement was also improved significantly.[57] Yet, despite these new tax burdens, there were no sustained public protests, nor is there evidence of significant tax bargaining and conflict behind the scenes. Even more notable was the absence of public mobilization around the introduction of the VAT. The VAT was introduced in the midst of elevated political tensions and mass political mobilization surrounding demands for democratization, but there is scant evidence that the new tax became a rallying point for the opposition. This stands in sharp contrast to the role of the VAT as a catalyst for broad-based political mobilization in Ghana at a similar moment in its political history. Finally, major increases in fuel prices and fuel taxes have likewise rarely been a source of significant political conflict, despite their broad impact and high level of visibility. This was particularly true in 1994, when both prices and taxes were increased, but no major public mobilization ensued.[58]

---

[56] Personal interview on 19 August 2008 with former Permanent Secretary, Ministry of Finance.
[57] Personal interview on 22 July 2008 with former Advisor to Ministry of Finance and KRA, on 8 August 2008 with former Director of Tax Policy, Ministry of Finance, and on 15 September 2008 with former Commissioner, VAT, KRA.
[58] Personal interview on 8 October 2008 with former Minister of Energy in Kibaki Government.

4.2 Taxation, responsiveness and accountability in Kenya 139

The only case in which there was relatively large-scale taxpayer mobilization was the response of mid-sized business taxpayers to the introduction of ETRs, but this ultimately resulted in neither the repeal of the law nor concessions by government. Aside from this example, debates over tax policy have largely been restricted to MPs and elites who have merely sought to defend established privileges and exemptions. The capital gains tax was suspended successfully in 1985 as the result of opposition from MPs and elites, while efforts to reintroduce the capital gains tax and to introduce the taxation of MPs' benefits were consistently rebuffed throughout the period covered here.[59]

At a relatively small scale, there have been a handful of direct tax bargains between MPs and the Executive, but there is little evidence of significant public engagement. The most interesting examples are narrow tax bargains in which the government offered MPs greater authority over public expenditure in an effort to secure their support for broader tax collection. In seeking to expand the RML, the government agreed to decentralize part of the fund, thus increasing the power wielded by MPs.[60] Likewise, in the wake of the 2002 elections, the creation of the CDFs was an explicit response to demands from MPs for greater control over public spending, and was at least partly motivated by the broader government goal of gaining support for increased tax collection.[61] These examples represent a modest expansion of governmental accountability, insofar as they contributed to increasing parliamentary authority at the expense of the Executive, but the absence of broader public engagement invites scepticism. Consistent with this scepticism, the new tax on mobile phone usage was initially earmarked for microfinance, rural electrification and HIV/AIDS programs, but there is no evidence that the funds were reliably allocated according to the original promise, indicative of the weak connection between parliament and broader popular demands for reciprocity around taxation.[62]

---

[59] As noted previously, a capital gains tax was passed into law in September 2014, just as this book was being finalized. However, at the time of writing, there remained uncertainty about implementation while, more importantly, the tax rate, at 5%, still remained far below that of neighbouring countries, consistent with the overall story being told here.

[60] Personal interview on 20 August 2008 with senior policy researcher on tax issues, Kenya Institute for Public Policy Research and Analysis.

[61] Personal interview on 29 August 2008 with two senior civil society leaders working on budget monitoring, on 30 August 2008 with researcher working on politics surrounding CDFs, and on 22 September 2008 with senior donor official.

[62] Personal interviews on 8 September 2008 with senior official, Fiscal and Monetary Affairs Department, Ministry of Finance, on 15 September 2008 with former Commissioner, VAT, KRA, on 20 August 2008 with senior policy researcher on tax issues, Kenya Institute for Public Policy Research and Analysis. In addition to arguments to

4.2.2 The importance of indirect tax bargaining

While there has thus been little evidence of direct tax bargaining historically in Kenya, the pattern is sharply different in relation to indirect tax bargaining. The ability of taxpayers to resist taxation by unpopular governments has created broad pressure for increased responsiveness and accountability, while taxation has played a role in catalysing the growth and strengthening of civil society. What follows presents evidence of both processes, and thus reinforces the importance of moving beyond a narrow analytical focus on direct tax bargaining alone.

Tax compliance, tax resistance and reform

Despite the relative absence of direct tax bargaining or of major public conflict over taxation, it is clear that the popularity and perceived legitimacy of successive Kenyan governments has shaped their ability to raise revenue. Resistance to taxation has contributed to the fiscal weakness of unpopular governments, and has provided added pressure for changes in government and positive incentives for subsequent reform.

The relative inability of governments with flagging popularity to raise tax revenue was modestly apparent during the first three decades after independence. From 1975–1978, the Kenyatta government experienced increasing tax collection difficulties as it began to lose public confidence. This pattern was reversed during the optimistic early days of the Moi government, as tax collection improved noticeably. As Moi's popularity declined after the mid-1980s, the government again experienced increasing difficulty sustaining tax collection and closing a growing fiscal deficit.[63] Finally, the elections of 1992, which imbued the government with some renewed legitimacy also set the stage for a dramatic period of tax reform and a major surge in revenue collection.[64]

While tax collection thus consistently tracked the fortunes of governments for the first three decades after independence, the political consequences were modest, as firmly entrenched governments successfully weathered the fiscal downturns that resulted from declining popularity. This began to change in the late 1990s, as tax resistance took on greater political importance. Revenues began to fall rapidly after 1997,

---

this effect by those interviewed, careful review of budgetary documents, and discussion with staff at the Ministry of Finance, offers no convincing evidence that funds were reliably and consistently used in the ways claimed during passage of the tax.

[63] Personal interviews on 8 August 2008 with former Director of Tax Policy, Ministry of Finance, on 19 August 2008 with former Permanent Secretary, Ministry of Finance, and on 20 August 2008 with Former Permanent Secretary, Ministry of Finance.

[64] Personal interviews on 8 August 2008 with former Director of Tax Policy, Ministry of Finance and on 22 July 2008 with former Advisor to Ministry of Finance and KRA.

4.2 Taxation, responsiveness and accountability in Kenya

and while this was driven to a significant degree by the economic crisis, it also reflected the fact that the declining popularity of the government was eroding administrative probity and encouraging citizens to engage in tax evasion and avoidance. This view is widely shared by tax officials, and some go so far as to describe this as a semi-explicit opposition strategy to weaken the Moi government in anticipation of important elections in 2002.[65]

The growing fiscal crisis undermined the ability of the government to implement popular public programs and reduced the capacity of the government to dispense patronage to sustain electoral support. These factors contributed to Moi's defeat in the 2002 election. Critically, the tax resistance that contributed to his defeat also created strong incentives for the incoming government to expand responsiveness and accountability in order to secure improved tax compliance and collection. This contention is supported by three key facts. First, the new government was responsible for substantial improvements in responsiveness and accountability by any available cross-country measure. Second, efforts to improve tax collection were facilitated by widely acknowledged improvements in the willingness of citizens to pay taxes.[66] Finally, there is evidence that, in implementing its reform programme, the government was explicitly motivated by the revenue imperative, as it repeatedly sought to connect tax compliance to key aspects of the reform agenda, including free primary education, the creation of the CDFs and aid independence. Thus, there is important evidence that tax conflicts contributed to the change in government and provided significant additional incentives for reform, thus contributing to the expansion of both responsiveness and accountability.

Events surrounding the outbreak of violence following the 2007 elections tell a similar story, as business sought to respond to the crisis. Because the outbreak of violence posed a major threat to Kenyan businesses,[67] the major business associations pushed the government for a peaceful settlement. Critically, as the conflict continued, parts of the

---

[65] Personal interviews on 8 August 2008 with former Director of Tax Policy, Ministry of Finance, on 15 September 2008 with former Commissioner, VAT, KRA, and on 20 August 2008 with Tax Officer, Domestic Tax Department, KRA.

[66] Personal interviews on 18 September 2008 with senior leader, Kenya Private Sector Association, on 15 September 2008 with former Commissioner, VAT, KRA, on 20 August 2008 with senior researcher on tax issues, Institute for Economic Affairs, on 11 September 2008 with senior policy researcher on petroleum prices and taxation, Kenya Institute for Public Policy Research and Analysis, and on 20 August 2008 with Tax Officer, Domestic Tax Department, KRA.

[67] Retrospective analysis of the economic costs of the crisis suggest a reduction of overall GDP by about 6% over the course of 2008–2009, while there were fears at the time of significantly greater economic disruption as the conflict continued (Guibert and Perez-Quiros 2012).

business community used their status as taxpayers to call for a resolution of the political impasse by explicitly threatening to withhold tax revenue if the government failed to make peace.[68] While there were diverse factors that contributed to the resolution of the post-election crisis, many observers feel that the role of the business community was significant, and that the need to sustain tax revenue played an important part in pushing the government towards peace.[69] Consistent with this view is the fact that the level of tax collection quickly returned to earlier levels in the aftermath of the violence, following earlier fears of a fiscal crisis, as the business community complied with tax demands from the crisis period. Ultimately, it was the threat of tax resistance by businesses that contributed to putting pressure on government to pursue a peaceful resolution more quickly than it otherwise may have. Indeed, one could argue that this was, strictly speaking, a case of direct tax bargaining, with the government making explicit concessions in order to secure continued tax compliance. However, the relatively invisible nature of this bargain, and the broad nature of the government "concession," makes this episode more akin to the earlier examples of indirect tax bargaining.

Taxation, civil society and public engagement
Taxation has also contributed to the expansion of responsiveness and accountability in Kenya by acting as a catalyst for the strengthening of civil society. This has been true of both business associations, for whom the threat of taxation has encouraged greater engagement, and broader civil society organizations, several of which have organized advocacy campaigns explicitly focused on the rights of taxpayers.

Business associations
While business associations have the potential to play an important role in supporting the expansion of responsiveness and accountability, research about business associations in the developing world has argued that, in practice, business associations have frequently sought narrow benefits for their most powerful members rather than pursuing broad-based improvements in governance (Olson 1965; Bräutigam, Rakner and Taylor 2002; Goldsmith 2002). The political challenge thus largely lies in shifting business associations from an essentially rent-seeking role to engaging

---

[68] Personal interview in September 2008 with prominent business leader and KAM and KEPSA member.
[69] Ibid., and interview on 18 September 2008 with senior leader, Kenya Private Sector Association. KEPSA, the umbrella organization for Kenyan business, has itself publicly sought to highlight its role in contributing to the 2008 negotiations. See also Owuor and Wisor (2014).

4.2 Taxation, responsiveness and accountability in Kenya

in "constructive contestation" with government (Handley 2008: 2). In Kenya, there is evidence that taxation has contributed to such a shift.

Under President Moi, the country's major business associations were primarily engaged in lobbying for narrow benefits rather than providing a unified voice for change. This reflected the fact that the Moi government offered significant scope for these kinds of narrow benefits. This dynamic began to change after the 2002 election in response to political opening, reduced opportunities for narrow rent-seeking, and the shifting burden of taxation. Whereas under Moi businesses allied with the government were able to secure formal and informal relief from paying their full share of taxes, the increasingly aggressive and balanced enforcement of taxation after 2002 provided stronger incentives for business to bargain with government on a collective basis. Correspondingly, taxes have remained near the top of the agenda for the large business associations, which have particularly argued for broadening the tax base. The government made at least halting efforts to respond to this demand, and business leaders report that the increased willingness of businesses to comply with tax laws has been driven in part by reciprocal efforts by the government to extend taxation to small- and medium-sized enterprises.[70]

While fairer enforcement of taxation has thus contributed to large business associations engaging more constructively with government, it has also directly catalysed the growth of business associations representing small- and medium-sized enterprises, which were historically excluded from the larger associations. The most high-profile example was the emergence of the UBA, which was founded in 2001 to oppose a government decision to require all traders to use Stock Cards, designed to monitor movements in their inventory of goods and thus curb tax evasion. The organization subsequently grew to greater prominence organizing resistance to the introduction of ETRs, and opted for further formalization and the creation of a permanent Secretariat in response to continued government efforts to improve tax collection from medium-sized firms.[71]

Taxation has also played a role in strengthening informal sector associations, including the Nairobi Informal Sector Confederation (NISCOF). NISCOF and similar associations gained prominence in response to political liberalization and growing government interest in engaging with

---

[70] Personal interviews on 18 September 2008 with senior leader, Kenya Private Sector Association and in September 2008 with prominent business leader and KAM and KEPSA member.
[71] Personal interviews on 28 August 2008 with senior leader and business official, United Business Association, and on 18 September 2008 with senior leader, Kenya Private Sector Association.

the sector, driven by a desire to expand the tax base. The Kenya Private Sector Association (KEPSA) has also supported the growth of NISCOF, with KEPSA members hoping to increase their political legitimacy and encourage the formalization of small firms.[72] Interestingly, informal sector associations are not focused simply on resisting taxation but also on bargaining directly with government. While bargaining is highly informal, NISCOF and others have hoped to exchange greater tax compliance for the simplification of business registration rules, a strengthened political voice and greater protection from the predation of municipal officers seeking bribes. As captured by Sheila Kamunyori (2007: 17) in her study of the association, "NISCOF was clear that street vendors would be willing to pay tax, in return for guaranteed services (or at least the right to demand these services)."

Civil society and taxpayer mobilization

While the threat posed by taxation has catalysed the growth and more active engagement of business associations, it also has prompted responses from a broader range of civil society organizations. These organizations have been organized explicitly around the idea that the payment of taxes entitles taxpayers to demand responsiveness and accountability from government. While these organizations have had a modest absolute impact on the behaviour of government, often owing to the unwillingness of government to make concessions, they point to the broader mobilizing potential of taxation and provide an indication of opportunities for future civil society engagement.

The Karen and Langata District Association (KLDA), which represents taxpayers from one of Nairobi's wealthiest neighbourhoods, challenged the right of the City Council to collect taxes in light of the absence of any transparency or accountability. The KLDA won a court decision in 1995 that suspended the right of the City Council to collect property taxes and mandated that taxes be placed in an escrow account until the City Council had put in place appropriately transparent financial accounts. Unfortunately, this decision resulted in a stalemate rather than leading to an effective tax bargain: taxes continued to be placed in the escrow as of the time of this research, with the KLDA demanding that it be given greater control over district development planning before releasing the funds.[73]

---

[72] Personal interview on 18 September 2008 with senior leader, Kenya Private Sector Association.
[73] Personal interview on 19 August 2008 with senior leader, Karen and Langata District Association.

The KLDA was followed by another wealthy group of taxpayers who created the We Can Do It (WCDI) campaign. The group challenged the right of the City Council to collect property taxes until such time as it could demonstrate improved accountability, and a court ruled in its favour in both 2001 and 2004. The WCDI campaign demanded that stakeholder boards be created to expand public participation in municipal management and also demanded that property taxes be based on the level of development of the property, as opposed to land area alone. Yet, as of the time of writing, there had been no compromise, with the local government unwilling to create stakeholder boards and claiming that property valuation based on the level of development was beyond the capacity of the council (Kelly 2000).[74]

Finally, the Kenya Alliance of Resident Associations (KARA) was founded in 1999 to connect and support residents' associations in their demands for improved government performance. While the organization has addressed a huge array of primarily urban development issues, the work of KARA is underpinned by the argument that tax payment provides residents with a basis for demanding improved performance from government. Although the organization was still young at the time of the research, the effort to link taxation and public accountability as a strategy for mobilizing public advocacy does appear to have meaningful resonance within the forums in which the organization operates.[75]

While all of these organizations have made some strides in linking taxation to broader demands for responsiveness and accountability, they are plagued by the fact that they have been largely unable to reach beyond relatively elite constituencies.[76] A more recent initiative has sought to achieve this broader outreach and make demands for public responsiveness and accountability on the basis of the status of its members as taxpayers. The National Taxpayers' Association (NTA) was launched in 2007 as a joint initiative of the Centre for Governance and Development (CGD) and the UK Department for International Development. The practical focus of the NTA has been on monitoring local expenditure under the CDFs, and this objective is shared with several other organizations in the country. The agenda thus remained focused primarily on expenditure, but there was an internal desire to engage more directly with issues of tax policy and administration. More generally, one of the goals of the NTA has been to make taxpayer rights a central theme

---

[74] Personal interview on 2 September 2008 with senior leader, We Can Do It campaign.
[75] Personal interview on 8 September 2008 with senior staff member, Kenya Alliance of Resident Associations.
[76] Personal interview on 28 August 2008 with senior leader, United Business Association.

underpinning and motivating advocacy efforts, and campaign organizers report significant success in this regard. To quote one leader of the campaign: "They [local residents] get really excited when you explain to them that they are actually the ones who fund the government, [and that] this can be negotiated."[77] The early work of the NTA thus presents important, although still tentative, evidence that taxation can be a catalyst for broad-based community organizing and demands for responsiveness and accountability.[78]

4.3 Explaining patterns of tax bargaining

There is significant evidence that while direct tax bargaining has been rare in Kenya, indirect tax bargaining has made an important contribution to the expansion of responsiveness and accountability. This finding is somewhat surprising, as on the surface Kenya would seem to be a case in which direct tax bargaining should be particularly likely. As noted earlier, it has a relatively strong private sector, and has enjoyed relative political openness and stability. In addition, Kenya has collected some of the highest levels of tax revenue of any country in the region continuously since independence, while it has a relatively active civil society. Perhaps most strikingly, data from the 2008 and 2012 rounds of the Afrobarometer survey indicate that Kenyans are comparatively likely to support tax avoidance and evasion when the government is deemed to be unaccountable.[79] Yet, this apparent willingness to resist unaccountable taxation has not been consistently transformed into effective collective action and bargaining with the government.[80]

---

[77] Personal interviews on 29 August 2008 with two senior civil society leaders working on budget monitoring.
[78] Ibid.
[79] The 2008 round of the Afrobarometer survey asked respondents whether they agreed with the statement that: "The department of taxes always has the right to make people pay taxes." Out of sixteen countries, Ghanaians had the second highest level of agreement, whereas Kenya was ninth. Ethiopia, which is the subject of the next chapter, was not surveyed. Additional countries and tax-related questions were added in the 2012 round of the survey, with Ghana now ranking first amongst twenty-nine countries in response to the same question, whereas Kenya ranked thirteenth. This pattern is repeated across a wide range of questions in the 2012 round of the survey, with Kenyans reporting a relatively high tax rate, significant difficulty of evasion, but a relatively strong resistance to unaccountable taxation (Aiko and Logan 2014).
[80] While this is only a very crude correlation, it does point towards the potential risks associated with studying the relationship between taxation and accountability through public opinion surveys or lab-in-the-field type experiments, as an expressed willingness to resist unaccountable taxes – or to mobilize in response to them – may not necessarily translate into concrete or effective political action.

4.3 Explaining patterns of tax bargaining   147

Table 4.1 *Kenya: the role of contextual factors*

Structural factor	Relevant contextual variables	Impact
Taxpayer capacity for collective action	• Government repression • Limited taxpayer unity, rooted in a combination of ethnic differences and pervasive rent-seeking • History of high taxation and limited public engagement, rooted in part in minority control of many significant business interests	• While repression was modest by regional standards, it still posed a barrier to bargaining in the 1980s in particular • Lack of unity amongst business taxpayers undermined the bargaining role of business associations until the late 1990s • Racial divisions undermined ability of anti-tax protests to gain a broader popular following, while historically high levels of taxation are comparatively normalized
The political salience of taxation	• Timing and gradualism in implementation of reform • Central government attention to transparency of CDFs	• Strategic use of timing and gradualism in reform has undermined the political salience of taxes, led by the VAT • Attention to CDFs raised the political salience of taxes from 2003 onwards
The potential and scope for tax resistance	• Heavy reliance on direct taxes from a strong private sector • Intra-elite business unity	• Strength of private sector offers a strong foundation for tax resistance. • Intra-elite fragmentation undermined the potential for collective tax resistance until the late 1990s, while greater business association unity enhanced the potential for tax resistance thereafter.
Revenue pressure facing government	• Economic and fiscal crisis of the late 1990s	• Fiscal crisis increased the vulnerability of the government to tax resistance
Institutions for bargaining	• Expanded scope for formal bargaining with business post-2002	• Shaped role of business in arguing for improved governance and, particularly, the end of post-election conflict in 2008

The goal of this final section is, therefore, to offer an explanation for both the relative absence of direct tax bargaining and for the comparative importance of indirect forms of tax bargaining (summarized in Table 4.1). As in Ghana, factors shaping taxpayer capacity for collective action loom large, although in Kenya it is the extent of (dis)unity amongst taxpayer interests – and particularly elite taxpayer interests – that appears to have been most critical in shaping capacity for collective action across a range of tax episodes. This question of elite unity has also figured centrally in shaping the potential for tax resistance. Meanwhile, individual tax episodes reveal clearly the importance of the political salience of taxation and of revenue pressure in shaping particular outcomes.

4.3.1 *Taxpayer capacity for collective action and the political salience of taxation*

The weakness of collective action in response to taxation in Kenya has been driven by the combination of government repression, starkly divided taxpayer interests and the roles of government strategy and of history in reducing the political salience of taxation.

Limited political openness

Despite a high degree of political stability and the persistence of nominal democracy, Kenyan politics remained relatively autocratic until the 2002 elections, with the period from the mid-1980s until the 1992 elections being particularly repressive. When asked why there was not more of a public response to taxation throughout the period, and particularly to the introduction of the VAT in 1990, most observers first point to the general absence of political liberties.[81] While there were large public protests leading up to the introduction of elections in 1992, this mass political action stood in contrast to the special interest driven tax politics of the period. However, repression alone is a clearly inadequate explanation: Ghanaian mobilization against the VAT makes clear that taxation can be a catalyst for protest even where the government remains only weakly democratic (Osei 2000). Meanwhile, reduced political repression since 2003 has not given rise to any dramatic examples of direct tax bargaining in Kenya, despite large increases in revenue collection. This points to the importance of additional factors more unique to the Kenyan context.

Divided taxpayer interests

The most critical factor appears to have been an absence of unified interests amongst taxpayers, which has denied them the political power

---

[81] Personal interviews on 19 August 2008 with former Permanent Secretary, Ministry of Finance, on 20 August 2008 with former Permanent Secretary, Ministry of Finance, and on 8 August 2008 with Former Director of Tax Policy, Ministry of Finance.

4.3 Explaining patterns of tax bargaining   149

and cohesion necessary to compel government concessions. This lack of cohesion has had two key dimensions: internal divisions amongst elite business taxpayers, rooted in a history of narrow rent-seeking, and the inability of business taxpayers to secure the support of the broader base of taxpayers. Both stand in contrast to the cross-cutting taxpayer unity exemplified by the *Kume Preko* protests in Ghana, while both appear, at least in part, to be rooted in divisive racial politics inherited from Kenya's colonial history as a settler colony.

Elite fragmentation and narrow benefit-seeking
When confronted with taxation, taxpayers may respond collectively with other taxpayers in an effort to secure a broad tax bargain with government, or may respond by seeking narrow benefits for themselves. For example, a business confronted with the increasingly assertive collection of corporate taxes may: (a) opt to work with other businesses to ensure that the government improves the business environment in exchange for tax compliance; or (b) work through individual contacts in government to ensure that it will be spared part of the new tax burden, or will receive narrow benefits in return. Historically, many Kenyan elites have preferred to pursue narrow benefits, thus undermining the potential for collective action and bargaining between taxpayers and governments.[82] This outcome is broadly consistent with the predictions of pioneering work by Margaret Levi (1988: 64), who has suggested that governments might seek to purchase the allegiance of a small number of influential taxpayers using "side payments" rather than engaging in tax bargaining with a broader group.

This pattern of narrow benefit-seeking was particularly apparent amongst many business elites at least until 2003, but appears to have shifted somewhat since then. A well-placed observer of the historical role played by the Kenya Alliance of Manufacturers, likely Kenya's strongest business association, captured this widely held view, explaining that "a few people got what they wanted, but they did not go after a whole business agenda for manufacturing."[83] This began to change most notably after the elections of 2002, as businesses began to adopt a more unified agenda, with the profile of the major business associations growing as a

---

[82] Personal interviews on 18 September 2008 with senior leader, Kenya Private Sector Association, on 15 September 2008 with former Commissioner, VAT, KRA, on 28 August 2008 with senior leader, United Business Association, on 20 August 2008 with senior researcher on tax issues, Institute for Economic Affairs, and on 20 August 2008 with Former Permanent Secretary, Ministry of Finance.
[83] Personal interview on 18 September 2008 with senior leader, Kenya Private Sector Association.

result.[84] As is discussed in greater detail in Chapter 6, this appears to reflect growing political openness – and the consequent expansion of the potential for bargaining – but also a decline in tax-related corruption and discretion, thus reducing the scope for narrow benefits and exemptions, and pushing businesses towards more collective strategies.[85]

The same pattern is apparent amongst the political elite. Parliament's refusal to pass laws taxing their benefits, or to reinstitute the capital gains tax, have been indicative of a class that is happy to tax others, secure in the knowledge that they will remain relatively less affected. This dynamic similarly is apparent in the poorly kept secret that, particularly under Moi, the politically well-connected frequently paid less tax than they should have by law, exemplified by the consistent failure of state-controlled firms to pay all of their taxes.[86] In an environment in which the relatively powerful are able to pursue narrow benefits and exemptions, it is little surprise that elites have historically not led efforts to catalyse public demands for reciprocity in taxation. Instead, by sharp contrast, these privileged elites have appeared to prefer to keep tax issues intentionally off of the political agenda, so as not to draw attention to their privilege.

The absence of popular support

While the ability of elites to pursue narrow benefits has eroded the likelihood of unified tax bargaining, an equally important issue has been the inability of small- and mid-sized businesses resisting taxation to garner significant popular support. Two examples stand out: the conflict over ETRs and the absence of conflict over fuel taxes.

While major protests erupted in response to government legislation requiring the use of ETRs by all VAT registered firms, those protests were undermined by the fact that the protesters, numerous as they were, never enjoyed broad-based popular support. The government successfully labelled those businesses "tax evaders," and in the public mind, this outweighed trader complaints about the costs of collection or a lack of government accountability.[87] This allowed the government to ignore the

---

[84] Ibid., and interview on 20 August 2008 with senior researcher on tax issues, Institute for Economic Affairs.

[85] Personal interviews on 18 September 2008 with senior leader, Kenya Private Sector Association, in September 2008 with prominent business leader and KAM and KEPSA member, and on 15 September 2008 with former Commissioner, VAT, KRA.

[86] Personal interview on 15 September 2008 with former Commissioner, VAT, KRA, on 18 September 2008 with senior leader, Kenya Private Sector Association, and on 20 August 2008 with former Permanent Secretary, Ministry of Finance.

[87] Personal interviews on 28 August 2008 with senior leader and official, United Business Association and on 15 September 2008 with former Commissioner, VAT, KRA.

widespread protests and press forward with the measure without making any meaningful concessions. In similar fashion, increases in fuel prices have consistently been met with complaints from public transport operators. Yet, despite the fact that the public bears the resulting higher costs of transport, the operators have never enjoyed broad public support in their protests against fuel taxes. It is widely believed that this has resulted from the deep unpopularity of public transport operators, who are viewed as reckless, disrespectful and – occasionally – criminal.[88] While the inability of different groups of taxpayers to find a united voice with which to bargain with government has diverse roots, these examples make clear that the absence of unity has undermined the likelihood of tax bargaining.

The role of racial divisions
While the absence of taxpayer unity has diverse sources – and is common to some extent across the case studies – Kenya's relatively unique racial divisions appear to have played an important role in exacerbating these dynamics. Particularly during the 1960s and 1970s, the willingness of parliament and the population to accept rapid increases in taxation was largely driven by a belief, with significant justification, that much of the tax burden would be borne by economically dominant Asians and Europeans. Thus, the unique racial characteristics of the country help to explain the fact that Kenya established a relatively effective tax system soon after independence.[89] While this dynamic became less explicit over time, concerns about tax evasion by Asian businesspeople remains a ubiquitous topic in discussions with tax officials, suggesting strongly that public support for effective tax administration continues to be shaped by support for taxing Asians and Europeans.[90]

The flip side of popular support for an effective system to tax Asians and Europeans has been public unwillingness to support tax

---

[88] The most dramatic evidence of this lack of popularity comes from 2004 when then-Minister for Transport, John Michuki, instituted major new regulatory and safety requirements for public transport operators. The operators staged a two-week strike over the perceived high cost of the measures, and completely shut down transport in the major urban centres. Yet, citizens as a group, despite being forced to walk enormous distances to work, continued to side with the government on the need for reform. Personal interviews on 20 August 2008 with senior policy researcher on tax issues, Kenya Institute for Public Policy Research and Analysis and in September 2008 with former matatu conductor and taxi company owner.
[89] Personal interviews on 20 August 2008 with former Permanent Secretary, Ministry of Finance and on 19 August 2008 with former Permanent Secretary, Ministry of Finance.
[90] Personal interviews on 15 September 2008 with former Commissioner, VAT, KRA, on 18 September 2008 with senior leader, Kenya Private Sector Association, on 8 September 2008 with senior official, Fiscal and Monetary Affairs Department, Ministry of Finance, and on 28 August 2008 with senior leader, United Business Association.

resistance and tax bargaining by those groups. This was displayed during the protests against ETRs, as the protesters were not only labelled tax evaders, but were specifically labelled *Asian* tax evaders, and this fatally undermined public support for their cause. The absence of public support, and the salience of the racial dimension, is more remarkable given that the Chairman of the UBA, which organized the protests, was an African, and that a significant part of the cost of increased prices would be borne by consumers. Ultimately, without public support, mid-sized businesses had little ability to bargain effectively with the government.[91]

While racial divisions have thus undermined the potential for business elites to garner broad-based support, they equally appear to have contributed to the rise of narrow rent-seeking by the business community and the corresponding absence of elite collective action around taxation. While difficult to quantify, it is relatively common to hear variants on the claim that "non-African businesses lack political support, and as a result their only options are to engage in tax evasion or seek individual benefits, often through bribery or collusion."[92] There is no evidence that Asians or Europeans have been disproportionately involved in such activities, but instead, there is a broad sense that these racial dynamics contributed to giving rise to a general mode of government-business interaction that was individualistic and patronage-based. Meanwhile, the fact that Europeans and Asians dominated the large business associations almost certainly weakened their ability to pursue a broad-based advocacy programme by courting public support.[93] By the same token, leaders within the large business community stress that the increasing prominence of African-owned businesses in the country has contributed to shifting the political dynamics linking the government and business since 2003.[94] Ultimately, the key message is that unique racial dynamics have contributed to the historical tendency of business associations to pursue narrower political agendas, to the exclusion of broader opportunities for tax bargaining, although this has appeared to be changing since 2003.

[91] Personal interviews on 28 August 2008 with senior leader and official, United Business Association.
[92] Personal interviews on 15 September 2008 with former Commissioner, VAT, KRA, on 8 August 2008 with former Director of Tax Policy, Ministry of Finance, and on 20 August 2008 with former Permanent Secretary, Ministry of Finance, amongst others.
[93] Personal interviews on 18 September 2008 with senior leader, Kenya Private Sector Association, on 28 August 2008 with senior leader, United Business Association, and in September 2008 with prominent business leader and KAM and KEPSA member.
[94] Personal interview on 18 September 2008 with senior leader, Kenya Private Sector Association.

Strategy, history and the political salience of taxation

Finally, while taxpayer potential for collective action has been limited by political repression and a lack of unity, it has also been undermined by the limited political salience of taxation. This has reflected both intentional government strategies and more idiosyncratic historical legacies of taxation in the country.

In the realm of the intentional, the government has relied on both strategic timing and gradualism in reform in an effort to avoid the politicization of tax changes – in sharp contrast to the political salience of the VAT and fuel taxes in Ghana. The most basic element of this strategy has been to implement controversial tax changes at moments of extensive political goodwill, rather than in moments of crisis. The most ambitious tax reforms undertaken by the government occurred following the elections of 1992 and 2002, both of which were periods of political goodwill and economic growth. The controversial capital gains tax in the 1970s was similarly implemented during the early phases of the coffee boom and was pitched in part as a tax on that new wealth. While the VAT was introduced in 1990, the most controversial elements of the tax – centred on rationalizing the rate structure and extending it to services – were put off until after the 1992 elections. The government was thus able to take advantage of popular goodwill to push through reforms that might otherwise have been highly controversial. Once the reforms had been implemented, it was unlikely that they would subsequently be reversed, although the capital gains tax was suspended in 1985. One senior official captured this dynamic succinctly: "You need to introduce new taxes at a time of boom. That is the politics of taxation."[95]

In the same spirit, the government consistently has pursued a policy of gradualism when undertaking any kind of economic reform, including in the realm of taxation, in order to minimize resistance.[96] This stands in contrast to many other countries in the region, which have often been characterized by rapid and clearly defined periods of reform, in part owing to the demands of international donors (O'Brien and Ryan 2001). Senior policymakers are transparent about the fact that gradualism has been a means to limit public attention and ensure that the impact is

---

[95] Personal interview on 8 September 2008 with senior official, Fiscal and Monetary Affairs Department, Ministry of Finance.

[96] The programme of economic liberalization, for example, was prominently proposed within government as early as 1982, but reforms were still being implemented in the late 1990s. Personal interviews on 22 August 2008 with former senior official and current Advisor to Central Bank of Kenya, on 19 August 2008 with former Permanent Secretary, Ministry of Finance, on 8 August 2008 with former Director of Tax Policy, Ministry of Finance, and on 20 August 2008 with former Permanent Secretary, Ministry of Finance.

spread over time and thus less likely to spark a reaction from either special interests or the public at large.[97] One of Kenya's most prominent economic policymakers reports gaining a measure of infamy with international organizations for arguing that "the more you involve people in reform the less likely you are to achieve your goals. The less transparent you are the more likely you are to succeed."[98] This view is widely shared by similarly placed officials, who propose that Kenya has been characterized by "reform by stealth"[99] and "reform by subterfuge,"[100] with the gradual implementation of the VAT serving as the clearest illustration in the realm of taxation.

While government strategy has thus figured prominently in reducing the political salience of taxation – and the consequent likelihood of taxpayer responses – Kenya's particular history of taxation also appears to have played a role. As noted earlier, Kenya is relatively unique in sub-Saharan Africa in having established a quite effective system of taxation immediately after independence. More importantly in this context, it did so with very little politicization, at least in part because taxes were understood by the African political majority to be levies primarily on Asian and European "others" who controlled much of the economy.[101]

While these racial divisions have continued to affect the (dis)unity of taxpayer interests, the long, uninterrupted history of relatively substantial taxation in Kenya also appears to have shaped expectations in a way that has discouraged collective action. Most simply, tax systems are highly path-dependent (Lieberman 2002), and once high taxes have been established they may be less likely to prompt opposition than when they are first introduced.[102] Discussion in Kenya suggests that taxpayers may be less likely to aggressively and publicly oppose taxation precisely because taxation has been a relatively consistent feature of life since independence, and has thus become normalized, even if unpopular. It is worth noting that the long history of tax collection may also promote indirect tax bargaining by contributing to the strengthening of civil society and

[97] Ibid.
[98] Personal interview on 22 August 2008 with former senior official and current Advisor to Central Bank of Kenya.
[99] Ibid.
[100] Personal interview on 22 July 2008 with former Advisor to Ministry of Finance and KRA.
[101] Personal interview on 19 August 2008 with former Permanent Secretary, Ministry of Finance, on 20 August 2008 with former Permanent Secretary, Ministry of Finance.
[102] Tellingly, this may undermine the utility of survey evidence about attitudes towards taxation across countries in understanding the likelihood tax bargaining. For example, respondents in two different countries may express similar attitudes towards the payment of "unjust" taxes, yet in practice, have very different preferences based on their historical experience of what level of taxation should be considered "just."

4.3 Explaining patterns of tax bargaining

broader, but quieter, public engagement – a notion that is consistent with the relatively widespread and explicit engagement of civil society organizations with taxation in Kenya, but not a notion that is easily empirically testable.

Perhaps as importantly, Kenya's history of relatively effective taxation is an important part of what has allowed the Kenyan government to sustain its gradualist and strategic approach to tax reform. The government has been able to implement taxation on its own timeline, and during moments of political goodwill, in large part because the tax system has remained relatively effective in generating revenue. This has limited the role of fiscal crisis and donors in forcing more rapid and decisive approaches to reform, while allowing the government to balance new tax demands against the parallel provision of new tax benefits. For example, major tax reforms from 1993–1995 were possible, in part, because large increases in total collection were accompanied by a government commitment to declining tax rates and improved customer service.[103] Similarly, the introduction of the VAT in 1990 included efforts to reform the hugely unpopular and burdensome system of tax refunds,[104] while the introduction of the RML in 1994 was eased by the fact that it reduced reliance on the unpopular system of road tolls.[105] In each case, reform generated significantly more revenue than had previously been the case, but in each case the existence of the earlier taxes, and the possibility of pointing to the relative benefits of the new system, improved the bargaining position of government and made it possible to lower the political salience of tax debates.

Finally, it is also worth noting that while the government has generally sought to reduce the political salience of taxation, there is evidence that it has also been able to selectively *increase* the political salience of taxation where it has been motivated to do so. This appears to have occurred over the course of the 2000s, with a variety of observers noting mounting popular attention to tax issues, with one well-placed observer going so far as to argue that "there is a huge amount of concern about tax and about how it is being used. A strong feeling that 'this is our money.'"[106] These sentiments stand in sharp contrast to earlier periods of Kenyan history and beg the question of what might explain increased public

---

[103] Personal interview on 8 September 2008 with senior official, Fiscal and Monetary Affairs Department, Ministry of Finance.
[104] Personal interview on 15 September 2008 with former Commissioner, VAT, KRA.
[105] Personal interviews on 20 August 2008 with senior policy researcher on tax issues, Kenya Institute for Public Policy Research and Analysis and on 8 October 2008 with former Minister of Energy in Kibaki Government.
[106] Personal interview on 22 September 2008 with senior donor official.

interest. While many factors have surely played a role, a central part of the story in the view of those involved has been the role of the CDFs in expanding public awareness and engagement. While the CDFs were initially a concession to MPs hoping to use them to entrench their local political positions, the Executive – which had harboured some scepticism about the CDFs – had an interest in ensuring that the funds were relatively well-monitored and deployed. To this end, significant measures were taken to draw public attention to the idea that the CDFs were "taxpayer money," including publishing publicly available lists of all approved CDF projects on an annual basis. One consequence, it appears, has been to raise awareness not only of the funds, but also of the broad message amongst taxpayers that government funds are "their money." This has, in turn, been reflected in expanded public engagement with tax issues post-2003, including the civil society initiatives noted earlier.[107]

4.3.2 Revenue pressure and the potential for tax resistance

The combination of repression, a lack of taxpayer unity and the limited political salience of taxation has thus curbed the potential for direct tax bargaining in Kenya. However, Kenya has also witnessed important instances in which tax resistance has generated pressure for significant governance changes, beginning in the late 1990s. At a broad level, the emergence of tax resistance as an important political strategy in Kenya is somewhat unsurprising, as Kenya has a very strong private sector, and is comparatively heavily reliant on relatively visible direct taxes. The more interesting analytical question is why instances of indirect tax bargaining have become more common over time. The answer appears to lie in the combination of changes in the potential for tax resistance and the revenue pressure facing the government.

To illustrate the role of these two variables, it is useful to focus on two instances in which tax resistance shaped subsequent governance outcomes: tax resistance preceding the 2002 elections, which contributed to the eventual removal of the Moi government from office, and the role of tax resistance by the business community in putting pressure on the government to put an end to post-election violence in 2008. In both cases the effectiveness of tax resistance as a political strategy was supported by elevated revenue pressure facing the government.

Leading up to the 2002 elections, a persistent economic crisis contributed to a reduced tax base, thus putting increasing pressure on

[107] Personal interviews on 22 September 2008 with senior donor official, on 30 August 2008 with researcher working on politics surrounding the CDFs, and on 29 August 2008 with two senior civil society leaders working on budget monitoring.

government finances and enhancing the impact of tax resistance by the business community. The role of revenue pressure is all the more apparent in the case of violence following the 2008 elections, as there was a widespread sentiment that continued violence could result in an economic and fiscal crisis. In both cases it was thus elevated revenue pressure that made threats of non-compliance by the business community particularly influential in shaping government incentives.

However, it is readily apparent that revenue pressure alone was not enough to empower the business community to put meaningful pressure on government. Most obviously, the government faced an acute fiscal crisis after the 1992 elections as a result of the Goldenberg scandal, but in that case the business community did not generate similar political pressures through tax resistance. The difference was that the business community remained highly divided in the early 1990s, thus reducing the scope for tax resistance to significantly affect government finances or incentives. While individual firms may have sought to pressure the government through tax resistance, this engagement of firms with the government was relatively ad hoc. By contrast, the growing unity of the business community by the late 1990s meant that tax resistance prior to the 2002 elections appeared to senior tax officials to be more widespread and systematic, and thus came to resemble an explicit political strategy.[108] This allowed a more meaningful impact on government finances, while generating clear incentives for the incoming government to be responsive. Finally, by 2008 tax resistance emerged as a relatively explicit business strategy for pressuring the government to resolve post-election violence, facilitated by even greater levels of business coherence.[109] In both cases, instances of indirect tax bargaining were thus underpinned by the combination of revenue pressure and significant business potential for engaging in tax resistance.

4.4 Conclusions

The Kenyan experience advances our understanding of tax bargaining in three particular ways. First, despite the relative absence of direct tax bargaining, it provides important evidence that tax bargaining more generally has contributed significantly to the expansion of responsiveness and

---

[108] Personal interviews on 8 August 2008 with former Director of Tax Policy, Ministry of Finance, on 15 September 2008 with former Commissioner, VAT, KRA, and on 20 August 2008 with Tax Officer, Domestic Tax Department, KRA.
[109] Personal interview in September 2008 with prominent business leader and KAM and KEPSA member.

accountability in Kenya. Second, it specifically highlights the importance of indirect tax bargaining. Discussions of tax bargaining instinctively have tended to focus on direct tax bargaining, involving the relatively explicit exchange of tax compliance for improved responsiveness and accountability. This is reflected most clearly in existing econometric approaches to the question, which have assumed a highly linear causal process. By contrast, the Kenyan experience has highlighted the importance of indirect tax bargaining through resistance to taxation imposed by unpopular governments and through the gradual strengthening of civil society and public engagement. Third, this chapter has shed significant light on the contextual factors that appear to shape the particular character and outcomes of tax bargaining. The analysis here has captured the extent to which diminished taxpayer potential for collective action and the limited political salience of taxation have collectively minimized the scope for direct tax bargaining. However, it equally has highlighted the ways in which growing potential for tax resistance has contributed to opening new paths to bargaining since the late 1990s. In both cases, questions of taxpayer unity and elite leadership have figured prominently in explaining outcomes, thus reinforcing a message that emerged comparatively tentatively from the earlier case study of Ghana. Collectively, the evidence in this chapter thus reinforces not only the role of direct and indirect tax bargaining in shaping political developments, but the extent to which these processes vary across countries and over time in response to differences in the social, economic and political contexts.

Appendix

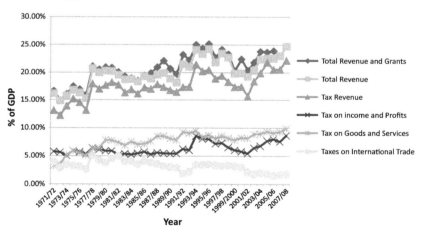

Figure 4.1 Kenya: composition of government revenue, 1971–2008.

Appendix

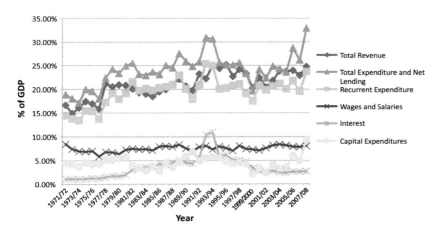

Figure 4.2 Kenya: government expenditure and revenue, 1971–2008.

5 The quiet politics of taxation in Ethiopia, 1974–2008

This final case study looks at the recent history of taxation in Ethiopia. The attraction of focusing on Ethiopia lies in significant part in the fact that it never experienced full-blown colonial rule on the scale seen elsewhere on the continent, and correspondingly presents a relatively unique environment in which to examine the political dynamics around taxation. As importantly, it presents a contemporary political and economic environment that is profoundly different from those found in Ghana and Kenya, thus offering new dimensions along which to consider the impact of context on the potential for tax bargaining.

Whereas European powers conquered almost the entirety of sub-Saharan Africa in the late nineteenth century, Ethiopian forces led by then-Emperor Menelik successfully rebuffed the Italian advance in 1896. Ethiopia retained its formal independence through the entire African colonial period, save for a brief period of Italian control from 1936 to 1941. The result was a comparatively indigenously led process of cultural, political and economic development, including the gradual development of a national tax system.

Interestingly, secondary sources point to the importance of conflicts over taxation during this early phase of state-building and consolidation, in ways totally distinct from experiences elsewhere on the continent. During the early modern Imperial period, this was reflected in repeated conflicts between successive Emperors, the Church and newly conquered areas in the south, as competing political authorities sought the resources with which to build a stronger and more centralized state. The period after the Italian occupation saw the emergence of more focused tax conflicts, as local resistance movements developed in response to state efforts to expand taxation and central government control. Thus, for example, the *Weyane* rebellion in Tigray in 1943 saw local landowners and populations successfully resist the re-imposition of taxes abolished by the Italians, whereas the *Bale* rebellion in the South in 1963 saw the emergence of armed resistance in response to the expanded taxation of land and of pastoralist groups (Tareke 1991; Zewde 1991). Perhaps most notably, the introduction of a new agricultural income tax in 1974 has been credited for contributing to the strengthening of the Ethiopian parliament (Schwab 1972), while it also gave rise to an additional armed uprising against the tax in Gojjam province (Schwab 1972; Tareke 1991; Zewde 1991). While interesting in their own right, these events have also shaped local understanding of tax debates, with local officials frequently recounting the long history of conflicts over taxation in Imperial Ethiopia in framing discussion of the comparative absence of tax debates during the more contemporary period.[1]

This unique history aside, modern Ethiopia since the removal of Emperor Haile Selassie in 1974 also provides a significant contrast to political and economic conditions in the cases examined so far. Whereas Ghana and Kenya were selected as case study countries owing in part to the a priori likelihood of tax bargaining, Ethiopia was selected owing to a set of characteristics that are expected to make tax bargaining comparatively *unlikely*. Four issues stand out. First, throughout the period 1974 to 2009, Ethiopia has remained a comparatively autocratic state, limiting *taxpayer capacity for collective action* and the scope of *institutions that could facilitate tax bargaining*. The socialist government that ruled until 1991 was exceptionally repressive, while under the current government space for public debate and competitive politics has remained sharply curtailed. Second, Ethiopia is one of the poorest, most agrarian countries in the world, and has a significantly weaker private sector than either Ghana or Kenya. This is expected to constrain both *the potential and scope for tax resistance* and *taxpayer capacity for collective action*. Third, Ethiopia is very heavily dependent on foreign aid, thus potentially reducing the *level of revenue pressure* facing the government, and consequent incentives to bargain with taxpayers. The socialist government that was in power until 1991 received significant aid, primarily from the Soviet Union, while the government in power since 1991 has received aid from the West worth an average of more than 10 per cent of GDP annually, and reaching almost 20 per cent of GDP from 2002 to 2004. Fourth, Ethiopia has an aforementioned long history of highly autocratic rule, which is, in the view of many, reinforced by a culturally ingrained conservatism and deference to established authority. While historic conflicts over taxation occasionally prompted tax resistance and armed rebellion, there is little consistent history of organized political contestation, thus further limiting *taxpayer*

---

[1] Personal interviews on 3 November 2008 with senior tax reform official, Ministry of Revenue, on 3 November 2008 with senior official working on regional fiscal relations, Federal Ministry of Finance and Economic Development, and on 19 November 2008 with Opposition Member of Parliament, amongst others.

capacity for collective action (Levine 1965: 3; Clapham 1988: 21–22; Tekle 1990: 45–47).

Aside from these broad social, economic and political characteristics, Ethiopia is also unique in being a federal state and in having experienced both civil war and an interstate war with Eritrea in the recent past. Taken together, these various factors make Ethiopia a compelling setting for providing new research insights. Ultimately, we find, as expected, that there has been relatively limited direct and indirect tax bargaining in Ethiopia since 1974, owing to the particular social, economic and political characteristics noted so far. Yet, despite the relative absence of tax bargaining at the national level, there is nonetheless important evidence of direct tax bargaining at the regional level, as well as evidence that the ability of the government to collect tax revenue has been shaped by public perceptions and levels of public support. These findings suggest that while the Ethiopian context has been particularly unfriendly to the emergence of both direct and indirect tax bargaining, the basic political processes of interest remain relevant.

As with the preceding chapters, what follows begins with an analytical narrative of the political economy of taxation in Ethiopia from 1974 to 2009, with detailed revenue figures presented in the appendix to the chapter. The subsequent sections then ask whether there is evidence of a relationship between taxation, responsiveness and accountability, and what contextual factors appear to explain patterns of tax bargaining in the country. Owing to the particularities of the Ethiopian political and fiscal environment the tax narrative is divided into three parts: (1) the period of socialist rule until 1991; (2) the period of Ethiopian People's Revolutionary Democratic Front (EPRDF) rule since 1991; and (3) a final section focused on regional taxation.

5.1 The Derg and the end of the feudal state, 1974–1991

Until 1974, Ethiopia was ruled by a succession of Emperors, with Haile Selassie holding power from 1930 onwards, aside from the brief period of Italian occupation. Against this background, the end of the Imperial system arrived suddenly in 1974, when Haile Selassie was overthrown by a diverse coalition of opposition forces that proceeded to implement a dramatic political, economic and social reorganization of society along socialist lines. In the most thorough history of the period, Clapham (1988) has argued forcefully that, for all the limitations of the new regime, the scale of change was undeniably revolutionary. This change in government thus marks a useful starting point for the analysis, and what follows provides an overview of the general politics and reforms of the revolutionary period before turning to the specifics of the fiscal evolution of the state from 1974 to 1991.

5.1.1 Revolution and the transformation of the state

Mid-level and junior military officers initially seized power in 1974 in the midst of a growing urban protest movement committed to a broadly socialist ideology. The Imperial regime had become unable to contain the growing political pressures emanating from a modernizing class of students who expressed outrage at the narrowness of Imperial rule and at the continued existence of exploitative relations in the countryside, where landowners continued to exercise enormous power over the peasantry. Yet, the urban unrest remained poorly organized, which created uncertainty about who would seize the leadership of the new movement and about the extent to which the socialist ideals of the protesters would be transformed into reality.

Over time, it was military officers who progressively asserted control. The military leadership was organized into an inclusive leadership committee known as the Derg, but by 1977 Mengistu Haile-Mariam had seized unrivalled control of the Derg through political manoeuvring and the removal of his major rivals through violence. Two major civilian rivals, the All-Ethiopia Socialist Movement (known by its Amharic acronym, Meison) and the Ethiopian People's Revolutionary Party (EPRP), confronted the Derg. Each professed socialist ideals and a desire for civilian government, but both were largely eliminated during a period of urban terror and violence that peaked during 1976–1977. The violence initially pitted the Derg and Meison against the EPRP, after which the Derg violently turned on its erstwhile allies.

Programmatically, while the Derg was not steeped in socialist ideology, it quickly adopted a broadly socialist programme of action focused on nationalization and the construction of a powerful central state. The centrepiece was the announcement of land reform in 1975. The proclamation nationalized all land and called for its equal distribution amongst the peasantry, who were to be organized into peasant associations (PAs). In a single stroke, this sought to fulfil a central promise of the revolution and decisively eliminate the power of the traditional landed classes. While parts of the former elite engaged in armed resistance, the most remarkable trait of the reform was its popularity, and the consequent speed and ruthlessness with which the old elite was swept away and replaced by the PAs. The reform served to improve the position of the peasantry, particularly in the South, and also dramatically enhanced the power of the government. Despite the differences in method, this push for greater centralization had much in common with earlier efforts dating back more than a century, as successive Emperors had confronted the challenge of strengthening the central government and curbing the power of landowners (Clapham 1988; Zewde 2002).

In subsequent years, land reform was followed by a series of policy pronouncements that were consistent with socialist ideology and a desire to expand state power. The government nationalized virtually all industry as well as a large share of urban property and housing. Urban areas were organized into *kebeles* (neighbourhoods), and individual *kebeles* were made responsible for local administration, land nationalization and security, with the last of these roles most apparent in the role of *kebele* defence squads during the urban terror campaign. In rural areas, the PAs initially enjoyed significant freedom of action, but it was not long before the government began to extend its control. By 1978, the government had seized increasing control over the marketing and transport of agricultural products, and was thus able to institute tightly enforced production quotas and price controls (Clapham 1988; Ottaway 1990).

Government efforts to transform the countryside took on progressively more ambitious forms over time. The initial creation of the PAs had been accompanied by incentives for the creation of cooperatives, but this initial programme proceeded gradually, and showed no benefits in terms of productivity. More ambitious was the villagization campaign that began in 1985. The goal was to permanently change the basic character of the countryside by relocating scattered peasant homes, which tended to be located near individual fields, into centralized villages. Despite the fact that promised improvements in service provision in these new villages often did not materialize, the implementation of the policy was remarkable, as millions of peasants literally knocked down their previous homes and moved them to new settlements. Moreover, while peasants often moved grudgingly, the power of the central government was such that villagization was largely achieved without recourse to overt violence (Brietzke 1976; Cohen and Isaksson 1987; Clapham 1988). This form of social engineering reached its climax in the government push to resettle peasants away from the densely populated and famine-prone North. While planned resettlements were not entirely new to Ethiopia, the government resettlement of a reported 600,000 people in the aftermath of the 1984–1985 famine was unparalleled, while subsequent plans to resettle an even larger share of the population appear only to have been prevented by the deteriorating position of the regime in the late 1980s (Clapham 1988).

5.1 The Derg and the end of the feudal state

While the government thus succeeded in building a massive administrative apparatus and in developing the capacity to profoundly reshape the lives of citizens, it remained unable to decisively solve the problem of armed insurgency in the North. Armed resistance to the regime emerged almost immediately in 1974, and was led by the Eritrean People's Liberation Front (EPLF) and the Tigray People's Liberation Front (TPLF). The resistance in Eritrea was unsurprising given longstanding secessionist ambitions in the region. By contrast, the resistance in Tigray was aimed at autonomy rather than independence, and reflected a deeply rooted, although more complex, regional identity. These resistance movements exercised a degree of control within their regional bases, and necessitated the continuous militarization of the country, including extremely high levels of military spending, significant military aid from the Soviet Union, and periodic conscription. That said, these resistance movements did not appear to pose a serious military threat to the state as a whole until suddenly claiming the initiative after 1988 amidst evidence of the internal collapse of the Ethiopian army and state (Clapham 1988).

5.1.2 *The fiscal basis of the socialist state*

The Derg period witnessed the rapid expansion of the role and reach of the state through nationalization, the strengthening of the administrative apparatus, and significant militarization. This needed to be matched by a corresponding growth of state revenues, despite the problems that revenue collection had posed for previous governments. In practice, the expansion of revenue was never sufficient to match the dramatic expansion of the state and the costs of endless warfare, and fiscal deficits began to accumulate in the 1980s. Revenue gains were nonetheless dramatic, with the difficulties of taxation in earlier periods largely overcome by nationalization and the destruction of the old elite.

Studying the political economy of taxation in a socialist state poses a particular challenge, as government control of economic activity implies that taxation is frequently hidden within the broader activities of the command economy. Extensive state control of the formerly private sector meant that tax compliance was assured, as a significant share of economic production was internal to the state. While government accounts officially distinguished between taxation and investment income, in a command economy the practical distinction would often have been merely a matter of accounting. In writing about the transition from Communism in the former Soviet Union, Gehlbach (2008: 20) clearly highlights the differences between taxation in a command economy and taxation in an open economy: "Laying claim to funds to run the state was largely an accounting matter when most productive assets were state owned. But with privatization and liberalization, bureaucracies had to be created to locate and encourage the transfer of what was now possessed by private actors." While remarkably little detailed information is available about taxation under the Derg regime, the basic message that state control internalized a significant share of taxation appears accurate. That said, a small private sector did survive, although interviews suggest that these firms often engaged in aggressive tax evasion, owing to cripplingly high tax rates on the private sector and the general hostility of the government to private enterprise.[2]

Within the agricultural sector, taxation retained its character as a transfer from private agents to the government to a significantly greater extent. The new government eliminated earlier agricultural taxes, but replaced them with a land-use tax and an agricultural income tax borne by individual producers, which together yielded roughly 5 per cent of government tax revenue annually, which is a similar proportion to what was collected by the Imperial government.[3] In addition to these official taxes, agricultural producers faced significant and increasing taxation through the system of agricultural price controls. In these cases, precise levels of taxation were hidden in prices, but the possibility of smuggling offered peasant producers both insight into the extent of government taxation and a means of tax evasion (Dercon and Ayalew 1995). Finally, the peasantry faced significant informal exactions by local officials to support the government's military campaigns, and this appears to have gradually contributed to disenchantment with the regime (Clapham 1988: 124–125).[4]

With these caveats in place, and bearing in mind the serious limitations of available data, it remains possible to chart broad revenue patterns over the period. In 1973/1974, government tax revenue had reached a historic high of 6.3 per cent of GDP, while total revenue excluding grants amounted to 7.1 per cent of GDP. By 1979/1980, tax revenue had grown to 8.6 per cent of GDP with total revenues of 10.3 per cent, while – after a period of stagnation – total revenue reached an all-time high of 16 per cent of GDP in 1988/1989. These figures further exclude both on-budget grant revenue and off-budget military assistance from foreign donors, the former of which is reported to have exceeded 3 per cent of GDP in

---

[2] Personal interviews on 25 November 2008 with senior official, Ministry of Revenue, on 30 October 2008 with former State Minister of Finance, on 3 November 2008 with senior tax reform official, Ministry of Revenue, and on 19 November 2008 with senior official, Addis Ababa Chamber of Commerce.
[3] Calculations by the author based on government data and data from the Imperial period provided in Yirko (1994).
[4] Personal interview on 6 November 2008 with leader of major research programme, IFPRI.

5.1 The Derg and the end of the feudal state

several years in the 1980s. Thus, at their height, the fiscal resources available to the Derg regime were more than double the highest levels achieved during the Imperial regime – and also far greater than those that have been available to subsequent governments, as discussed later in this chapter.

These revenue gains came from four primary sources: business income taxes, government investment income, export taxes on coffee, and excise taxes on alcohol. The excise tax on alcohol was simply a case of the government levying a large tax on a good that was easy to tax and faced inelastic demand. There is no evidence that this generated any particular political debate within the broader context of state control. More interesting is the rapid expansion of government investment income, which appears to have been dominated by revenue from state-owned firms and urban housing, although available data does not allow for a specific categorization. Unlike in most countries in the region, state-run enterprises appear to have been reasonably efficient throughout much of the period, thus sustaining their contribution to state investment income. Much of the growth of business income tax revenue similarly flowed from these nationalized firms, with the division between taxation and profits largely a question of accounting. Finally, remaining private firms also certainly contributed somewhat to these totals, although specific information is unavailable (Clapham 1988: 124–125).

The surge in export taxes from coffee reflected a combination of high global prices in the second half of the 1970s and a long-term government decision to reduce the share of the world price that was returned to producers. After world prices returned to normal in the 1980s, the Derg government held the distinction of paying a smaller share of the world price to producers than any other government in Africa. The effect of these policies was that export taxes on coffee increased from 0.6 per cent of GDP in 1974/1975 to a high of 3 per cent of GDP in 1977/1978, before settling at close to 1.5 per cent of GDP until 1985 (Clapham 1988: 184; Dercon and Ayalew 1995; Dercon 2001: 10).

Taking a broader view of government policy, land reform initially implied a marked increase in peasant welfare, as rural producers were freed from the exactions of landlords and the collection of land and agricultural taxes was temporarily virtually eliminated. But it was not long before the government had replaced old burdens with new ones in an effort to finance its programme of industrialization and militarization (Love 1989). This began with the introduction of the agricultural income tax and land use fee, and was followed by the more burdensome exactions imposed through price controls at below world market prices. While implicit taxes on coffee were most important to public revenue, the most notorious example was the forced delivery of quotas of grain at far below market prices (Dercon 2001: 4–6). These formal agricultural exactions were matched by the regular burdens imposed by military conscription, the need for communities to directly support their conscripts and requirements of forced labour on government projects. Overall, the peasantry, which initially was highly supportive of the new regime as a result of land reform, became increasingly disenchanted because of these increasing burdens, although overt protest remained virtually unheard-of given the extensive repressive apparatus of the state (Clapham 1988).

5.1.3 Fiscal dimensions of crisis and collapse, 1988–1991

Amongst the most remarkable aspects of the Derg government is that it succeeded in dramatically extending the power of the state for more than a decade, but then collapsed both suddenly and completely from 1988 onwards. While there had been a longstanding guerrilla war in the North, the Ethiopian army possessed an overwhelming numerical and technical advantage, and appeared firmly in control in mid-1987. Yet, by 1990 the overthrow of the regime appeared inevitable, and it was completed with surprisingly limited bloodshed in 1991 (Clapham 1988).

The obvious explanation for this sudden collapse lay within the military itself. By 1987, morale in the military was declining after a decade of forced conscription and seemingly endless warfare, and this was undoubtedly a factor in explaining the earliest military defeats in late 1987. The situation was exacerbated when these early defeats prompted an attempted military coup, which not only further fractured morale, but also led to the imprisonment or execution of a significant part of the senior military leadership. In the aftermath of these events, the TPLF in particular made large gains against weakened government forces (Clapham 1988).

What this focus on the military overlooks is the broader fiscal collapse of the state and its consequences for the military campaign. The year 1989 marked not only a military turning point, but also a fiscal turning point, as revenue peaked in 1988/1989 and began a staggeringly rapid decline the following year. In 1988/1989, tax revenue stood at 9.7 per cent of GDP and total government revenue, including grants, stood at 19.3 per cent of GDP. Two years later, in 1990/1991, those values had fallen to 7.2 per cent and 11.1 per cent, respectively, with the latter figure likely less than the level of military spending alone during the years of peak spending from 1987/1988 through 1989/1990.[5] Put quite simply,

---

[5] Data on expenditure varies significantly across sources. Bevan (2001) estimates that defence spending over the period of 1986–1987 to 1990–1991 averaged about 9%

the government reached a point at which it could no longer afford to maintain the war effort, which accelerated its defeat.[6]

The fiscal collapse was in part the product of military losses, as lost territory implied lost tax revenue and disrupted transport networks. But this explanation is insufficient in light of the small revenues collected in the North and the massive scale of actual revenue losses. Instead, the collapse of state revenue seems to have emerged from three major factors. First, grants from the Soviet Union declined substantially in 1989–1990 following the fall of the Berlin Wall. Second, the fiscal collapse reflected the accumulated weight of a decade of excessively large deficits and overly demanding taxation. As the fiscal needs of the regime became increasingly onerous in the second half of the 1980s, the government appears to have dramatically increased retention of investment income from state-owned enterprises. This eventually proved unsustainable, crippling those enterprises and government revenue along with them (Bevan and Pradhan 1994; Bevan 2001). Finally, those interviewed suggest that with morale declining and the stability of the government now in question, the population became increasingly unwilling to bear the fiscal exactions of the government and tax compliance declined.[7]

5.2 Liberalization and decentralization under the EPRDF, 1991–2008

In late 1991, the Ethiopian People's Revolutionary Democratic Front (EPRDF) officially seized power (Bevan 1994). The EPRDF was thoroughly dominated by the TPLF but also incorporated other smaller regional parties. Meanwhile, the EPLF, which had been an equal partner in the campaign to oust the Derg, did not join the new government, preferring to focus exclusively on achieving independence for Eritrea. Both the TPLF and the EPLF shared the socialist convictions of the Derg, but they were faced with the practical reality of a country crippled by warfare and deprived of the support it had once received from the Soviet Union. In response to these practical realities, the new

---

of GDP, while Clapham (1988) reports a speech in which Mengistu announced that military spending in 1987–1988 amounted to 15% of GDP. Even allowing for some under-recording of GDP during these years, it is likely that total government revenue in 1990–1991 was below levels of military spending alone in previous years.

[6] Personal interview on 18 November 2008 with economist, IMF and on 3 November 2008 with senior tax reform official, Ministry of Revenue.

[7] Personal interviews on 3 November 2008 with senior tax reform official, Ministry of Revenue, on 25 November 2008 with senior official, Ministry of Revenue, and on 30 October 2008 with former State Minister of Finance.

government quickly entered into partnership with the international community and embarked on a programme of economic and political liberalization.

The new economic reform programme built on reforms adopted by the Derg in its final years, as the previous government had similarly been compelled by crisis to face the need for reform (Clapham 1988; Bevan 1994; Naudé 1998). Meanwhile, the most dramatic step taken by the new government was the rapid promulgation of a new constitution in 1995, which enshrined a high degree of formal decentralization and effectively confirmed Eritrean independence. Building on the highly developed administrative systems put in place by the Derg government, major expenditure tasks were devolved to ten new regional governments. However, the more limited decentralization of revenue collection meant that regional governments continued to rely heavily on block grants from the central government (Chole 1994; Bevan 2001; Gudina 2006). Decentralization reflected the ideological convictions of the TPLF and EPLF, as well as the practical need to resolve the regional tensions unleashed by the aggressively centralizing agenda of the Derg (Tareke 1991: 206). That said, actual policy divergence between the central and regional governments expanded very gradually, owing to the lack of policymaking capacity in the regions and the ability of the central government to exercise political control over regional governments (Bevan 2001; Fiseha 2006).

The change in government in 1991 thus brought with it dramatic economic and political changes. From 1991 until the time of writing the EPRDF has remained relatively firmly entrenched in power, pursuing halting political liberalization while facilitating significant economic liberalization and renewed economic growth. What follows focuses particularly on the fiscal dimension of reform and is organized around several relatively distinct periods in the reform process.

5.2.1 *The EPRDF and economic liberalization, 1992–1998*

With few other options available, the new government embarked on a World Bank and IMF sponsored structural adjustment programme in 1992. Immediate economic reforms included a large devaluation of the Ethiopian Birr, the abolition of most price controls, the liberalization of agricultural marketing, significant reductions in import duties and some financial sector liberalization. The immediate result of the economic reform programme, which was aided by favourable weather, was a sharp improvement in economic growth. That said, reform followed a persistently gradualist approach, consistent with government ideology,

5.2 Liberalization and decentralization under the EPRDF

and some donors were expressing frustration with the pace of reform by 1996 (Abegaz 2001; Dercon 2001).[8]

In many respects the most remarkable aspect of the economic transition was the rapid fiscal recovery. In general, countries emerging from civil war can be expected to achieve fiscal recovery through three channels: expanded international aid, reduced military spending and the recovery of tax revenues. The last two are generally expected to be slow and difficult processes, owing to the cost of demobilizing the military, the complexity of rebuilding administrative capacity and the challenge of establishing norms of tax compliance (Bevan 2001).

Yet Ethiopia succeeded in advancing extremely quickly on all three fronts. Foreign aid exceeded 10 per cent of GDP by 1993, while military spending fell precipitously, from more than 40 per cent of total spending at the height of the civil war to an average of 10.8 per cent of spending from 1991/1992 to 1995/1996 (Bevan 2001). Meanwhile, tax revenues expanded from 5.7 per cent of GDP in 1992/1993 to 7.5 per cent in 1993/1994 and had reached 9.3 per cent of GDP by 1996/1997. Non-tax revenue likewise increased rapidly owing to the recovery of state controlled industries and proceeds from privatization.

Gains in tax revenue, which were primarily from income and trade taxes, are largely attributable to economic recovery, as administrative capacity was limited, administrative reform was gradual and policy reform was largely limited to reducing income tax rates and customs tariffs. Yet, the fact that the tax administration was able to achieve a significant measure of effectiveness was remarkable in the wake of an extended civil war and a profound political and economic transition. It appears attributable to the near total absence of visible political opposition, a strong bureaucratic culture and a surprising degree of administrative continuity in the midst of profound political upheavals. To take a very narrow example, the coordinator of the eventual EPRDF tax reform programme had originally joined the tax administration in the 1960s under Emperor Haile Selassie.[9]

From the perspective of rural citizens, the most significant tax reform of the period was the abolition of marketing and price controls, along with other forms of forced exactions from the peasantry. While precise estimates are difficult, it is clear that the peasantry experienced an immediate and significant improvement in welfare (Dercon 2001).[10] The experience

---

[8] Personal interview on 18 November 2008 with economist, IMF.
[9] Personal interviews on 3 November 2008 with senior tax reform official, Ministry of Revenue, and on 5 November 2008 with senior tax official, Ministry of Revenue.
[10] Personal interview on 6 November 2008 with leader of major research programme, IFPRI.

of agricultural taxation also offers a further illustration of the resilience of bureaucratic and tax norms. The collection of the agricultural income tax and the land use fee had collapsed almost entirely in 1991/1992, but by the following year, under a new government, compliance was as high or higher than ever.[11] Overall, the government was motivated to reduce demands on the peasantry by a combination of ideology, external pressure and a desire to secure the political support of rural citizens.[12]

5.2.2 War with Eritrea, 1998–1999

The highly successful transition to peace and stability was dramatically interrupted by the outbreak of war with newly independent Eritrea in 1998. The conflict was narrowly centred on a land dispute over the newly drawn border, but reflected a deeply rooted disagreement over the extent to which Eritrea would remain closely tied to Ethiopia. Putting aside the complex roots of the conflict (Clapham 1988; Lata 2003), the issue of interest here is the fiscal consequences of the war, which involved a significant military mobilization that lasted until the year 2000 (Addison and Ndikumana 2003: 246–247).

Based on official government data, defence spending increased from 1.5 per cent of GDP in 1996/1997 to 10.3 per cent of GDP in 1999/2000. This, in turn, led total recurrent expenditure to increase from 12.8 per cent of GDP in 1997/1998 to 20.6 per cent of GDP in 1999/2000, as the government increased defence spending while largely sustaining spending on social services at pre-war levels. To pay for this massive increase in recurrent expenditure the government significantly reduced capital expenditures and dramatically increased the size of the fiscal deficit. Capital spending fell from almost 8 per cent of GDP per annum from 1996/1997 through 1998/1999 to only 5 per cent of GDP in 1999/2000. Meanwhile, the budget deficit rose to 7.4 per cent and 9.3 per cent of GDP during the two years of the war, after never previously exceeding 4 per cent under the EPRDF. This vast increase in the deficit reflected not only the increase in defence spending, but also the consequences of the suspension of some donor funding in response to the outbreak of war.

Warfare has historically been a dominant motive for major tax reform, and both theory and intuition supported this expectation as the Ethiopian

---

[11] While the share of GDP accounted for by these two taxes was slightly lower than previously, this was despite the fact that there had been no increase in nominal tax rates despite significant inflation and a large devaluation. Thus levels of compliance had likely increased, or at least remained stable. Authors' calculations based on data from the Ministry of Finance.

[12] Personal interview on 30 October 2008 with former State Minister of Finance.

5.2 Liberalization and decentralization under the EPRDF

deficit grew rapidly (Tilly 1992; Addison, Chowdhury and Murshed 2004). However, while there is some evidence that the war motivated increased attention to revenue mobilization in Ethiopia, this impact appears to have been more modest than may have been expected. During the war, the government introduced a 10 per cent surcharge on imports, while a major tax reform, which is discussed in detail in the next section, was initiated in 2001 and led to relatively large revenue increases (Addison and Ndikumana 2003).[13] Yet, despite the timing of tax reform, senior officials who were involved in the reform programme are adamant that the fiscal pressure created by the war was not the dominant motivation. They point to the fact that extensive background work for the reform programme was initiated prior to the outbreak of war.[14] Moreover, they argue that political infighting within the EPRDF at the end of the war meant that the Minister of Finance was too preoccupied for such a reform program to have taken root if it had not been initiated much earlier (Medhane and Young 2003).[15] In fact, senior officials cite significantly increased pressure from the IMF, as opposed to domestic priorities, as an essential factor in motivating the acceleration of the tax reform programme, although it is possible that the war played a role in making the IMF a more forceful advocate for increased tax collection.[16]

Why, then, did the very large deficits incurred during the war not create greater pressure for tax reform? The answer seems to lie in the fact that the long-term fiscal consequences of the war were significantly more modest than might have been expected, and this is attributable to three major factors. First, the deficits accumulated during the war, while large, were smaller than would otherwise have been the case owing to an unprecedented surge in privatization receipts, which exceeded 5 per cent of total revenue in both years of the war. Second, in 1999 Russia agreed to forgive 80 per cent of the former-Soviet debts incurred by the Derg government as part of a broader agreement with the Paris Club of large lending nations (Martin and Johnson 2005). This amounted to $4.8 billion of debt forgiveness, and ensured that total debt repayments, which would have been expected to expand dramatically because of borrowing during the war, remained manageable. Finally, the end of the war

---

[13] Personal interview on 10 December 2008 with senior official, Federal Ministry of Finance and Economic Development.
[14] Personal interviews on 3 November 2008 with senior tax reform official, Ministry of Revenue and on 5 November 2008 with senior tax official, Ministry of Revenue.
[15] Personal interview on 30 October 2008 with former State Minister of Finance.
[16] Personal interviews on 30 October 2008 with former State Minister of Finance, on 3 November 2008 with senior tax reform official, Ministry of Revenue, and on 5 November 2008 with senior tax official, Ministry of Revenue.

witnessed the rapid resumption of high levels of foreign aid, thus helping to reduce fiscal pressure on the government.[17]

5.2.3 Accelerated reform, 2000–2004

The period following the war was one of accelerated reform, and this was broadly attributable to the combination of changing priorities within the TPLF leadership and a more assertive stance by donors. The government drew praise from international observers for re-energizing the process of economic reform and continuing to strengthen the role of regional governments. At the same time, the government began to focus more heavily on infrastructure investment and industry-specific incentives as it sought to pursue an economic model based on the experience of fast growing economies in East Asia. Finally, political liberalization advanced significantly, as a relatively vocal opposition emerged and it appeared that the 2005 national elections would be the first genuinely competitive national elections in Ethiopia's history.

The pace of reform was equally rapid with respect to taxation, as plans initiated in the late 1990s were progressively rolled out beginning in 2001. A combination of administrative and policy reform contributed to the growth of tax revenue from 9.2 per cent of GDP in 1999/2000 to 12.1 per cent of GDP in 2003/2004. This revenue growth was given a further boost by a substantial increase in trade taxes in 2003/2004, driven in part by rising imports to supply growing infrastructure investment.[18]

Administrative reform included the creation of a Ministry of Revenue that enjoyed greater autonomy from the Ministry of Finance, internal reorganization, the introduction of Taxpayer Identification Numbers, the introduction of a basic IT system and a new emphasis on taxpayer outreach and education.[19] Notable for its absence was any effort to significantly increase salaries, as had occurred in many other countries in the region, and this reflected a commitment to maintaining established norms of equity within the civil service.[20] Given the conformist bureaucratic culture in the country (Tekle 1990: 45) implementation was

---

[17] Personal interviews on 19 November 2008 with senior economic researcher and economic advisor to the President and on 10 December 2008 with senior official, Federal Ministry of Finance and Economic Development.

[18] Personal interview on 10 December 2008 with senior official, Federal Ministry of Finance and Economic Development.

[19] Personal interviews on 3 November 2008 with senior tax reform official, Ministry of Revenue and on 5 November 2008 with senior tax official, Ministry of Revenue.

[20] Personal interview on 5 November 2008 with senior tax official, Ministry of Revenue and on 30 October 2008 with former State Minister of Finance.

5.2 Liberalization and decentralization under the EPRDF 175

predictably both gradual and relatively without controversy.[21] The impact of the administrative changes, and overall increasing attention to tax administration, appears to have been mixed. There were substantial jumps in both trade and sales tax collection quite immediately, but income tax collection stagnated, aside from a brief spike in revenue in 2001/2002 that resulted from a tax amnesty programme.

The period also witnessed three major policy initiatives: the introduction of a value-added tax (VAT), the reform and expansion of the presumptive tax system, and the introduction of a withholding tax on imports. The most straightforward was the withholding tax on imports, an administratively simple means to compel compliance with existing income taxes, although it does not appear to have had a particularly large revenue impact. It is interesting that it does not appear to have prompted any effective resistance from businesses despite the fact that it effectively enforced the prepayment of a share of income taxes.[22]

The implementation of the VAT was designed to be gradual, owing to the limits of administrative capacity.[23] Beginning 1 January 2003, the tax administration initially targeted larger firms as it gradually expanded the tax net. Revenue gains during the first two years were meaningful, although not spectacular, as overall collection increased by between 5 per cent and 10 per cent relative to the former sales tax, with most of the gains occurring through collections on imports. While there were some complaints from taxpayers, especially related to the penalties for evasion, the implementation experienced little political controversy (Teffera 2004).[24] One of the most notable features of the new VAT was that it provided significantly fewer exemptions for basic goods than the previous sales tax, thus increasing the tax burden for low-income consumers (Munoz and Cho 2004). Yet this too does not appear to have generated any significant political response.[25] The largest controversy was over the distribution of revenue and administrative responsibility between the regional and central governments, with the central government ultimately retaining the bulk of revenue as well as primary responsibility for administering the tax (Yesegat 2008).[26]

---

[21] Personal interviews on 5 November 2008 with senior tax official, Ministry of Revenue, on 25 November 2008 with senior official, Ministry of Revenue, on 3 November 2008 with senior tax reform official, Ministry of Revenue, and on 18 November 2008 with senior official, Ministry of Revenue.
[22] Personal interviews on 3 November 2008 with senior tax reform official, Ministry of Revenue and on 30 October 2008 with former State Minister of Finance.
[23] Ibid., and interview on 5 November 2008 with senior tax official, Ministry of Revenue.
[24] Ibid.   [25] Ibid.
[26] Personal interviews on 28 October 2008 with senior official, Oromia Bureau of Revenue, on 25 November 2008 with former senior official, Tigray Bureau of Revenue, and on 20 January 2009 with international tax advisor to the regional governments.

Despite the attention given to the new VAT, it was the new presumptive tax regime that proved to be both the most important reform in revenue terms and the only measure to generate significant political controversy. Under Ethiopian law, firms were divided into three categories based on turnover: Category A was more than 500,000 Birr, Category B was between 100,000 and 500,000 Birr, and Category C was less than 100,000 Birr. Category C firms were not expected to maintain detailed financial accounts, while many Category B firms similarly did not do so. Instead of being subject to income tax and the VAT, these firms were required to pay a presumptive tax on income and a 2 per cent tax on turnover. Both were deemed to imply a reduced compliance burden, as they only required measuring total turnover. In the relatively more complex case of presumptive taxation, tax liability was assessed by estimating turnover, applying a predetermined industry-specific profit rate and then taxing the resultant profits at the standard income tax rate.

This basic system had existed prior to 2001 but had been weakly enforced in many areas owing to a lack of government commitment and problems with the system for assessing turnover, under which individual tax assessors estimated turnover on an annual basis. Under the new system, local Tax Assessment Committees, that included both government officials and local business representatives, were charged with estimating turnover every three years, in hopes of thereby increasing coverage and reducing corruption and abuse (Jordan 1999). More importantly, the regional governments, which were responsible for implementing the new version of the tax, dramatically increased enforcement.[27]

The result of the new system was that income and profit tax collection in the regions increased dramatically from 1.16 per cent of national GDP in 1999/2000 to 1.73 per cent in 2003/2004. Tax officials are adamant that the new system also succeeded in reducing levels of arbitrariness, abuse and corruption. Yet the new system became the subject of significant taxpayer unhappiness, as tax liabilities increased dramatically, more than doubling in many cases. While these increases were generally justified according to the letter of the law, the suddenness of the increases and the lack of explanation from government fed public unhappiness and bred mistrust, despite the creation of the Tax Assessment Committees (Warner, Ergano, Bekele and Moges 2005). Moreover, the

---

[27] Personal interviews on 28 October 2008 with senior official, Oromia Bureau of Revenue, on 25 November 2008 with former senior official, Tigray Bureau of Revenue, on 2 December 2008 with senior official, Tigray Bureau of Revenue, on 21 October 2008 with professor of economics, University of Addis Ababa, on 4 December 2008 with former senior official, Amhara Bureau of Revenue, and on 4 December 2008 with senior official, Tax Audit and Enforcement, Amhara Bureau of Revenue.

predetermined profit rates used to calculate tax liabilities were, by the admission of many tax officials, excessively high, and while this had been relatively inconsequential when implementation was lax, it became crippling for many business as the government tightened enforcement. Such was the level of public unhappiness in the Amhara region in particular that the government began studies in 2004 to evaluate the fairness of the assigned profit rates.[28]

5.2.4 Taxation and the 2005 elections

The 2005 national elections were expected to be a watershed moment in the process of political liberalization, as the ruling party had permitted the emergence of an organized and vocal opposition for the first time. In practice, the election became a moment of renewed political repression. While most observers believe that the ruling party legitimately received the largest number of votes nationally, unexpectedly strong opposition in Addis Ababa and the three largest regions led the government to resort to electoral fraud to guarantee its dominance. A significant part of the opposition opted for public demonstrations and a decision to boycott parliament. The government responded with widespread arrests and the violent disruption of public gatherings. As of the end of 2014, the political atmosphere remained highly repressive, with few signs that subsequent elections would offer the possibility of significant contestation (Lyons 2006; Arriola 2008).

The failed elections had major consequences for taxation. In the run-up to the elections, the government sought to buy support through the provision of targeted tax concessions. While this general point was made almost universally in interviews, it is difficult to gather more specific information on this topic owing to the reluctance of officials to discuss potentially politicized issues.[29] However, two examples were repeatedly

---

[28] Personal interviews on 28 October 2008 with senior revenue official, Federal Ministry of Finance and Economic Development, on 5 November 2008 with senior tax official, Ministry of Revenue, on 28 October 2008 with senior official, Oromia Bureau of Revenue, on 21 October 2008 with professor of economics, University of Addis Ababa, on 4 December 2008 with former senior official, Amhara Bureau of Revenue, and on 4 December 2008 with senior official, Tax Audit and Enforcement, Amhara Bureau of Revenue.

[29] Personal interviews on 21 October 2008 with senior official working on budgeting and IT reform, Federal Ministry of Finance and Economic Development, on 19 November 2008 with Opposition Member of Parliament, on 10 December 2008 with leading opposition political party figure and former member of Parliament, on 10 December 2008 with senior official, Federal Ministry of Finance and Economic Development, on 19 November 2008 with senior economic researcher and economic advisor to the President, and on 21 October 2008 with two professors of economics, University of Addis Ababa.

mentioned. The first was the provision of a growing range of trade tax exemptions to favoured sectors. The government plausibly attributes these decisions to an increasingly interventionist industrial strategy, but some well-placed individuals argue that there was also a political motive.[30] It is certainly clear that there was a significant fall in trade tax collection in the year preceding the election, despite continued increases in imports.

The second, and more widely acknowledged, example was a decision by the government to suspend certain types of fines in Addis Ababa, where the opposition was strongest, including the high profile abolishment of various fines and arrears affecting taxi drivers.[31] Addis Ababa was the most tightly contested political district in the country, and as a local taxi driver explained, "the government told us that they would eliminate these fines if the taxi drivers would vote for them." Others describe the measures in equally stark terms: they were "one of the strategies to buy people."[32] Ultimately, there is a general feeling that these measures did relatively little to secure additional support for the government, as the tax concessions were perceived to be short-term and opportunistic.[33] But while the concessions are viewed as having been of modest practical importance, these pre-election concessions indicate that the government perceived a meaningful link between taxation and its political popularity, even in the absence of visible public opposition to taxation.

The election results had a much more profound impact on tax collection, as the results alerted the government more unambiguously to its growing unpopularity. While the government turned to political repression in the wake of the elections, it also took highly visible steps to try to shore up its popularity outside the capital. The government sent officials throughout the regions to hold public consultations about the roots of public opposition. Despite their clear limitations, these forums appear to have at least provided some opportunities for public feedback, and one of

---

[30] Personal interviews on 10 December 2008 with senior official, Federal Ministry of Finance and Economic Development, and on 19 November 2008 with senior economic researcher and economic advisor to the President.

[31] Personal interviews on 10 December 2008 with leading opposition political party figure and former member of Parliament, on 19 November 2008 with Opposition Member of Parliament, and on 6 November 2008 with leader of major research programme, IFPRI. In the particular area of taxes on taxis, this narrative is confirmed widely by taxi drivers themselves. Specific informants made reference to the idea that the government effectively granted widespread tax amnesties for arrears in the same year, but it was impossible to confirm this claim with absolute certainty owing to the political sensitivity of the issues.

[32] Personal interview on 19 November 2008 with Opposition Member of Parliament.

[33] Ibid., and interview on 10 December 2008 with leading opposition political party figure and former Member of Parliament.

5.2 Liberalization and decentralization under the EPRDF 179

the issues that emerged strongly was public unhappiness with taxation, and particularly with the new presumptive tax system.[34]

The government immediately responded with a dramatic reduction in presumptive taxation, achieved by way of a sharp reduction in the presumptive profit rates used to calculate tax liabilities. Although presumptive taxation is formally under the control of regional governments, the reduction in profit rates was nationwide, and appears to have been heavily dictated by the central government.[35] While the government had initiated an internal review of presumptive profit rates a year earlier, there is widespread agreement that both the suddenness and the depth of the rate reductions were politically motivated.[36] This view is supported by the fact that rate cuts were frequently accompanied by significant efforts to improve public dialogue and consultation surrounding the tax, while several regions also implemented a corresponding reduction in agricultural tax rates in order to maintain horizontal equity.[37] While many tax administrators believed that the original profit rates had been too high, they were equally opposed to the sharp cuts, which severely undermined regional government tax revenue.[38] Presumptive tax collection immediately declined from 1.67 per cent to 1.24 per cent of GDP and collection of rural land use fees declined from 0.48 per cent to 0.17 per cent of GDP. These losses amounted to almost 25 per cent of regional tax collection, thus generating a significant decline in regional fiscal welfare (Warner, Ergano, Bekele and Moges 2005).

In considering the impact of the tax changes following the elections, what is perhaps most striking is their somewhat contradictory character.

---

[34] Personal interviews on 4 December 2008 with senior official, Tax Audit and Enforcement, Amhara Bureau of Revenue, on 4 December 2008 with former senior official, Amhara Bureau of Revenue, and on 10 December 2008 with leading opposition political party figure and former member of Parliament.

[35] Personal interviews on 28 October 2008 with senior official, Oromia Bureau of Revenue, on 20 January 2009 with international tax advisor to the regional governments, and on 4 December 2008 with former senior official, Amhara Bureau of Revenue.

[36] Personal interviews on 28 October 2008 with senior revenue official, Federal Ministry of Finance and Economic Development, on 30 October 2008 with former State Minister of Finance, and on 3 November 2008 with senior tax reform official, Ministry of Revenue.

[37] Personal interviews on 28 October 2008 with senior official, Oromia Bureau of Revenue, on 4 December 2008 with senior official, Tax Audit and Enforcement, Amhara Bureau of Revenue, on 20 January 2009 with international tax advisor to the regional governments, and on 10 December 2008 with leading opposition political party figure and former member of Parliament.

[38] Personal interviews on 25 November 2008 with former senior official, Tigray Bureau of Revenue, on 28 October 2008 with senior official, Oromia Bureau of Revenue, on 28 October 2008 with senior revenue official, Federal Ministry of Finance and Economic Development, on 5 November 2008 with senior tax official, Ministry of Revenue, and on 20 January 2009 with international tax advisor to the regional governments.

On the one hand, there is little doubt that the decision to reduce tax rates reflected a government desire to garner public support, as the tax cuts were fiscally significant and were spread across the majority of the low and middle-income population. On the other hand, there are some reasons to believe that the changes in taxation were simultaneously an effort by the government to punish its opponents and centralize political control. Most widely accepted is the belief that the reduction in regional taxes was designed in part to make the regional governments more reliant on transfers from the central government, and thus to reduce their independence (Warner, Ergano, Bekele and Moges 2005). Having experienced unexpected political resistance, the central government was reasserting its control. A second issue lies in the fact that the tax changes, while reducing taxes across the board, also made regional tax systems more regressive. Changes to the presumptive tax regime reduced the overall tax burden on mid-sized (Category B) firms much more substantially than the tax burden on small-firms (Category C).[39] In similar fashion, the changes in agricultural taxation generally reduced collection from larger farms most dramatically, while the benefits to smaller farms were comparatively modest (Warner, Beyede, Asaminew and Sibhatu 2005; Warner, Ergano, Bekele and Moges 2005). In both cases, some observers believe that these redistributive shifts were intentional, based on the rationale that the government wished to punish the poor, who were more likely to support the opposition (Arriola 2008). This possibility is a reminder that in some cases governments may respond to public opposition to taxation not only with compromises, but also through implicit or explicit threats.

5.2.5 *Post-election revenue shortfalls, 2005–2007*

While changes in regional taxation were the most explicit tax event of the post-election period, they were part of a much broader revenue downturn that appears to be attributable to the elections. Overall tax revenue declined significantly from 12.1 per cent of GDP in 2003/2004 to 10.1 per cent in 2006/2007, thus reversing many of the gains of previous years. Declining revenue resulted from a continuous decline in direct tax

---

[39] While the change in presumptive tax rates applied equally to both medium and small firms, the aggregate effect of this change was to make the taxation of firms more regressive, because SMEs are subject to two major taxes: a flat 2% tax on turnover and the progressive presumptive tax on profits. By reducing the relative importance of the presumptive tax, the progressivity of the business tax system as a whole was sharply reduced, implying that much of the benefit of the tax change flowed to relatively better off mid-sized businesses.

5.2 Liberalization and decentralization under the EPRDF 181

collection, stagnation in domestic VAT collection, and a marked decline in the collection of import VAT and customs duties. While the revenue downturn undoubtedly had multiple causes, interviews suggest that it was at least in part the result of government reluctance to crack down on tax evasion in the aftermath of the elections.[40]

In accounting for revenue performance that fell short of expectations, observers point in part to explanations grounded in technical barriers to collection. One prominent issue is the simple lack of funding for tax administration. In the case of the VAT, which is indicative of a broader pattern, Teffera (2004) points to the fact that funding for administration was estimated to be less than 0.8 per cent of total collection, which is significantly below the level of 1–2 per cent recommended by international tax experts, and provides limited resources for audit functions in particular (Yesegat 2008: 14). While committed administrative effort was sufficient to overcome limited resources for a time, administrators argue that the lack of capacity became an increasingly severe problem as the number of taxpayers increased.[41] Yesegat (2008) also points to problems related to the distribution of administrative responsibility between the central and regional governments, particularly after regional governments were granted greater responsibility for VAT collection beginning in 2004. Finally, the period in question witnessed a significant increase in tax incentives and exemptions, which further helps to account for falling rates of VAT and trade tax collection.[42]

While such technical explanations are important, the magnitude of the revenue decline demands consideration of political factors. At a basic level, the expansion of exemptions, while officially motivated by the need to provide incentives for investment and growth, almost certainly also embodied political motives. More strikingly, a senior tax official explains that "after the election they told us you cannot take all the people to court... [as a result] taxpayers got relaxed... they knew that we were

---

[40] Personal interviews on 30 October 2008 with former State Minister of Finance, on 3 November 2008 with senior tax reform official, Ministry of Revenue, on 7 November 2008 with private sector senior accountant, former official of VAT Department, Ministry of Finance and Economic Development, on 25 November 2008 with senior official, Ministry of Revenue, and on 19 November 2008 with Opposition Member of Parliament.
[41] Personal interviews on 25 November 2008 with senior official, Ministry of Revenue, on 5 November 2008 with senior tax official, Ministry of Revenue, and on 3 November 2008 with senior tax reform official, Ministry of Revenue.
[42] Personal interviews on 10 December 2008 with senior official, Federal Ministry of Finance and Economic Development, on 5 November 2008 with donor official, private sector development programme, and on 19 November 2008 with senior official, Addis Ababa Chamber of Commerce.

not in a position to enforce it the way we did before."[43] This reduced aggressiveness of enforcement is consistent with the government response to unhappiness with the presumptive tax, and offers a more complete explanation for the sharp fall in tax collection.

In addition to these factors, there is also a widely held belief that the government was attempting to extend its political control over the tax administration. In the aftermath of the election, a major administrative reorganization was ushered in as part of a broader government programme of Business Process Reengineering. The domestic taxation and customs departments were brought together under the Federal Inland Revenue and Customs Authority, which replaced the Ministry of Revenue. This was accompanied by efforts to merge activities that were being duplicated, reorganize business processes along functional lines, reassign large portions of the existing staff, and train a large group of recent university graduates to join the administration. The motivation for the programme was largely technical, but it is also widely believed to have had political undertones, as the government sought to reassert bureaucratic control after the elections. Regardless of the actual politicization of the reform programme, the impression of politicization appears to have made administrators particularly cautious, which, along with the general disruption caused by rapid and centrally mandated reorganization, weakened the effectiveness of administration.[44]

While officials are very guarded in discussing the impact of the elections on the activities of government, the overall body of evidence suggests strongly that political considerations must figure prominently in explaining falling tax revenue. It seems relatively clear that businesses took advantage of the reticence of the government to aggressively pursue tax evaders, and that political turmoil undermined the effectiveness of administration. It is more difficult to ascertain whether political alienation reduced the willingness of taxpayers to comply with taxation, but sharply declining revenue in the absence of a clear explanation is certainly indicative of that possibility. While political opposition was sharply repressed in the aftermath of the election, perhaps the strongest evidence of quiet resistance to taxation lies in the fact that the government avoided adopting significant new tax revenue measures despite a marked

---

[43] Personal interview on 3 November 2008 with senior tax reform official, Ministry of Revenue.
[44] Personal interviews on 25 November 2008 with senior official, Ministry of Revenue, on 21 October 2008 with senior official working on budgeting and IT reform, Federal Ministry of Finance and Economic Development, on 13 November 2008 with World Bank official, public financial management project, and on 14 November 2008 with donor official working on tax capacity building.

5.2 Liberalization and decentralization under the EPRDF 183

deterioration in its fiscal position, and significant external pressure for reform.[45]

5.2.6 Renewed revenue focus, 2008–2009

Following a period of declining tax collection after the elections, the government slowly began to refocus attention on revenue issues from the beginning of 2007. The profit rates used for calculating presumptive tax liabilities were increased, although to a level still well below that which existed before the election, while all of the highland regions of the country also increased agricultural tax rates during this period.[46] More generally, the highest levels of government began to pay increasing attention to taxation. The first highly visible step was the 2007 reintroduction of the import surtax, initially introduced during the war with Eritrea.[47] In late 2008, the government issued an official proclamation about the need to increase collection from large and small taxpayers alike, with a special focus on the largest 13,000 taxpayers. At the same time, Parliament passed new laws that, at least in principle, significantly expanded the power of the tax administration to use penalties, coercion and required withholding in order to collect the VAT.[48]

This resurgence in government attention to taxation from 2007 onwards seems to have reflected changes in the political environment and the deteriorating finances of the government. Politically, the turmoil surrounding the elections had subsided, and more importantly, the opposition had been decimated. With the opposition weak and divided, and public discontent largely silenced, the government appears to have felt more secure in seeking to reinvigorate tax collection.[49] Meanwhile, external pressure from donors for increased tax collection had been mounting in response to significant fiscal deficits. The Ethiopian government had developed a reputation for resisting donor demands in the belief that aid would ultimately be forthcoming regardless. However, there is

---

[45] Personal interviews on 18 November 2008 with economist, IMF, on 13 November 2008 with World Bank official, public financial management project, and on 19 November 2008 with senior economic researcher and economic advisor to the President.
[46] Personal interviews on 28 October 2008 with senior official, Oromia Bureau of Revenue and on 30 October 2008 with former State Minister of Finance.
[47] Personal interview on 10 December 2008 with senior official, Federal Ministry of Finance and Economic Development.
[48] Personal interviews on 30 October 2008 with former State Minister of Finance and on 3 November 2008 with senior tax reform official, Ministry of Revenue.
[49] Personal interview on 30 October 2008 with former State Minister of Finance.

evidence that donors were becoming more assertive at the same time that reduced tax revenue was making the government more dependent on aid revenues.

Ultimately, the most dramatic revenue measure taken during this period related not to tax per se, but its mirror image: the removal of long-standing fuel subsidies, particularly for kerosene, estimated to have been worth about US$800 million.[50] Whereas increases in fuel prices in Ghana have historically been a significant trigger for public mobilization, such public mobilization did not, unsurprisingly, emerge in Ethiopia in the face of government repression. That said, the removal of the fuel subsidy did receive greater public attention than other tax changes, and elicited a degree of public anger, reflecting its visibility and broader incidence. Seeking to minimize any public response, the government announced that the savings from removing the subsidy would be put towards reducing rapidly rising food prices, through a combination of grain purchases and removing the VAT and turnover tax on certain food products (IMF 2008; Admassie 2013).[51] That said, it is unclear whether the informal earmarking of newly available revenues for reductions in food prices was a direct response to pressure emerging in response to increased fuel prices. Many suspect, instead, that food subsidies were planned anyway, and that the government merely used them as a convenient justification for the fuel price increase. Meanwhile, senior officials similarly question whether the combined value of new subsidies and reduced taxes on foodstuffs was equivalent to the significant revenue gains accruing to the government from the removal of fuel subsidies, although detailed data is not available.[52]

In any case, despite a seemingly genuine government commitment to rebuilding tax collection, actual increases in tax revenue were slow to arrive. Instead, tax collection continued to decline despite the government's apparent efforts, reaching a low of 8.6 per cent of GDP in 2008/2009. It was only in 2009/2010 that tax revenue began to increase, and only in 2012/2013 that tax collection had returned to the levels achieved prior to the 2005 elections. The government's struggles in seeking to reinvigorate tax collection after the elections appear to have reflected the continued disruption caused by administrative reorganization, but also problems in achieving compliance and enforcement amidst

---

[50] www.reuters.com/article/2008/10/04/us-ethiopia-fuel-idUSTRE49318S20081004.
[51] Personal interview on 30 October 2008 with former State Minister of Finance, on 18 November 2008 with economist, IMF, and on 25 November 2008 with senior official, Ministry of Revenue.
[52] Personal interview on 30 October 2008 with former State Minister of Finance.

a lack of popular support. While there was little space for popular mobilization against the government after 2005, patterns of tax collection thus appear to have in part reflected quieter forms of resistance.[53]

5.3 The dynamics of regional government taxation

Having explored broad trends in national and regional taxation, it is useful to turn briefly to exploring divergent tax trends across regions within Ethiopia to further highlight key features of the political economy of taxation in the country. The motivation for doing so lies in the fact that Ethiopia is relatively unique in sub-Saharan Africa in the extent of fiscal decentralization. Regional governments collect upwards of 25 per cent of total government revenue, with the most important revenue coming from the taxation of SMEs, land use fees, regional sales and excise taxes and a variety of non-tax fees and levies. As already noted, changes in regional taxation can have a significant impact on overall levels of tax collection, while comparisons across regions can correspondingly hold important lessons.

With this in mind, what follows highlights a series of additional insights offered by comparing developments in Ethiopia's two most influential regions: Amhara and Tigray. Amhara has been the site of the most pronounced tax controversies in recent years, while it has historically been the centre of economic and political power in the country. Meanwhile, Tigray is home to the TPLF, which dominates the ruling EPRDF party, and has thus emerged as the centre of national political power since 1991. Divergent outcomes across these two regions are indicative of patterns that are repeated elsewhere, and shed further light on four major issues: the centrality of political allegiance to tax compliance, the local nature of tax politics, the importance of implementation strategies and the politics of land taxation. Collectively, these features of regional taxation offer additional insights into the political dynamics surrounding taxation and the potential for tax bargaining.

5.3.1 Political loyalty and tax performance

Theory predicts that citizens who feel a stronger connection to their governments will be more likely to comply with taxation, and that administrators that feel greater loyalty to the government will be more effective (Lieberman 2002; Kasara 2005). This prediction is borne out at the

---

[53] Ibid., and interview on 28 October 2008 with senior official, Oromia Bureau of Revenue, and on 25 November 2008 with senior official, Ministry of Revenue.

national level by declining tax revenue in the wake of the 2005 elections, and is similarly highlighted by comparing the Tigray and Amhara regions. Through its domination of the EPRDF, the Tigray-based TPLF effectively dominates all of the regional governments. And, as expected, Tigray appears, within the limits of available data, to be the most effective tax-collecting region in the country.[54] Moreover, anecdotal evidence suggests overwhelmingly that local leaders and politicians in the region are uniquely successful in mobilizing non-tax community resources for local development projects.[55] By contrast, the Amhara region was the centre of power in the country during the later Imperial period but is now politically dominated by the EPRDF. This has led to a high degree of resistance to the ruling party, as reflected in relatively strong electoral support for the opposition in the 2005 election (Arriola 2008). This tension is reflected in patterns of taxation, as the Amhara region has been a relatively poor tax collector throughout much of the period since 1991. This began to change with the arrival in 2000 of a new regional governor who was committed to improving tax collection, but the region subsequently became the site of the most virulent opposition to the new presumptive tax regime.[56]

5.3.2 Government taxation versus community contributions

One of the more remarkable features of tax collection in both regions, and particularly in Tigray, is the widespread belief that citizens are more willing to contribute significant resources – both cash and in kind – to locally controlled community development projects than to the payment of taxes. Even more striking is the belief that local politicians are likely to encourage citizens to contribute to such projects rather than paying their taxes, thus eroding the political will for more aggressive tax collection.[57] At a general level, this seems to point to the absence of

---

[54] Personal interviews on 25 November 2008 with former senior official, Tigray Bureau of Revenue, and on 20 January 2009 with international tax advisor to the regional governments.

[55] Personal interviews on 2 December 2008 with senior official, Tigray Bureau of Revenue, on 25 November 2008 with former senior official, Tigray Bureau of Revenue, and on 21 October 2008 with professor of economics, University of Addis Ababa.

[56] Personal interviews on 4 December 2008 with former senior official, Amhara Bureau of Revenue, 4 December 2008 with senior official, Tax Audit and Enforcement, Amhara Bureau of Revenue, on 20 January 2009 with international tax advisor to the regional governments, and on 3 November 2008 with senior tax reform official, Ministry of Revenue.

[57] Personal interviews on 2 December 2008 with senior official, Tigray Bureau of Revenue, on 25 November 2008 with former senior official, Tigray Bureau of Revenue, and on 21 October 2008 with professor of economics, University of Addis Ababa.

5.3 The dynamics of regional government taxation

confidence amongst taxpayers that tax payments to the regional government will result in corresponding local benefits, and this pattern of reliance on community initiatives funded by voluntary contributions is repeated elsewhere in sub-Saharan Africa (Chazan 1983; Guyer 1992).[58]

The fact that Tigray is particularly well known for its community development projects is rooted in history. Tigray has long maintained a strong sense of regional and sub-regional independence (Levine 1965: 2). Local rulers were very autonomous throughout Ethiopia's long history and often displayed limited loyalty to the centre in times of turmoil. More recently, Tigray was persistently resistant to Haile Selassie's rule, as exemplified by the *weyane* rebellion, and was the site of continuous guerrilla warfare against the Derg regime. The guerrilla war fostered not only a sense of regional autonomy but also a culture of self-reliance, and it is this element of local history that seems to explain the high level of community contributions as well as the preference for locally controlled community development projects. While the rise to power of the TPLF has encouraged a willingness to comply with regional taxes as well (Young 1997), continued reliance on local development projects even in the ruling party's home region is reflective of significant distrust of government and of the difficulties of fostering productive bargaining around formal taxes where trust is limited.

5.3.3 Reform strategies and public responses

One of the most dramatic differences in taxation between the two regions is their divergent experience of the new presumptive tax regime. Despite the absence of public protest, which has rarely been a feature of Ethiopian politics, the presumptive tax regime became hugely unpopular in the Amhara region and a political liability for the government. By contrast, the new tax was introduced with little public opposition in Tigray.[59] While the generally more cooperative relationship between government and citizens in Tigray played some role, those involved strenuously point to the importance of implementation strategy. Amhara was the first region to implement the new tax and did so particularly aggressively, leading

---

[58] In a more recent study from Sierra Leone, Jibao, Prichard and van den Boogaard (2014) find much more positive popular opinion of informal taxes paid to community development organizations as compared to formal taxes paid to the government.
[59] Personal interviews on 4 December 2008 with senior official, Tax Audit and Enforcement, Amhara Bureau of Revenue, on 21 October 2008 with professor of economics, University of Addis Ababa, on 4 December 2008 with former senior official, Amhara Bureau of Revenue, and on 20 January 2009 with international tax advisor to the regional governments.

businesses to frequently experience 100–300 per cent increases in their tax payments. Public opposition became particularly acute because the change was sudden and lacked transparency. So severe was public opposition that after the election the regional government provided tax refunds, amounting to a reported 11 million birr (US$1.1 million), to all of those taxpayers who had been over taxed relative to the reduced rates introduced in 2005.[60] By contrast, tax administrators in Tigray emphasize their explicit and successful efforts to avoid Amhara's fate by introducing the reforms slowly, engaging in extensive public dialogue, and involving important stakeholders like the local Chamber of Commerce.[61] As was the case in Kenya, it appears that gradualist reform strategies have served to minimize popular resistance, while fostering incremental improvements in accountability, whereas more abrupt tax increases have been more likely to prompt change through confrontation between taxpayers and governments.

5.3.4 The politics of agricultural and land taxation

Moving away from a strict comparison of Amhara and Tigray, it is useful to conclude this discussion of regional government taxation by looking in more detail at the experience of agricultural and land taxes. In most countries in sub-Saharan Africa agricultural and land taxes are poorly enforced, owing to the lack of administrative capacity and the likelihood of aggressive public resistance. By contrast, successive Ethiopian governments have maintained an extensive system of land taxation and, remarkably, this system does not appear to have been a source of significant contemporary political conflict.

The absence of political conflict is, undoubtedly, partly explained by political repression and the inherited legacy of government control. At the simplest level peasants dare not challenge the government, which controls access to nationalized rural land.[62] This implicit connection between tax payments and land rights dates to Haile Selassie's tax reform efforts in the 1940s. A tax officer from the Imperial government explains that "peasants thought that the tax slip was for the land – that this slip

---

[60] Personal interviews on 4 December 2008 with former senior official, Amhara Bureau of Revenue and on 4 December 2008 with senior official, Tax Audit and Enforcement, Amhara Bureau of Revenue.

[61] Personal interviews on 21 October 2008 with professor of economics, University of Addis Ababa and on 25 November 2008 with former senior official, Tigray Bureau of Revenue.

[62] Personal interview on 23 October 2008 with former Member of Parliament under EPRDF.

recognized their control of the land. So they were willing to pay."⁶³ This mindset has persisted to the present, despite changes in government and land tenure rules. Reporting the results of a survey of peasant farmers, Kassahun (2006: 19) explains that "all responding farmers confirmed that paying land tax is unquestionable. The annual payment implicitly grants land security where their name as land owner is updated on the government's master document."

Related to this connection between tax payment and land rights is a broader sense that under Haile Selassie land and agricultural taxes became a part of peasant efforts to claim rights as citizens. Zewde (1991: 192) has argued that as a result of the expansion of taxation, "the term *gabbar* [peasant] lost its exploitative associations and assumed the more respectable connotation of taxpayer." An official from the period explains that paying tax "was a matter of existence," as it allowed the peasantry to connect themselves to the Emperor and the national community.⁶⁴ Another official explains that during the reign of Haile Selassie, "rural people carried their tax receipt like an identity card."⁶⁵ While these officials believe that this connection between tax payments and citizenship has been eroded over time, there remains a clear view amongst many observers both that rural people continue to see a connection between taxation, land right and citizenship and that these connections play a role in limiting rural resistance to taxation.⁶⁶

5.4 Taxation, responsiveness and accountability in contemporary Ethiopia

Having presented this extended narrative of the political economy of taxation in Ethiopia since 1974, two key analytical questions remain. First, does this narrative provide evidence that tax bargaining has played a role in the expansion of responsiveness and accountability? Second, what can we say about the role of Ethiopia's particular historical, social, political and economic characteristics in shaping patterns of tax bargaining?

---

[63] Personal interview on 3 November 2008 with senior tax reform official, Ministry of Revenue.
[64] Ibid.
[65] Personal interview on 4 December 2008 with former senior official, Amhara Bureau of Revenue.
[66] Personal interview on 3 November 2008 with senior tax reform official, Ministry of Revenue, on 4 December 2008 with former senior official, Amhara Bureau of Revenue, on 23 October 2008 with former member of Parliament under EPRDF, on 19 November 2008 with opposition member of Parliament, and on 25 November 2008 with senior official, Ministry of Revenue.

Ultimately, the evidence suggests that tax bargaining has played a comparatively small role in shaping political outcomes in Ethiopia: not only has direct tax bargaining been rare, but taxation also has played little role in encouraging the growth of civil society. Moreover, while there is evidence that taxpayers have engaged in tax resistance when successive governments have been particularly unpopular, the political consequences have been more muted than in either Ghana or Kenya. This finding is not entirely surprising: social, economic and political conditions in Ethiopia all appear to militate against an important role for tax bargaining. Important factors include the highly autocratic character of politics, the weakness of domestic economic forces, the heavy reliance of the government on foreign aid and historical and cultural contexts that seems likely to discourage tax conflicts. However, we do nonetheless observe a handful of politically significant episodes of both direct and indirect tax bargaining. That this is true in spite of all of the factors that would seem to militate against it causes those episodes to take on greater analytical significance.

With this in mind, the discussion to follow proceeds in two parts: the first section reviews the relative absence of direct tax bargaining and of public engagement around tax issues more generally, while the second section considers the more limited evidence of both direct and indirect tax bargaining. This sets the stage for a more detailed discussion of the contextual factors that appear to have shaped the comparatively limited potential for tax bargaining in Ethiopia.

5.4.1 The limited role of tax bargaining in Ethiopia

The most glaring feature of the political economy of taxation in contemporary Ethiopia is the extent to which overt political conflict over taxation at the national level has been virtually non-existent. Not only is there no evidence of direct tax bargaining; even civil society engagement with tax issues has been extremely rare, with even the major business associations playing a primarily informational, rather than advocacy, role.[67] The series of events most resembling direct tax bargaining surrounded the removal of fuel subsidies in 2008, with the government announcing that the

---

[67] Those involved with the major business associations are explicit about their essentially service delivery role, and the sharp constraints on their political engagement, drawing a clear contrast with the more activist role of business associations elsewhere. Personal interviews on 19 November 2008 with senior official, Addis Ababa Chamber of Commerce, on 6 November 2008 with donor official working with Addis Ababa Chamber of Commerce and on 5 November 2008 with donor official, private sector development programme.

5.4 Contemporary Ethiopia

revenue saved would be devoted to reducing high food prices through a combination of subsidies and reduced taxes. However, as noted earlier, senior officials are sceptical either that the government was motivated primarily by public pressure, or that the bulk of the revenue saved through the elimination of the fuel subsidies was, in fact, committed to reducing food prices.[68]

The pattern of limited public engagement and bargaining is particularly unsurprising during the period of socialist rule, owing to both the repressive power wielded by the government and the hidden character of taxation in a state-controlled economy. The Derg regime was remarkable in the context of low-income countries for its ability to penetrate society, even in rural areas, and thus stifle political dissent. Aside from the absence of open political contestation, there was a widespread popular belief that even private activities and views could be uncovered and punished by the government (Clapham 1988). In such an environment of repression, the absence of direct tax bargaining was a virtual certainty. As importantly, the socialist economic system placed most non-agricultural economic activity under the direct control of the state, and thus obscured the very concept of taxation. For state-owned enterprises, "taxation" was little more than a bookkeeping matter, as the government simply claimed a share of profits as taxation. In this context, there was little scope for tax bargaining as conceived here, as state ownership of large economic enterprises implied that the state was both taxpayer and tax collector.[69]

The situation was somewhat different in the agricultural sector, where smallholder farming continued to be the dominant form of production despite the government push for collectivization. Yet even in agriculture the strict enforcement of price controls meant that taxation was hidden in the low prices paid to producers, and tax evasion could only be achieved through smuggling. Meanwhile, the fact that the government had nationalized all agricultural land increased the vulnerability of the peasantry and their incentives to comply with land and agricultural tax requirements.[70] Ultimately, state control of economic activity significantly curtailed the potential for both direct and indirect tax bargaining. As Easter (2008: 74) writes about tax bargaining in communist Russia and Poland, which were even further under government control,

---

[68] Personal interview on 30 October 2008 with former State Minister of Finance.
[69] Personal interview on 23 October 2008 with former member of Parliament under EPRDF, on 3 November 2008 with senior tax reform official, Ministry of Revenue, and on 30 October 2008 with former State Minister of Finance.
[70] Personal interview on 23 October 2008 with former Member of Parliament under EPRDF.

"communist states did not require a compliance strategy to collect taxes. Instead they extracted hidden taxes indirectly through the administrative structures of the command economy." Given that taxation was embedded in the structure of the command economy, tax resistance and tax bargaining were, by definition, intertwined with challenges to the broader structure of economic activity and economic incentives. In this context, it is difficult to distinguish grievances related to taxation from more general opposition to government control of the economy (Clapham 1988).

The arrival in power of the EPRDF brought with it a degree of political liberalization and the dismantling of the nationalized economic system. The former implied the potential for limited forms of public opposition to the regime, while the latter re-established taxation as a distinct feature of economic management, potentially subject to more direct tax bargaining. Nonetheless, public engagement with tax issues remained extremely limited, and direct tax bargaining at the national level virtually non-existent. This pattern was first apparent in the immediate aftermath of the arrival in government of the EPRDF in 1991. The new government oversaw the reorientation of the tax system towards the taxation of new private enterprises, but there was virtually no public engagement.

While the ease with which the new tax system was implemented is less remarkable given the massive changes associated with the transition, and the goodwill that greeted the new government,[71] the absence of public engagement during a new round of tax reform beginning in 2001 is more striking. During this period the government introduced a new VAT and dramatically increased levels of revenue collection by improving enforcement of trade, income and goods and services taxes. Yet the public response was muted. Most notable was the absence of a public response to the VAT, which reduced the range of tax exemptions available for basic goods and thus increased prices that directly affected the majority of the population.[72] What is particularly noteworthy during this period is not simply the absence of tax bargaining, but the absence of engagement with tax issues amongst the two groups that would be most expected to take an active interest: the political opposition and business associations. During interviews, members of the political opposition were adamant in arguing that tax issues had not been a significant political focus, and that they had been largely a non-issue in parliamentary debates during

---

[71] Personal interviews on 30 October 2008 with former State Minister of Finance, on 3 November 2008 with senior tax reform official, Ministry of Revenue, and on 25 November 2008 with senior official, Ministry of Revenue.
[72] Ibid.

5.4 Contemporary Ethiopia

the period.[73] In the case of business associations, there was a significant interest in tax issues within the Chamber of Commerce, but engagement was strictly limited to an educational, rather than advocacy, role.[74]

The one exception to the near total absence of direct tax bargaining at the national level appears to lie in efforts by the tax administration since 1991 to increase the transparency and openness of the tax system, with the goal of enhancing compliance. While it is tempting to dismiss these efforts, given the fact that public outreach and transparency remain comparatively limited, leading tax officials speak with pride about these efforts and are adamant that progress has been made.[75] While these changes are specific to the realm of taxation, they hold the potential to quietly challenge the tendency towards hierarchical organization in public administration, and government more generally. Moreover, a transparent tax system can increase public understanding of government activities and affect taxpayer expectations of reciprocity.[76] While it would be foolish to overstate these factors, it would be equally foolish to ignore the extent to which such subtle changes may be significant in shaping long term public engagement in a historically tightly controlled political context.

5.4.2 The quiet politics of tax bargaining

While the absence of public debate about tax issues, and of direct forms of tax bargaining at the national level, is noteworthy, it is not entirely surprising. In the context of a highly autocratic government, public contestation of government policy is extremely difficult. However, there are alternative avenues through which taxation has shaped broader political outcomes. While such cases have also been relatively infrequent in Ethiopia, two issues warrant attention: the importance of relatively direct tax bargaining at the regional government level and the potential for indirect tax bargaining through tax resistance.

---

[73] Personal interviews on 19 November 2008 with opposition member of Parliament, and on 10 December 2008 with leading opposition political party figure and former Member of Parliament.
[74] Personal interviews on 19 November 2008 with senior official, Addis Ababa Chamber of Commerce, on 6 November 2008 with donor official working with Addis Ababa Chamber of Commerce, and on 5 November 2008 with donor official, private sector development programme.
[75] Personal interviews on 3 November 2008 with senior tax reform official, Ministry of Revenue, on 5 November 2008 with senior tax official, Ministry of Revenue, and on 4 December 2008 with senior official, Tax Audit and Enforcement, Amhara Bureau of Revenue.
[76] Personal interview on 10 December 2008 with leading opposition political party figure and former Member of Parliament.

Tax bargaining at the subnational level

While tax bargaining, and public engagement with taxation more generally, has been rare at the national level in Ethiopia, there is evidence that regional taxation has been more contentious, and has yielded meaningful gains in responsiveness and accountability. This finding is consistent with the arguments of proponents of fiscal decentralization, who have long argued that constructive engagement between citizens and government may be more likely when governing decisions are decentralized, and thus closer to citizens (Bird and Vaillancourt 1998).

The most important example of direct tax bargaining in contemporary Ethiopia surrounds the presumptive taxation of small businesses. When introducing the reformed presumptive tax in 2001, the government stressed that Tax Assessment Committees, comprised of members of both government and the business community, would conduct assessment of the tax. This appears to have been a pre-emptive concession aimed at curbing public opposition to the new tax by increasing public participation and oversight.[77] Yet, even with the establishment of the Committees, increased enforcement of the tax generated significant unhappiness amongst taxpayers.

While the absence of a culture of public protest, coupled with the autocratic character of the government, ensured that conflict over the tax occurred relatively quietly, there is no doubt that the regional and central governments were well aware of public hostility to the tax. The government initially set up a commission to study the fairness of the new tax, but the 2005 elections led the government to believe that unhappiness with the tax was significantly undermining its popularity.[78] This led the government to suddenly reduce rates and also to introduce broader measures to expand public consultation, particularly in the Amhara region. This included nationwide consultations conducted by the EPRDF, while since then regional governments have made continuous efforts to be more transparent in communicating with taxpayers about the need for taxation and the use of tax revenues.[79] A senior tax official from Amhara

---

[77] Personal interviews on 28 October 2008 with senior official, Oromia Bureau of Revenue, on 25 November 2008 with former senior official, Tigray Bureau of Revenue, and on 4 December 2008 with former senior official, Amhara Bureau of Revenue.

[78] Personal interviews on 3 November 2008 with senior tax reform official, Ministry of Revenue, on 28 October 2008 with senior revenue official, Federal Ministry of Finance and Economic Development, and on 4 December 2008 with senior official, Tax Audit and Enforcement, Amhara Bureau of Revenue.

[79] Personal interviews on 4 December 2008 with senior official, Tax Audit and Enforcement, Amhara Bureau of Revenue, on 10 December 2008 with leading opposition political party figure and former member of Parliament, and on 4 December 2008 with former senior official, Amhara Bureau of Revenue.

5.4 Contemporary Ethiopia

explains that "[now] we negotiate with society, we discuss with society... [we explain] why the government is imposing tax on the society, [and provide] transparency to society, [with taxpayers as] active participants in the assessment process." The same official also contends that this amounted to a process of "door to door negotiation by political leaders."[80]

It is, of course, important not to overemphasize the importance of these reforms. The creation of assessment committees and the expansion of transparency certainly constitute gains in accountability, but both are also relatively limited in their scope. That said, there is a sense amongst at least some stakeholders that the expansion of consultation and transparency around taxation may be an important force in changing the political expectations of citizens.[81] Increased transparency stands to increase public expectations about the connection between taxation and public services, while – in a broader sense – these reforms create a modest space for dialogue within a political environment that has remained relatively repressive and closed dating back to the Imperial period.

The fact that this bargaining revolved around a regional tax on small businesses, as opposed to a national tax on larger firms, points to the potential importance of such smaller taxes for prompting direct tax bargaining and public engagement. The experience of taxation in pastoral regions reinforces that broad message. While the government and pastoralist taxpayers have failed to achieve an effective tax bargain, the ongoing debate highlights both the ability of taxation to prompt bargaining between taxpayers and government and the potential for tax bargaining to be an entry point for broader governance gains.

The taxation of pastoralists has long been a source of conflict in Ethiopia, although the small revenue implications have prevented this conflict from being a major political issue. The government has generally sought to tax reluctant pastoralists using a combination of movement controls, customs points and market taxes, and has justified these taxes on the grounds that pastoralists should be expected to contribute tax revenue in exchange for government services. Such controls could, moreover, aid government efforts to monitor livestock levels and establish how much tax should be collected. Pastoralists have responded to these

---

[80] Personal interview on 4 December 2008 with senior official, Tax Audit and Enforcement, Amhara Bureau of Revenue.

[81] Ibid., and interviews on 10 December 2008 with leading opposition political party figure and former member of Parliament, on 4 December 2008 with former senior official, Amhara Bureau of Revenue, on 3 November 2008 with senior tax reform official, Ministry of Revenue, and on 21 October 2008 with senior official working on budgeting and IT reform, Federal Ministry of Finance and Economic Development.

efforts with hostility, for two reasons. First, pastoralists complain that government efforts to impose movement controls and customs points undermine the basic nature of pastoral livelihoods, which rely on mobility and adaptability. Second, pastoralists contend that the very low level of existing government services does not justify the levels of taxation being demanded.

Disagreement over movement controls and taxation has bred occasionally violent conflict that dates at least as far back as 1963, when anger amongst pastoralists at the imposition of tax-related movement controls contributed to the outbreak of the Bale uprising (Tareke 1991). In more recent years conflict between pastoralists and state officials, including the military, has led to occasional violence and, more frequently, the seizure of livestock and other pastoralist assets. In aggregate terms, the government has expended significant resources, and bred significant animosity, without achieving meaningful revenue gains. Meanwhile, the uncertainty, violence and seizures encountered by pastoralists, coupled with the absence of effective services, appear to entail costs that exceed the burden of potential taxation (Pastoralist Communication Initiative 2005, 2006; Devereux 2006; Prichard 2007).

At a gathering of pastoralists and policymakers convened in December 2006,[82] the nature of the tax conflict was succinctly summarized by a government official: "The pastoralists are saying that they don't receive services, so they shouldn't have to pay tax. The government says the pastoralists don't pay tax, so they don't deserve services." Both sides expressed an understanding of the potential benefits of a mutually acceptable and conciliatory tax bargain, but neither side has been able to overcome the antagonism that characterizes the current relationship. At the same gathering, senior pastoralist leaders provided clear indications that they would, in principle, support greater tax compliance in exchange for better services and reduced harassment by the government. One leader went so far as to ask, "If pastoralists are not paying taxes, are they in a position to demand services?" The message for this research is clear: regional government taxation, which involves direct interaction between taxpayers and the government, holds significant potential to spur tax bargaining and the benefits are potentially large. Yet, despite these potential gains effective tax bargaining can be extremely difficult in the context of deep mistrust.

---

[82] The gathering was organized by the Pastoralist Communication Initiative, and was held at the Institute of Development Studies, Brighton, UK, 3–8 December 2006.

Tax compliance, tax resistance and incentives for reform

While experience at the regional level thus provides some evidence of direct tax bargaining, there is compelling evidence that, as in Ghana and Kenya, levels of tax collection have fallen in response to growing popular unhappiness with the government. This has not contributed to changes in government to the same extent as has been the case in Ghana and Kenya. However, it clearly reinforces the message that over the long-term tax resistance by unhappy taxpayers may contribute to the removal of unpopular governments and to producing positive incentives for greater responsiveness and accountability in states that are reliant on tax revenue.

The first Ethiopian example relates to the overthrow of the Derg government, which was accelerated by a fiscal crisis to which tax resistance was at least a minor contributor. While the immediate cause of the fall of the Derg regime lay in declining morale and military defeat, this outcome was underpinned by the dramatic collapse of state finances. This was shaped in part by the loss of financial support from the Soviet Union, but a dramatic fall in domestic revenue collection accounted for the largest part of the decline in government revenue. During the final stages of the civil war, domestic revenue fell from almost 20 per cent to only 11 per cent of GDP, at a time when the fiscal demands on the state were at their height. This narrative minimally makes clear that fiscal issues contributed pivotally to the fall of the Derg government. Had the government enjoyed access to large non-tax revenues, the conflict likely would have continued much longer, and been much more destructive. Conversely, the state's reliance on tax revenue increased its vulnerability and hastened its defeat, and a subsequent transition to a reformist (although still autocratic) government. The experience thus speaks unambiguously to the broad role of tax reliance in having shaped the political prospects of the Derg regime.

However, the more specific question posed by this research is whether the decline in government revenue can be attributed in part to tax resistance by taxpayers engaging in a form of quiet political resistance. On one hand, it is clear that tax resistance per se was not the dominant cause of declining government revenue: The largest revenue losses are widely attributed to the loss of transport networks and territory during the war, coupled with the collapse of revenues from state-owned enterprises that appeared to wilt after several years in which the government had directed profits aggressively to the war effort (Bevan and Pradhan 1994; Bevan 2001). Meanwhile, the scope for tax resistance within the state-owned sector was inherently limited.

On the other hand, interviews and secondary sources are consistent with at least some role for tax resistance in shaping outcomes. There is some suggestion that part of the declining performance of state-owned enterprises may be attributed to the declining popularity of the regime in its final years, and correspondingly declining commitment amongst those employed by the state. However, while highly intuitive, it has been impossible to substantiate this possibility with certainty given the paucity of available data and detailed research evidence from the period.[83] Meanwhile, within the realm of agriculture, there is at least anecdotal evidence that the growing unpopularity of the regime, and its efforts to extract ever more revenue to sustain the war effort, met with increasing resistance in rural areas in the late 1980s (Webb, von Braun and Yohannes 1992: 63). This was reflected in a declining collection of agricultural and land taxes in the last years of the war, as well as by a sharp decline in official coffee production during the same years, which suggests that smuggling was also increasing as an implicit form of resistance to state control (Dercon and Ayalew 1995: 1799; Naudé 1998). These declines in formal market exactions are likely to have been indicative of a larger decline in the ability of the state to draw on extensive but informal exactions from the peasantry to support its military campaigns.

Ultimately, there is very clear evidence that fiscal crisis played an important role in the fall of the Derg, and evidence that tax resistance played at least some role in contributing to this fiscal crisis. It is, unfortunately, difficult to discern the precise contribution of tax resistance to the broader fiscal collapse. It is not difficult to construct a narrative in which much of the fiscal decline is attributed to the combination of tax resistance and smuggling by agriculturalists and passive resistance by those employed by state-owned enterprises. That said, the paucity of data, and the general difficulty of accessing information from this period, means that any strong conclusions are necessarily somewhat speculative. In any event, however, the evidence available is fully consistent with discussion in previous chapters about the potential for tax resistance to contribute to expanded responsiveness and accountability by contributing to changes in government.

This same potential for tax resistance to act as a catalyst for political change is reinforced by the Ethiopian experience around the 2005 elections. While taxation was not a major campaign issue, the government came to believe that taxation was an important driver of public

---

[83] Personal interview on 3 November 2008 with senior tax reform official, Ministry of Revenue.

opposition. In response, the government both reduced certain tax rates and allowed tax enforcement to become more lax in the aftermath of the election.[84] The result was a sharp decline in the share of tax revenue in GDP in the years following the election. While taxpayers did not resist taxation in the classic sense of anti-tax protests or aggressive tax evasion, by expressing their displeasure informally, and exploiting the declining aggressiveness of government tax enforcement, they nonetheless precipitated a fall in tax revenue. Indeed, even after the formal opposition had been decimated after the 2005 election the government continued to experience falling revenue collection through the 2008/2009 fiscal year, with levels of collection only returning to the levels that had existed prior to 2005 in 2012/2013.

While the fall in tax revenue contributed to economic imbalances, it did not ultimately lead to a change in government or force the government to expand responsiveness and accountability. The episode nonetheless provides confirmation of the broader claim that public unhappiness with government can frequently lead to declining tax revenue, and thus increase the *likelihood* of changes in government and of reform. In highly autocratic settings like Ethiopia, where direct tax bargaining is highly constrained, the fact that taxpayers were able to force substantially reduced levels of government tax collection offered them an alternative avenue through which to create pressure for change.

5.5 Explaining outcomes: political, economic and social barriers to tax bargaining

The discussion so far has highlighted an important example of direct tax bargaining around presumptive taxation as well as evidence that the popularity of the government has shaped revenue-raising capacity. This evidence supports the belief that tax bargaining can be an important contributor to the expansion of responsiveness and accountability. However, the broader message is that tax bargaining, both direct and indirect, has been comparatively rare in contemporary Ethiopia. As has already been noted, this is not entirely surprising, as the political, economic and social conditions that prevail in Ethiopia are precisely those that we expect to make tax bargaining particularly unlikely. The discussion so far has

---

[84] Personal interviews on 30 October 2008 with former State Minister of Finance, on 3 November 2008 with senior tax reform official, Ministry of Revenue, on 25 November 2008 with senior official, Ministry of Revenue, on 19 November 2008 with Opposition Member of Parliament, and on 18 November 2008 with economist, IMF.

alluded to the roles of political repression, the weakness of the private sector, foreign aid and history in shaping the relative weakness of tax bargaining. What follows aims to link these insights more explicitly to the model developed in Chapter 2 by looking at the ways in which the Ethiopian context has constrained taxpayer capacity for collective action, reduced the scope for tax resistance, limited access to institutions for tax bargaining, minimized the political salience of taxation, and limited the revenue pressure facing the government (summarized in Table 5.1).

5.5.1 Taxpayer potential for collective action

At the core of the relative absence of tax bargaining in Ethiopia have been sharp constraints on the potential for collective action. This has reflected the quite obvious repressiveness of the regime but, as in Kenya, also reflects more idiosyncratic features of the Ethiopian context, led by the weakness and fragmentation of the private sector and the particular national history of taxation.

Effective repression

Beginning with the comparatively obvious, Ethiopia has been amongst the most politically repressive states in Africa throughout its modern history, with stark consequences for the potential for collective action by opposition groups. This was particularly true of the Derg regime, but has continued under the EPRDF. This has been reflected in a wide array of informants who have noted taxpayers' preferences for quieter forms of resistance, and the sharp constraints on public protest.[85] It has also, indirectly, been reflected in the striking reluctance of state officials to discuss even moderately controversial topics, including the decline in tax collection and enforcement following the 2005 elections. Underlying the particular effectiveness of repression is the widely noted reach of the Ethiopian state, which has long shown much greater capacity than most countries in the region to exercise authority down to the local level.[86]

---

[85] Personal interviews on 28 October 2008 with senior official, Oromia Bureau of Revenue, on 21 October 2008 with professor of economics, University of Addis Ababa, on 28 October 2008 with senior revenue official, Federal Ministry of Finance and Economic Development, on 19 November 2008 with Opposition Member of Parliament, and on 3 November 2008 with senior tax reform official, Ministry of Revenue.

[86] Personal interviews on 23 October 2008 with former member of Parliament under EPRDF, on 16 October 2008 with former director of budget management reform programme, Federal Ministry of Finance and Economic Development, on 21 October 2008 with senior official working on budgeting and IT reform, Federal Ministry of Finance and Economic Development, and on 20 January 2009 with international tax advisor to the regional governments.

5.5 Explaining outcomes

Table 5.1 *Ethiopia: the role of contextual factors*

Structural factor	Relevant contextual variables	Impact
Taxpayer capacity for collective action	• Government repression • Weak and fragmented private sector • Weak civil society • Little history of organized and peaceful collective action	• No evidence of public mobilization in response to taxation • Private sector more focused on securing narrow bargains than broader governance gains • Limited cases of direct tax bargaining resulted from quietly expressed taxpayer anger and electoral threats
Institutions for bargaining	• Few institutional channels for bargaining • Creation of such channels at the regional level is one outcome of tax bargaining	• Little dialogue between taxpayers and government, further limiting scope for direct tax bargaining • Some evidence that forums for regional engagement around tax issues have enhanced limited forms of bargaining
The political salience of taxation	• Very gradualist approach to reform • Little modern history of mobilization around tax issues • Limited elite leadership in publicizing tax debates	• Further reduces extent of popular engagement with tax issues
The potential and scope for tax resistance	• Weak and fragmented private sector • Significant public and ruling party ownership of major sectors • Significant reliance on direct taxes at the regional level	• Despite challenges, significant evidence of tax resistance since 2005, although without an impact on national level responsiveness and accountability • More scope for resistance, and thus bargaining, at the regional level, with modest government concessions
Revenue pressure facing government	• High levels of foreign aid reduce revenue pressure	• Government has faced little incentive to compromise with taxpayers in search of revenue, even when tax collection has declined sharply

The weakness and fragmentation of the private sector

The effectiveness of repression has, in turn, been reinforced by the comparative weakness and fragmentation of the private sector, in contrast to the prominent bargaining role of the private sector in Kenya and Ghana. This has been driven by four elements: the overall weakness of the economy, the direct repression of private sector political action, fragmentation resulting from mistrust between businesses, and fragmentation resulting from heavy reliance on sector specific government support.

Ethiopia is one of the lowest income and most rural countries in the world, which on its own would significantly weaken the political power wielded by the private sector. This has been reinforced by both the ideology and general repressiveness of successive regimes, which have viewed the private sector as a potential threat, as reflected in regular state rhetoric about the dangers of private sector "rent-seekers" seeking to take advantage of the population at large (Vaughn and Gebremichael 2011). Under the Derg regime business associations were correspondingly dominated by the state and state-owned enterprises. The EPRDF has in principle allowed some opening of space for the major business associations, but in practice this space has been sharply constrained. Most notably, there have remained sharp controls on the political activities of business associations, leading to the imprisonment of some leaders, while, illustratively, the very building in which the Addis Ababa Chamber of Commerce was housed remained government owned until 2008. The result is that the major business associations have remained focused on acting primarily as service providers to business, through the provision of training and networking, rather than pursuing an advocacy role.[87]

While this weakness of business associations is relatively straightforward, more subtle is the fragmentation of interests within the business community, which has further undermined any potential for collective action. This is widely attributed at least in part to the historical evolution of a highly distrustful business culture, the roots of which are beyond the scope of this study (World Bank 2009; Vaughn and Gebremichael 2011). However, divisions within the business community also reflect government policy. At a broad level, the government has retained a proactive industrial policy, which gives the state a role in shaping access to credit,

---

[87] Personal interviews on 19 November 2008 with senior official, Addis Ababa Chamber of Commerce, on 6 November 2008 with donor official working with Addis Ababa Chamber of Commerce, and on 5 November 2008 with donor official, private sector development programme.

5.5 Explaining outcomes

contracts and other economic opportunities. This alone has encouraged bilateral, rather than collective, bargaining with the state by key business actors seeking opportunities. This has, in turn, been reinforced by the government, which has actively promoted the development of sectoral business associations, while side-lining broader Chambers of Commerce. This has reflected in part a government desire to provide targeted support to key sectors of the economy (Vaughn and Gebremichael 2011). However, this focus on sector-based engagement with the business community has also served an intentionally political purpose: it has fragmented the organization of business interests further, and generated structural incentives for businesses to pursue individual or sectoral bargaining around taxation, rather than developing a more broad-based agenda.[88] This pattern mirrors the fragmentation of the business community in Kenya until the late 1990s.

Finally, both the weakness of business associations and the overall fragmentation of business interests have been exacerbated by the prominent role of state owned enterprises and "endowment" companies within the Ethiopian economy. While gradually being privatized, the state-owned sector remains large in Ethiopia, with a senior tax official estimating that about 20 per cent of the 500 largest taxpayers are SOEs.[89] These firms have, unsurprisingly, played a passive political role, or have been absent entirely from the Chambers of Commerce, while they appear to be particularly tax compliant (Vaughn and Gebremichael 2011; World Bank 2009: 50–52).[90] This situation is further complicated by the presence of so-called endowment firms; that is, private firms owned by endowment funds closely linked to the ruling party, and initially created using funds accumulated during the civil war against the Derg regime. While technically private firms, these firms are closely aligned with the ruling party, and are thus unlikely to play an active political role, while they have been accused in some circles of exacerbating the tendency towards

---

[88] Personal interviews on 19 November 2008 with senior official, Addis Ababa Chamber of Commerce, on 6 November 2008 with donor official working with Addis Ababa Chamber of Commerce, and on 5 November 2008 with donor official, private sector development programme.

[89] Personal interview on 18 November 2008 with senior official, Ministry of Revenue. Interestingly, information on the share of state-owned or endowment firms in tax revenue, and in the economy overall, were very sensitive at the time of the research, with tax officials reporting that they do not compile specific figures. This appears to reflect opposition accusations that these firms receive significant advantages from government, and a corresponding desire to downplay questions about SOEs.

[90] Personal interviews on 6 November 2008 with donor official working with Addis Ababa Chamber of Commerce and On 19 November 2008 with senior official, Addis Ababa Chamber of Commerce.

bilateral bargaining with the state (World Bank 2009: 54–55; Vaughn and Gebremichael 2011).[91]

The legacies of history
A final part of the story appears to lie in the possibility that a long history of highly coercive taxation in Ethiopia may have shaped the more general extent to which taxpayers expect reciprocity for their tax payments. If taxation is not perceived as a form of exchange, with expectations of reciprocity, then the likelihood that taxpayers will make demands for reciprocal concessions from government will clearly be sharply reduced. This possibility is raised much more frequently in Ethiopia than elsewhere in the region, reflecting the highly coercive origins of taxation in Ethiopia, both in tributes levied by successive Emperors during the Imperial period and in the government controls of the Derg period. In interviews there is a widespread sense that many taxpayers view tax payments as a means to achieve recognition by the state and basic claims to land, but that there is often little expectation of reciprocity in terms of service provision. In this sense, taxes continue to be perceived primarily as "tributes" to the King or ruler, particularly amongst rural populations. In this vein, it is telling that the Amharic word, *geber*, which roughly translates as "tribute," continues to be used to refer to agricultural and land taxes (Kassahun 2006).[92]

The extent to which taxpayers may not think of taxation in terms of reciprocity should not, of course, be overstated. Outside observers have long been tempted to make similar claims about the ignorance of taxpayers throughout sub-Saharan Africa, but limited survey evidence has consistently found that even rural taxpayers have much stronger expectations of reciprocity than has often been assumed (Fjeldstad and Semboja 2001; Aiko and Logan 2014). While similar survey evidence is not available in Ethiopia, the question of perceptions of taxation is

---

[91] Personal interviews on 19 November 2008 with Opposition Member of Parliament, on 6 November 2008 with donor official working with Addis Ababa Chamber of Commerce, and on 25 November 2008 with former senior official, Tigray Bureau of Revenue. As detailed in Vaughn and Gebremichael (2011), there is significant speculation and uncertainty about the role of these firms. Many local actors, particularly from the opposition, feel that these firms receive very large and uncompetitive benefits from the government, and channel significant resources back to the political leadership. By contrast, recent research suggests comparatively moderate and declining advantages granted by the state, and a limited role in funding the ruling party. These debates are, however, beyond the scope of the discussion here.

[92] Personal interviews on 3 November 2008 with senior tax reform official, Ministry of Revenue, on 19 November 2008 with Opposition Member of Parliament, on 21 October 2008 with two professors of economics, University of Addis Ababa, and on 20 January 2009 with international tax advisor to the regional governments.

5.5 Explaining outcomes

complex, and the evidence here very partial. That said, both interviews and intuition suggest that Ethiopian history may have made expectations of reciprocity around taxation relatively weak, particularly in rural areas, with possible consequences for tax bargaining.

5.5.2 Bargaining institutions and the political salience of taxation

While the primary barrier to direct tax bargaining has thus been the particular weakness of taxpayer capacity for collective action, this has been reinforced by the near total absence of meaningful institutions to facilitate tax bargaining, and the generally limited political salience of taxation. Opposition politicians are forthright in explaining that tax issues have not played a central role in formal opposition politics, and that tax issues have rarely figured in parliamentary sessions or debates.[93] In the same way, and despite moves towards greater openness and transparency, the national tax agency has remained relatively isolated from the population at large, with few opportunities for engagement. Meanwhile, broader public attention to tax issues has remained rare, with little coverage in the popular press, and a pervasive sense that taxpayers have limited understanding of the details of the tax system.[94]

The lack of political salience appears to reflect a combination of Ethiopia's repressive history, government strategy and the weakness of elite engagement. Given Ethiopia's long history of highly coercive taxation – particularly under the Derg government – many senior officials feel that a lack of recent attention to tax issues reflects the fact that the tax systems is, at a minimum, viewed as vastly improved relative to earlier periods.[95] This has, in turn, facilitated a broader government strategy of gradualism in tax reform, which, as in Kenya, has been designed to obscure major changes and minimize popular engagement and resistance.[96] Finally, one of the lessons from Ghana and Kenya is

---

[93] Personal interviews on 19 November 2008 with Opposition Member of Parliament and on 10 December 2008 with leading opposition political party figure and former Member of Parliament.
[94] Personal interviews on 21 October 2008 with professor of economics, University of Addis Ababa, on 6 November 2008 with donor official working with Addis Ababa Chamber of Commerce, and on 19 November 2008 with Opposition Member of Parliament.
[95] Personal interviews on 30 October 2008 with former State Minister of Finance, on 3 November 2008 with senior tax reform official, Ministry of Revenue, and on 25 November 2008 with senior official, Ministry of Revenue.
[96] Personal interviews on 25 November 2008 with senior official, Ministry of Revenue, on 18 November 2008 with economist, IMF, on 3 November 2008 with senior tax reform official, Ministry of Revenue, and on 21 October 2008 with professor of economics, University of Addis Ababa.

that it is elites who play a critical role in making taxation issues politically salient to the bulk of the population, and the weakness of elite engagement in Ethiopia – particularly by the business community – has thus further undermined popular attention to tax issues.

Tellingly, Ethiopia offers a limited set of examples that appear to reveal the added potential for tax bargaining where reform has been less gradual, and where channels for institutional engagement have been available. This is most notable at the regional level, where debates about the presumptive tax have been made possible in part because it is comparatively "visible" to individual taxpayers. More strikingly, the presumptive tax generated a dramatically stronger public reaction in Amhara, where rates were increased quickly and very visibly, whereas it encountered much less resistance in other states, where it was intentionally introduced gradually and with little fanfare.[97] Meanwhile, representatives across several regions note the extent to which assessment committees made up of a combination of government officials and local business representatives offered an important channel through which public unhappiness was transmitted to the government.[98]

5.5.3 The potential for tax resistance and role of revenue pressure

Substantial barriers to collective action have thus restricted the potential for direct tax bargaining. Against this background, a reasonable expectation is that taxpayers may, instead, bargain indirectly with the state through politically motivated tax resistance. And, indeed, there is significant evidence that the ability of the government to collect tax revenue has been undermined by its declining popularity and expanded tax resistance since 2005. However, this resistance has generally failed to elicit significant concessions from the government. This pattern appears to reflect both the repressive strength of the state and the relative absence of revenue pressure that might have compelled the government to make concessions in the face of reduced tax collection.

As already noted, quiet forms of tax resistance have been significant in Ethiopia, and have successfully constrained government revenue, despite

---

[97] Personal interviews on 21 October 2008 with professor of economics, University of Addis Ababa, on 25 November 2008 with former senior official, Tigray Bureau of Revenue, on 4 December 2008 with former senior official, Amhara Bureau of Revenue, on 4 December 2008 with senior official, Tax Audit and Enforcement, Amhara Bureau of Revenue, and on 20 January 2009 with international tax advisor to the regional governments.

[98] Personal interviews on 21 October 2008 with professor of economics, University of Addis Ababa, on 25 November 2008 with former senior official, Tigray Bureau of Revenue, and on 28 October 2008 with senior official, Oromia Bureau of Revenue.

5.5 Explaining outcomes

the weakness and fragmentation of the private sector. During the period after 2005, taxpayers appear to have expanded evasion and avoidance efforts, while the government became more reluctant to pursue aggressive tax enforcement in the face of popular resistance, while also reducing the rates of smaller, primarily regional, taxes.[99] The effectiveness of this tax resistance appears to have been aided by the relative weakness of the tax administration – and its corresponding struggles to enforce taxes[100] – as well as by the prevalence of highly visible direct taxes at the regional level, which fell particularly sharply from 2005 onwards.

However, unlike in Ghana and Kenya, this tax resistance does not appear either to have significantly weakened the government, or to have generated effective pressure for the expansion of responsiveness and accountability. Part of the explanation undoubtedly lies in the entrenched political position of the government, and the limited threat posed by the political opposition. However, the political ineffectiveness of tax resistance also appears to reflect government access to significant alternative sources of revenue. Throughout the period under study Ethiopia remained heavily dependent on foreign aid. From 1990 to 2008 Ethiopia received an average of more than 10 per cent of GDP annually in foreign aid from OECD countries, while the level of aid reached almost 20 per cent of GDP from 2002 through 2004. In parallel, the government began to receive increasing aid from China beginning in 2000 – accelerating around 2005 – with China emerging as a major source of development finance, although the Chinese government does not produce aggregate figures on total aid flows by country (Hackenesch 2013).[101] In most years the level of foreign aid thus matched or exceeded total revenue from tax collection. Multiple authors have predicted that such high levels of aid dependence may discourage long-term levels of tax collection – and, by extension, opportunities for tax bargaining. And while there is little support for a negative impact of aid on tax collection *on average* across countries, it remains

---

[99] Personal interviews on 30 October 2008 with former State Minister of Finance, on 3 November 2008 with senior tax reform official, Ministry of Revenue, on 25 November 2008 with senior official, Ministry of Revenue, on 19 November 2008 with Opposition Member of Parliament, and on 18 November 2008 with economist, IMF.

[100] Personal interviews on 25 November 2008 with senior official, Ministry of Revenue, on 5 November 2008 with senior tax official, Ministry of Revenue, and on 3 November 2008 with senior tax reform official, Ministry of Revenue.

[101] Not only does the government not provide aggregate figures by country, but it also does not strictly follow OECD guidelines for the classification of development assistance. Moreover, China has become a major provider of export credits to Africa, which, while not strictly speaking a form of aid, has offered additional access to development financing. While the details are thus somewhat unclear, the significance of Chinese financing is now widely accepted. See Hackenesch (2013).

entirely possible that access to alternative revenue sources may reduce incentives for governments to make concessions to resistant taxpayers in times of crisis (Moore 1998; Bräutigam and Knack 2004).[102]

This logic offers the most convincing explanation for the relative absence of government concessions in the face of sharply declining tax revenue following the 2005 elections. While tax collection declined dramatically during this period, the fiscal consequences of sharply reduced tax collection were mitigated by the fact that foreign aid from OECD countries continued at levels averaging more than 10 per cent of GDP, alongside rapidly increasing aid from China. In the absence of aid it is difficult to avoid the conclusion that the government would have been significantly less able to weather the reduction in tax revenue, and thus would likely have faced stronger incentives to bargain with taxpayers rather than simply reducing collection.[103] This topic is discussed at greater length in the concluding chapter.

5.6 Conclusions

For the most part since 1974 successive Ethiopian governments have been able to achieve reasonable levels of tax collection almost entirely through the use of coercion. This was overwhelmingly true under the Derg regime, but even since the arrival of the EPRDF major tax reforms have generally been greeted by passive acceptance or tax evasion, with little evidence of direct tax bargaining or civil society engagement. At the national level neither business associations, civil society organizations, nor the political opposition have engaged actively with tax issues. But while the relative absence of easily observable tax bargaining is striking, it is not particularly surprising. Social, political and economic conditions in Ethiopia present a perfect storm of factors that are expected to reduce the likelihood of tax bargaining: repressive politics, a weak private sector, dependence on foreign aid and a long history of coercive taxation.

Given that Ethiopia is thus a setting in which tax bargaining is particularly *unlikely*, the fact that there is nonetheless meaningful, if limited, evidence of tax bargaining offers support to the broader ideas being explored by this book. Most obviously, tax bargaining around the

---

[102] While some research has suggested a consistently negative impact of aid on tax collection (Gupta et al. 2004; Benedek et al. 2014), more recent research indicates that this relationship is not robust, thus suggesting that aid may sometimes discourage tax collection, but that outcomes are likely to vary significantly according to the broader context (Clist and Morrissey 2011; Prichard, Brun, and Morrissey 2012; Morrissey, Prichard and Torrance 2014).

[103] Personal interview on 10 December 2008 with leading opposition political party figure and former Member of Parliament.

5.6 Conclusions

presumptive tax on small businesses at the regional government level was clear cut, and resulted in important gains in accountability in an environment in which political repression was otherwise increasing. While the gains were modest in absolute terms, in a context of such limited opportunities, outcomes that create space for political engagement and reshape political expectations remain noteworthy.[104] This is likewise true of the broader trend towards building a more transparent tax system at the national level.

As important is evidence that the ability of the government to raise tax revenue has been substantially shaped by levels of popular support. While falling tax revenue after the 2005 elections did not result in a change in government or in major concessions, the episode offers further support for the argument that taxpayers can exercise political power through quiet resistance to taxation, even in a repressive political environment. Over the long-term there is every reason to believe that the ability of taxpayers to exercise such indirect political influence through tax resistance will increase the likelihood of more responsive and accountable government.

Of particular interest is evidence that tax bargaining in Ethiopia has been particularly prevalent at the regional level. It is small business taxation at the regional government level that offers the clearest evidence of direct tax bargaining, while it is at the regional level that taxes declined most rapidly in the face of public resistance immediately before and after the 2005 elections. On one hand, it is unsurprising that tax bargaining may be more pronounced, and more visible, at the regional government level, where governments rely more on highly visible direct taxes, and where the distance between taxpayers and governments is comparatively modest. On the other hand, Moore (2008) has argued that more coercive forms of taxation may be more likely at the subnational level, where low-incomes, a weak private sector, access to large central government transfers, and the limited mobility of agricultural producers may reduce the scope for collective action and tax resistance. While it may not thus be universally the case that tax bargaining is more likely at the subnational level, Ethiopian experience highlights the reasons why this might sometimes be the case, and the potential that this offers.

Ultimately, the evidence in this chapter, taken on its own, would constitute weak evidence at best of the role of tax bargaining in shaping the responsiveness and accountability of governments. However, when considered in conjunction with the two previous case studies, the evidence in this chapter offers important confirmation of the importance of tax bargaining, as well as the clearest insights into the importance of

[104] Ibid.

contextual factors in shaping particular outcomes. In a repressive environment like Ethiopia, the importance of taxation in shaping broader political outcomes will invariably be indirect and difficult to observe, but this chapter has made clear that the basic political mechanisms of interest are no less relevant. Meanwhile, preliminary evidence of enhanced tax bargaining at the subnational level is suggestive of important avenues for future research.

Appendix

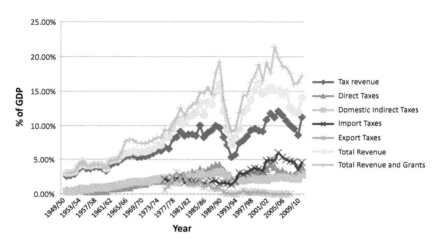

Figure 5.1 Ethiopia: composition of revenue, 1949–2010.

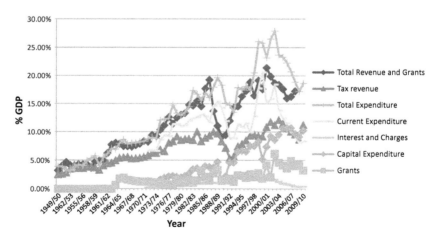

Figure 5.2 Ethiopia: expenditure and revenue, 1949–2010.

Appendix 211

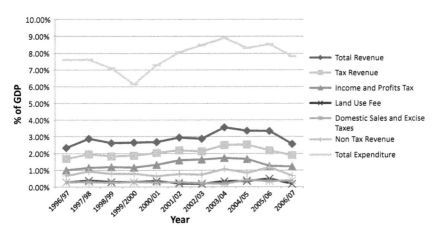

Figure 5.3 Ethiopia: composition of regional tax revenue, 1996–2007.

6 Understanding tax bargaining
Complexity and contingency

The research presented in this book has been both broad and exploratory. Each chapter has sought to tell part of the larger story, and each individual tax episode has had its own messages. This chapter takes stock of the entirety of the evidence presented so far and synthesizes it into a set of key insights and lessons. The first part of the chapter summarizes evidence that the need for taxation has, indeed, been linked to broader gains in responsiveness and accountability. While this finding is consistent with conventional wisdom, the case study evidence summarized here provides a much more substantial empirical foundation for existing claims. The remainder of the chapter explores in more detail how, and when, taxation has been linked to the expansion of responsiveness and accountability in practice. It begins with an exploration of the multiple alternative causal processes that have linked taxation, responsiveness and accountability. This is followed by a detailed review of the role of a variety of contextual factors in shaping both the likelihood and form of tax bargaining. Collectively, these elements provide a sharper departure from existing research, as they move the analysis beyond comparatively broad existing claims and towards capturing a more complex and contingent reality.

6.1 Taxation, responsiveness and accountability: reviewing the evidence

This book began with a review of existing cross-country studies of the relationship between taxation and accountability, followed by a brief presentation of new econometric findings. Those new findings were based on the use of dramatically improved data, and a wider range of econometric strategies. The goal was to provide a robust picture of both the extent *and limits* of what cross-country econometric evidence can tell us about the relationship between taxation and accountability.

The first message from the econometric evidence was that the results are entirely *consistent* with the existence of a causal relationship between taxation and accountability. The new econometric tests leave little

6.1 Taxation, responsiveness and accountability

question that countries that are more reliant on tax revenue, as a share of total government revenue, are more likely to be democratic, as predicted by the theory developed in this book. Tellingly, the *tax reliance* variable has significantly greater explanatory power across all of the models than the level of GDP, suggesting that the composition of government revenue may be the strongest available predictor of patterns of democracy across countries.

However, while cross-country results are consistent with the existence of a relationship between taxation, responsiveness and accountability, the second message is that they are quite clearly not *sufficient* evidence, in two senses. Narrowly, it is not possible to isolate the role of *tax bargaining* specifically in driving the broader relationship between tax reliance and democracy, as distinct from the possibility that this relationship is driven entirely by the antidemocratic effects of resource wealth. More broadly, the cross-country econometric results are insufficient because they are unable to offer nuanced insight into the potentially diverse causal processes that may link taxation, responsiveness and accountability, or into the contextual factors that are likely to shape divergent outcomes across countries or over time. Indeed, the inconclusiveness of the econometric results can, from one perspective, be understood as confirmation that *if* a relationship between taxation, responsiveness and accountability exists, it is likely to be significantly more complex and contingent than what is suggested by many standard accounts. The strongest message emerging from the econometric tests has thus been that there is a need for complementary country-level evidence that can capture the complexity and contingency of the causal processes of interest. This message has provided the impetus for the core contribution of this book.

In moving towards a country-level investigation of these relationships the initial challenge has been methodological, as the relationship between taxation, responsiveness and accountability is not easily amenable to case study research. Although the intuition behind tax bargaining is clear, its practical manifestations are likely to be frequently implicit, indirect, long-term and embedded in broader processes of political change, making empirical observation difficult. The solution pursued here has been the development of a detailed theoretical model, coupled with clearly defined outcomes of interest, to aid the process of organizing and making sense of the case study evidence.

The model began by defining two general *mechanisms* through which the need for taxation may expand the political power wielded by taxpayers. First, tax reliance may expand opportunities for taxpayers to engage in *tax resistance*, and thus create incentives for governments to make concessions to taxpayers in order to improve tax compliance and increase tax revenue. Second, increased taxation may encourage *public engagement and collective action* amongst taxpayers seeking to ensure that they benefit from their tax payments. These two mechanisms were, in turn, expected to drive three more specific *causal processes*, capturing different patterns of interaction between taxpayers and governments. While these causal processes were not expected to capture some of the relatively implicit and unobservable ways in which tax reliance may shape levels of responsiveness and accountability, they provided a clear empirical basis for evaluating the case study evidence.

The first causal process was termed *direct tax bargaining*, and captured cases in which governments respond to taxpayer demands by making relatively explicit concessions aimed at securing increased tax collection and curtailing public opposition. The second and third causal processes were jointly termed *indirect tax bargaining*, as they aimed to capture cases in which governments do not make reciprocal concessions to taxpayers, but in which the need for taxation nonetheless contributes to longer-term political change. Thus, *tax resistance and changes in government* captured cases in which resistance to taxation weakens the fiscal base of an incumbent government, creates pressure for a change in government and provides positive incentives for an incoming government to make concessions to taxpayers in order to improve tax collection in the future. Meanwhile, *strengthened political capabilities of taxpayers* captured cases in which taxation contributes to strengthening civil society and opening up new spaces for political engagement, with long-term implications for the expansion of responsiveness and accountability. These latter two processes went beyond standard models of tax bargaining in aiming to capture difficult-to-observe processes that are less explicit than direct tax bargaining, but rely on a comparable causal logic.

With this model serving as an analytical foundation, the case study chapters have presented historical narratives of the political economy of taxation, with a focus on the political dynamics surrounding particular *tax episodes*. The analysis of political processes surrounding these tax episodes has provided the basis upon which to evaluate the presence, or absence, of a relationship between taxation and the expansion of responsiveness and accountability. The primary challenge in evaluating the evidence has been that we do not expect to observe evidence of direct or indirect tax bargaining during *every* tax episode. Taxation remains a fundamentally coercive process and there will inevitably be instances in which taxpayers are unable to mount an effective response, or in which governments increase tax collection irrespective of the protests of taxpayers. While such processes may nonetheless contribute to political change over the long-term in relatively subtle ways, the focus of empirical case

6.1 Taxation, responsiveness and accountability

study research is necessarily on observable forms of tax bargaining. The corresponding question was thus not whether *every* tax increase or tax debate would result in observable tax bargaining, but whether the case studies would confirm that bargaining over taxation has been, and can be, an important factor in contributing to the expansion of responsiveness and accountability.

With this in mind, Table 6.1 provides a general summary of the political implications of the most important tax episodes from the case study chapters. Particular tax episodes and outcomes are categorized as being representative of one of the three causal processes identified by the model, or as falling into a fourth category, *taxation without bargaining*, which captures instances in which significant increases in taxation did not yield observable evidence of tax bargaining. In addition, instances of direct tax bargaining are disaggregated into three broad types of outcomes: "improved provision of public services," "changes in tax policy and administration," and "broad expansions of accountability." The same is not possible in cases of indirect tax bargaining, which have involved broader, longer-term and less specific impacts on governance outcomes.

The overall body of evidence makes clear that tax bargaining has in many instances been an important catalyst for the expansion of responsiveness and accountability. There are clear examples of each of the three hypothesized causal processes in each of the three case study countries. Moreover, these examples are substantively important, with tax bargaining contributing in significant ways to the expansion of public services, to changes in the way that taxes are administered and to processes of political liberalization. While there have been clear differences in the form and extent of tax bargaining across countries, the fact that there has been visible evidence of tax bargaining even in Ethiopia, where social, political and economic conditions would seem to militate against it, is particularly striking. That said, this summary of the case study evidence equally highlights a variety of cases of *taxation without bargaining*. These include the relative absence of a strong response to the introduction of the VAT in both Kenya and Ethiopia, the lack of controversy surrounding large increases in tax collection in Kenya in the early 1990s, and the limited public response to a variety of tax changes in Ethiopia since 1991. These episodes are a clear reminder that the presence of taxation is by no means a guarantee that governments will bargain with taxpayers or make any important concessions to them (Fjeldstad and Therkildsen 2008).

Finally, there is no evidence that particular varieties of tax bargaining have been associated with specific types of outcomes. Within the case study countries, direct tax bargaining has contributed to improvements in services, significant reforms of tax policy and administration,

Table 6.1 *Summary of key episodes of tax bargaining*

Taxation without bargaining	Direct tax bargaining	Tax resistance and changes in government	Strengthened political capabilities of taxpayers
Ghana: • Tax Reforms 1982–1990 • Tax increases and fuel price increases 2001–2003 *Kenya:* • Introduction of VAT 1991–1996 • Major increase in tax collection 1993–1996 • Major increase in tax collection 1963–1972 • Fuel price increases 1994–1996 *Ethiopia:* • Tax increases under the Derg 1974–1989 • Increased tax collection 1991–1998 • Increased collection of national taxes 2001–2005 • Increased tax collection 2007–2008	*Improved Provision of Public Services* *Ghana:* VAT increase earmarked for GET Fund 2000 *Ghana:* VAT increase (NHIL) earmarked for NHIS 2003 *Ghana:* Communications Tax earmarked for Youth Employment Scheme 2008 *Kenya:* Road Maintenance Levy 1994 *Kenya:* Business associations' demands for resolution of post-election violence *Changes in Tax Policy and Administration* *All countries:* Increased transparency in tax administration and taxpayer education *Ethiopia:* Tax Assessment Committees for presumptive taxation 2001 *Ghana:* Associational taxation for informal sector *Ghana and Kenya:* Increased taxation of SMEs to gain the support of the business community *Broad Expansions of Accountability* *Ghana:* Anti-VAT protests and political liberalization 1995 *Ghana:* Resistance to fuel price increases and increased inclusiveness in decision-making 1993 *Ethiopia:* Expanded public consultation around presumptive tax 2005	*Kenya 1998–2002:* • Sharp decline in tax revenue resulting from reduced economic growth as well as aggressive evasion by government opponents • Change of government in 2002 elections aided by fiscal crisis • Significant increase in responsiveness and accountability following elections, accompanied by steep increase in tax collection *Ghana 1998–2000:* • Declining tax revenue and growing deficit owing to tax resistance and resistance to increased fuel prices • Change of government in 2000 election contributes to political liberalization • Dramatically improved tax collection after elections *Ethiopia 1989–1991:* • Fiscal crisis exacerbated by rural tax resistance and smuggling • Fiscal crisis central to overthrow of Derg government • Rapid fiscal recovery after transition	*Ghana:* • Association of Ghana Industries (1999–) • Ghana Union of Traders Association (1989, 2007–) • Committee for Joint Action (1995–) *Kenya:* • Kenya Manufacturers Associations and Kenya Private Sector Associations (2002–) • United Business Association (2001, 2005–) • Nairobi Informal Sector Confederation (2002–) • Karen and Langata District Associations (1995–) • Kenya Alliance of Residents' Associations (1999–) • National Taxpayers' Association (2007–) *Ethiopia:* • The mobilization of regional business associations around oversight of presumptive taxes on small businesses

and broader expansions of accountability. Drawing such explicit links is more difficult in cases of indirect tax bargaining, but it is minimally clear that governments coming to power following episodes of tax resistance have similarly courted favour with taxpayers in diverse ways. Following elections in 2002, for example, the newly elected Kenyan government sought to encourage tax compliance through explicit references to a combination of reform of the tax administration, the expansion of free primary education and a desire to reduce aid dependence and increase local accountability.

Ultimately, this absence of any strict correspondence between processes and outcomes is unsurprising. This book proposed that the need for governments to rely on taxing their own citizens is best understood as increasing the effective bargaining power of those taxpayers. Specific outcomes will depend on the particular priorities of those taxpayers and on the particular ruling strategies of governments, as they bargain with one another. As Levi (1999: 115) has previously argued, "it is the ruler who extends the franchise and other rights in order to promote joint ventures with subjects whose cooperation the ruler requires to maximize his own revenue." That is, faced with the same pressure from taxpayers, different governments will almost certainly make different types of concessions depending on their circumstances and priorities. By the same token, taxpayer demands are likely to reflect particular social and political circumstances at a given moment in time, as well as the policy preferences of leading groups. Timmons (2005) has most forcefully argued that different groups of taxpayers may have substantially different priorities, with individual episodes of tax bargaining correspondingly likely to reflect the priorities of those groups that are most affected.

6.2   Causal processes and outcomes

While the case study results provide significant evidence of the potential for conflict over taxation to be a catalyst for broader governance gains, the most novel research contribution lies in offering a better understanding of the specifics of how, and when, this relationship has emerged in practice. As indicated by the results captured in Table 6.1, the case study evidence has confirmed the importance of three related, but ultimately distinct, causal processes through which the need for taxation has contributed to the expansion of responsiveness and accountability. These three causal processes move us beyond the core intuition of existing models, providing both a more nuanced understanding of tax bargaining in practice and a clearer picture of the ways in which processes of tax bargaining are embedded within broader processes of contestation and political change. What follows correspondingly captures the key characteristics of these three causal processes by summarizing key examples from the case studies.

6.2.1 Direct tax bargaining

The term *direct tax bargaining* refers to cases in which governments have relatively explicitly conceded increased responsiveness and accountability in an effort to increase acceptance of taxation by citizens. The framework laid out in Chapter 2 proposed that direct tax bargaining is likely to result in three observable types of outcomes, which are a subset of the broader concepts of responsiveness and accountability: (1) broad expansions of accountability; (2) improved provision of public services; and (3) changes in tax policy and administration. The case studies provide significant examples of each type of outcome, reviewed here in turn.

The most dramatic example of direct tax bargaining was the broad expansion of accountability that followed anti-VAT protests in Ghana. In 1995, the Ghanaian government introduced a new value-added tax, and this prompted what were likely the largest public protests of the previous fifteen years. The unexpected protests quickly led the government to repeal the new law, which was only reintroduced, in revised form, in 1998. More important than the repeal of the tax itself was the fact that the protests came to incorporate much broader demands for political liberalization, which, once catalysed, persisted beyond the repeal of the tax itself. This put pressure on the government, which had remained highly hierarchical, to move towards a more inclusive governing style. The government recognized that such a shift would be required both to calm the immediate anger unleashed by the tax protests and in order to regain the political legitimacy necessary to raise revenue in the future. There is correspondingly near universal agreement in Ghana that the VAT protests were integral to the broader process of political liberalization during this period.

A subsequent example from Ghana highlights the important role of tax bargaining in prompting sustained, and institutionalized, improvements in public service provision. In 2000 and 2003, successive Ghanaian governments sought to introduce increases in the VAT rate. These plans were met by public outcry, and in response, the government agreed to commit all new tax revenues to specific, and popular, social programs. This resulted in the creation of the Ghana Education Trust Fund to support higher education and educational infrastructure and a new National Health Insurance Scheme. Moreover, both funds were accompanied by the creation of new Boards of Directors intended to achieve a measure of transparency in the management of the funds. While significant concerns have been raised about the desirability and credibility of these promises over the long-term, there is little dispute about the fact that the government explicitly conceded targeted public spending, and a degree of increased oversight and transparency, in exchange for public acceptance of new taxation.

Finally, conflict over the presumptive tax on small businesses in Ethiopia prompted the government to marginally increase the transparency of the tax system itself and to introduce new spaces for public engagement. Presumptive taxation had always held the potential for controversy owing to the subjective nature of tax assessment and the high level of direct interaction between tax collectors and taxpayers. Thus, when the government sought improved enforcement of the tax beginning in 2001, it also pre-emptively decided to establish Tax Assessment Committees, composed of representatives from both government and the business community, to increase public confidence in assessment procedures. Despite this measure, the dramatic increase in enforcement led to significant controversy. While political repression in Ethiopia prevented this opposition from erupting into explicit protests, the government came to believe that unhappiness with the tax was a significant factor in its lack of success in controversial elections in 2005. In response, the government reduced rates and, as importantly, took further steps to expand transparency, most notably by creating new public forums in which citizens could raise questions and concerns about tax collection and public expenditure. Both the creation of these forums and the introduction of the Tax Assessment Committees were modest measures, but in a relatively closed political environment they can reasonably be seen as incremental processes for institutionalizing consultation and participation, if not formal accountability. While the subsequent crackdown on political freedoms in Ethiopia has limited any broader gains in accountability, this does not negate the positive pressure generated by conflicts over taxation.

6.2.2 Tax resistance and changes in government

The case studies also capture important evidence of the importance of *tax resistance and changes in government* to the emergence of responsiveness and accountability. This causal process captures cases in which citizens have resisted taxation by an unpopular government, thus creating pressure for a change in government and positive incentives for future reform. These processes hold much in common with cases of direct tax bargaining, but are distinguished by being comparatively long-term and implicit, and correspondingly more likely to be overlooked. To be fully persuasive these cases require evidence that (1) tax resistance contributed to declining tax revenue, (2) fiscal crisis contributed to a change in government, and (3) the new government ushered in important improvements in responsiveness and accountability. In addition to these factors, the most compelling cases were those in which incoming governments experienced significant revenue gains after explicitly linking governance improvements to efforts to increase tax collection.

The most clear-cut example comes from Kenya, where revenue collection declined dramatically after controversial elections in 1997. Part of the decline was attributable to declining economic growth, but well placed observers are nearly unanimous in arguing that it was also the result of relatively explicit efforts by supporters of the opposition to evade existing taxes, resist new taxes and weaken the fiscal position of the government. The success of this tax resistance contributed to a growing fiscal crisis, which, in turn, made a change in government in the 2002 elections more likely. As importantly, having witnessed the struggles of its predecessor, the incoming government made tax reform a major priority and sought to explicitly link efforts to increase tax collection to success in increasing accountability, strengthening the fairness of the tax system, and expanding popular social programs. Thus we have a clear case in which tax resistance, largely by elites, created added pressure for a change in government and provided positive incentives for future reform. This message is reinforced by evidence that when violence broke out after the 2007 elections the business community used the threat of non-compliance with taxation as an important means to gain leverage over the government in calling for a peaceful resolution.

A similar pattern was apparent in Ghana, where government controlled fuel prices were the central issue. As noted previously, while government controlled fuel prices are not technically taxes, changes in fuel prices were fiscally and behaviourally equivalent to taxes, with higher prices for consumers entailing greater government revenue. In the late 1990s, global fuel prices began to rise, which implied fiscal losses for the government if domestic fuel prices remained unchanged. The government hoped to raise domestic fuel prices along with global prices, but such increases were judged to be politically impossible owing to relentless public opposition driven by frustration with the declining pace of political liberalization. The inability of the government to raise fuel prices was, in turn, central to a growing fiscal crisis, and to this day remains a source of frustration to prominent figures in the government at the time. As in Kenya, the fiscal crisis contributed to a change of government in the 2000 elections. As importantly, the incoming government learned from the fiscal struggles of its predecessor, and quickly made tax reform, including increased fuel

6.2 Causal processes and outcomes

prices, a major priority linked explicitly to broader political liberalization. Thus, again, resistance to taxation created pressure for a change in government and generated positive incentives for the incoming government to adopt a reformist agenda.

In Ethiopia, tax resistance has not played an equally decisive role, but there is nonetheless evidence of the ability of taxpayers to use tax resistance as a means to respond to political repression. Under the Derg regime, political opposition was aggressively controlled, while even the potential for tax resistance was reduced by government control over a significant portion of economic activity. Tax resistance in rural areas appears, nonetheless, to have played a limited role in accelerating the fiscal crisis that was central to the eventual overthrow of the government in 1991, while there are difficult-to-verify suggestions that the growing unpopularity of the government may similarly have undermined profits within state-owned firms. While the incoming government remained autocratic, it undoubtedly marked a move towards political liberalization and greater responsiveness.

More than a decade later the potential importance of tax resistance was again apparent, as tax collection fell sharply in the aftermath of highly controversial elections in 2005. In this case it was the government that pre-emptively decided to cut tax rates and ease the aggressiveness of tax enforcement, but that choice was a response to quiet, but increasingly apparent, public opposition. The sharp fall in tax revenue after 2005 did not lead to a change in government, as the EPRDF was firmly entrenched in power and managed to aggressively repress the opposition. However, the fact that quiet public opposition was sufficient to generate a sharp fall in tax revenue collection even in a relatively repressive environment provides powerful confirmation of the ability of taxpayers to weaken unpopular regimes through their opposition to tax collection.

While tax resistance is thus an important mechanism for taxpayers to generate pressure for expanded responsiveness and accountability, it is important to bear in mind that tax resistance is a relatively blunt political instrument. While aggressive tax resistance can weaken an unpopular incumbent, it cannot guarantee that a new government will be more responsive and accountable than its predecessor. The basic message is nonetheless clear: when a government is reliant on tax revenue taxpayers have the potential to threaten the regime through tax resistance. In some cases that threat will contribute to direct tax bargaining, but, even where it does not, tax resistance can be a means to undermine repressive regimes, thus opening the door to reform. This causal process is comparatively complex, and intertwined with broader political developments, and as a result has received little attention in existing research. However, these narratives are very consistent with the implicit and conflictual character of tax bargaining historically in early modern Europe, and thus add important breadth to contemporary understanding of the links between taxation, responsiveness and accountability.

6.2.3 Strengthened political capabilities of taxpayers

Finally, the case studies capture instances in which increases in taxation have acted as a catalyst for *strengthening the political capabilities of taxpayers*, thus contributing to long-term demands for responsiveness and accountability. While taxation may contribute to long-term levels of political engagement in relatively invisible ways, this research has focused on cases in which conflicts over taxation have contributed to strengthening visible civil society networks and organizations, which have in turn made broader demands for the expansion of responsiveness and accountability.

The experience of the Committee for Joint Action (CJA) in Ghana speaks clearly to the potential centrality of taxation to the mobilizing efforts of civil society actors. The CJA was initially founded in the aftermath of the anti-VAT protests, emerging as an informal heir to the broader Alliance for Change, which directed the 1995 *Kume Preko* protests. While conflict over taxation figured centrally in the origins of the CJA, it subsequently grew beyond its initial founding, emerging as an important organizer of mass public mobilization around issues of political liberalization, corruption and poverty reduction. Yet even as the CJA has grown to encompass a much wider vision and focus, its efforts have continued to be profoundly shaped by tax debates. Since 1995, the CJA has repeatedly used frustration over tax related issues, including high fuel prices, as a central theme for mobilizing public protests aimed at demanding broader improvements in government performance. In the words of one of the CJA's leaders, quoted earlier: "Taxes have always provided a focal point for public mobilization. Have provided momentum for the resistance."

The Centre for Governance and Development (CGD) in Kenya has made more explicit use of the idea that taxation can be a catalyst for public engagement over the longer-term. The CGD was already supporting local level expenditure monitoring when, in 2005, it decided to participate in the founding of a National Taxpayers' Association (NTA). The goal of the NTA was to explicitly link tax-related concerns and advocacy to existing activities related to expenditure monitoring. The NTA organizers believed that by reinforcing community ownership of public revenues they could encourage more active public engagement. While still in its infancy, the campaign has found that the message that tax payment can be a basis for making claims on the government has significant public resonance, and has the potential to become an increasingly important basis for public engagement and advocacy.

Finally, the case studies have highlighted a wide array of instances in which taxes have played a role in catalysing enhanced, and more constructive, political engagement amongst business associations. In some ways these examples are particularly interesting, as business associations are viewed by some as a key component of improved governance in the developing world, but have remained very weak throughout sub-Saharan Africa (Doner and Schneider 2000; Handley 2008). The central question about business associations in the region has long been whether they would act as narrow rent-seeking organizations (Olson 1965; Goldsmith 2002), or whether they would become productive interest groups engaged in processes of "constructive contestation" with government (Bräutigam, Rakner and Taylor 2002; Handley 2008: 2).

One of the key insights from earlier research is that the emergence of constructively engaged business associations requires the emergence of a unified set of interests that encourages cooperation and collective action. Because taxation, when equitably applied, often represents a common threat to a large segment of the business community, it has played an important role in spurring precisely this kind of unified engagement with government. This has, in turn, had lasting implications for the ability of business associations to become active in demanding greater responsiveness and accountability from government. The impact of taxation on the activities of business associations can be seen throughout the case studies, both amongst large business associations, including the Association of Ghana Industries and the Kenya Private Sector Association, and amongst associations representing small and medium enterprises, including the United Business Association in Kenya and the Ghana Union of Traders Association.

6.3 Contextual factors and tax bargaining

Having identified these multiple causal processes linking taxation, responsiveness and accountability, the final aim of this book has been to begin to understand the contextual factors shaping the likelihood and the form of tax bargaining. This is a particularly ambitious goal given the complexity of the processes involved, but is equally essential. The empirical evidence presented here makes clear that while direct and indirect forms of tax bargaining have played an important role in the case study countries, such processes have been highly varied and far from guaranteed. The Ghanaian case study captured extensive evidence of direct tax bargaining, while indirect tax bargaining figured more prominently in the Kenyan case. In Ethiopia, observable evidence of tax bargaining was comparatively rare, owing to a range of social, economic and political barriers. Meanwhile, patterns of tax bargaining have varied substantially over time and across tax episodes within each individual case. Understanding the sources of this variation is essential to understanding where positive outcomes are likely and, critically, how they may be fostered and supported more effectively.

Of course, the range of contextual factors that may shape outcomes is potentially limitless. Tax bargaining is embedded within broader processes of political contestation, and is thus likely to be shaped by the entire range of factors shaping the bargaining power and preferences of competing groups. The key analytical challenge has thus been to develop a manageable and flexible framework for analysing the role of context in shaping outcomes.

At the broadest level, the contextual factors that are expected to shape tax bargaining are those that *strengthen the capacity for demand-making amongst taxpayers through tax resistance and collective action*; and those that *strengthen the incentives for governments to make reciprocal concessions*. The analytical model in Chapter 2 subsequently sought to disaggregate the analysis slightly further, highlighting five structural factors that are expected to shape the extent and character of tax bargaining: *Revenue pressure facing governments, the scope and potential for tax resistance, factors affecting taxpayer capacity for collective action, the existence of institutions that facilitate tax bargaining* and *the political salience of taxation*. These structural factors are attractive because each captures an analytically distinct pathway through which contextual factors may shape outcomes. In turn, each *structural factor* is expected to reflect more idiosyncratic and country-specific *contextual variables*, which are individually distinct but which shape the potential for tax bargaining in analytically comparable ways.

In seeking to assess the role of these different structural factors in shaping outcomes, the analysis in this book has sought to exploit variation in tax bargaining *across countries*, but also to exploit variation in tax bargaining *within countries over time*, in response to changes in key contextual factors. Thus, for example, democratization in Ghana in the mid-1990s has made it possible to compare the dynamics of tax bargaining before and after democratization, while keeping a variety of country specific variables relatively unchanged. Each individual chapter has concluded with a discussion of the contextual factors that appear to have been pivotal in shaping specific outcomes within each case. What follows pulls the case study evidence together more systematically. The discussion is organized around the structural factors that are the focus of the model, while it highlights specific contextual variables that have been most important in shaping outcomes in the cases examined here. Finally, this section concludes with a set of broader reflections about those factors that have been most important, setting the stage for discussion of the policy implications of these findings in the concluding chapter.

6.3.1 Revenue pressure facing governments

The first structural factor expected to shape the potential for tax bargaining is the level of *revenue pressure* facing governments. Governments that would ideally raise additional revenue, but which do not face acute pressure to do so, will have greater flexibility in responding to tax resistance. While they may opt to make concessions to support increased revenue collection, they equally have the option of tolerating reduced tax collection rather than making unwanted concessions to taxpayers. By contrast, governments facing urgent revenue needs will have strong incentives to make reciprocal concessions to taxpayers to encourage tax collection. While a government facing significant revenue pressure may refuse to make concessions nonetheless, it may find itself crippled by even a small downturn in revenue, thus raising the likelihood of losing power.

Of course, a variety of distinct contextual variables may shape the level of revenue pressure facing governments. The most frequently cited variable is access to significant non-tax revenue, most often from non-renewable natural resources. By offering governments greater fiscal flexibility, access to such non-tax revenue is expected, on average, to reduce pressure on governments to make concessions to taxpayers in the face of declining revenue. This in part explains why governments with extensive access to non-tax revenue raise far fewer taxes: they would rather forego additional revenue than risk politically costly efforts to impose new taxes, which might spark popular demands for responsiveness and accountability (Bornhorst, Gupta and Thornton 2008; McGuirk 2013).

While the case studies here do not focus explicitly on the role of natural resource wealth, they have instead captured the role of a variety of additional contextual variables – including high deficits, economic downturns and external pressure – that have shaped the revenue pressure facing governments in more idiosyncratic ways. In Ghana, anti-VAT protests in 1995 emerged in part because the government sought to introduce the new VAT law extremely quickly and with little consultation. This was, in turn, a response to acute revenue pressure resulting from high spending before the 1992 elections and mounting donor pressure. This revenue pressure not only set the stage for the initial protests, but equally put pressure on the government to subsequently re-engage the opposition in an effort to reintroduce the tax. Without increased revenue pressure and the urgency that it engendered, it is possible, and even likely, that the VAT protests would never have occurred on the scale that they did. It seems equally possible that the government would not have engaged in such extensive subsequent compromise with the opposition had it not faced an urgent need to reintroduce the tax.

While this example points to the importance of revenue pressure in driving direct tax bargaining, there is equally evidence that revenue pressure has made governments more vulnerable to tax resistance. In Ghana, public opposition to the expansion of taxation (including the raising of fuel prices) became politically pivotal in the late 1990s, as a mounting fiscal deficit precipitated the defeat of the incumbent government in elections in 2000. However, the political impact of tax resistance was contingent on mounting revenue pressure resulting from additional sources as well, including increased public spending prior to the 1996 elections, stagnant economic growth and rising global fuel prices. In Kenya, purposeful tax resistance played a similarly important role in undermining the Moi government in the late 1990s. And, again, tax resistance proved particularly pivotal only in the context of the broader revenue pressure facing the government as a result of stagnating economic growth.

A final example relates to the apparent role of foreign aid in curbing the potential for tax bargaining in Ethiopia. Before and after contested elections in 2005 one of the strategies pursued by the government to court public support was a sharp reduction in tax collection. The result was a decline in tax collection from 12.6 per cent of GDP in 2004 to only 9.6 per cent of GDP in 2008. Such a dramatic decline in public revenue appears to have been facilitated by continued high levels of foreign assistance, with total Official Development Assistance (ODA) remaining above 12 per cent of GDP in 2008, alongside increasing financing from China. In the language adopted here, foreign aid reduced the revenue pressure facing the Ethiopian government following the 2005 elections, thus making it easier for the government to reduce tax collection and the corresponding potential for public mobilization and opposition.

6.3.2 *The potential and scope for tax resistance*

Classic models of tax bargaining developed by Bates and Lien (1985) and Levi (1988) both centre on the extent to which the *potential for tax resistance* by taxpayers creates incentives for rulers to make governing concessions in an effort to encourage "quasi-voluntary" compliance. A wide variety of factors may influence the extent of this potential for tax resistance,[1] but the case studies point most strongly towards the importance of two contextual variables: (1) the strength of elites and the private sector, and (2) variation in tax types and other features of the tax system. What follows considers each variable in turn.

The strength of elites and the private sector
In Tilly's (1992) accounts linking taxation and state-building in early modern Europe the economic power wielded by the capitalist class is the decisive factor in shaping processes of tax bargaining. Where the capitalist class was powerful, tax bargaining was likely; whereas countries that lacked a strong capitalist class tended to pursue more coercive forms of taxation. The reason for this pattern was simple: capitalists controlled valuable and mobile economic resources and the state could only secure access to those resources through bargaining. It was comparatively easy for capitalists to evade taxation, owing to the extent, secrecy and mobility of their assets, or to draw on their greater resources to resist taxation directly. This logic has been most recently re-emphasized by Moore (2008: 40–42) who has argued that in contemporary developing countries bargaining will be most pronounced in countries with strong private sectors capable of engaging in tax evasion, tax resistance and collective action, while tax bargaining will be comparatively unlikely in poor and agrarian contexts.

These predictions are borne out by the case study evidence, as the comparatively strong private sectors in Kenya and Ghana have contributed in important ways to tax bargaining, while the weakness of the private sector in Ethiopia has significantly weakened the potential for bargaining around taxation. In Kenya, the ability of wealthy individuals and businesses to engage in aggressive tax evasion has been central to episodes of direct and indirect tax bargaining. Tax resistance during the late 1990s contributed to deepening the fiscal crisis and to a change in government in 2002, and this tax resistance was driven to a large extent by large business taxpayers. A similar pattern emerged when violence broke out

---

[1] Bates and Lien (1985), for example, specifically highlight the role of mobility in increasing potential for tax evasion and resistance, and, by extension, the bargaining power of mobile taxpayers. However, this focus on mobility is comparatively abstract and stands in for the more general notion that tax bargaining will reflect the ability of taxpayers to gain leverage through the extent of the threat of evasion. Taken most literally, the focus on mobility points towards the potential leverage enjoyed by highly mobile international firms, and this leverage is reflected in widespread investment incentives enjoyed by those firms. However, such narrow benefits are not the primary focus here, as described in Chapter 2.

following elections in 2007, as large Kenyan firms played an important role in pressuring the government to achieve a resolution of the conflict, in part through threats of non-compliance with taxation.

By contrast, the weakness of the private sector in Ethiopia has contributed to a lack of direct involvement in processes of tax bargaining. Alongside the relatively small size of the private sector, the government in Ethiopia has continued to play an unusually prominent role in managing the economy, while the ruling party continues to control important areas of economic activity. This prominent government role in shaping access to economic opportunities appears, in turn, to have played a continuing role in limiting the ability of opposition figures to use tax resistance as a political strategy, with business leaders expressing a greater wariness about challenging the tax demands of the state than in the other case study countries. To be clear, businesses *did* resist and evade taxation following the 2005 elections, and this *did* contribute to declining government revenue. However, the potential for such resistance – and its consequent impact – was constrained by the weakness of the independent private sector.

Part of this weakness reflected the limited economic power of the Ethiopian private sector. However, all of the case studies make clear that the ability of the private sector to secure governance gains through politically motivated tax resistance has depended not only on the economic strength of the private sector, but also on its unity. While political unity amongst private sector interests is particularly important to the potential for collective action, successful tax resistance has also turned on a measure of implicit or explicit coordination amongst larger firms. In Kenya in the late 1990s, officials report a measure of implicit coordination and political intent as leading firms expanded their tax evasion. This both multiplied the revenue impact of resistance and strengthened incentives for the incoming government to respond. Likewise, the threat of tax resistance after the disputed elections in 2007 became more effective because of a degree of unity amongst business actors. In the same vein, the lack of unity amongst businesses in Ethiopia – split between private businesses, endowment companies and SOEs, and also divided along sectoral lines – has minimized the potential for crosscutting efforts to expanded resistance and evasion.

Features of the tax system and tax reform

While the importance of elites to the potential for politically influential tax resistance is thus apparent, existing research suggests that particular features of the tax system may also shape the scope for tax evasion and resistance. This logic is most commonly reflected in the prediction that

6.3 Contextual factors and tax bargaining

direct taxes – and personal and corporate income taxes in particular – will be central to processes of tax bargaining, as income taxes are particularly important to the taxation of elites and pose the greatest threat of evasion (Moore 1998; Lieberman 2002; Mahon 2005). Empirically, examples of politically influential tax resistance from the case studies have, indeed, revolved to at least some extent around income taxation. Tax resistance in Kenya in the late 1990s included a significant decline in the collection of direct taxes, as predicted by theory, while threats of non-compliance following electoral violence in 2007 similarly centred on corporate tax payments. Perhaps more strikingly, the only meaningful evidence of direct tax bargaining in Ethiopia surrounded presumptive taxes collected at the subnational level, with the presumptive taxes distinguished by their high degree of visibility, direct interaction between taxpayers and tax officials, and significant scope for negotiation and evasion.

However, the case study evidence suggests that a narrow focus on tax types can be misleading, with a corresponding need to also consider the roles of *tax administration* and *features of the reform process* in shaping the potential for tax resistance. The role of tax administration is particularly intuitive: where the administration is more vulnerable to corruption, collusion and ineffective enforcement, the potential for evasion, and the corresponding importance of quasi-voluntary compliance, will be amplified. This was part of the story in Kenya, where purposeful tax evasion in the late 1990s was facilitated by an increasingly de-motivated tax administration, which opened new spaces for evasion and collusion. Ethiopian officials similarly cite diminished administrative effectiveness, and significant administrative uncertainty, following the 2005 elections as an important contributor to reduced tax collection

Meanwhile, the importance of the *process of tax reform* lies in the fact that resistance to taxation may occur through evasion, but may also occur through popular resistance that makes tax increases politically unfeasible. In turn, the likelihood that taxes will be effectively blocked by public opposition depends in significant part on the extent to which the reform process makes proposed tax increases politically salient, thus inviting popular resistance. This was the case in Ghana, where the fiscal crisis of the late 1990s was amplified by the inability of the government to raise government-controlled fuel prices, or to increase VAT rates as quickly as hoped, in the face of generalized public opposition. This resistance to indirect taxes was made possible by the unusual salience of these taxes in the public consciousness following the 1995 anti-VAT protests, which made the reform processes the subject of unusually significant public scrutiny. This question of the political salience of taxation is taken up in greater detail later in this chapter.

6.3.3 Factors affecting taxpayer capacity for collective action

While formal models of tax bargaining have tended to emphasize the importance of tax resistance in spurring governing concessions, more recent studies have tended to stress the potential for taxation to act as a catalyst for collective action and political mobilization. However, the potential for collective action in response to taxation is expected to be highly dependent on context, given the existence of significant and well-known barriers to collective action. Following the model developed in Chapter 2, what follows highlights three factors that appear to have been particularly influential in shaping the potential for tax bargaining: the extent of political openness, the unity of taxpayer interests, particularly amongst elites, and the nature of established expectations.

Political openness, repression and tax bargaining

The strongest prediction from theory is that tax bargaining, at least in relatively observable forms, is likely to be comparatively rare where governments are relatively repressive. While both tax resistance and collective action may be more difficult in repressive environments owing to the risk of retaliation by the state, it is the scope for collective action that is likely to be most sharply limited.

The case study evidence is consistent with these predictions, with tax bargaining having been significantly more limited in comparatively repressive contexts. This is most apparent in Ethiopia, where public engagement with tax issues was virtually non-existent under the Derg and where visible public action around tax issues has remained very rare under the EPRDF since 1991. In Ghana, tax bargaining was similarly rare under military rule from 1981 to 1992, despite dramatic increases in tax collection, while more visible and direct forms of tax bargaining emerged following moves towards democratization. In Kenya, key stakeholders likewise attribute the absence of direct tax bargaining in the 1980s and 1990s to the relatively repressive character of the government, while visible public conflict over taxation has expanded since 2002.

However, while tax bargaining appears less frequent in repressive contexts, it has not been entirely absent but has, instead, frequently taken less visible and direct forms. Taxpayers in repressive environments have instead relied on comparatively indirect and implicit modes of bargaining, led by tax resistance through tax evasion. In Kenya, taxpayers did not engage in significant tax related collective action during the 1990s, owing at least in part to restrictions on political freedom, but they did protest through aggressive tax resistance during the latter half of the decade. In

Ethiopia, conflict over the presumptive tax on small businesses led the government to make modest concessions to taxpayers, but, consistent with the difficulty of collective action in repressive environments, taxpayers expressed their grievances not through protests, but quietly through tax resistance, voting and informal channels. As such, the extent of political openness is best understood as impacting both the likelihood *and* the form of tax bargaining, with political repression minimizing the scope for collective action and more direct forms of tax bargaining.

Elite leadership and the importance of unified interests
While collective action is thus crucially dependent on the broad political environment, research elsewhere has long argued that leadership from elites, including small but influential middle classes in low-income countries, is often critical to the success of collective action. Elites enjoy access to critical political resources and have the profile and means to play a role in crystalizing disparate grievances (McAdam, Tarrow and Tilly 2001: 142–143). Moreover, they are likely to be particularly important to public mobilization around taxation as a result of bearing the largest share of the tax burden. Again, the case study evidence is consistent with this prediction. However, it also adds nuance by drawing attention both to the importance, and challenge, of achieving elite unity around a set of collective demands, and to the importance of interrogating the ability of elite groups to gain the support of broader constituencies.

The importance of elite leadership is most clearly demonstrated by the anti-VAT protests in Ghana. Despite the mass character of the protests themselves, it was elite groups, including the political opposition, who were crucial to mobilizing broader public engagement, and transforming the protests into a major political uprising. Ninsin (2007: 94) stresses the elite dimension, going so far as to argue that "those sporadic mass actions were part of opposition politics.... They were therefore not driven by citizens' free will to effect policy changes." While this may be an overly pessimistic assessment of citizen action, it serves to stress the critical role of elite politics.

Elite leadership is similarly apparent in the genesis of the largest tax protests to have occurred in Kenya, which surrounded the introduction of Electronic Tax Registers (ETRs) for medium sized businesses. In this case it was the owners of medium sized businesses, organized through the United Business Association (UBA), who were at the forefront of large-scale protests across the largest cities in the country. The activities of residents' associations in Kenya similarly have been dominated by elites. The most concerted collective action has been undertaken by the Karen and Langata District Association (KLDA), which represents what has historically been Nairobi's most wealthy neighbourhood. More broadly, the emergence of increasingly regular consultation between the government and large business associations around tax issues in both Ghana and Kenya speaks to the important institutional position occupied by elite economic actors in shaping tax debates.

However, the case studies make clear that elite leadership in prompting governance-enhancing tax bargaining depends critically on the emergence of relatively unified interests amongst those elite groups – and their ability to gain the support of broader constituencies. In Ghana the political opposition had been divided and ineffective prior to the 1995 anti-VAT protests. Earlier tax increases had not prompted significant popular resistance, owing in part to the ability of the government to frame tax increases as an effort to target a narrow group of formerly corrupt elites. The success of the anti-VAT protests lay in bringing together leading opposition politicians, prominent members of civil society, large and small businesses, and citizens at large, all unified around calls for the repeal of the tax and for political liberalization.

Even more striking is the extent to which a lack of unity ultimately undermined protests against ETRs in Kenya. While the UBA was successful in mobilizing large protests in multiple cities, these protests failed almost entirely to catalyse broader popular action or demands for responsiveness and accountability. Instead, the protesters found themselves without support from the public or other elites, both of whom labelled the protesters 'Asian tax evaders' rather than allies. Given this lack of public support, the government was able to press through the ETR requirement without making meaningful concessions to the protesting businesses. This is consistent with a wider range of experiences in Kenya, as successive governments framed new taxes as targeting minority Whites and Asians, thus fragmenting taxpayers' interests and reducing the likelihood of collective action.

While the importance of achieving unified elite interests is not itself surprising, these cases highlight the basic difficulties inherent in achieving such unity – as well as potential avenues for encouraging greater collective action. Margaret Levi (1988) has argued that elites will frequently respond to the threat of taxation not through support for collective demands but by seeking narrow privileges and benefits ("side-payments"). The intuition is straightforward: for elite taxpayers it may frequently be more rational to engage directly with governments in search of special privileges or tax exemptions (both formal and informal) than to engage in attempting to spur collective action and collective demands. Likewise, governments may prefer to grant narrow benefits to powerful

6.3 Contextual factors and tax bargaining

taxpayers, rather than making broader based concessions. This is consistent with the conclusions of studies of business associations in low-income countries, which have argued that business associations have often functioned as narrow, highly personalized, rent-seeking organizations, rather than venues for pressing for broader governance gains (Olson 1965; Goldsmith 2002). It is equally consistent with continuing concern that the widespread use of tax exemptions in developing countries may undermine the emergence of more effective demands for democratic accountability (Therkildsen 2012).

And, indeed, precisely this pattern is apparent in looking at the historical evolution of business associations in the case study countries. Until at least the late 1990s the private sector in Kenya was characterized by extensive rent-seeking, with many businesses responding to taxation by seeking individual benefits and exemptions rather than broader political influence for the sector. The result was the development of close individual links between businesses and the state, while business associations played little role in engaging with tax issues or pressing for improved governance. Instead, business associations acted largely as vehicles for advancing the individual ambitions of particular firms and individuals. In Ghana, the role of business associations was still more limited prior to the mid-1990s, as they lacked any significant and autonomous institutional strength, and individual businesses sought benefits through bilateral ties to the government (Handley 2008). However, in both countries this dynamic began to shift towards the end of the 1990s, as businesses began to privilege collective demands to a greater degree, and began to develop into more cohesive organizations with a broader role in national debates. This has been most obviously reflected in the emergence in both countries of institutionalized spaces through which governments seek to consult business associations.

While the tendency of business actors to pursue narrow benefits thus represents an important barrier to collective action around taxation, the more recent shift towards greater cohesiveness also holds potentially important lessons. This shift in the behaviour of business associations appears to reflect a variety of factors, including expanded autonomy in the wake of democratization and economic liberalization.[2] However,

---

[2] In the most extensive existing work on business associations in Africa, Handley (2008) stresses the lack of autonomy of business associations across much of the continent owing to dependence on the central state and the absence of institutionalized channels for dialogue. With economic liberalization, this dependence on the state has declined, while new institutional spaces have been created, although the extent of these patterns should not be overstated.

subtle changes in tax systems have also played a role in shifting bargaining incentives. Alongside processes of economic liberalization, governments in both Ghana and Kenya took steps to enforce taxation more uniformly amongst large businesses, and, in so doing, reduced opportunities for individual exemptions. In both countries this was particularly true in relation to newly instituted value-added taxes, although enforcement of corporate income taxes also become more uniform over time in both countries. By confronting the business community with a relatively uniform "threat," and diminished opportunities for bilateral bargaining, these changes strengthened incentives for collective action, with implication beyond the narrow realm of tax policy. This should not, of course, be overstated: in both countries formal and informal tax exemptions remain common for the politically well connected, and business associations in Ghana in particular remain relatively weakly institutionalized (Doner and Schneider 2000; Handley 2008). However, this broad pattern speaks to the potential for more uniform application of tax policy to generate more unified and collective business interests, and thus to spur tax bargaining.

Pre-existing organizations and linkages

The growing role of business associations speaks to a broader message: the potential for shifting tax bargaining away from the search for narrow benefits, and towards more collective demands for improved governance, has depended critically on the existence of organizations capable of translating dispersed interests into collective action. While public mobilization in Ghana in response to the introduction of the VAT in 1995 was crucially dependent on the existence of unified demands amongst elites, the extension of the protests to a much wider constituency was made possible by the role of broader based organizations, led by opposition political parties and representatives of the pro-democracy movement. It was these organizations that were positioned to rally broader public grievances in response to a tax that is widely felt to have been only poorly understood by much of the public.

This pattern was repeated after the end of the protests in Ghana, as the CJA was created as a loose coalition linking civil society leaders and opposition political figures. Critically, the CJA was not a large civil society organization in the conventional sense, with few regular programs, members or staff. It was, instead, a loose coalition that sought to preserve key political ties, inherit the legacy of the anti-VAT protests, and retain the reputation and capacity for mass political mobilization. Consistent with these goals, this latent capacity for public mobilization has repeatedly proven valuable, as the CJA has played a regular role in

6.3 Contextual factors and tax bargaining 235

mobilizing broader public engagement around tax and revenue issues. This has particularly involved mobilization in response to upward changes in previously government-controlled fuel prices, but the latent potential for mobilization was equally apparent in response to subsequent increases in the VAT rate in particular.

While the CJA thus emerged as an institution capable of leading periodic mass mobilization in response to tax and revenue issues, civil society organizations in Kenya are indicative of a more conventional civil society role in spurring public engagement with tax issues. Although comparatively limited in scope, both the Karen and Langata District Association (KLDA) and the Kenya Alliance of Resident Associations (KARA) played important roles in mobilizing urban constituencies around questions of reciprocity in the use of tax revenue. Meanwhile, in smaller towns the Centre for Governance and Development (CGD) has sought to leverage its existing role in public expenditure monitoring in order to raise awareness about tax issues and mobilize public concerns. These examples appear to speak to the potential role for such organizations in bringing tax debates to broader constituencies.

Finally, we see instances in which business associations have played a similar role as catalysts for collective action beyond their narrow membership. At a broad level, we see evidence of the role of business associations in both Ghana and Kenya in spurring public debate around tax issues and government spending. By contrast, the weakness of the Chamber of Commerce in Ethiopia, which has strictly avoided playing an advocacy role in relation to tax issues, has seemed to contribute to stifling tax debates more broadly. However, the most interesting potential role of business associations is revealed in the activities of those representing small and medium sized firms. In Kenya, the United Business Association (UBA), which represents medium sized businesses, was a lynchpin in the mobilization of public protests in response to the introduction of ETRs. While the absence of public support, described earlier, undermined the eventual effectiveness of these efforts, they speak to the potential role of broad-based business associations. This potential is similarly apparent in Ghana, where the Ghana Union of Traders Association (GUTA) has allowed small businesses to make reciprocal demands for market services in exchange for tax payments, and where the Ghana Private Road Transport Union (GPRTU) was successful in negotiating reciprocal benefits in exchange for tax payments by their members. While these latter examples do not amount to particularly broad based tax bargains, they move beyond the realm "side payments" to elites and point to the potential for smaller business associations to unify disparate interests in pursuit of incremental gains.

The nature of expectations

Finally, previous research has suggested that the potential for collective action around taxation is also likely to depend on whether taxpayers have developed expectations of reciprocity around taxation or consider tax demands to be excessive and inconsistent with established notions of fairness (Tilly 1992: 101). This is consistent with broader arguments holding that accountability cannot be divorced from expectations and norms, as these expectations dictate the types of demands that citizens consider legitimate and warranted (Grant and Keohane 2005: 31).

This possibility is difficult to assess empirically, but the available evidence is generally supportive of the idea that expectations can play an important role – and that this may be an important entry point for thinking about how tax bargaining may be fostered. The most striking example of the importance of expectations comes from Ethiopia, where a wide range of observers attribute the relative lack of public mobilization in response to taxation in part to the absence of strong expectations of reciprocity, particularly in rural areas. This has been attributed in part to the recent history of extremely coercive taxation under the Derg government. More provocatively, there are widespread suggestions that those in rural areas often think of agricultural and property taxation in tributary rather than reciprocal terms, reflecting the norms and expectations that surrounded the paying of tribute during the Imperial period.

The case of repeated public mobilization around increases in the VAT in Ghana shares some of these characteristics. There is a widely held sense that the initial anti-VAT protests, and the earmarking of the subsequent increase in the VAT for the Ghana Education Trust Fund, contributed to establishing particular expectations of reciprocity. With those expectations established, tax earmarking has become a repeated feature of Ghanaian tax debates in subsequent years, despite being comparatively uncommon elsewhere in the region.

A growing body of research has refuted any broad generalizations about the absence of expectations of reciprocity in low-income countries (Fjeldstad and Semboja 2001). However, it remains likely that expectations of reciprocity will vary in their intensity and character, with both historical differences and recent experiences of conflict over taxation likely to contribute to this variation. It is this possibility that underpins the work of the Centre for Governance and Development in Kenya, which has sought to explicitly link discussion of tax collection to the monitoring of public spending at the local government level. Underlying their approach is a belief that by highlighting the connections between revenue and expenditure they can alter citizens' expectations of reciprocity

6.3 Contextual factors and tax bargaining

around taxation, and by doing so transform tax payment into an entry point for more active demands for improved governance.

6.3.4 Political institutions and the potential for bargaining

The preceding discussion has already highlighted the importance of political openness in creating space for collective action and relatively explicit forms of direct tax bargaining. However, while broad political openness can create space for collective action, more inclusive political institutions can also shape the extent and character of tax bargaining in more specific ways. They can do so by providing spaces for direct interaction and bargaining between taxpayers and the state, by extending political time horizons, and by providing a context for expanded trust between taxpayers and governments (Skocpol 1992).

Representative institutions and tax bargaining

Levi (1988) and North and Weingast (1989) have argued that representative institutions may facilitate relatively explicit bargaining between governments and taxpayers by providing a forum for aggregating taxpayer interests and demands. Indeed, they propose that historically rulers agreed to establish representative institutions in part in order to facilitate credible bargaining over taxation, as an alternative to more drawn-out protest and conflict.

The prediction that representative institutions will facilitate explicit forms of direct tax bargaining is clearly borne out by experiences in Ghana. When the government sought to introduce the VAT in 1995 it did so at a time when the opposition was boycotting parliament, thus rendering organized political bargaining unlikely. As a result the implementation of the VAT was undertaken hastily and was met by large public protests, with the political opposition playing a leading role. The resulting tax bargain did not emerge from any explicit agreement between protesters and the government, but from what Moore (2008) has termed "mutual behaviour adjustment," as the government repealed the tax and opted to adopt a more inclusive governing style in order to prevent similar protests in the future.

Part of the government reaction to the anti-VAT protests was a greater commitment to ensuring that the elections held in 1996 were perceived to be fair, thus encouraging the entry of the opposition into parliament. This, in turn, facilitated more explicit forms of direct tax bargaining in the future. The reintroduction of the VAT was achieved peacefully in 1998 after significant consultation and bargaining between the government and the opposition. Later increases in the VAT rate likewise prompted public opposition, but that opposition was resolved through explicit bargaining in parliament that resulted in additional revenue being earmarked for the Ghana Education Trust Fund and the National Health Insurance Scheme. The same pattern was followed by other taxes, as the extension of the National Reconstruction Levy included explicit concessions to the business community, while part of the revenue from the Communications Tax in 2008 was earmarked for youth employment. The basic message is that once the role of parliament was strengthened, so too was the potential for relatively explicit forms of direct tax bargaining.

Of course, while "inclusive political institutions" is a useful short hand, specific institutions invariably empower certain groups more than others. This is, in turn, likely to be reflected in the nature of resultant tax bargains. The case studies offer only relatively limited evidence on this point – in part because it is difficult to gauge which groups are "most empowered" in particular instances and whether a given tax bargain benefits them disproportionately. The most noteworthy trend is the growth of forums in both Ghana and Kenya through which the larger business community has been offered unique spaces for dialogue with the government. It is possible to discern moments in which this appears to have offered businesses additional leverage over policy decisions, as with the creation of a venture capital fund in Ghana in order to mute opposition to the National Reconstruction Levy. This echoes a similar concern raised by Moore (2014), who has noted growing dialogue between tax agencies and the private sector, and the corresponding risk of disproportionate policy influence for the latter. There are therefore grounds for focusing attention on the development of more inclusive forums in which to discuss tax issues, in order to balance the unique access enjoyed by larger business associations.

Democratic politics, political time horizons and incentives to bargain

While political institutions thus appear to have played an important role in facilitating direct tax bargaining, institutions may also affect *incentives to bargain* through their impact on political time horizons. Levi (1999: 115) has argued that because it is ultimately political leaders who decide whether to bargain or not, "only secure and relatively powerful rulers will act in this way; insecure rulers will grant exemptions to those whose alliance is necessary to protect power." The intuition is straightforward: because tax bargains are likely to carry benefits to rulers over the long-term by increasing revenue collection, it is rulers with long time horizons who will have the strongest incentives to pursue these bargains. By contrast, rulers with short time horizons have little incentive to make concessions today to improve the fiscal position of subsequent rulers. This intuition is consistent with broader arguments that stress the importance of long time horizons in prompting investments in state capacity and institutional development (Olson 1993; Kelsall et al. 2010; Besley and Persson 2011). Consistent with this logic, public officials in both Ghana and Kenya explained that they are frequently unwilling to bear the political costs of strengthening taxation owing to a fear that the benefits will be reaped by future governments led by the opposition.

Given the importance of time horizons, the more interesting analytical question is thus what political institutions are likely to give rise to long time horizons, and thus potentially facilitate tax bargaining. In principle, well-entrenched autocratic rulers could have particularly long time horizons, and thus be more amendable to tax bargaining. However, within the case studies here, any positive bargaining incentives associated with long time horizons appear to have been outweighed by the tendency of autocratic governments to turn to coercion in seeking to strengthen tax enforcement.

Of greater interest is the potential influence of elections on time horizons for revenue generation. On the one hand, elections frequently make individual tenures in power shorter, and may thus shorten political time horizons. On the other hand, institutionalized democracy may serve to create longer effective time horizons through the likelihood that power will alternate and that political actors who lose an election may subsequently return to power (Olson 1993). Consistent with the potential benefits of democracy, political officials in Ghana explained that the growing regularity of elections, and corresponding assurances of alternation in power, had begun to facilitate cooperative bargaining over the expansion of taxation. However, this remains an area in which additional research is needed, as the relationship between elections and effective political time horizons will undoubtedly vary across contexts.

Trust and informal institutions

The final important role of political institutions lies in the potential of both formal and informal institutions to shape levels of trust between taxpayers and governments, with consequences for the potential for bargaining. The intuitive importance of trust rests on the necessity of credible commitment: direct tax bargaining requires that citizens trust that promises made by governments will be implemented and sustained, while governments must believe that increased tax collection will similarly endure (North and Weingast 1989). If governments do not believe that concessions will, in fact, lead to increased tax compliance, they will have significantly weaker incentives to make such concessions (Gehlbach 2008). If citizens have sufficiently low trust in a government's willingness to provide reciprocal benefits, they will not be willing to comply with taxes beyond what can be compelled through coercion. This is the conclusion drawn by Fjeldstad and Semboja (2001) in writing about taxation in rural Tanzania, where they argue that citizens do, in principle, embrace the idea of a fiscal bargain, but are, in practice, frequently unwilling to voluntarily comply with taxes because of extremely low levels of trust in government.

While the intuition surrounding the role of trust in tax bargaining is clear, case studies can offer at best imperfect evidence given the difficulty of measuring relevant levels of trust. With that caveat in mind, the importance of trust is most explicitly illustrated by the unique, but revealing, case of tax disputes between the government of Ethiopia and pastoralist communities. A lack of trust has led the government to demand tax payments before providing better services, while pastoralists have long demanded better services, and treatment in general, before complying with taxes. The result has been perpetual conflict, despite the fact that tax bargaining is acknowledged by both groups of stakeholders to hold the potential for significant mutual benefit, as well as being a potential entry point for broader engagement between the two groups.

A slightly different set of insights emerges from experiences in Ghana, where tax earmarking has been successfully used as a strategy to increase trust and thus facilitate reciprocal bargaining around tax increases. Initial government efforts to increase the VAT rate faced sharp public opposition owing to a lack of public confidence that increased revenue would be used productively. In response, the government not only promised to allocate the new tax revenue to supporting investments in education through the GET Fund, but also to put in place new oversight mechanisms for the funds. Having taken steps to build public trust that the money would be used effectively, public support for the tax quickly increased – despite general unhappiness with the government, which was resoundingly defeated in subsequent elections. Tellingly, this gain in trust appears to have had durable consequences, as the earmarking strategy was subsequently replicated by the incoming government in building public support for the introduction of the National Health Insurance Levy and the Communications Tax. Although the overall efficacy of tax earmarking is likely to remain controversial, and demands further research, these episodes speak to the potential for tax earmarking to function as a strategy for building trust around fiscal issues in contexts where such trust is initially limited (Bird and Jun 2005; Flores-Macias 2012).

6.3.5 *The political salience of taxation*

The final structural factor shaping the extent and character of tax bargaining is the political salience of taxation. The basic intuition is so straightforward as to be banal: alongside factors discussed already, collective action in response to taxation will be more likely where taxpayers are more keenly aware of the taxes that they pay. At this level of generality, the importance of political salience is self-evident, as there can generally be no collective action where citizens are not aware of the taxes that they pay. The question of interest is thus not whether the political salience of taxation matters, but what factors are critical in determining the political salience of taxation in particular contexts.

Interest in this question has historically revolved around what Martin and Gabay (2007: 2) term "the visibility hypothesis," which predicts that income taxes, and other taxes paid directly by individual taxpayers to tax authorities, will be more visible, and thus more politicized. By contrast, import taxes, which are collected at the border, and goods and services taxes, which are collected at the point of sale and then remitted to the government by individual businesses, are expected to be less visible to individual taxpayers, and thus less likely to provoke a political response. This prediction is intuitively appealing, and would appear to be particularly relevant to developing countries, where goods and services taxes are often hidden by the absence of receipts and by the fact that small retailers, on whom most consumers rely, frequently do not collect goods and services taxes directly (Bird and Gendron 2007).

However, despite the common prediction that income taxes will be more politicized than goods and services taxes, the case study evidence is significantly more mixed. There certainly is evidence of the politicization of taxes that are paid directly to the government. Tax resistance in Kenya has consistently revolved around income taxes, while efforts by various residents' associations to demand reciprocity for tax payments have focused primarily on direct property taxes. Similarly, the lone example of direct tax bargaining in Ethiopia since 1974 has revolved around the highly visible presumptive tax on small businesses, despite the fact that it comprises a relatively small share of total tax collection.

However, while direct taxes have been politicized, so too have supposedly "invisible" taxes on goods and services. In Ghana, far and away the most contentious taxes have been the VAT and taxes on fuel. The original introduction of the VAT led to the largest tax protests observed in any of the case study countries, while subsequent increases in the VAT rate required the earmarking of revenue for popular public services in order to minimize political opposition. Meanwhile significant changes in fuel prices, which remained functionally equivalent to tax changes as long as prices remained government controlled, led to public resistance in a wide range of cases. Similarly, in Kenya efforts by the government to strengthen VAT enforcement through the requirement that medium-sized firms use ETRs led to significant public protests.

The message is that while awareness certainly does matter, the simple dichotomy between direct taxes and indirect taxes is an insufficient means to capture levels of awareness and political salience. This conclusion echoes the work of Martin and Gabay (2007: 2), who have concluded – based on evidence from the United States – that analysis needs to move beyond the crude distinction between direct and indirect taxes in order to focus on "the ease with which [the tax] burden can be traced to the actions of policymakers." This does not imply that the distinction between direct and indirect taxes is irrelevant. The almost complete absence of a public response to the initial implementation of the VAT in either Kenya or Ethiopia suggests that goods and services taxes are, indeed, often somewhat hidden from public view. Instead, the case study evidence suggests that awareness and political salience are also shaped by other factors, including the reform strategies adopted by governments and the role of elites and civil society in encouraging public awareness and engagement.

The importance of the reform process itself is particularly evident in Kenya, where the government consistently adopted a gradualist approach to reform, with reform leaders openly describing their efforts to pursue reform "by stealth" in order to reduce public scrutiny. Unlike the decisive implementation of the VAT in most developing countries, the Kenyan VAT was implemented over the course of six years, with incremental changes over time used as a strategy to avoid public debate and controversy. By contrast, the most important episodes of tax bargaining in Ghana and Ethiopia occurred when reform was undertaken hastily and very publicly. This was true of the original introduction of the VAT in Ghana, and of the introduction of the presumptive tax on small businesses in Ethiopia. The latter notably produced major controversy in the Amhara region, where it was introduced relatively suddenly, but less controversy elsewhere, where it was phased in gradually.

Echoing the discussion earlier, political elites and leaders within civil society also appear to have played a key role in politicizing taxes that may not otherwise have been visible or politically salient to individual taxpayers. This reflects the fact that while individual taxpayers are often not fully aware of the burden of the VAT in their purchases, business owners feel this tax quite directly, while political elites are aware of the broader revenue being raised. As such, the extent to which goods and services taxes become politically salient is often a reflection of the success of business owners and elites in placing those taxes on the public agenda. The fact that the VAT prompted major protests in Ghana, and has remained a prominent and controversial issue since, reflects the fact that both political elites and organized civil society were actively involved in transforming the otherwise relatively invisible VAT into an issue of national concern. The 1995 anti-VAT protests were largely attributable to a public belief, fed by elites, civil society and the media, that the new tax was going to cause major price increases. In subsequent years resistance to increases in the VAT rate again originated with the political opposition and organized civil society, both of whom mediated public understanding. Thus, the evidence suggests that when certain taxes do not prompt a significant public response an important part of the explanation is likely to lie not only in simple distinctions between tax types, but in the actions of business owners, politicians, civil society and the media, all of whom play an important role in shaping the political salience of individual taxes.

6.3.6 *Political repression, elite power and the potential for tax bargaining*

The preceding discussion has highlighted a wide range of structural factors and more specific contextual variables that have shaped the extent and character of tax bargaining. The final challenge lies in offering a more holistic view of the role of contextual factors in shaping the potential for tax bargaining to act as a spur to expanded responsiveness and accountability.

The most striking single message is the central importance of political openness, and associated political institutions, in shaping the potential for tax bargaining. Across the case studies, repressive regimes have been relatively successful in curbing collective action in response to taxation, even when tax collection has been rising rapidly, thus curbing relatively direct and visible forms of tax bargaining. This has been reinforced by the absence of inclusive political institutions, which elsewhere have proven pivotal in facilitating comparatively direct and explicit forms of tax bargaining.

The importance of political openness has a straightforward, but nonetheless striking, implication: while tax bargaining can be an important factor contributing to the expansion of accountability, expanded accountability also plays a crucial role in facilitating tax bargaining. Seen optimistically, this implies the potential for the emergence of virtuous circles linking improvements in accountability and the expansion of tax bargaining: improvements in accountability may serve to enhance the ability of citizens to bargain over taxation, and thus demand the further expansion of accountability. However, the interconnectedness of tax bargaining and accountability also carries a second, less promising, implication: that tax bargaining is likely to be most difficult in contexts in which expanded responsiveness and accountability are most needed. This latter message is particularly striking because recent policy engagement has often been based implicitly on the hope that tax bargaining may offer a useful entry point to improved governance *particularly* where formal institutions of accountability are weak.

Against this background, what does the evidence here suggests about the potential for tax bargaining in low-income and politically repressive contexts? The broad message is straightforward: while the potential for tax bargaining in such contexts is comparatively limited in absolute terms, tax bargaining can nonetheless offer a rare source of political leverage to taxpayers in contexts in which few such opportunities exist. While tax bargaining has been rare in Ethiopia, it has not been non-existent, revolving around a combination of subnational action and the ability of taxpayers to resist taxation even in the face of repression. This resistance has weakened the fiscal position of repressive governments and, at least in the case of the presumptive tax, compelled the government to make certain concessions.

While these examples highlight observable political gains, they also confirm the broader causal logic of tax bargaining and reinforce the message that reliance on tax revenue may also subtly strengthen pressures for greater responsiveness and accountability in relatively less observable ways. The Ethiopian government clearly understood that modest governance concessions would be important in order to encourage tax compliance, reflecting the subtle pressures facing a government in need of tax revenue. Likewise, the government decision to sharply reduce tax collection in the wake of the 2005 elections was an implicit acknowledgement that taxation held the potential to be a catalyst for popular resistance. This suggests that even in poor, repressive, contexts governments that are more reliant on taxation are, all else equal, more likely to be confronted by a politicized citizenry and to face incentives to improve performance in order to secure tax compliance.

The second message that emerges centrally throughout the analysis is the critical role of elites in shaping the potential for tax bargaining. Elites are more able to engage in effective tax resistance because resistance by elites can have a significant impact on the overall fiscal position of governments. Elites are likewise critical to collective action because they possess the political resources necessary to make effective demands on government and to mobilize broader constituencies. And, most basically, elites play an important role in mediating the political salience of taxation,

6.3 Contextual factors and tax bargaining

and thus facilitating broader based collective action. Even where tax bargaining has involved a relatively broad base of taxpayers, as with the 1995 anti-VAT protests in Ghana, it is clear that the strength of taxpayer demands has depended critically on elite involvement. More generally, the strength of the private sector appears to have played an important role in shaping opportunities for tax bargaining.

The central role of elites raises concerns that the benefits of tax bargaining will be biased towards the interests of already powerful groups or, of greater concern, that any potential benefits of tax bargaining may be displaced by more narrow rent-seeking by those same elite groups. This possibility was raised more than two decades ago by Levi (1988), who noted the possibility that narrow elite-based rent-seeking would dominate the potential for more broad-based, governance-enhancing forms of tax bargaining. And, indeed, the case study evidence here reflects these risks, particularly in Kenya where narrow rent-seeking by elites long undermined more broad based tax bargaining.

However, the case studies also reflect two more optimistic messages. First, in a variety of cases we observe overlap between the interests of elites and the broader base of taxpayers, thus generating more broad-based gains. This has sometimes reflected a simple commonality of interests, as, for example, with the push for improved governance in Kenya in the late 1990s (resulting in the removal of the Moi government) and the push for an end to post-election violence in 2008. It has also reflected the fact that elites have often sought to mobilize broader constituencies when bargaining with governments over taxation in order to expand their political influence. This was most obviously true of the 1995 *Kume Preko* protests in Ghana, which were elite-led, but which came to include a much broader political constituency. It is also apparent when speaking to business associations in Kenya, which have sought to incorporate small firms within their ranks in an effort to expand their political legitimacy and influence.[3] Second, the case studies reveal the extent to which the progressive rationalization of tax systems over the past decade, and particularly efforts to limit discretion in the granting of exemptions, has contributed to reducing the scope for elites to engage in narrow rent-seeking, and thus to encouraging more collective tax bargaining. While discretionary tax exemptions and other forms of rent-seeking remain commonplace, there is relatively clear evidence that curbing the most discretionary abuses has helped to open new spaces for governance-enhancing tax bargaining.

---

[3] Personal interview on 18 September 2008 with senior leader, Kenya Private Sector Association.

This points towards the final broad message from the case studies: characteristics of tax reform, and of tax systems more generally, have played a meaningful role in shaping outcomes, in three major ways. First, as noted previously, equity in the application of tax rules has served to encourage collective action, whereas highly discretionary systems have tended to fragment popular resistance and encourage comparatively narrow forms of bargaining and rent-seeking. Second, differences in the implementation of tax reform have had large implications for the political salience of those reform efforts, and the corresponding likelihood of popular responses. Third, all else being equal, direct taxes – including regional taxes in Ethiopia – appear to have offered greater opportunities for tax bargaining, owing both to the scope for tax resistance and the greater likelihood that these highly visible taxes will prompt popular resistance. The potential policy implications of these findings are discussed at greater length in the concluding chapter.

6.4 Conclusions

This book began with the contention that despite growing attention to the potential links between taxation, responsiveness and accountability in developing countries, existing research has provided only a limited empirical basis for such claims, while saying little about how, and when, such connections are likely to emerge in practice. The case study evidence summarized in this chapter serves to provide a firmer empirical basis for existing claims, while providing new insights into the specific causal processes at work and the contextual factors most important to shaping the strength of these connections.

The analysis has focused on the importance of three particular causal processes – *direct tax bargaining, tax resistance and changes in government* and *expanded political capabilities of taxpayers* – and has provided evidence that all three processes have contributed to broader governance gains in the case study countries. These examples alone are indicative of the importance of taxation to broader political outcomes. However, it is equally important to emphasize again that they are unlikely to capture the entire range of ways in which tax reliance may contribute to the expansion of responsiveness and accountability, as some such processes are likely to be subtle and difficult to observe. The experience of taxation may prompt subtle changes in the expectations and political behaviour of taxpayers, or the need to tax may subtly alter government decision-making, but in ways that are invisible individually, but cumulatively important. As such, the actual importance of reliance on taxation to the expansion of responsiveness and accountability is likely to be still greater than the

6.4 Conclusions

sum of the examples presented here, which capture only the most visible manifestations of the underlying causal mechanisms.

While identifying these alternative causal processes has provided the core of the analysis, the more ambitious and challenging goal has been to shed light on the contextual factors shaping the likelihood and character of tax bargaining. This emphasis on the importance of context reflects two straightforward rationales. First, while taxation has frequently contributed to broader gains in responsiveness and accountability, taxation remains a fundamentally coercive endeavour, and positive governance gains are far from guaranteed. Second, tax bargaining is best understood not as a discreet and relatively self-contained political process, but as a concept that captures the multiple ways in which explicit and implicit conflicts over taxation may contribute to shaping broader processes of political contestation between states and citizens. For both reasons, contextual factors are expected to figure centrally in shaping particular outcomes.

The contextual factors identified here range from broad characteristics of the political, economic and fiscal environment to more idiosyncratic factors shaping prospects for collective action in relation to tax issues. The former factors are expected to drive broad patterns of cross-country variation in the extent and form of tax bargaining. The latter factors include specific features of tax systems and tax reform that are potentially more amendable to explicit targeting by key stakeholders. While broad political and economic factors have tended to make tax bargaining more limited and challenging in comparatively repressive and low-income environments, a key message from the case studies is that tax bargaining has nonetheless remained possible even in the most difficult contexts. Meanwhile, more idiosyncratic factors related particularly to the character of tax systems and tax reform offer insights into how positive processes of tax bargaining may be encouraged. These policy implications are taken up in the concluding chapter.

7 Looking forward
Broader messages, policy lessons and directions for future research

The idea that taxation may lie near the heart of broader processes of state-building, economic development and political change grows out of a rich intellectual history, as the importance of taxation figures prominently in seminal works addressing trajectories of economic and political change in early modern Europe and elsewhere (Mann 1986; Levi 1988; North 1990; Tilly 1992). More recently, attention to the importance of taxation in shaping political outcomes in developing countries has expanded significantly, and has been particularly prominent in discussions of the causes of poor governance in many resource rich states (Moore 1998, 2004, 2008; Herbst 2000; Bates 2001; Ross 2004; Collier 2009). As Martin, Mehrotra and Prasad (2009: 1) write in their recent volume on the emergence of a "new fiscal sociology": "Everyone knows that taxation is important."

Against this backdrop, the conclusion that taxation has, in fact, been an important catalyst for the expansion of responsiveness and accountability in contemporary developing countries may appear rather unremarkable. However, while claims about the potential connections between taxation, responsiveness and accountability have become increasingly widespread, this has occurred in spite of the absence of a strong foundation of empirical evidence. This absence of detailed empirical evidence has had two important consequences. First, it has yielded an academic debate that has often lacked depth and nuance, making it difficult to incorporate questions of fiscal politics into broader accounts of politics and political change in low-income countries. Second, it has prevented the translation of broad ideas about taxation, responsiveness and accountability into specific policy advice for national and international actors. This brief final chapter is correspondingly devoted to addressing these issues, before concluding with a discussion of directions for future research.

7.1 A broader and more nuanced understanding of tax bargaining

Reflecting the persuasiveness of historical experiences, and the clear intuition underlying models of tax bargaining, many scholars have been quick to embrace the existence of important connections between taxation, responsiveness and accountability. However, this embrace has been partial and incomplete. In the absence of detailed country-level research, discussion of the links between taxation and broader political outcomes has remained compartmentalized and absent from most mainstream accounts of politics and political change in low-income countries. Meanwhile, wider debate has frequently proven polarizing and sometimes simplistic, characterized by a focus on relatively abstract and general claims.

In recent decades, natural resource wealth has come to be seen as a key determinant of governance outcomes, and thus as a key element of any discussion of political dynamics in resource-dependent states. As noted in the introduction to this book, this has been reflected in a small but growing group of studies that have identified access to natural resource wealth as a critical determinant of broader governing incentives and development outcomes (Doner, Ritchie and Slater 2005; Besley and Persson 2011). By contrast, the politics surrounding taxation has received widespread attention as a set of abstract ideas about the long-term evolution of governance outcomes, but has continued to receive comparatively limited attention in country-level political narratives in low-income countries. Within accounts of national political dynamics there is frequently little, if any, acknowledgement of the ways in which patterns of taxation, and episodes of conflict over taxation, may shape broader governance outcomes. Most of the tax episodes described in this book are entirely absent from prominent country-level narratives, with even the anti-VAT protests in Ghana receiving significant attention in only a handful of sources. The absence of greater attention to the political implications of taxation, and broader fiscal dynamics, in country-level political accounts seems likely to have been a direct reflection of the absence of detailed narratives capturing specific causal processes linking taxation to broader governance outcomes. Simply put, researchers have not known what to look for in giving conflicts over taxation a more prominent place in explaining broader political outcomes.

Instead, research into the governance implications of taxation has remained a somewhat specialized field, with tax bargaining frequently viewed as a relatively compartmentalized set of processes through which tax compliance may be exchanged relatively explicitly for reciprocal concessions from governments. Research in this area has thus focused on finding evidence that particular groups of taxpayers have consented to a particular set of taxes and received a specific set of benefits in return.[1] Such processes – dubbed direct tax bargaining in this book – are clearly important, but offer a narrow view of the possible connections between taxation and broader governance outcomes. By contrast, a core aim of this book has been to situate tax bargaining explicitly within broader political processes. It proposes that tax bargaining is best understood as a broad concept capturing the multiple ways in which reliance on taxation may strengthen the bargaining power of taxpayers, and increase incentives for government to make governing concessions. It is thus intimately connected to, and embedded within, broader processes of political contestation and change. Seen through this lens, the role of conflicts over taxation in shaping political outcomes lies not only in instances of direct tax bargaining, but in the more subtle ways in which debates over taxation shape political power, incentives and engagement. By exploring these multifaceted processes empirically in three countries, a core goal of this book has thus been to suggest the ways in which the politics of revenue-raising can be more fully incorporated into country-level political narratives.

In locating the importance of tax bargaining within broader processes of political contestation, this book has sought not only to broaden attention to these issues, but also to confront the development of a sometimes overly simplistic and polarizing debate. In the absence of systematic country-level evidence, there has been a tendency amongst sceptics and supporters alike – particularly in policy circles – to simplify a more complex reality, and thus distort the nature of the connections between taxation, responsiveness and accountability. Sceptics have pointed to the absence of clear-cut, easily measurable and predictable examples of direct tax bargaining and taken this as evidence that there is no meaningful relationship. In doing so, they have risked overlooking the more subtle ways in which reliance on taxation may shift political incentives and outcomes in more diverse and long-term ways. Meanwhile, those who have embraced the importance of taxation to broader governance outcomes have sometimes done so uncritically, assuming that expanded taxation will inevitably drive broader gains in accountability. In doing so, they have lost sight of the fact that taxation remains a fundamentally coercive act, and over long periods may fail to generate any meaningful opportunities

---

[1] Perhaps the best example is the work of Gehlbach (2008), who argues that post-Soviet states have systematically favoured large, immobile and easily taxed firms. He views this as a classic, although unconventional, tax bargain, in which those firms that pay the largest share of taxes receive reciprocal benefits from the state. It is one of the most detailed existing studies of tax bargaining, but addresses only one specific way in which taxation and governance may be connected.

for governance-enhancing bargaining. This book has sought to chart a middle ground, arguing that while taxation can be a spur to broader governance gains, these outcomes are context-specific, and are dependent on a broad set of variables shaping the power wielded by taxpayers and the potential for bargaining. This, in turn, shifts the analytical focus towards understanding where positive forms of tax bargaining are most likely to emerge, and how they might be fostered.

7.2 From broad claims to specific policy implications

Even as interest in the potential connections between taxation, responsiveness and accountability has expanded over the past decade, the potential policy implications have remained vague. The basic message has been simple: Countries should seek to strengthen domestic tax collection, given the promise that greater reliance on tax collection may spur virtuous processes of tax bargaining. Reflecting this message, important policy statements from the Organisation for Economic Cooperation and Development (OECD), the IMF and various bilateral donors have explicitly cited the potential governance benefits of taxation as motivation for expanding support for tax reform programs (OECD 2008, 2010; IMF 2011).[2] Similar messages have been echoed by national authorities and tax administrators within low-income countries, and by national and international civil society organizations.[3] Although this basic policy prescription finds support in the evidence presented in this book, it is also overly simplistic. While the expansion of taxation *may* lead to broader governance gains, this outcome is far from guaranteed. Governments may impose new taxes coercively, while successfully resisting reciprocal demands from taxpayers. Alternatively, governments may opt to strike narrow bargains with a subset of powerful taxpayers – through tax exemptions or the delivery of specific benefits – in order to fragment broader taxpayer resistance and avoid broader concessions. Which of these outcomes predominates depends critically on the overarching

---

[2] In an example of the broad appeal of these ideas, the connections between taxation and governance reform were featured prominently in an address by Secretary of State Hilary Clinton delivered at the OECD on 26 May 2011.

[3] For example, a core objective of the African Tax Administration Forum (ATAF) is "Improving good governance and accountability between state and citizens" (www.ataftax.net/en/about.html). This sentiment was echoed by the Commissioner General of the Uganda Revenue Agency, Allen Kagina, who argued to her colleagues in a 2009 speech at the launch of ATAF: "We should elevate ourselves from being just tax collectors and tax administrators to being state builders." Amongst civil society organizations, these same questions have been central to the work of, amongst others, the Tax Justice Network-Africa and Christian Aid.

political and economic context. The policy challenge therefore lies not simply in expanding taxation, but in understanding how to approach the expansion of taxation in a way that is most conducive to governance-enhancing tax bargaining.

This question demands significant caution, as the instances of tax bargaining captured in this book are embedded within broader processes of political contestation, and are deeply rooted in the particular histories, and economic and political characteristics, of individual countries. Such complex processes are not easily translated into straightforward policy prescriptions given the wide range of relevant variables. This book has, however, highlighted five sets of factors that appear to have been particularly influential in shaping the potential for tax bargaining: (1) the extent of revenue pressure facing governments; (2) the potential and scope for tax resistance; (3) factors affecting taxpayer capacity for collective action; (4) the nature of political institutions; and (5) the political salience of taxation. In translating these findings into policy advice, the broad message is that the potential for tax bargaining depends not only on *how much* tax revenue is collected, but on *how* those taxes are collected – and on the broader political and economic context for bargaining. By understanding the variables that have shaped the potential for tax bargaining, it becomes possible to begin to pinpoint specific policy options for enabling these processes.

Some of the factors identified in this book are not easily amenable to influence by prospective reformers. This includes, most notably, the extent of revenue pressure, the nature of political institutions and the strength of the private sector. While it may be true that tax bargaining is more likely where governments do not have access to natural resource wealth, or where democratic institutions are stronger, this is largely beyond the control of reformers. By contrast, a subset of contextual variables related more closely to characteristics of the tax system itself offer potential entry points for those seeking to foster tax bargaining. Building from the evidence presented in the previous chapter, what follows thus highlights five types of reforms that may contribute to fostering processes of governance-enhancing tax bargaining: (1) expanding the political salience of taxation, including through an emphasis on direct taxes; (2) increasing horizontal equity in the tax system; (3) directly encouraging bargaining and collective action; (4) expanding transparency and engagement; and (5) creating institutionalized spaces for tax bargaining.[4]

---

[4] The discussion here draws in part on Prichard (2010), which includes a range of evidence from developing countries that is broadly consistent with the claims made here. That

7.2 From broad claims to specific policy   253

Having presented these relatively specific reform messages, this section then concludes by considering some broader implications for aid donors.

7.2.1 Expanding the political salience of taxation

The most straightforward message emerging from the analysis presented so far is that the scope for direct and indirect tax bargaining is crucially dependent on public awareness and the broader political salience of taxation. While this is highly intuitive, it remains an important starting point, given that public debate about taxation has generally been relatively limited in low-income countries in recent decades. At a broad level, this reflects the fact that the trajectory of reform in many developing countries has been driven to a large extent by transnational networks of experts, as reflected in the commonality of reform experiences across countries (Fjeldstad and Moore 2008: 238–242). At the same time, the political salience of taxation is frequently low owing at least in part to the very limited reach of national direct taxes and the consequent fact that, at the national level, most taxpayers are primarily or exclusively subject to indirect taxes, many of which are themselves not collected at the final point of sale. In the case studies highlighted here, and in developing countries more generally, the few hundred largest taxpayers frequently pay more than two thirds of total income and sales taxes, while national income taxes frequently affect only a very small percentage of the economically active population (Fjeldstad and Moore 2008: 256).[5]

Relatively low levels of awareness and political salience suggest two starting points for fostering the potential for tax bargaining. First, investments in taxpayer education and outreach may be a first step towards fostering greater public engagement with the tax system, and the prospect of broader governance gains. While specific evidence remains limited, available information suggests that taxpayers frequently only have a relatively vague understanding of what taxes they pay, of the specific rules surrounding these taxes or of how much revenue is collected by governments. Similarly, while there have not yet been any systematic studies of the impact of taxpayer outreach programs in developing countries,

---

said, the discussion here represents a further evolution of that earlier work, while it is grounded more explicitly in the case study evidence presented in this book.

[5] While data is inevitably problematic, in 2009 the Ghanaian tax authorities reported that in a country of almost 25 million the total number of individuals registered to pay income taxes was 1.285 million. Greater than 95% of these taxpayers had income taxes deducted directly from their pay checks at source, such that the total number of income tax filers was dramatically lower, although precise figures are not available (Prichard and Bentum 2009: 61).

anecdotal research and interviews are suggestive of significant demand for them amongst tax authorities and of their potential to encourage significantly expanded engagement and trust (Durand and Thorp 1998; Abrie and Doussy 2006; OECD 2013).

Alongside the value of outreach and education is the potential value of attempting to broaden the direct tax net, thus expanding the portion of the population that bears a direct tax burden.[6] This study has raised important cautions about assuming that direct taxes will always be more "visible" than indirect taxes, as the "visibility" of taxes frequently hinges on the role of elites civil society and the media in fostering public debate about particular taxes. However, it remains likely that a broader constituency would be engaged in tax debates if it felt the tax burden more directly. While this goal may be achieved to some extent through the expansion of enforcement of traditional income taxes on individuals and businesses, these taxes are unlikely to reach the low-income majority. Instead, any dramatic expansion of the direct tax net is likely to involve some combination of taxes focused on small businesses in the informal sector and the expansion of local government taxation, with a focus on property taxes (Joshi and Ayee 2008; Jibao and Prichard 2013, forthcoming; Joshi, Prichard and Heady 2014). Such taxes have historically received limited attention from tax reformers because of their comparatively modest revenue yields, but the evidence presented in this book suggests that they may be politically significant, thus arguing for greater research and attention.

7.2.2 *Increasing horizontal equity in the tax system*

At the core of many episodes of tax bargaining is the importance of collective action by taxpayers seeking to make reciprocal demands on governments. A key challenge for prospective reformers correspondingly lies in facilitating and encouraging collective action around tax questions. Elite taxpayers are likely to be particularly important, owing to the fact that they are both the largest taxpayers and wield significant political influence, including through their ability to mobilize broader

---

[6] This possibility has been raised by Fjeldstad and Moore (2008: 255), although in more speculative and intuitive form. Mirroring the discussion here they write: "Imagine that tax reformers... wanted to encourage constructive engagement between governments and citizens over tax issues. What would they then do?... They would want to engage the attention and political energies of a substantial fraction of their citizens in taxation issues by raising taxes from them. The felt experience of paying taxes should not be confined to small numbers of companies and very rich people. It should be shared sufficiently widely to secure the prominence of taxation issues on the public political agenda."

7.2 From broad claims to specific policy

constituencies. However, collective tax bargaining by elite taxpayers in search of broad governance gains has been relatively uncommon. Instead, they have frequently exploited their political influence in order to pursue narrow benefits, often seeking to escape taxation by seeking tax exemptions and by using their political influence to blunt the effectiveness of tax enforcement.

The effectiveness of these narrow strategies has not only undermined revenue collection, but has fragmented the interests of elite groups and reduced incentives for them to bargain collectively with government in search of broader concessions. The corollary of this pattern is that efforts to increase equity in tax enforcement, and thus curb the availability of politically motivated tax exemptions, hold the potential to shift elite taxpayers towards more collective bargaining strategies. Whereas exemptions can fragment elite bargaining interests, the case studies have presented evidence that where business elites have been confronted by a uniform tax burden, they have been more likely to make collective demands for reciprocity and improved governance. This possibility has been most apparent in Ghana and Kenya, where large businesses historically relied on individual political connections in order to secure narrow tax exemptions and privileges. In both countries this began to change when governments began to enforce taxation amongst elites more equitably, thus generating shared concerns within the business community and catalysing business associations to adopt more collective agendas.[7] Notably, the key variable in these episodes was equity in enforcement, rather than the overall extent of taxation, as rates were frequently reduced at the same time that enforcement was expanded. In both cases there remains scope for significant further progress in increasing the equity of tax enforcement, but there is clear evidence that preliminary changes in tax enforcement played an important role in shifting business incentives.[8]

---

[7] While the research in this book highlights the importance of efforts by national governments to improve equity in tax enforcement, recent research has also begun to stress inequitable patterns of tax enforcement resulting from the greater ability of larger companies and wealthy individuals to reduce tax burdens through the use of tax havens (Picciotto 2013). As such, efforts to reform the international tax system may equally be important in encouraging collective tax bargaining by elites, although this remains an area in need of additional research.

[8] There are, of course, clear political reasons why consistent taxation of economic elites has proven elusive across the developing world, and an extensive policy literature has long focused on the revenue and economic efficiency to be gained by curbing the use of tax incentives and exemptions (Klemm 2009). The evidence in this book goes one step further in stressing the potential for horizontal equity in enforcement to also drive broader political changes, thus providing additional impetus for making horizontal equity a central reform priority.

7.2.3 *Directly supporting bargaining and collective action*

While increasing equity in tax enforcement appears to be an important strategy for fostering collective action and engagement, an alternative strategy lies in seeking to directly support civil society organizations, the media, business associations and parliamentarians to engage with tax issues. This reflects both the ability of these groups to bargain directly with government and their critical role in increasing the salience of tax debates amongst taxpayers more broadly. However, despite the centrality of taxation to processes of state formation historically, engagement with tax issues beyond small groups of experts has generally remained limited in low-income countries (Fjeldstad and Moore 2008).

There has been limited research on specific strategies for encouraging engagement with tax issues by a broader set of groups, but the case study evidence presented in this book speaks strongly to the potential benefits. Key examples of tax bargaining have depended to a significant degree on the expanding engagement of business associations, of parliamentarians and on the engagement of civil society groups, as with the CJA in Ghana. The case studies have also presented the possibility that business associations representing small and informal businesses may be able to play an important bargaining role, although these activities remain in their infancy. Engagement by all of these groups has, at times, included explicit financial support from external actors, while in other cases they have been facilitated by government efforts to open spaces for dialogue with a broader range of stakeholders.[9] Both types of strategies warrant expanded study and consideration.

7.2.4 *Expanding transparency and engagement*

While reforms to the tax system designed to foster awareness, equity and engagement offer important entry points to encourage tax bargaining, the broader expansion of transparency around both revenue collection and the budgeting process has the potential to further all of these goals.[10] Greater transparency can serve to raise tax awareness, but can also make a greater contribution to fostering positive public engagement and bargaining. Transparency around both revenue and budgeting can establish more explicit links between taxation and expenditure, thus fostering

---

[9] This is consistent with observations by Doner and Schneider (2000) about factors potentially contributing to strengthening the positive role of business associations.
[10] This again bears much in common with the more intuitive claims of Fjeldstad and Moore (2008: 255) who suggested that reformers seeking to foster tax bargaining would "want to levy taxes as consensually and transparently as possible."

7.2 From broad claims to specific policy

expectations of reciprocity and trust – the foundations for constructive demand-making in relation to taxation. In the absence of expectations of reciprocity, or basic information about the content of government spending, it is likely to remain difficult for citizen groups to become mobilized effectively. Meanwhile, the absence of trust can frequently be amongst the most fundamental barriers to tax bargaining, as taxpayers have little confidence in government promises and correspondingly prefer simple tax evasion to longer-term bargaining.

Consistent with these expectations, government outreach and transparency around the establishment of Constituency Development Funds in Kenya helped to generate expectations of reciprocity, while providing citizens a basis for assessing the extent to which public revenue was being translated into improved outputs. This provided a foundation for greater engagement. Meanwhile, the case studies point towards a range of cases in which improved transparency has contributed to incremental improvements in trust by allowing taxpayers to clearly see their tax payments translated into desired outcomes. This was the case, for example, with the introduction of associational taxation on small businesses in Ghana, which paved the way for the progressive institutionalization of the taxation of small firms. Meanwhile, these conclusions are supported by a small number of other studies looking at the potential benefits of transparency for developing greater trust around taxation (Bahiigwa et al. 2004; Korsun and Meagher 2004: 164; Ssewakiryanga 2004). That said, it is important to stress that expanded transparency does not simply imply publishing tax data, but requires efforts to ensure that this is done in a way that is broadly accessible and can be understood by taxpayers – including potentially working with partners that can play a role in communicating data to broader groups of taxpayers.

A more radical option is to move beyond the general expansion of transparency by explicitly earmarking specific taxes for particular types of public spending. The aim of such tax earmarking is to build greater trust between governments and taxpayers, while providing a foundation for improved monitoring of public expenditures. The case for such tax earmarking is particularly strong in low-income countries where trust is frequently limited and monitoring particularly difficult. Within the case studies explored here this strategy has been widely applied in Ghana, where the government twice linked increases in the VAT to specific, and popular, areas of public service delivery. Consistent with predictions, this practice served to increase trust amongst taxpayers while also making it somewhat easier for the public to monitor government performance. However, tax earmarking carries with it important risks. Fiscal experts have long opposed tax earmarking on the basis that it reduces fiscal flexibility in the long-term, and potentially undermines the public goods character of taxation by linking it to specific, and potentially narrow, benefits. More proximately, tax earmarking can be misleading, as it may be used to achieve political ends without actually affecting spending decisions, owing to the fungibility of government resources (Bird and Jun 2005). Both of these risks have been a source of debate in the Ghanaian cases described in this book.

Given that tax earmarking involves inevitable trade-offs, two broad policy messages appear warranted. The first is that the potential benefits of tax earmarking warrant greater attention and research in low trust environments, but tax earmarking should generally be limited in scope, resistant to fungibility and easily monitored (Prichard 2010: 34–35).[11] The second message is that more informal efforts to link revenues and expenditures may be desirable in many cases. In this way, governments may transparently highlight the purposes to which additional revenue will be used, and provide avenues for public monitoring, but stop short of permanently earmarking revenues for specific purposes. This type of "informal earmarking" was employed with some success in Kenya, where the post-2002 government linked new revenue collection to a series of popular new programs, while similar examples have been noted in recent studies elsewhere (see, for example, Jibao and Prichard 2013, forthcoming).

7.2.5 *Creating institutionalized spaces for tax bargaining*

While transparency may thus play a role in expanding political salience, changing expectations, building trust and encouraging engagement, the creation of institutionalized spaces for public engagement around taxation may further facilitate tax bargaining by expanding the scope for comparatively consensual interaction between taxpayers and governments. The case studies in this book have pointed clearly to the importance of political institutions in facilitating comparatively direct forms of tax bargaining, and while tax reformers may have little influence over national institutions, reform at the level of tax administration may contribute

---

[11] In a recent example of such research, Flores-Macías (2014) highlights the example of Colombia's "democratic security taxes," whereby the government secured compliance with a temporary wealth tax by earmarking revenue for security forces and putting in place explicit mechanisms for overseeing the use of the new revenue. This example has thus proven successful in building trust and expanding collection, but is subject to concerns about fiscal flexibility and about allowing elites to direct tax payments to specific spending priorities, rather than to a broader set of public goods.

to similar goals. This may involve the creation of regular forums for consultation or the inclusion of citizen representatives more directly in aspects of tax administration. We see examples of the former in the expansion of such consultative forums in all of the case study countries, and most notably through the institutionalization of consultation with business leaders. Meanwhile, the inclusion of businesses directly in overseeing tax assessment has occurred in both Ghana and Ethiopia, with similar examples also appearing in research elsewhere (Ssewakiryanga 2004; Prichard 2010: 31). Whereas research has frequently spoken of "pockets of productivity" within otherwise weak public administrations (Leonard 2010), it may equally be possible to imagine "pockets of inclusion or consultation" in relation to taxation, as an incremental step towards building a foundation for more responsive and accountable governance.

7.2.6 Broader implications for aid donors

Having highlighted a set of specific policy implications for prospective reformers seeking to foster expanded tax bargaining, it is useful to step back and consider the broader implications of the research findings for aid donors. Over the past decade, the focus of discussions linking aid, donors and tax bargaining has been on the possibility that high levels of foreign aid may, much like natural resource wealth, discourage local tax collection. The implication has been that an unintended consequence of aid may be to undermine the potential for tax bargaining, and, more broadly, weaken ties between states and citizens (Moore 1998; Bräutigam and Knack 2004; Moss, Pettersson, and van de Walle 2006; Eubank 2012).

However, more recent research has shown that – unlike natural resource revenue – access to aid *does not* consistently lead to lower levels of tax collection in recipient countries (Clist and Morrissey 2011; Clist 2014; Morrissey, Prichard and Torrance 2014). While aid may in some cases reduce incentives for tax collection, it is equally possible that aid may contribute to increased collection through the impacts of technical assistance, conditionality and broader pressures to expand public spending (Prichard, Brun, and Morrissey 2012; Morrissey, Prichard and Torrance 2014). There is a corresponding need for a more nuanced view of the impact of aid on the potential for tax bargaining, with potentially important messages for donors.

While aid does not consistently reduce incentives for domestic taxation and tax bargaining, it remains possible that it may contribute to reduced tax effort at particular moments in particular countries (Eubank 2012).

While not the primary focus here, this possibility appears periodically in the case study chapters: for example, the Kenyan government increased tax collection in the wake of declining aid in the early 1990s, while the decision by the Ethiopian government to dramatically reduce tax collection after the 2005 elections appears to have been made possible in part by continued high levels of aid. In the latter case, it seems very plausible that the ability of the government to rely on aid revenue, and thus to reduce taxation in the face of public unhappiness, may have freed the government from the need to bargain with citizens over revenue collection. More generally, high levels of foreign aid also may reduce the political leverage wielded by taxpayers, by relieving the revenue pressure facing governments. This is not to say that donors should not deliver aid, or that donors should not deliver aid in times of fiscal crisis. It is simply a reminder that while aid does not consistently lead to reduced tax collection, it remains necessary for donors to be aware that aid may, in some cases, undermine the ability of taxpayers to put pressure on, and bargain with, their governments. As has been increasingly noted, irrespective of claims of technocratic neutrality, the provision of aid almost invariably has broader, and often unintended, political implications, and donors have an important responsibility to "do no harm" (OECD 2009, Booth 2011).

Moving beyond the impact of aid on aggregate incentives for tax collection, the most important impact of donors on the potential for tax bargaining may stem from their influence of the setting of tax reform priorities. This reflects an extensive literature documenting the often-pivotal role of international networks, international organizations, and bilateral donors in shaping the broad contours of tax reform efforts in recent decades (Mahon 2004; Sanchez 2006; Bird 2008; Fjeldstad and Moore 2008; Keen 2013). The discussion so far has highlighted the extent to which tax bargaining is dependent on particular features of tax policy and administration, thus pointing towards specific reform strategies for increasing the likelihood of governance-enhancing tax bargaining. Keen (2013) has argued that the reform priorities advocated by the IMF and others closely match the types of reform priorities suggested by a "governance enhancing" tax reform agenda (Prichard 2010).[12] Indeed, there is no doubt that international organizations have been supportive of a focus on many of the key issues raised here: horizontal equity, transparency,

---

[12] While this book presents the most refined statement on what such a "governance enhancing" tax reform agenda would entail, an earlier and less developed version of these arguments first appeared in a report published by OECD in 2010, while similar ideas began to circulate in policy circles around this time. Keen's (2013) work was a response in part to those ideas and, by extension, to the ideas presented here.

public education, consultation and greater engagement by civil society. However, they have, in the view of most observers, tended to make these goals secondary priorities, with the primary focus on increasing revenue collection and minimizing market distortions (Barbone et al. 1999; IEG 2008). This has meant that the types of issues highlighted here have been more easily overlooked during the process of implementing reform. More optimistically, there is evidence that this emphasis has begun to shift in recent years, and a continued shift towards emphasizing process related aspects of tax reform promises to create a more supportive environment for tax bargaining (IMF 2011).

Finally, while these policy suggestions draw on a combination of the case study evidence in this book and broader research, it remains important to acknowledge that they remain both preliminary and somewhat speculative. There is still much more to learn about when tax bargaining is likely, what forms it might take, and how it may be encouraged, through both a broader range of case studies and more in-depth study of individual possibilities. It is equally important to remember that even if these strategies are desirable in principle in order to strengthen the links between taxation, responsiveness and accountability, that does not necessarily imply that governments and tax reformers will be quick to adopt them – indeed, many of these suggestions have long been advocated by tax reformers, albeit for different reasons. There thus remains an equal need for research exploring how such reform strategies may be advanced more effectively.[13] Despite these caveats, the discussion here highlights potentially useful entry points for seeking to strengthen domestic processes of political dialogue and contestation around taxation, as a foundation for achieving broader governance gains.

7.3 Limitations and future research

As noted in the introductory chapter, this book has sought to explore an expansive, diverse and difficult-to-observe set of political processes at a relatively macro level of analysis. The case studies have each covered several decades while seeking to draw broad conclusions about relevant causal processes and contextual variables. The adoption of this

---

[13] Such research has recently begun to expand rapidly, much of it linked to the International Centre for Tax and Development. This has included research into the political economy of property tax reform, informal sector taxation, the reform of tax exemption regimes, the use of tax earmarking, and broader efforts to increase horizontal equity in the taxation of elites. See, for example, Fjeldstad and Heggstad (2012), Flores-Macias (2014), Fairfield (2013), Joshi, Prichard and Heady (2014), Moore (2014) and Jibao and Prichard (2013, forthcoming).

relatively ambitious and exploratory research agenda has reflected the nature of the existing literature, which offered limited guidance about key features of tax bargaining in contemporary developing countries. A broad research agenda was correspondingly necessary to begin to empirically map key elements of the relationship between taxation, responsiveness and accountability. Having identified the main features of this relationship, there remains significant scope for more tailored studies to fill remaining gaps or deepen our understanding of important issues raised here. This section highlights five limitations of this study, and five corresponding avenues for future research.

First, this research has focused on a particular set of countries and, while they capture significant variation in the key variables of interest, there is a strong case for broadening the range of cases still further. Exploring the political dynamics surrounding taxation in states with significant resource wealth appears to hold particular interest and promise. While such studies may provide additional insight into the relative absence of tax bargaining in such countries, it would also allow for asking whether processes of tax bargaining may still be possible and significant even where levels of tax collection are comparatively low. This book has argued that there is likely to be less tax bargaining in resource rich states for two reasons: lower levels of tax collection, with consequently weaker incentives for collective action by taxpayers, and lower levels of revenue pressure, with consequently diminished incentives for governments to bargain with taxpayers engaged in tax resistance. However, there are nonetheless moments at which even resource rich states are compelled to increase tax collection, or in which they face acute revenue pressure, often in response to falling resource revenues. Research into the broader politics of taxation in such states, particularly during times of crisis, thus holds the potential to extend this research in an important direction.[14] A similar opportunity lies in studying the potential role of tax bargaining in post-conflict settings. Recent work has suggested that the need for many post-conflict states to rebuild tax collection from very low levels may offer an important opportunity to make revenue-raising processes an entry point for pursuing broader governance gains, including strengthening engagement and trust between taxpayers and the state (Boyce and O'Donnell 2007; Ghani and Lockhart 2008; Jibao and

---

[14] There is important ongoing research looking at tax collection, and the potential for tax bargaining, in Nigeria. Much of this research has focused specifically on developments in Lagos State, where the Governor has invested heavily in strengthening tax collection while providing significantly improved public services to citizens (Cheeseman 2013). Alternative research has begun to look at the potential for tax reform in Angola to contribute to broader governance improvements (Fjeldstad, Jensen and Orre 2012).

7.3 Limitations and future research

Prichard 2013, forthcoming). However, despite this potential, taxation has rarely been a priority in post-conflict contexts, nor has research yet told us much about the particular challenges of tax collection in post-conflict environments.

A second possible direction for future research lies at the local government level, thus moving beyond the focus here on national and regional government taxation. While the vast majority of tax revenue in sub-Saharan Africa and elsewhere in the developing world is collected at the national level, the majority of taxpayers experience taxation most directly at the local government level, through an array of taxes, fees and levies involving comparatively small sums. Local government taxation generally involves more direct interaction between taxpayers and tax collectors, while connections between revenue and public expenditure are potentially more direct. Collectively, these features of local government taxation make it appear to be a particularly likely setting for relatively direct tax bargaining, with this expectation mirroring broader claims about the potential for decentralization to contribute to improved accountability (Agrawal and Ribot 1999; Bardhan 2002; Faguet 2004). However, tax collection at the local government level also poses particular barriers to tax bargaining, rooted in the potential for tax collection and governance at the local government level to be particularly coercive, exclusive and elite dominated (Crook and Manor 1998; Crook 2003; Crook and Sverrisson 2003; Devarajan, Khemani and Shah 2009). Consistent with this risk, the small body of existing research at the local government level is very mixed, with some studies reporting tentative evidence of a positive connection between taxation, responsiveness and accountability (Gadenne 2014 Hoffman and Gibson 2005; Jibao and Prichard 2013, forthcoming), and others finding that tax relationships at the local government level are dominated by coercion and conflict (Fjeldstad and Semboja 2001; Bernstein and Lü 2008; Fjeldstad and Therkildsen 2008). With existing evidence quite mixed, there remains scope for significantly more research investigating the contexts in which the comparatively intimate tax relationship at the local government level may become a catalyst for broader governance gains.

Alongside these opportunities to expand research to new settings, there are also a number of areas in which the initial insights provided in this book may be deepened. Most obviously, this book has focused on capturing a subset of relatively observable causal processes that have linked taxation to the expansion of responsiveness and accountability. As has been noted repeatedly, this is likely to overlook some of the less observable ways in which the need for taxation may shape broader governance outcomes. While this book has argued that the observable processes captured in the case studies are very likely to be indicative of the existence of these more subtle processes, additional research and evidence would be of obvious value. The most immediate possibility is that the experience of being taxed may have subtle, long-term, impacts on the political engagement and expectations of taxpayers. One strategy lies in detailed surveys, which may, for example, capture how taxpayer perceptions of the tax system shape broader views of government, or how taxpayer views of government change over time in response to changes in taxation. Such strategies are crucially dependent on the quality of the underlying survey data, and while this has so far remained a barrier to high quality research, opportunities to more accurately capture the impacts of taxation on individual taxpayers will expand as the quality of data improves (Fjeldstad and Semboja 2001; McGuirk 2013). An alternative strategy, similarly reflected in recent work, is reliance on field experiments to attempt to capture the impact of taxation on taxpayer attitudes and behaviours (Paler 2013; Martin 2014). While this type of research demands a level of abstraction from the practical barriers to political change, it can nonetheless offer important insights into the micro-level dynamics of interest. Finally, econometric analysis at the subnational level has the potential to continue to shed new light on difficult-to-observe features of the relationship between taxation, responsiveness and accountability (Hoffman and Gibson 2005; Gadenne 2014).

A fourth potential direction for future research lies in further exploring the importance of the contextual factors that appear to shape the potential for tax bargaining. The factors highlighted in this book are supported by a combination of the case study evidence here, a small number of similar studies and predictions emerging from historical experience. However, the overall sample size on which these conclusions are based remains relatively small, while there have not been any other studies explicitly seeking to test these possibilities in contemporary developing countries. Having now identified a set of factors that appear to have played a critical role in shaping outcomes, there is an opportunity to more explicitly focus attention of the importance of particular contextual factors, asking whether variation in those factors yields consistently different outcomes across a wider range of cases. That said, the inherent complexity of many of the causal processes of interest, coupled with the fact that tax bargaining has been relatively infrequent, is likely to render such a research agenda very challenging. Again a promising strategy may lie in subnational research: at that level there are better prospects for observing comparatively small-scale political interactions around taxation in detail. Similarly, there are likely to be opportunities for more precise comparison, identifying specific differences between otherwise

7.3 Limitations and future research

similar localities and exploring the implications of those differences for contestation and bargaining around taxation. The ultimate goal is not to arrive at a highly deterministic model, as processes of tax bargaining will invariably be contingent and connected to broader processes of political contestation. However, better understanding those factors that make particular environments more conducive to tax bargaining is of both academic and practical importance.

A final consideration for future research is that while this book has focused on the connections between taxation, responsiveness and accountability, there are a variety of other ways in which the need for taxation may shape broader governance and development outcomes. One possibility is that reliance on taxation may contribute to strengthening broader state capacity. Collecting significant tax revenue is amongst the most administratively demanding tasks facing the state, and is interconnected with many other elements of effective state capacity. It may thus act as a leading edge of broader administrative strengthening and reform (Bräutigam and Knack 2004; Bräutigam 2008a; Prichard and Leonard 2010). The need to rely on tax revenue may also make governments more likely to adopt growth-promoting policies, owing to their common interest in promoting the prosperity of taxpayers in order to maximize tax revenues (Bates 2001).[15] Both possibilities are closely related to the issues investigated here and additional research in these areas could offer potentially rich insights into the broader importance of taxation to statebuilding, governance and development.

This last point is suggestive of the broader potential of research that is focused on the importance of taxation, and sources of government revenue more broadly, to development outcomes. While this book has focused specifically on the potentially positive implications of taxation for the expansion of responsiveness and accountability, it is also part of a broader resurgence of interest in the broad field of fiscal sociology; that is, in the possibility that understanding the sources of government revenue may be central to understanding development outcomes more broadly. This resurgence has included now extensive research into the resource curse, as well as research that has used the study of taxation in order to illuminate the character of the broader political bargains underpinning different states (Lieberman 2002; Slater 2010; Schneider 2012; Hassan and Prichard 2013). However, the potential for research

---

[15] In a recent study, Gehlbach (2008) highlights a more nuanced variant of this idea, arguing more specifically that governments will have incentives to promote the prosperity of individuals or firms that are likely to make the largest contribution to state tax revenue.

focused on understanding the development implications of differences in the fiscal foundations of states is much broader, reflecting the diversity of sources of government finance – both licit and illicit – in developing countries.

Most obvious is the potential for continued research into the implications of foreign aid for governing incentives (Moss, Pettersson and van de Walle 2006; OECD 2009; Prichard, Brun, and Morrissey 2012). More recently, Moore (2012) has highlighted a variety of other, often off-budget, revenue sources that play important roles particularly in countries facing significant governance challenges – and which frequently finance particular factions within the state disproportionately. These include state involvement in illicit activities such as the drug trade, the growing role of sovereign wealth funds, revenue derived from control over the allocation and development of property, and revenue derived from offshore finance and other enclave economic activities. Of course, scholars have long recognized that these different sources of revenue exist; what is new is the recognition that these seemingly disparate topics are all closely interconnected in analytical terms. By shaping the ways that states and governments are financed, these disparate sources of revenue are all likely to shape the ways in which different states are governed. In highlighting the role of taxation in shaping the relationship between citizens and states, this book has thus also pointed towards the analytical potential of research that views the fiscal foundations of states as critical to explaining development outcomes. The ability to raise revenue is amongst the most basic features of statehood, and both taxation and broader sources of government financing warrant a more central place in the study of politics in developing countries.

Key interviews

Ghana

Title	Location	Date
Program Director, Leading Budget and Tax Advocacy Network	Accra	25/02/2009
Senior Auditor, Large Taxpayers Unit	Accra	20/02/2009
Senior Official, Internal Revenue Service	Accra	13/02/2009
Program Officer, PUFMARP Project, World Bank	Accra	09/09/2008
International advisor to Ministry of Health	Accra	23/04/2008
Former Commissioner, Internal Revenue Service	Accra	21/04/2008
Former Senior Tax Collector, Internal Revenue Service, Current Tax Consultant	Accra	21/04/2008
Former Deputy Minister of Finance	Accra	20/04/2008
Senior Official, Youth Employment Scheme, Ministry of Manpower, Youth and Employment	Accra	17/04/2008
Former Commissioner, Internal Revenue Service	Accra	16/04/2008
Senior Official, Bank of Ghana	Accra	16/04/2008
Opposition Member of Parliament and Member of Parliamentary Finance Committee	Accra	15/04/2008
Senior Budget Official, Ministry of Finance and Economic Planning	Accra	15/04/2008
Government Member of Parliament and Member of Parliamentary Finance Committee	Accra	14/04/2008
Official, International Monetary Fund	Accra	11/04/2008
Director, Leading Civil Society Advocacy Network	Accra	10/04/2008
Former Deputy Minister of Finance and Senior Official in PNDC and NDC Governments	Accra	10/04/2008
Director, Leading Ghanaian Economic Policy Think Tank, Former Senior Member of PNDC Economic Management Team	Accra	02/04/2008
Country Officer, World Bank	Accra	02/04/2008
Senior Official, Ghana National Chamber of Commerce and Industry	Accra	27/03/2008
Program Coordinator, Civil Society Organization Working on Budget Management	Accra	26/03/2008

(*cont.*)

Key interviews

Title	Location	Date
Senior Budget Expert, NGO Advocacy Initiative	Accra	26/03/2008
Senior Official, Ghana National Chamber of Commerce and Industry	Accra	25/03/2008
Director, Leading Advocacy NGO	Accra	25/03/2008
Senior Advisor, NDC Senior Leadership	Accra	25/03/2008
Senior NDC and Government Official	Accra	25/03/2008
Senior Official, Canadian International Development Agency	Accra	24/03/2008
Former Minister in PNDC and NDC Governments	Accra	21/03/2008
Senior Advisor to President Atta-Mills	Accra	21/03/2008
Senior Official, International NGO Working on Informal Sector Taxation	Accra	20/03/2008
Senior Researcher, Association of Ghana Industries	Accra	18/03/2008
Senior Official, Associations of Ghana Industries	Accra	18/03/2008
Budget Official, Ministry of Finance and Economic Planning	Accra	18/03/2008
Senior Official, Ghana Union of Traders Association	Accra	18/03/2008
Professor, Institute of Statistical, Social and Economic Research, University of Ghana	Accra	17/03/2008
Senior Donor Official, Tax Reform Program	Accra	17/03/2008
Senior Leader, Committee for Joint Action	Accra	17/03/2008
Budget Analyst, Ministry of Finance	Accra	14/03/2008
Professor, University of Ghana; Former Auditor, Internal Revenue Service	Accra	14/03/2008
Senior Official, Research, Planning and Monitoring, Revenue Agencies Governing Board	Accra	13/03/2008
Coordinator, Civil Society Budget Monitoring Project	Accra	12/03/2008
Director of Finance, Leading Civil Society Organization Working on Budget Issues	Accra	12/03/2008
Senior Official, Ghana National Petroleum Authority	Accra	10/03/2008
Senior Official, Tax Policy Unit, Ministry of Finance and Economic Planning	Accra	10/03/2008
Senior Official, Tax Policy Unit, Ministry of Finance and Economic Planning	Accra	10/03/2008
Deputy Commissioner, Internal Revenue Service	Accra	10/03/2008
Professor, Institute of Statistical, Social and Economic Research, University of Ghana	Accra	04/03/2008
Senior Collector, Customs, Excise and Preventive Service	Accra	03/03/2008
Assistant Deputy Commissioner, Internal Revenue Service	Accra	03/03/2008
Data Management Official, VAT Service	Accra	03/03/2008
Senior Official, Customs, Excise and Preventive Service	Accra	03/03/2008
Senior Official, Private Enterprise Foundation	Accra	28/02/2008
Senior Official, VAT Service	Accra	27/02/2008
Leading Political Journalist	Accra	27/02/2008
Professor, Faculty of Social Studies, University of Ghana	Accra	19/02/2008
Deputy Director, Leading Human Rights NGO	Accra	19/02/2008
Senior Donor Official	Accra	19/02/2008
Former Leader of Tax Reform Program, and Senior Official in Ministry of Finance	Over Phone	18/01/2008

Kenya

Title	Location	Date
Former Minister of Energy	Nairobi	08/10/2008
Former matatu conductor and taxi company owner	Nairobi	Repeated Interviews 09/2008
Prominent Business Leader, KAM and KEPSA member	Nairobi	Repeated Interviews 09/2008
Former Commissioner, Domestic Tax Department, Kenya Revenue Authority	Nairobi	26/09/2008
Senior Official, IT Division, Kenya Revenue Authority	Nairobi	24/09/2008
Senior Donor Official	Nairobi	22/09/2008
Senior Leader, Kenya Private Sector Association	Nairobi	18/09/2008
Senior Civil Society Leader Working on Tax Issues	Nairobi	17/09/2008
Senior staff member, Leading NGO working on corruption issues	Nairobi	16/09/2008
Senior Policy Researcher on Budget Issues, Kenya Institute for Public Policy Research and Analysis	Nairobi	16/09/2008
Former Commissioner, VAT, Kenya Revenue Authority	Nairobi	15/09/2008
Senior Policy Researcher on Petroleum Prices and Taxation, Kenya Institute for Public Policy Research and Analysis	Nairobi	11/09/2009
Governance Advisor, UK Department for International Development	Nairobi	09/09/2008
Senior Official, Fiscal and Monetary Affairs Department, Ministry of Finance	Nairobi	08/09/2008
Senior Staff Member, Kenya Alliance of Resident Associations	Nairobi	08/09/2008
Senior Leader, We Can Do It campaign	Nairobi	02/09/2008
Researcher working on politics surrounding the Constituency Development Funds	Nairobi	30/08/2008
Senior Civil Society Leader working on Budget Monitoring	Nairobi	29/08/2008
Senior Civil Society Leader working on Budget Monitoring	Nairobi	28/08/2008
Official, United Business Association	Nairobi	28/08/2008
Senior Leader, United Business Associations	Nairobi	28/08/2008
Former Senior Official and Current Adviser to Central Bank of Kenya	Nairobi	22/08/2008
Senior Policy Researcher on Tax Issues, Kenya Institute for Public Policy Research and Analysis	Nairobi	20/08/2008
Senior Researcher on Tax Issues, Institute for Economic Affairs	Nairobi	20/08/2008
Researcher working on tax and governance questions, University of Nairobi	Nairobi	20/08/2008

(cont.)

Title	Location	Date
Former Permanent Secretary, Ministry of Finance	Nairobi	20/08/2008
Tax Officer, Domestic Tax Department, Kenya Revenue Authority	Nairobi	20/08/2008
Senior Leader, Karen and Langata District Association	Nairobi	19/08/2008
Former Permanent Secretary, Ministry of Finance	Nairobi	19/08/2008
Senior Official, Research, Monitoring and Planning, Kenya Revenue Authority	Nairobi	18/08/2008
Consultant to National Taxpayers' Association	Nairobi	12/08/2008
Researcher working on politics surrounding informal sector taxation	Nairobi	11/08/2008
Former Director of Tax Policy, Ministry of Finance	Nairobi	08/08/2008
Former Advisor to Ministry of Finance and Kenya Revenue Agency	Nairobi	22/07/2008

Ethiopia

Title	Location	Date
Former director of budget management reform program, Federal Ministry of Finance and Economic Development	Addis Ababa	16/10/2008
International Tax Advisor to the Regional Governments	Over Phone	20/10/2009
Senior Official, Federal Ministry of Finance and Economic Development	Addis Ababa	10/12/2008
Leading figure and former member of parliament, leading opposition political party	Addis Ababa	10/12/2008
Senior Official, Tax Audit and Enforcement, Amhara Bureau of Revenue	Bahir Dar, Amhara	04/12/2008
Former Senior Official, Amhara Bureau of Revenue	Bahir Dar, Amhara	04/12/2008
Former Member of Parliament under EPRDF	Addis Ababa	02/12/2008
Senior Official, Tigray Bureau of Finance and Economic Development	Mek'ele, Tigray	02/12/2008
Senior Official, Tigray Bureau of Revenue	Mek'ele, Tigray	02/12/2008
Former Senior Official, Tigray Bureau of Revenue	Addis Ababa	25/11/2008
Senior Official, Ministry of Revenue	Addis Ababa	25/11/2008
Senior Official, Addis Ababa Chamber of Commerce	Addis Ababa	19/11/2008
Senior economic researcher and economic advisor to the President	Addis Ababa	19/11/2008
Opposition Member of Parliament	Addis Ababa	19/11/2008

Key interviews

Title	Location	Date
Economist, International Monetary Fund	Addis Ababa	18/11/2008
Senior official, Ministry of Revenue	Addis Ababa	18/11/2008
Ambassador from leading donor country	Addis Ababa	18/11/2008
Senior official, IT Reform Program, Ministry of Revenue	Addis Ababa	14/11/2008
Donor official working on tax capacity building	Addis Ababa	14/11/2008
World Bank Official, Public Financial Management Project	Addis Ababa	13/11/2008
Private sector senior accountant, Former official of VAT Department, Ministry of Revenue	Addis Ababa	07/11/2008
Donor Official working with Addis Ababa Chamber of Commerce	Addis Ababa	06/11/2008
Leader of major research program, IFPRI	Addis Ababa	06/11/2008
Donor official, Private Sector Development Program	Addis Ababa	05/11/2008
Senior Tax Official, Ministry of Revenue	Addis Ababa	05/11/2008
Senior Official working on regional fiscal relations, Federal Ministry of Finance and Economic Development	Addis Ababa	03/11/2008
Senior tax reform official, Ministry of Revenue	Addis Ababa	03/11/2008
Prominent Political Journalist	Addis Ababa	Repeated Interviews Oct. – Nov. 2008
Former State Minister of Finance	Addis Ababa	30/10/2008
Senior Official, Oromia Bureau of Revenue	Addis Ababa	28/10/2008
Senior Revenue Official, Federal Ministry of Finance and Economic Development	Addis Ababa	28/10/2008
Senior Official, Central Bank	Addis Ababa	24/10/2008
Senior official working on budgeting and IT reform, Federal Ministry of Finance and Economic Development	Addis Ababa	21/10/2008
Professor of Economics, University of Addis Ababa	Addis Ababa	21/10/2008
Professor of Economics, University of Addis Ababa	Addis Ababa	21/10/2008
Senior government official dealing with pastoralist issues	Brighton, UK	06/12/2006

References

Abegaz, Berhanu 2001. 'Ethiopia,' in *Aid and Reform in Africa: Lessons from Ten Case Studies*, edited by S. Devarajan, D. Dollar and T. Holmgren. Washington, DC: World Bank, pp. 167–226.

Abrie, W. and E. Doussy 2006. 'Tax Compliance Obstacles Encountered by Small and Medium Enterprises in South Africa.' *Meditari Accountancy Research* 14(1): 1–13.

Acemoglu, D., S. Johnson, P. Querubin and J. A. Robinson 2008. *When Does Policy Reform Work? The Case of Central Bank Independence.* NBER Working Paper 14033.

Acemoglu, D., S. Johnson, J. A. Robinson and P. Yared 2008. 'Income and Democracy.' *American Economic Review* 98(3): 808–842.

Acemoglu, Daron and James A. Robinson 2006. *Economic Origins of Dictatorship and Democracy.* Cambridge: Cambridge University Press.

Adams, Charles 1998. *Those Dirty Rotten Taxes: The Tax Revolts that Built America.* New York: The Free Press.

Addison, Tony, Abdur Chowdhury and S. Mansoob Murshed 2004. 'The Fiscal Dimensions of Conflict and Reconstruction,' in *Fiscal Policy for Development: Poverty, Reconstruction and Growth*, edited by T. Addison and A. Roe. Basingstoke: Palgrave Macmillan, pp. 260–273.

Addison, Tony and Leonce Ndikumana 2003. 'Overcoming the Fiscal Crisis of the African State,' in *From Conflict to Recovery in Africa*, edited by T. Addison. Oxford: Oxford University Press, pp. 240–262.

Admassie, Assefa 2013. *The Political Economy of Food Price: The Case of Ethiopia.* WIDER Working Paper NO. 2013/001. Helsinki: UNU-WIDER.

Agrawal, Arun and Jesse Ribot 1999. 'Accountability in Decentralization: A Framework with South Asian and West African Cases.' *The Journal of Developing Areas* 33(4): 473–502.

Aiko, R. and C. Logan 2014. 'Africa's Willing Taxpayers Thwarted by Opaque Tax Systems, Corruption.' *Afrobarometer Policy Paper* 7.

Alexeev, M. and R. Conrad 2009. 'The Elusive Curse of Oil.' *The Review of Economics and Statistics* 91(3): 586–598.

Ali, M., O. Fjeldstad and I. Sjursen 2014. 'To Pay or Not to Pay? Citizens' Attitudes Toward Taxation in Kenya, Tanzania, Uganda and South Africa.' *World Development* 64: 828–842.

Alm, James, Isabel Sanchez and Ana de Juan 1995. 'Economic and Noneconomic Factors in Tax Compliance.' *Kyklos* 48(1): 3–18.

Amponsah, Nicholas 2007. 'Institutions and Economic Performance: Ghana's Experience Under the Fourth Republic, 1992–2002', in *Ghana: One Decade of the Liberal State*, edited by K. Boafo-Arthur. Dakar: CODESRIA, pp. 106–127.
Andersen, J. and S. Aslaksen 2013. 'Oil and Political Survival.' *Journal of Development Studies* 100: 89–106.
Andersen, J. and M. Ross 2014. 'Big Oil Change: A Closer Look at the Haber-Menaldo Analysis.' *Comparative Political Studies*.
Arriola, Leonard 2008. 'Ethnicity, Economic Conditions and Opposition Support: Evidence from Ethiopia's 2005 Elections.' *Northeast African Studies* 10(1): 115–144.
Ascher, William 1989. 'Risk, Politics and Tax Reform: Lessons from Some Latin American Experiences', in *Tax Reform in Developing Countries*, edited by M. Gillis. Durham: Duke University Press.
Aslaksen, Silje 2010. 'Oil and Democracy: More than a Cross-Country Correlation?' *Journal of Peace Research* 47(4): 421–431.
Assibey-Mensah, George 1999. 'The Value-Added Tax in Ghana', *Public Budgeting and Finance* 19: 76–89.
Auriol, Emmanuelle and Michael Warlters 2005. 'Taxation Base in Developing Countries', *Journal of Public Economics* 89(4): 625–646.
Bahiigwa, Godfrey, Frank Ellis, Odd-Helge Fjeldstad and Vegard Iversen 2004. 'Rural Taxation in Uganda: Implications for Growth, Income Distribution, Local Government Revenue and Poverty Reduction', EPRC Research Series Number 35. Economic Policy Research Center.
Bahl, Roy 1998. 'China: Evaluating the Impact of Intergovernmental Fiscal Reform,' *Fiscal Decentralization in Developing Countries*, edited by R. Bird and F. Vaillancourt. Cambridge: Cambridge University Press, pp. 49–77.
Bailyn, Bernard 1967. *The Ideological Origins of the American Revolution*. Cambridge, MA: Harvard University Press.
Barbone, Luca, Arindam Das-Gupta, Luc De Wolf and Anna Hansson 1999. *Reforming Tax Systems: The World Bank Record in the 1990s*. World Bank Policy Research Working Paper 2237. Washington, DC: World Bank.
Bardhan, Pranab 2002. 'Decentralization of Governance and Development.' *The Journal of Economic Perspectives* 16(4): 185–205.
Barkan, Joel and Michael Chege 1989. 'Decentralizing the State: District Focus and the Politics of Reallocation in Kenya.' *The Journal of Modern African Studies* 27(3): 431–453.
Baskaran, T. and A. Bigsten 2013. 'Fiscal Capacity and the Quality of Government in Sub-Saharan Africa.' *World Development* 45(3): 92–107.
Bates, Robert 2008. *When Things Fell Apart: State Failure in Late-Century Africa*. Cambridge: Cambridge University Press.
Bates, Robert 2001. *Prosperity and Violence: The Political Economy of Development*. New York: W.W. Norton & Company.
Bates, Robert 1989. 'A Political Scientist Looks at Tax Reform,' in *Tax Reform in Developing Countries*, edited by M. Gillis. Durham: Duke University Press, pp. 473–491.

Bates, Robert. 1981. *Markets and States in Tropical Africa: The Political Basis of Agricultural Policies*. Berkeley: University of California Press.

Bates, Robert and Da-Hsiang Lien 1985. 'A Note on Taxation, Development and Representative Government.' *Politics and Society* 14(53): 53–70.

Beblawi, H. and G. Luciani 1987. *The Rentier State*. London: Croom Helm.

Benedek, Dora, Ernesto Crivelli, Sanjeev Gupta, and Priscilla Muthoora. 2014. 'Foreign Aid and Revenue: Still a Crowding Out Effect?' *FinanzArchiv: Public Finance Analysis* no. 70(1): 67–96.

Bennett, Andrew and Colin Elman 2006. 'Complex Causal Relations and Case Study Methods: The Example of Path Dependence.' *Political Analysis* 14: 250–267.

Berenson, Marc 2006. 'Don't Mess With Taxes! How Poles and Russians Pay Their Dues', Princeton: Department of Politics, Princeton University.

Bergman, Marcelo 2002. 'Who Pays for Social Policy? A Study on Taxes and Trust.' *Journal of Social Policy* 31(2): 289–305.

Bergman, Marcelo. 2003. 'Tax Reforms and Tax Compliance: The Divergent Paths of Chile and Argentina.' *Journal of Latin American Studies* 35: 593–624.

Bernstein, Thomas and Xiaobo Lü 2008. 'Taxation and Coercion in Rural China,' in *Taxation and State Building in Developing Countries: Capacity and Consent*, edited by D. Bräutigam, O.-H. Fjeldstad and M. Moore, pp. 89–113.

Besley, Timothy and Torsten Persson 2011. *Pillars of Prosperity: The Political Economics of Development Clusters*. Princeton: Princeton University Press.

Bevan, David 2001. 'The Fiscal Dimensions of Ethiopia's Transition and Reconstruction.' *UNU-WIDER Discussion Paper No 2001/56*. Geneva: UNU-WIDER.

Bevan, David 1994. 'Economic Aspects of the Ethiopian Transition from War to Peace,' in *Some Economic Consequences of the Transition from Civil War to Peace*, edited by J.-P. Azam, D. Bevan, P. Collier, S. Dercon, J. W. Gunning and S. Pradhan. Washington, DC: World Bank, pp. 109–188.

Bevan, David and Sanjay Pradhan 1994. 'Fiscal Aspects of the Transition from War to Peace: With Illustrations from Uganda and Ethiopia,' in *Some Economic Consequences of the Transition from Civil War to Peace*, edited by J.-P. Azam, D. Bevan, P. Collier, S. Dercon, J. W. Gunning and S. Pradhan. Washington, DC: World Bank, pp. 87–108.

Bird, Richard 2008. 'Tax Challenges Facing Developing Countries,' *Institute for International Business Working Paper* 12. Toronto: University of Toronto.

Bird, Richard and Pierre-Pascal Gendron 2007. *The VAT in Developing and Transitional Countries*. Cambridge: Cambridge University Press.

Bird, Richard and Joosung Jun 2005. *Earmarking in Theory and Korean Practice, International Studies Working Paper 05–15*. Atlanta, GA: Andrew Young School of Policy Studies, Georgia State University.

Bird, Richard, Jorge Martinez-Vazquez and Benno Torgler 2004. 'Societal Institutions and Tax Effort in Developing Countries,' *International Tax Program Working Paper 04/011*. Toronto: Joseph L. Rotman School of Business, University of Toronto.

Bird, Richard and Francois Vaillancourt 1998. 'Fiscal Decentralizaiton in Developing Countries: An Overview,' in *Fiscal Decentralization in Developing Countries*, edited by R. Bird and F. Vaillancourt. Cambridge: Cambridge University Press, pp. 1–48.

Bird, Richard and Eric Zolt 2007. *'Technology and Taxation in Developing Countries: From Hand to Mouse.'* Toronto: University of Toronto.

Bird, Richard and Eric Zolt 2005. 'Redistribution via Taxation: The Limited Role of the Personal Income Tax in Developing Countries.' *International Tax Program Working Paper 05/08*. Toronto: Joseph L. Rotman School of Management, University of Toronto.

Blundell, Richard and Stephen Bond 1998. 'Initial Conditions and Moment Restrictions in Dynamic Panel Data Models.' *Journal of Econometrics* 87(1): 115–143.

Boahen, A. 1997. 'Ghana: Conflict Reoriented,' in *Governance as Conflict Management*, edited by I.W. Zartman. Washington, DC: The Brookings Institution, pp. 95–148.

Boahen, A. 1989. *The Ghanaian Sphinx: Reflections on the Contemporary History of Ghana 1972–1987*. Nigeria: Sankofa Educational Publishers.

Booth, D. 2011. 'Aid Effectiveness: Bringing Country Ownership (and Politics) Back In,' Overseas Development Institute Working Paper 336.

Bornhorst, F., S. Gupta and J. Thornton 2008. 'Natural Resource Endowments, Governance and the Domestic Revenue Effort: Evidence from a Panel of Countries.' IMF Working Paper 08/170.

Bosco, Luigi and Luigi Mittone 1997. 'Tax Evasion and Moral Constraints: Some Experimental Evidence.' *Kyklos* 50(3): 297–324.

Boyce, James and Madalene O'Donnell, eds. 2007. *Peace and the Public Purse: Building State Capacity After Violent Conflict*. Boulder: Lynne Rienner.

Boylan, Delia 1996. 'Taxation and Transition: The Politics of the 1990 Chilean Tax Reform.' *Latin American Research Review* 31(1): 7–31.

Brady, Henry, David Collier and Jason Seawright 2006. 'Toward a Pluralistic Vision of Methodology.' *Political Analysis* 14: 353–368.

Brand, Laurie 1992. 'Economic and Political Liberalization in a Rentier Economy: The Case of the Hashemite Kingdom of Jordan,' in *Privatization and Liberalization in the Middle East*, edited by I. Harik and D. Sullivan. Bloomington: Indiana University Press, pp. 167–188.

Bräutigam, Deborah 2008a. 'Introduction: Taxation and State-Building in Developing Countries,' in *Taxation and State Building in Developing Countries: Capacity and Consent*, edited by D. Bräutigam, O.-H. Fjeldstad and M. Moore, pp. 1–33.

Bräutigam, Deborah 2008b. 'Contingent Capacity: Export Taxation and State-Building in Mauritius,' in *Taxation and State Building in Developing Countries: Capacity and Consent*, edited by D. Bräutigam, O.-H. Fjeldstad and M. Moore, pp. 135–159.

Bräutigam, Deborah 2002. 'Building Leviathan: Revenue, State Capacity and Governance.' *IDS Bulletin* 33(2): 10–20.

Bräutigam, Deborah, Odd-Helge Fjeldstad and Mick Moore (eds.) 2008. *Taxation and State Building in Developing Countries: Capacity and Consent*. Cambridge: Cambridge University Press.

Bräutigam, Deborah and Stephen Knack 2004. 'Foreign Aid, Institutions and Governance in Sub-Saharan Africa.' *Economic Development and Cultural Change* 52: 255–285.
Bräutigam, Deborah, Lise Rakner and Scott Taylor 2002. 'Business Associations and Growth Coalitions in Sub-Saharan Africa.' *Journal of Modern African Studies* 40(4): 519–547.
Brewer, John 1989. *The Sinews of Power: War, Money and the English State, 1688–1783*. New York: Alfred A. Knopf.
Brietzke, Paul 1976. 'Land Reform in Revolutionary Ethiopia.' *The Journal of Modern African Studies* 14(4): 637–660.
Broms, Rasmus 2014. 'Putting Up or Shutting Up: On the Individual-Level Relationship between Taxpaying and Political Interest in a Developmental Context.' *Journal of Development Studies* 51(1): 93–109.
Brun, Jean-Francois, Gerard Chambas and Samuel Guerineau 2008. 'Aide et Mobilisation Fiscale Dans Les Pays en Developpement.' *CERDI, Etudes et Documents E 2008.12*. Clermont-Ferrand: CERDI.
Brunnschweiler, Christa N. 2008. 'Cursing the Blessings? Natural Resource Abundance, Institutions, and Economic Growth.' *World Development* 36(3): 399–419.
Brunnschweiler, Christa N. and Erwin H. Bulte 2008. 'The Resource Curse Revisited and Revised: A Tale of Paradoxes and Red Herrings.' *Journal of Environmental Economics and Management* 55(3): 248–264.
Bulir, Ales 1998. 'The Price Incentive to Smuggle and the Cocoa Supply in Ghana, 1950–96.' *IMF Working Paper 98/88*. Washington, DC: International Monetary Fund.
Bush, Barbara and Josephine Maltby 2004. 'Taxation in West Africa: Transforming the Colonial Subject into the "Governable Person."' *Critical Perspectives on Accounting* 15(1): 5–34.
Caselli, Francesco and Tom Cunningham 2009. 'Leader Behaviour and the Natural Resource.' *Oxford Economic Papers* 61: 628–650.
Centeno, Angel 1997. 'Blood and Debt-War and Taxation in Nineteenth-Century Latin America.' *American Journal of Sociology* 102(6): 1565–1605.
Centeno, Miguel Angel 2002. *Blood and Debt: War and the Nation-State in Latin America*. University Park: Pennsylvania State University Press.
Chaudhry, Kiren Aziz 1997. *The Price of Wealth: Economies and Institutions in the Middle East*. Ithaca: Cornell University Press.
Chaudhry, Kiren Aziz 1989. 'The Price of Wealth: Business and State in Labor Remittance and Oil Economies.' *International Organization* 43(1): 101–145.
Chazan, Naomi 1988. 'Patterns of State-Society Incorporation and Disengagement,' in *The Precarious Balance: State and Society in Africa*, edited by D. Rothchild and N. Chazan. Boulder: Westview Press, pp. 121–148.
Chazan, Naomi 1983. *An Anatomy of Ghanaian Politics: Managing Political Recession, 1969–82*. Boulder: Westview Press.
Cheeseman, N. 2013. 'Public Goods, Taxation, and the Evolution of a Social Contract in Lagos, Nigeria.' Annual Meeting of the American Political Science Association, Chicago, IL.

References

Cheeseman, Nicholas and Robert Griffiths 2006. 'Increasing Tax Revenue in Sub-Saharan Africa: The Case of Kenya.' *Oxford Council on Good Governance Economy Analysis* 6. Oxford: Oxford Council on Good Governance.

Cheibub, J.A., Gandhi, J. and Vreeland, J.R. 2010. 'Democracy and Dictatorship Revisited.' *Public Choice* 143(2), 1–2: 67–101.

Cheibub, Jose Antonio 1998. 'Political Regimes and the Extractive Capacity of Governments: Taxation in Democracies and Dictatorships.' *World Politics* 50(3): 349–376.

Chole, Eshetu 1994. 'Issues of Vertical Imbalance,' in *Fiscal Decentralization in Ethiopia*, edited by Eshetu Chole. Addis Ababa: Addis Ababa University Press, pp. 168–190.

Clapham, Christopher 1988. *Transformation and Continuity in Revolutionary Ethiopia* Cambridge: Cambridge University Press.

Clist, P. and Oliver Morrissey 2011. 'Aid and Tax Revenue: Signs of a Positive Effect since the 1980s.' *Journal of International Development* 23(2): 165–180.

Clist, Paul 2014. *'Foreign Aid and Domestic Taxation: Multiple Sources, One Conclusion.'* ICTD Working Paper 20. Brighton: Institute of Development Studies.

Cohen, John and Nils-Ivar Isaksson 1987. 'Villagisation in Ethiopia's Arsi Region.' *The Journal of Modern African Studies* 25(3): 435–464.

Collier, David, Henry Brady and Jason Seawright 2004. 'Sources of Leverage in Causal Inference: Toward an Alternative View of Methodology,' in *Rethinking Social Inquiry: Diverse Tools, Shared Standards*, edited by Henry Brady and David Collier. Oxford: Rowan and Littlefield, 229–265.

Collier, Paul 2009. *Wars, Guns and Votes: Democracy in Dangerous Places*. New York: Harper.

Collier, Paul 2006. 'Is Aid Oil? An Analysis of Whether Africa Can Absorb More Aid.' *World Development* 34(9): 1482–1497.

Collier, Paul and Anke Hoeffler 2004. 'Greed and Grievance in Civil War.' *Oxford Economic Papers* 56(4): 563–596.

Collier, Paul and Anke Hoeffler 1998. 'On Economic Causes of Civil War.' *Oxford Economic Papers* 50(4): 563–573.

Collier, Paul, Anke Hoeffler and Dominic Rohner 2009. Beyond Greed and Grievance: Feasibilty and Civil War. *Oxford Economic Papers* 61(1): 1–27.

Cotet, Anca M. and Kevin K. Tsui 2013. 'Oil and Conflict: What Does the Cross Country Evidence Really Show?' *American Economic Journal: Macroeconomics* 5(1): 49–80.

Crook, Richard 2003. 'Decentralisation and Poverty Reduction in Africa: The Politics of Local-Central Relations.' *Public Administration and Development* 23(1): 77–88.

Crook, Richard and James Manor 1998. *Democracy and Decentralisation in South Asia and West Africa: Participation, Accountability and Performance*. Cambridge: Cambridge University Press.

Crook, Richard and Alan Sverrisson 2003. 'Does Decentralization Contribute to Poverty Reduction? Surveying the Evidence,' in *Changing Paths: International Development and the New Politics of Inclusion*, edited by Peter P. Houtzager and Mick Moore. Ann Arbor: University of Michigan Press, 233–259.

Crystal, Jill 1990. *Oil and Politics in the Gulf: Rulers and Merchants in Kuwait and Qatar.* Cambridge: Cambridge University Press.

Cummings, Ronald, Jorge Martinez-Vazquez, Michael McKee and Benno Torgler 2005. 'Effects of Tax Morale on Tax Compliance: Experimental and Survey Evidence.' *CREMA Working Paper 2005–29*: Center for Research in Economics, Management and the Arts (CREMA).

Daunton, Martin 2001. *Trusting Leviathan: The Politics of Taxation in Britain, 1799–1914.* Cambridge: Cambridge University Press.

Dercon, Stefan 2001. *The Impact of Economic Reforms on Households in Rural Ethiopia 1989–1995.* Oxford: Center for the Study of African Economies, Oxford University.

Dercon, Stefan and Lulseged Ayalew 1995. 'Smuggling and Supply Response: Coffee in Ethiopia,' *World Development* 23(10): 1795–1813.

Devarajan, S., H. Ehrhart, T.M. Le and G. Raballand 2011. *'Direct Redistribution, Taxation and Accountability in Oil-Rich Economies: A Proposal.' Center for Global Development Working Paper* 281. Washington, DC: Center for Global Development.

Devarajan, Shantayanan, Stuti Khemani and Shekhar Shah 2009. 'The Politics of Partial Decentralization' in *Does Decentralization Enhance Service Delivery and Poverty Reduction?* edited by Ehtisham Ahmad and Giorgio Brosio. Cheltenham: Edward Elgar, pp. 102–121.

Devereux, Stephen 2006. 'Vulnerable Livelihoods in Somali Region, Ethiopia.' *IDS Research Report* 57. Brighton: Institute of Development Studies.

Diamond, Larry 2010. 'Why Are There No Arab Democracies?' *Journal of Democracy* 21(1): 93–112.

Doner, Richard, Bryan Ritchie and Dan Slater 2005. 'Systemic Vulnerability and the Origins of Developmental States: Northeast and Southeast Asia in Comparative Perspective.' *International Organization* 59: 327–361.

Doner, Richard and Ben Ross Schneider 2000. 'Business Associations and Economic Development: Why Some Associations Contribute More Than Others.' *Business and Politics* 2(3): 261–288.

Dunning, Thad 2008. *Crude Democracy: Natural Resource Wealth and Political Regimes.* Cambridge: Cambridge University Press.

Durand, Francisco and Rosemary Thorp 1998. 'Reforming the State: A Study of the Peruvian Tax Reform.' *Oxford Development Studies* 26(2): 133–151.

Easter, Gerald 2012. *Capital, Coercion and Post-Communist States.* Ithaca: Cornell University Press.

Easter, Gerald 2008. 'Capacity, Consent and Tax Collection in Post-Communist States,' in *Taxation and State Building in Developing Countries: Capacity and Consent*, edited by D. Bräutigam, O.-H. Fjeldstad and M. Moore, pp. 64–88.

Ertman, Thomas 1997. *Birth of the Leviathan: Building States and Regimes in Medieval and Early Modern Europe.* Cambridge: Cambridge University Press.

Esfahani, Hadi Salehi 2001. 'A Political Economy Model of Resource Pricing with Evidence from the Fuel Market', Champaign: Department of Economics, University of Illinois at Urbana-Champaign.

Eubank, Nicholas 2012. 'Taxation, Political Accountability and Foreign Aid: Lessons from Somaliland.' *The Journal of Development Studies* 48(4): 465–480.

Faguet, Jean-Paul 2004. 'Does Decentralization Increase Government Responsiveness to Local Needs? Evidence from Bolivia.' *Journal of Public Economics* 88(3–4): 867–893.

Fairfield, Tasha 2013. 'Going Where the Money Is: Strategies for Taxing Economic Elites in Unequal Democracies.' *World Development* 47: 42–57.

Fearon, J. 1995. 'Rationalist Explanations for War.' *International Organization* 49(3): 379–414.

Fearon, James and David Laitin 2003. 'Ethnicity, Insurgency and Civil War.' *American Political Science Review* 97(1): 75–90.

Fiseha, Assefa 2006. 'Theory Versus Practice in the Implementation of Ethiopia's Ethnic Federalism,' in *Ethnic Federalism: The Ethiopian Experience in Comparative Perspective*, edited by D. Thurton. Oxford: James Currey, pp. 131–164.

Fjeldstad, O., S. Jensen and A. Orre 2012. *Taking Stock of the Tax Reform Process in Angola... and Why Tax Incentives Should be Avoided*. Bergen, Norway: Chr. Michelsen Institute and Centro de Estudos e Investigação Científica.

Fjeldstad, Odd-Helge 2005. 'Corruption in Tax Administration: Lessons from Institutional Reforms in Uganda.' *CMI Working Paper* 2005: 10. Bergen: Chr. Michelsen Institute.

Fjeldstad, Odd-Helge 2001. 'Taxation, Coercion and Donors: Local Government Tax Enforcement in Tanzania.' *Journal of Modern African Studies* 39(2): 289–306.

Fjeldstad, Odd-Helge and Kari Heggstad 2012. '*Local Government Revenue Mobilization in Anglophone Africa.*' *ICTD Working Paper* 7. Brighton: International Center for Tax and Development.

Fjeldstad, Odd-Helge, Lucas Katera and Erasto Ngalewa 2009. 'Outsourcing Revenue Collection to Private Agents: Experiences from Local Authorities in Tanzania.' *REPOA Special Paper 09.28*. Dar es Salaam: REPOA.

Fjeldstad, Odd-Helge and Mick Moore 2008. 'Tax Reform and State-Building in a Globalised World,' in *Taxation and State Building in Developing Countries: Capacity and Consent*, edited by D. Bräutigam, O.-H. Fjeldstad and M. Moore, pp. 235–260.

Fjeldstad, Odd-Helge, Colette Schulz-Herzenberg and Ingrid Hoem Sjursen 2012. '*Peoples' View of Taxation in Africa: Theories, Evidence and an Agenda for Future Research.*' *ICTD Working Paper* 8. Brighton: Institute of Development Studies.

Fjeldstad, Odd-Helge and Joseph Semboja 2001. 'Why People Pay Taxes: The Case of the Development Levy in Tanzania.' *World Development* 29(12): 2059–2074.

Fjeldstad, Odd-Helge and Ole Therkildsen 2008. 'Mass Taxation and State-Society Relations in East Africa,' in *Taxation and State Building in Developing Countries: Capacity and Consent*, edited by D. Bräutigam, O.-H. Fjeldstad and M. Moore, pp. 114–134.

Flores-Macias, G. 2014. 'Financing Security Through Elite Taxation: The Case of Colombia's 'Democratic Security Taxes.' *Studies in Comparative International Development* 49(4): 477–500.

References

Frempong, Alexander 2007. 'Political Conflict and Elite Consensus in the Liberal State,' in *Ghana: One Decade of the Liberal State*, edited by K. Boafo-Arthur. Dakar: CODESRIA, pp. 128–164.

Frimpong-Ansah, Jonathan H. 1991. *The Vampire State in Africa: The Political Economy of Decline in Ghana*. London: James Currey.

Gadenne, Lucie 2014. *Tax Me, but Spend Wisely: Sources of Public Finance and Government Accountability*. University College London.

Gauthier, Bernard and Ritva Reinikka 2006. 'Shifting Tax Burdens Through Exemptions and Evasion: An Empirical Investigation of Uganda.' *Journal of African Economies* 15(3): 373–398.

Gehlbach, Scott 2008. *Representation through Taxation: Revenue, Politics and Development in Postcommunist States*. Cambridge: Cambridge University Press.

Gervasoni, Carlos 2010. 'A Rentier Theory of Subnational Regimes: Fiscal Federalism, Democracy and Authoritarianism in the Argentine Provinces.' *World Politics* 62(2): 302–340.

Ghani, Ashraf and Clare Lockhart 2008. *Fixing Failed Sates: A Framework for Rebuilding a Fractured World*. Oxford: Oxford University Press.

Glenday, Graham 1997. 'Capacity Building in the Context of the Kenya Tax Modernization Program,' in *Getting Good Government: Capacity Building in the Public Sectors of Developing Countries*, edited by M. Grindle. Cambridge: Harvard University Press, pp. 333–366.

Goetz, Anne Marie and Rob Jenkins 2005. *Reinventing Accountability: Making Democracy Work for Human Development*. New York: Palgrave Macmillan.

Goldsmith, Arthur 2002. 'Business Associations and Better Governance in Africa.' *Public Administration and Development* 22(1): 39–49.

Gordon, Roger and Wei Li 2009. 'Tax Structures in Developing Countries: Many Puzzles and a Possible Explanation.' *Journal of Public Economies* 93: 856–866.

Grant, Ruth and Robert Keohane 2005. 'Accountability and Abuses of Power in World Politics.' *American Political Science Review* 99(1): 29–43.

GSM Association 2007. 'Taxation and the Growth of Mobile in East Africa.' GSM Association. *Online at* www.gsma.com/publicpolicy/wp-content/uploads/2012/03/taxationandthegrowthofmobileineastafrica2007.pdf

Gudina, Merera 2006. 'Contradictory Interpretations of Ethiopian History: The Need for New Consensus,' in *Ethnic Federalism: The Ethiopian Experience in Comparative Perspective*, edited by D. Thurton. Oxford: James Currey, pp. 119–130.

Guibert, L. andPerez-Quiros, G. 2012. *Measuring the Economic Cost of the 2007/2008 Post-Election Violence in Kenya*. Pamplona, Spain: Navarra Center for International Development.

Gupta, Abhijit Sen 2007. 'Determinants of Tax Revenue Efforts in Developing Countries.' *IMF Working Paper 07/184*. Washington, DC: International Monetary Fund.

Gupta, Sanjeev, Benedict Clemens, Alexander Pivovarsky and Erwin Tiongson 2004. 'Foreign Aid and Revenue Response: Does the Composition of Aid Matter?' in *Helping Countries Develop: The Role of Fiscal Policy*, edited by S. Gupta, B. Clemens and G. Inchauste. Washington, DC: International Monetary Fund, pp. 385–406.

References

Gupta, Sanjeev and Walter Mahler 1995. 'Taxation of Petroleum Products: Theory and Empirical Evidence.' *Energy Economics* 17(2): 101–116.

Guyer, Jane 1992. 'Representation Without Taxation: An Essay on Democracy in Rural Nigeria: 1952–1990.' *African Studies Review* 35(1): 41–79.

Gwilliam, Ken and Zmarak Shalizi 1999. 'Road Funds, User Charges and Taxes.' *The World Bank Research Observer* 14(2): 159–185.

Haber, Stephen and Victor Menaldo 2011. 'Do Natural Resources Fuel Authoritarianism? A Reappraisal of the Resource Curse.' *American Political Science Review* 1: 1–26.

Hackenesch, Christine 2013. 'Aid Donor Meets Strategic Partner? The European Union's and China's Relations with Ethiopia.' *Journal of Current Chinese Affairs* 42: 7–36.

Hall, Peter A. and Rosemary C.R. Taylor 1996. 'Political Science and the Three New Institutionalisms.' *Political Studies* 44(5): 936–957.

Handley, Antoinette 2008. *Business and the State in Africa: Economic Policy Making in the Neo-Liberal Era*. Cambridge: Cambridge University Press.

Hassan, Mirza and Wilson Prichard 2013. *'The Political Economy of Tax Reform in Bangladesh: Political Settlements, Informal Institutions and the Negotiation of Reform.'* IDS Working Paper 14. Brighton: Institute of Development Studies.

Hausman, J. and McFadden, D. 1984. 'Specification Tests for the Multinomial Logit Model.' *Econometrica* 52(5): 1219–1240.

Hausman, J.A. 1978. 'Specification Tests in Econometrics.' *Econometrica* 46(6): 1251–1271.

Havro, Govril and Javier Santiso 2011. *'Benefiting the Resource Rich: How can International Development Policy Help Tame the Resource Curse?'* IDS Working Paper. Brighton: Institute of Development Studies.

Hedstrom, P. and P. Ylikoski 2010. 'Causal Mechanisms in the Social Sciences.' *Annual Review of Sociology* 36(1): 49–67.

Helmke, G. and S. Levitsky 2004. 'Informal Institutions and Comparative Politics: A Research Agenda.' *Perspectives on Politics* 2(4): 725–740.

Herb, Michael 2005. 'No Representation Without Taxation? Rents, Development and Democracy.' *Comparative Politics* 37(3): 297–316.

Herb, Michael 2003. 'Taxation and Representation.' *Studies in Comparative International Development* 38(3): 3–31.

Herbst, Jeffrey 2000. *States and Power in Africa: Comparative Lessons in Authority and Control*. Princeton: Princeton University Press.

Herbst, Jeffrey 1993. *The Politics of Reform in Ghana, 1982–1991*. Berkeley: University of California Press.

Herrera, Y. and Kapur, D. 2007. 'Improving Data Quality: Actors, Incentives and Capabilities.' *Political Analysis* 15: 365–386.

Hirschman, Albert 1970. *Exit, Voice and Loyalty: Responses to Decline in Firms, Organizations and States*. Cambridge, MA: Harvard University Press.

Hoffman, Barak and Clark Gibson 2005. *Fiscal Governance and Pubic Services: Evidence from Tanzania and Zambia*. San Diego: Department of Political Science, University of California, San Diego.

Humphreys, Marcartan 2005. 'Natural Resources, Conflict and Conflict Resolution.' *The Journal of Conflict Resolution* 49(4): 508–537.

Huntington, Samuel P. 1993. *The Third Wave: Democratization in the Late Twentieth Century*. Norman: University of Oklahoma Press.

IEG 2008. *Public Sector Reform: What Works and Why? An IEG Evaluation of World Bank Support*. Washington, DC: World Bank.

IMF 2011. *Revenue Mobilization in Developing Countries*. Washington, DC: World Bank.

IMF 2008. *The Balance of Payments Impact of the Food and Fuel Price Shocks on Low-Income African Countries: A Country-by-Country Assessment*. Washington, DC: IMF Africa Department.

Iversen, Vegard, Odd-Helge Fjeldstad, Godfrey Bahiigwa, Frank Ellis and Robert James 2006. 'Private Tax Collection – Remnant of the Past or a Way Forward? Evidence From Rural Uganda.' *Public Administration and Development* 26(2): 317–328.

Jensen, Nathan and Leonard Wantchekon 2004. 'Resource Wealth and Political Regimes in Africa.' *Comparative Political Studies* 37(7): 816–841.

Jerven, M. 2013a. *Poor Numbers: How We Are Misled by African Development Statistics and What to Do about It*. Ithaca: Cornell University Press.

Jerven, M. 2013b. 'For Richer, For Poorer: GDP Revisions and Africa's Statistical Tragedy.' *African Affairs* 112(446): 138–147.

Jerven, M. 2013c. 'Comparability of GDP Estimates in Sub-Saharan Africa: The Effect of Revisions in Sources and Methods Since Structural Adjustment.' *Review of Income and Wealth* 59(S1): S16–S36.

Jerven, M. and M.E. Duncan 2012. 'Revising GDP Estimates in Sub-Saharan Africa: Lessons from Ghana.' *The African Statistical Journal* 15(1): 13–22.

Jibao, S., Prichard, W. and van den Boogaard, V. 2014. 'Informal taxation in peripheral regions in post-conflict Sierra Leone', Paper presented at the *CEPA and SLRC 13th Annual Symposium on Post-War Development in Asia and Africa*, Colombo, Sri Lanka.

Jibao, Samuel and Wilson Prichard 2013. *Rebuilding Local Government Finances After Conflict: The Political Economy of Property Taxation in Post-Conflict Sierra Leone'*, ICTD Working Paper 12. Brighton: Institute of Development Studies.

Jibao, Samuel and Wilson Prichard forthcoming. The Political Economy of Property Tax in Africa: Explaining Reform Outcomes in Sierra Leone. *African Affairs*.Jordan, John 1999. *Ethiopia: Documents on Tax Administration and Policy Reforms, Volume I*. Addis Ababa: Ethiopian Federal Ministry of Finance and Economic Development.

Joshi, A., W. Prichard and C. Heady 2014. 'Taxing the Informal Economy: Challenges, Possibilities and Remaining Questions.' *Journal of Development Studies* 50(10): 1325–1347.

Joshi, Anuradha and Joseph Ayee 2008. 'Associational Taxation: A Pathway into the Informal Sector,' in *Taxation and State Building in Developing Countries: Capacity and Consent*, edited by D. Bräutigam, O.-H. Fjeldstad and M. Moore, pp. 183–211

Juul, Kristine 2006. 'Decentralization, Local Taxation and Citizenship in Senegal.' *Development and Change* 37(4): 821–846.

Kamunyori, Sheila 2007. *A Growing Space for Dialogue: The Case of Street Vending in Nairobi's Central Business District*. Cambridge, MA: Department of Urban Studies and Planning, Massachusetts Institute of Technology.

Karingi, Stephen Njuguna and Bernadette Wanjala 2005. 'The Tax Reform Experience of Kenya.' UNU-Wider Research Paper 2005/67: UNU-WIDER.

Karl, Terry Lynn 1997. *The Paradox of Plenty: Oil Booms and Petro-States*. Berkeley: University of California Press.

Kasara, K. and Suryanarayan, P. 2014. 'When do the Rich Vote Less than the Poor and Why? Explaining Turnout Inequality across the World.' *American Journal of Political Science*.

Kasara, Kimuli 2005. *Tax Me if You Can: Ethnic Geography, Democracy, and the Taxation of Agriculture in Africa*. Palo Alto: Department of Political Science, Stanford University.

Kassahun, Daniel 2006. *Towards the Development of Differential Land Taxation System in Ethiopia*. Addis Ababa: Forum for Social Studies.

Keen, Michael 2013. 'Taxation and Development – Again,' in *Critical Issues in Taxation and Development*, edited by George Zodrow and Clemens Fuest. Cambridge: MIT Press, pp. 13-41

Keen, Michael and Alejandro Simone 2004. 'Is Tax Competition Harming Developing Countries More Than Developed?' *Tax Notes International* 34(13): 1317–1326.

Kelly, Roy 2000. 'Designing a Property Tax Reform Strategy for Sub-Saharan Africa: An Analytical Framework Applied to Kenya.' *Public Budgeting and Finance* 1: 36–52.

Kelsall, T., D. Booth, D. Cammack and F. Golooba-Mutebi 2010. 'Developmental Patrimonialism? Questioning the Orthodoxy on Political Governance and Economic Progress in Africa.' *Africa Power and Politics Working Paper* 9. Online at http://r4d.dfid.gov.uk/Output/183560/

Kimenyi, Mwangi 2005. *Efficiency and Efficacy of Kenya's Constituency Development Fund: Theory and Evidence*, Storrs, CT: University of Connecticut, Department of Economics.

Klemm, Alexander 2009. *Causes, Benefits and Risks of Business Tax Incentives'*, IMF Working Paper 09/21. Washington, DC: International Monetary Fund.

Kolstad, Ivar and Arne Wiig 2009. 'Is Transparency the Key to Reducing Corruption in Resource-Rich Countries?' *World Development* 37(3): 521–533.

Korsun, Georges and Patrick Meagher 2004. 'Failure by Design? Fiscal Decentralization in West Africa,' in *Devolution and Development: Governance Prospects in Decentralizing States*, edited by Mwangi Kimenyi and Patrick Meagher. Aldershot: Ashgate, pp. 137–196.

Lata, Leenco 2003. 'The Ethiopian-Eritrea War.' *Review of African Political Economy* 30(97): 369–388.

Lawson, Andrew, Emmanuel Gyimah-Boadi, Ato Ghartey, Adom Ghartey, Tony Killick, Zaniab Kizilbash Agha and Tim Williamson 2007. *Joint Evaluation of Multi-Donor Budget Support to Ghana: Evaluation Results and Recommendations on Future Design & Management of Ghana MDBS*, Accra: Centre for Democratic Development.

Bodea, Cristina and Adrienne LeBas. 2014. 'The Origins of Voluntary Compliance: Attitudes toward Taxation in Urban Nigeria.' *British Journal of Political Science*.

Legovini, Arianna 2002. *Kenya: Macroeconomic Evolution Since Independence*, Geneva: United National Development Program.

Leonard, David 2010. '"Pockets" of Effective Agencies in Weak Governance States: Where Are They Likely and Why Does It Matter?', *Public Administration and Development* 30(2): 91–101.

Leonard, David 1991. *African Successes: Four Public Managers of Kenyan Rural Development*. Berkeley: University of California Press.

Levi, Margaret 1999. 'Death and Taxes: Extractive Equality and the Development of Democratic Institutions,' in *Democracy's Value*, edited by Ian Shapiro and Casiano Hacker-Cordon. Cambridge: Cambridge University Press, pp. 112–131.

Levi, Margaret 1988. *Of Rule and Revenue*. Berkeley: University of California Press.

Levi, Margaret and Audrey Sacks 2005. 'Achieving Good Government – And, Maybe, Legitimacy.' Presented at the *New Frontiers of Social Policy Conference*. Arusha: World Bank.

Levine, Donald 1965. *Wax and Gold: Tradition and Innovation in Ethiopian Culture*. Chicago: University of Chicago Press.

Lieberman, Evan 2005. 'Nested Analysis as a Mixed-Methods Strategy for Comparative Research.' *American Political Science Review* 99(3): 435–452.

Lieberman, Evan 2002. *Race and Regionalism in the Politics of Taxation in Brazil and South Africa*. Cambridge: Cambridge University Press.

Lin, Justin Yifu and Zhiqiang Liu 2000. 'Fiscal Decentralization and Economic Growth in China.' *Economic Development and Cultural Change* 49(1): 1–21.

Lindberg, Staffan 2009. 'Byzantine Complexity: Making Sense of Accountability.' *Committee on Concepts and Methods Working Paper Series*. Mexico City: International Political Science Association.

Love, Roy 1989. 'Funding the Ethiopian State: Who Pays.' *Review of African Political Economy* 16(44): 18–26.

Luciani, G. 1990. 'Allocation vs. Production States: A Theoretical Framework,' in *The Arab State*, edited by G. Luciani. Los Angeles: University of California Press, pp. 65–84.

Lyons, Terrence 2006. *Ethiopia in 2005: The Beginning of a Transition?* Washington, DC: Center for Strategic and International Studies.

Mahdavy, H. 1970. 'The Patterns and Problems of Economic Development in Rentier States: The Case of Iran,' in *Studies in the Economic History of the Middle East from the Rise of Islam to the Present Day*, edited by M. Cook. London: Oxford University Press, pp. 428–467.

Mahon, James 2005. 'Liberal States and Fiscal Contracts: Aspects of the Political Economy of Public Finance,' presented at the *Annual Meeting of the American Political Science Association*. Washington, DC.

Mahon, James 2004. 'Causes of Tax Reform in Latin America, 1977–95.' *Latin American Research Review* 39(1): 4–31.

References

Mamdani, Mahmood 1996. *Citizen and Subject: Contemporary Africa and the Legacy of Late Colonialism*. Princeton: Princeton University Press.

Manin, Bernard, Adam Przeworski and Susan Stokes 1999. 'Introduction,' in *Democracy, Accountability and Representation*, edited by A. Przeworski, S. Stokes and B. Manin. Cambridge: Cambridge University Press, pp. 1–26.

Mann, Michael 1986. *The Sources of Social Power: A History of Power from the Beginning to A.D. 1760*. Vol. 1. Cambridge: Cambridge University Press.

: Martin, I., A. Mehrotra and M. Prasad 2009. *The New Fiscal Sociology: Taxation in Comparative and Historical Perspective*. Cambridge: Cambridge University Press.

Martin, Isaac and Nadav Gabay 2007. *'Do Visible Taxes Cause Protest? Tax Policy and Tax Protest in Rich Democracies'*, La Jolla, CA: Department of Sociology, University of California-San Diego.

Martin, Lucy 2014. *'Taxation, Loss Aversion, and Accountability: Theory and Experimental Evidence for Taxation's Effect on Citizen Behavior'*, Unpublished working paper, Yale University. Online at http://sites.duke.edu/2014bmp/files/2014/10/Martin_TaxAcc.pdf.

Martin, Matthew 1993. 'Neither Phoenix nor Icarus: Negotiating Economic Reform in Ghana and Zambia, 1983–92,' in *Hemmed In: Responses to Africa's Economic Decline*, edited by T. Callaghy and J. Ravenhill. New York: Columbia University Press, pp. 130–179.

Martin, Matthew and Alison Johnson 2005. *Ethiopia's Debt Sustainability: From Paris Club to MDGs*. London: Debt Relief International.

McAdam, Doug, Sidney Tarrow and Charles Tilly 2001. *Dynamics of Contention*. Cambridge: Cambridge University Press.

McCleary, William 1991. 'The Earmarking of Government Revenue: A Review of Some World Bank Experience.' *World Bank Research Observer* 6(1): 81–104.

McGuirk, Eoin 2013. 'The Illusory Leader: Natural Resources, Taxation and Accountability.' *Public Choice* 154(3): 285–313.

McMillan, Margaret 2001. 'Why Kill the Golden Goose? A Political-Economy Model of Export Taxation.' *The Review of Economics and Statistics* 83(1): 170–184.

Medhane, Tadesse and John Young 2003. 'TPLF: Reform or Decline.' *Review of African Political Economy* 30(97): 389–403.

Mehlum, H., Karl Ove Moene and R. Torvik 2006. 'Institutions and the Resource Curse.' *The Economic Journal* 116: 1–20.

Moehler, Devra 2008. *Distrusting Democrats: Outcomes of Participatory Constitution Making*. Ann Arbor: University of Michigan Press.

Moore, Barrington 1966. *The Social Origins of Dictatorship and Democracy: Lord and Peasant in the Making of the Modern World*. Boston: Beacon.

Moore, Mick 2014. 'Revenue Reform and Statebuilding in Anglophone Africa.' *World Development* 60: 99–122.

Moore, Mick 2012. 'The Practical Political Economy of Illicit Flows,' in *Draining Development? Controlling Flows of Illicit Funds from Developing Countries*, edited by P. Reuter. Washington, DC: World Bank, pp. 457–482.

Moore, Mick 2008. 'Between Coercion and Contract: Competing Narratives on Taxation and Governance,' in *Taxation and State Building in Developing Countries: Capacity and Consent*, edited by D. Bräutigam, O.-H. Fjeldstad and M. Moore, pp. 34–63.

Moore, Mick 2007. 'How Does Taxation Affect the Quality of Governance?' *IDS Working Paper* 280. Brighton: Institute of Development Studies.

Moore, Mick 2004. 'Taxation and the Political Agenda, North and South.' *Forum for Development Studies* 31(1): 7–32.

Moore, Mick 2001. 'Political Underdevelopment: What Causes "Bad Governance"?' *Public Management Review* 3(3): 385–418.

Moore, Mick 1998. 'Death Without Taxes: Democracy, State Capacity and Aid Dependence in the Fourth World,' in *The Democratic Developmental State: Politics and Institutional Reform*, edited by M. Robinson and G. White. Oxford: Oxford University Press, pp. 67–88.

Morgan, Edmund and Helen Morgan 1953. *The Stamp Act Crisis: Prologue to Revolution*. New York: Collier Books.

Morrison, K.M. 2014. *Nontaxation and Representation: The Fiscal Foundations of Political Stability*. Cambridge: Cambridge University Press.

Morrison, Kevin 2009. 'Oil, Nontax Revenue and the Redistributional Foundations of Regime Stability.' *International Organization* 63(1): 107–138.

Morrissey, Oliver, Wilson Prichard and Samantha Torrance 2014. 'Aid and Taxation: Exploring the Behavioral Relationship.' *ICTD Working Paper* 21. Brighton: Institute of Development Studies.

Morton, Andrew 1998. *Moi: The Making of an African Statesman*. London: Michael O'Mara Books Limited.

Moss, Todd, Gunilla Pettersson and Nicolas van de Walle 2006. *An Aid-Institutions Paradox? A Review Essay on Aid Dependency and State Building in Sub-Saharan Africa*. CGD Working Paper 74. Washington, DC: Center for Global Development.

Moyi, Eliud and Eric Ronge 2006. *Taxation and Tax Modernization in Kenya: A Diagnosis of Performance and Options for Further Reform*. Nairobi: Institute of Economic Affairs.

Munoz, Sonia and Stanley Sang-Wook Cho 2004. 'Social Impact of a Tax Reform: The Case of Ethiopia.' in *Helping Countries Develop: The Role of Fiscal Policy*, edited by S. Gupta, B. Clemens and G. Inchauste. Washington, DC: International Monetary Fund.

Muriithi, Moses and Eliud Moyi 2003. 'Tax Reforms and Revenue Mobilization in Kenya.' *AERC Research Paper* 131. Nairobi: African Economic Research Consortium.

Naudé, Willem 1998. 'On Ethiopia's Economic Transition and Beyond.' *African Development Review* 10(2).

Newell, Peter and Joanna Wheeler 2006. 'Rights, Resources and the Politics of Accountability: An Introduction,' in *Rights, Resources and the Politics of Accountability*, edited by P. Newell and J. Wheeler. London: Zed Books, pp. 1–36.

Nickell, S. 1981. 'Biases in Dynamic Models with Fixed Effects.' *Econometrica*, 49: 1417–1426.

Ninsin, Kwame 2007. 'Markets and Liberal Democracy,' in *Ghana: One Decade of the Liberal State*, edited by K. Boafo-Arthur. Dakar: CODESRIA, pp. 86–105.

North, D. 1990. *Institutions, Institutional Change and Economic Performance*. Cambridge: Cambridge University Press.

North, Douglass, John Wallis and Barry Weingast 2009. *Violence and Social Orders: A Conceptual Framework for Interpreting Recorded Human History*, Cambridge: Cambridge University Press.

North, Douglass C. and Barry Weingast 1989. 'Constitutions and Commitment: The Evolution of Institutions Governing Public Choice in Seventeenth-Century England.' *The Journal of Economic History* 49(4): 803–832.

Nugent, Paul 1999. 'Living in the Past: Urban, Rural and Ethnic Themes in the 1992 and 1996 elections in Ghana.' *Journal of Modern African Studies* 37(2): 287–319.

Nugent, Paul 1995. *Big Men, Small Boys and Politics in Ghana: Power, Ideology and the Burden of History 1982–94*. London: Pinter.

Nyangira, Nicholas 1987. 'Ethnicity, Class and Politics in Kenya,' in *The Political Economy of Kenya*, edited by M.G. Schatzberg. New York: Praeger, pp. 15–32.

O'Brien, F. and T. Ryan 2001. 'Kenya,' in *Aid and Reform in Africa*, edited by S. Devarajan, D. Dollar and T. Holmgren. Washington, DC: World Bank, pp. 469–532.

OECD 2013. *Building Tax Culture, Compliance and Citizenship: A Global Source Book on Taxpayer Education*. Paris: OECD.

OECD 2010. *Citizen-State Relations: Improving Governance Through Tax Reform*. Paris: OECD.

OECD 2009. *Do No Harm: International Support for State Building*. Paris: OECD.

OECD 2008. *Governance, Taxation and Accountability: Issues and Practices*. Paris: OECD.

Olson, Mancur 1993. 'Dictatorship, Democracy and Development.' *American Political Science Review* 87(3): 567–576.

Olson, Mancur 1965. *The Logic of Collective Action: Public Goods and the Theory of Groups*. Cambridge: Harvard University Press.

Osei, Philip 2000. 'Political Liberalisation and the Implementation of Value Added Tax in Ghana.' *Journal of Modern African Studies* 38(2): 255–278.

Osei, Robert and Peter Quartey 2005. 'Tax Reforms in Ghana.' *UNU-WIDER Research Paper No. 2005/66*. Geneva: UNU-WIDER.

Ottaway, Marina 1990. 'Introduction: The Crisis of the Ethiopian State and Economy,' in *The Political Economy of Ethiopia*, edited by M. Ottaway. New York: Praeger, pp. 1–10.

Owuor, V. and Wisor, S. 2014. 'The Role of Kenya's Private Sector in Peacebuilding: The Case of the 2013 Election Cycle.' *One Earth Future Research Report*. Broomfield, CO: One Earth Future.

Palan, Ronen, Richard Murphy and Christian Chavagneux 2010. *Tax Havens: How Globalization Really Works*. Ithaca, NY: Cornell University Press.

Paler, Laura 2013. 'Keeping the Public Purse: An Experiment in Windfalls, Taxes, and the Incentives to Restrain Government.' *American Political Science Review* 107(4): 706–725.

Pastoralist Communication Initiative 2006. *Peace, Trade and Unity: Reporting from the Horn of Africa Regional Pastoralist Gathering.* Addis Ababa: UN OCHA-PCI.

Pastoralist Communication Initiative 2005. *Rain, Prosperity and Peace: Reporting from the Global Pastoralist Gathering.* Addis Ababa: UN OCHA-PCI.

Pesaran, M. Hashem and Smith, Ron 1995. 'Estimating Long-Run Relationships from Dynamic Heterogeneous Panels.' *Journal of Econometrics* 68(1): 79–113.

Picciotto, Sol 2013. *'Is the International Tax System Fit for Purpose, Particularly for Developing Countries?' ICTD Working Paper* 13. Brighton: International Centre for Tax and Development.

Prichard, W., Cobham, A. and Goodall, A. 2014. 'The ICTD Government Revenue Dataset.' *IDS Working Paper* 19. Brighton: Institute of Development Studies.

Prichard, Wilson 2010. 'Taxation and State Building: Towards a Governance Focused Tax Reform Agenda.' *IDS Working Paper* 341. Brighton: Institute of Development Studies.

Prichard, Wilson 2009. 'The Politics of Taxation and Implications for Accountability in Ghana 1981–2008.' *IDS Working Paper* 330. Brighton: Institute of Development Studies.

Prichard, Wilson 2007. 'The Role of IGAD in Shaping Livestock Policy in the Horn of Africa: Understanding the International System, International Actors and Implications for Reform.' *IGAD Livestock Policy Initiative Working Paper.* Addis Ababa: IGAD.

Prichard, Wilson and Isaac Bentum 2009. *Taxation and Development in Ghana: Finance, Equity and Accountability.* London: Tax Justice Network.

Prichard, Wilson, Jean-Francois Brun and Oliver Morrissey 2012. 'Donors, Aid and Taxation in Developing Countries: An Overview.' *ICTD Working Paper* 6. Brighton: International Centre for Tax and Development.

Prichard, Wilson and Samuel Jibao 2013. 'Rebuilding Local Government Finance After Conflict: The Political Economy of Property Tax Reform in Post-Conflict Sierra Leone.' *ICTD Working Paper* 12. Brighton: International Centre for Tax and Development.

Prichard, Wilson and David Leonard 2010. 'Does Reliance on Tax Revenue Build State Capacity in Africa?' *International Review of Administrative Sciences* 76(4): 653–675.

Prichard, Wilson, Paola Salardi, and Paul Segal 2014. 'Taxation, Non-Tax Revenue and Democracy: New Evidence Using New Cross-Country Data.' *ICTD Working Paper* 23. Brighton: Institute of Development Studies.

Ramsay, K. 2011. 'Revisiting the Resource Curse: Natural Disasters, the Price of Oil and Democracy.' *International Organization* 65(3): 507–529.

Roodman, David 2006. 'How to Do xtabond2: An Introduction to "Difference" and "System" GMM in Stata.' *Center for Global Development Working Paper Number* 103. Washington, DC: Center for Global Development.

Ross, Michael 2014. *What Have We Learned About the Resource Curse?* Los Angeles: UCLA Department of Political Science.

References

Ross, Michael 2012. *The Oil Curse: How Petroleum Wealth Shapes the Development of Nations*. Princeton: Princeton University Press.
Ross, Michael 2009. *Oil and Democracy Revisited*. Los Angeles: UCLA Department of Political Science.
Ross, Michael 2004. 'Does Taxation Lead to Representation?' *British Journal of Political Science* 34: 229–249.
Ross, Michael 2001. 'Does Oil Hinder Democracy?' *World Politics* 53: 325–361.
Sanchez, Omar 2006. 'Tax Systems Reform in Latin America: Domestic and International Causes.' *Review of International Political Economy* 13(5): 772–801.
Schedler, Andreas 1999. 'Conceptualizing Accountability,' *The Self-Restraining State: Power and Accountability in New Democracies*, edited by A. Schedler, L. Diamond and M.F. Plattner. Boulder: Lynne Rienner Publishers, pp. 13–28.
Schneider, A. 2012. *State Building and Tax Regimes in Central America*. Cambridge: Cambridge University Press.
Scholz, John and Mark Lubell 1998. 'Adaptive Political Attitudes: Duty, Trust and Fear as Monitors of Tax Policy.' *American Journal of Political Science* 42(3): 903–920.
Schumpeter, Joseph 1991[1918]. 'The Crisis of the Tax State,' in *Joseph A. Schumpeter. The Economic and Sociology of Capitalism*, edited by R.A. Swedberg. Princeton: Princeton University Press, pp. 99–140.
Schwab, Peter 1972. *Decision-Making in Ethiopia: A Study of the Political Process*. London: C. Hurst and Company.
Scott, James 1985. *Weapons of the Weak: Everyday Forms of Peasant Resistance*. New Haven: Yale University Press.
Scott, James C. 1987. 'How Peasants Rebel: Resistance without Protest and without Organization: Peasant Opposition to the Islamic Zakat and the Christian Tithe.' *Comparative Studies in Society and History* 29(3): 417–452.
Simensen, Jarle 1974. 'Rural Mass Action in the Context of Anti-Colonial Protest: The Asafo Movement of Akim Abuakwa, Ghana.' *Canadian Journal of African Studies* 8(1): 25–41.
Skocpol, Theda 1992. *Protecting Soldiers and Mothers: The Political Origins of Social Policy in the United States*. Cambridge, MA: Harvard University Press.
Slater, Dan 2010. *Ordering Power: Contentious Politics and Authoritarian Leviathans in Southeast Asia*. Cambridge: Cambridge University Press.
Smith, B. 2007. *Hard Times in the Land of Plenty: Oil Politics in Iran and Indonesia*. Ithaca, NY: Cornell University Press.
Smith, B. 2004. 'Oil Wealth and Regime Survival in the Developing World, 1960-99.' *American Journal of Political Science* 48(2): 232–246.
Snyder, Richard and Ravi Bhavnani 2005. 'Diamonds, Blood and Taxes: A Revenue-Centered Framework for Explaining Political Order.' *The Journal of Conflict Resolution* 49(4): 563–597.
Soliman, S. 2011. *The Autumn of Dictatorship: Fiscal Crisis and Political Change in Egypt under Mubarak*. Stanford: Stanford University Press.
Southall, Roger 1999. 'Re-forming the State: Kleptocracy and the Political Transformation in Kenya.' *Review of African Political Economy* 26(79): 93–108.

Ssewakiryanga, Richard 2004. 'Revenue Realities: Citizen Engagement and Local Government Fiscal Processes in Uganda.' LOGP Link Conference on Resources, Citizens and Democratic Local Governance, 5–9 December 2004. Porto Alegre, Brazil.

Stryker, Dirk, Emmanuel Dumeau, Jennifer Wohl, Peter Haymond, Andrew Cook and Katherine Coon 1990. *Trade, Exchange Rate and Agricultural Pricing Policies in Ghana*. Washington, DC: World Bank.

Tareke, Gebru 1991. *Ethiopia: Power and Protest*. Cambridge: Cambridge University Press.

Teffera, Arega Hailu 2004. 'Assessment of the Value Added Tax Implementation in Ethiopia.' Presented at the *Second International Conference on the Ethiopian Economy*. Addis Ababa.

Tekle, Amare 1990. 'Continuity and Change in Ethiopian Politics,' in *The Political Economy of Ethiopia*, edited by M. Ottaway. New York: Preager Publishers, pp. 31–52.

Terkper, Seth 1998. *Ghana: Tax Administration Reforms (1985–1993)*. Cambridge, MA: International Tax Program, Harvard University.

Therkildsen, O. 2012. 'Democratisation in Tanzania: No Taxation without Exemptions.' Paper presented at the Meeting of the American Political Science Association, New Orleans.

Throup, David and Charles Hornsby 1998. *Multi-Party Politics in Kenya*. Oxford: James Currey.

Tilly, Charles 2007. *Extraction and Democracy*. New York: Columbia University.

Tilly, Charles 1992. *Coercion, Capital and European States: AD 990–1992*. Oxford: Blackwell Publishers.

Tilly, Charles 1975. 'Reflections on the History of European State-Making,' in *The Formation of National States in Western Europe*, edited by C. Tilly. Princeton: Princeton University Press.

Timmons, Jeffrey 2005. 'The Fiscal Contract: States, Taxes and Public Services.' *World Politics* 57: 530–567.

Torgler, Benno 2005. 'Tax Morale in Latin America.' *Public Choice* 122: 133–157.

Torvik, R. 2009. 'Why Do Some Resource Abundant Countries Succeed While Others Do Not?' *Oxford Review of Economic Policy* 25(2): 241–256.

Tsui, K. 2010. 'More Oil, Less Democracy? Theory and Evidence from Crude Oil Discoveries.' *Economic Journal* 121(551): 89–115.

van der Ploeg, F. 2011. 'Natural Resources: Curse or Blessing?' *Journal of Economic Literature* 49(2): 366–420.

van de Walle, Dirk 1998. *Libya since Independence: Oil and State Building*. Ithaca: Cornell University Press.

Vaughn, S. and Gebremichael, M. 2011. 'Rethinking Business and Politics in Ethiopia: The Role of EFFORT, the Endowment Fund for the Rehabilitation of Tigray.' *Africa Power and Politics Research Report 02*. Overseas Development Institute, London, UK: Africa Power and Politics Programme.

Vijverberg, W. 2011. *Testing for IIA with the Hausman-McFadden Test IZA Discussion Paper No. 5826.* Bonn: Institute for the Study of Labor Law.

Wantchekon, Leonard 2002. 'Why Do Resource Dependent Countries Have Authoritarian Governments?' *Journal of African Finance and Economic Development* 2: 57–77.

Waris, Attiya 2008. 'Taxation Without Principles: A Historical Analysis of the Kenyan Taxation System.' *Kenya Law Review* 272.

Warner, James M., Fantahun Beyede, Kagnew Asaminew and Bahita Sibhatu 2005. 'Estimating the Revenue Potential for the Amhara National Regional State.' *Decentralization Support Activity Project Outside Report* 44. Addis Ababa: DSA Project, Ministry of Finance.

Warner, James M., Degela Ergano, Asrat Bekele and Sewagegn Moges 2005. 'Estimating the Current Revenue Potential for the SNNPR.' *Decentralization Support Activity Project Outside Report* 45. Addis Ababa: DSA Project, Ministry of Finance.

Wasike, Wilson 2001. 'Road Infrastructure Policies in Kenya: Historical Trends and Current Challenges.' *KIPPRA Working Paper* 1. Nairobi: KIPPRA.

Webb, Patrick, Joachim von Braun and Yisehac Yohannes 1992. 'Famine in Ethiopia: Policy Implications of Coping Failure at National and Household Levels.' *IFPRI Research Report* 92. Washington, DC: International Food Policy Research Institute.

Weyland, Kurt 1997. '"Growth with Equity" in Chile's New Democracy?' *Latin American Research Review* 32(1): 37–67.

Whitehead, Laurence and George Gray-Molina 2003. 'Political Capabilities over the Long Run,' in *Changing Paths: International Development and the New Politics of Inclusion*, edited by P. Houtzager and M. Moore. Ann Arbor: University of Michigan Press, pp. 32–57.

Widner, Jennifer 1993. 'The Discovery of "Politics": Smallholder Responses to the Cocoa Crisis of 1988–90 in Cote D'Ivoire,' in *Hemmed In: Responses to Africa's Economic Decline*, edited by T. Callaghy and J. Ravenhill. New York: Columbia University Press, pp. 279–331.

Wiens, D., Paul Poast and William Roberts Clark 2014. 'The Political Resource Curse: An Empirical Re-Evaluation.' *Political Research Quarterly* 67(4): 783–794.

World Bank 2009. *Toward the Competitive Frontier: Strategies for Improving Ethiopia's Investment Climate*. Washington, DC: World Bank.

Yates, D. 1996. *The Rentier State in Africa: Oil Rent Dependency and Neocolonialism in the Republic of Gabon*. Trenton: Africa World Press.

Yesegat, Wollela 2008. 'Value Added Tax Administration in Ethiopia: A Reflection of Problems.' *eJournal of Tax Research* 6(2): 145–168.

Yirko, Wogene 1994. 'History of the Post-War Ethiopian Fiscal System,' in *Fiscal Decentralization in Ethiopia*, edited by Eshetu Chole. Addis Ababa: Addis Ababa University Press, pp. 19–60.

Young, Crawford 1986. 'Africa's Colonial Legacy,' in *Strategies for African Development*, edited by J. Whitaker and R. Berg. Los Angeles: University of California Press, pp. 25–51.

Young, John 1997. *Peasant Revolution in Ethiopia: The Tigray People's Liberation Front, 1975–1991*. Cambridge: Cambridge University Press.

Zewde, Bahru 2002. *A History of Modern Ethiopia 1855–1991*. 2nd ed. Oxford: James Currey.

Zewde, Bahru 1991. *A History of Modern Ethiopia, 1855–1974*. 1st ed. Oxford: James Currey.

Index

Accra Metropolitan Authority 108
advocacy campaigns 107–08, 142, 145–46, 152, 223
Afrobarometer 25, 146
agriculture and land tax 52, 161, 166–67, 179–80, 188–89, 236
agricultural price controls 164, 166–67, 170, 171–72, 191, 198–99
All Ethiopia Socialist Movement (Meison) 163
Alliance for Change 100, 107, 222
Argentina 26
Association of Ghana Industries (AGI) 108–09, 223
autocracy
 transition between autocracy and democracy 10, 15, 17, 20–21, 46

Bale rebellion 160, 196
Bangladesh 56 n.4
bargaining *see* tax bargaining
Bates, Robert 33, 35, 39, 49, 60, 226, 227 n.1
benefit seeking, narrow 149–50, 232–33, 245, 255
Boston Tea Party 53, 62
Brazil 26, 27 n.20
business associations 29, 70, 223, 231–35, 238, 245, 255–56
 Ethiopia 3, 190, 192, 193, 202–03, 206
 Ghana 104, 108–09, 113
 Kenya 3, 141–44, 150, 152
Business Process Reengineering 182

capital gains tax 124, 136–37, 139, 150, 153
Central America 27 n.20
Centre for Governance and Development (CGD) 145, 222, 235, 236
Chaudhry, Kiren Aziz 25, 27 n.21
Chile 27

China 33 n.27, 207–08, 226
Citizens' Vetting Committees (CVCs) 87
civil society organizations 29, 68, 75, 222, 256
 Ethiopia 190, 208
 Ghana 106–08, 111–16, 234, 243
 Kenya 144–46, 154–55, 235
cocoa production and taxes 86–88, 98
Cocoa Marketing Board (CMB) 86
coercion 7, 8, 25, 78, 239, 263
 early modern Europe 49–51, 54, 69, 74
 Ethiopia 183, 208
 Ghana 98–99
coffee boom and taxes 123, 124, 153, 167, 198
collective action by taxpayers 6–7, 55–63, 68–75, 78–83, 223–24, 230–37, 262–63
 Ethiopia 161–62, 200–05
 Ghana 111–13
 Kenya 146–56, 158
Committee for Joint Action 107–08, 222
Common Correlated Effects version of the Mean Group estimator (CCE-MG) 15, 17, 19, 45, 46
Common Market for Eastern and Southern Africa (COMESA) 131
Communications Tax 96, 102, 238, 240
community development projects 186–87
Constituency Development Funds (CDFs) 134, 257
contextual factors affecting tax bargaining 36–43, 68–77, 81–82, 111–16, 223–47, 264
corporate tax 87–89, 125, 131, 149, 229, 234
country-level research, importance of 24–28, 249
Criminal Libel Act 110
Customs, Excise and Preventive Services (CEPS) 85, 93

debt relief
    Ghana 94–95
democratization 21, 224, 233
    Ethiopia 177–80
    Ghana 40, 91, 99, 100, 230
    Kenya 126, 138
Derg 162–69, 191, 197–98, 202–05, 208, 230, 236
development outcomes 32, 34, 35, 39, 249, 265–66

East Asian developmental states 35, 174
Eastern Europe 51
econometric evidence, cross-country 4, 8–24, 212–23
    sub-national 264
Economic Recovery Program (ERP) 84, 85
Egypt 61
elections 38
    Ethiopia 174, 177–80, 219
    Ghana 1, 90–94, 115, 225–26, 239
    Kenya 124, 126, 128–30, 137, 156–57, 217, 220
Electronic Tax Registers (ETRs) 135, 139, 143, 150, 152, 231, 242
elite groups 27 n.20, 31, 51, 74–75, 227–28, 231–34, 243–46
    Ghana 111–13
    Kenya 136, 149–50, 152
England 50, 51, 53, 68, 70
Eritrea 62, 165, 169, 172–74
Eritrean People's Liberation Front (EPLF) 165, 169, 170
Error Correction Mechanism (ECM) 17, 45–46
Ethiopia
    agricultural and land tax 161, 166–68, 172, 179, 183, 188–89
    barriers to tax bargaining 161, 190–93, 199–208
    business associations 3, 190, 192–93, 202–03
    coercion 183, 208
    collective action by taxpayers 161–62, 200–05
    community development projects 186–87
    democratization 177–80
    elections 174, 177–80, 219
    fiscal crisis 168–69, 198
    foreign aid 161, 169, 170–71, 173–74, 183, 207–08
    political economy of taxation 160–85
    presumptive tax 176, 179, 187–88
    tax bargaining at regional level 162, 185–89, 194–96
    tax resistance and changes in government 160–62, 197–99, 206–08
    value-added tax 175–77, 181
Ethiopian People's Revolutionary Democratic Front (EPRDF) 169–85, 192, 194, 202
Ethiopian People's Revolutionary Party (EPRP) 163
Europe, early modern
    coercion 49–51, 54, 69, 74

Federal Inland Revenue and Customs Authority 182
fiscal crisis 72
    Ethiopia 168–69, 198
    Ghana 84–90
    Kenya 141, 155
"fiscal social contract" 5, 87
fiscal sociology 32, 248, 265
foreign aid 5–8, 37, 72, 226, 266
    aid dependence 6, 37, 135, 141, 207–08, 217
    Ethiopia 161, 169, 170–01, 173–74, 183, 207–08
    Ghana 90, 115
    Kenya 125, 126, 128, 135, 141
    implications for donors 259–61
France 52–53, 54, 58, 60
    Estates General 52, 60
    French Revolution 53, 60
    Third Estate 52–53
Freedom House index 110, 133
fuel prices 220, 222
    Ethiopia 184
    Ghana 88–89, 93, 113, 114, 226, 229, 235, 242
    Kenya 130, 138, 151, 220

Gabay, Nadav 77, 241, 242
Generalized method of moments (GMM) 15, 17, 19, 21, 44–45, 46
Ghana
    absence of tax bargaining 98–99
    associational taxation 105
    business associations 104, 108–09, 113
    cocoa taxes 86, 88, 98
    coercion 98–99
    collective action by taxpayers 99–101, 106–09, 111–13
    Culture of Silence 84
    debt relief 94–95
    democratization 40, 91, 99, 100, 230
    direct tax bargaining 1–2, 99–106
    elections 1, 90–94, 115, 22–26, 239
    fiscal crisis 84–90
    Flat Rate VAT Scheme 104, 106

Index 295

foreign aid 90, 115
fuel taxes 89, 90–91, 93
institutions for tax bargaining 113–14
political economy of taxation 84–97
revenue pressure 85–87, 115–16
tax earmarking 101–04
tax resistance and changes in government 109–11, 115
value-added tax 2, 91–92, 100, 104, 106
Ghana Education Trust (GET) Fund 93, 218, 236, 238
Ghana Private Road Transport Union (GPRTU) 105, 113, 235
Ghana Union of Traders Association (GUTA) 99, 106, 108, 109, 113, 235
Goldenberg Scandal 128, 157
goods and services taxes 122–23, 125, 192, 241–43
Government Revenue Database (GRD) 11, 13
Graduated Personal Tax (GPT) 120, 121
Great Britain 51, 53
  British Parliament 51–53
  Glorious Revolution 52
Gulf War 89

Haber, Stephen 10, 15, 45–46
Highly Indebted Poor Countries (HIPC) 94, 95, 96
history
  legacies of taxation 204–05
  lessons from history 49–54

ideology 49, 163, 164, 172
  Ethiopia 166–67, 171, 175–76, 192
income tax 26, 27 n.20, 73, 77, 229, 234, 241, 253–54
  Ghana 94, 98–99
  Kenya 120–21, 122, 123, 125, 129
Indonesia 24, 57 n.5
institutions
  of accountability 64–67, 75–76, 101, 110, 239, 244
  for tax bargaining 75–76, 83–84, 113–14, 161, 200, 205–06, 237–38
International Centre for Tax and Development (ICTD) 11, 13, 14
International Monetary Fund (IMF) 251, 260
  Article IV reports 12 n.9
  Ethiopia 170, 173
  Ghana 84, 87, 88, 90, 91, 92, 95
  Governance Finance Statistics (GFS) 10
  Kenya 122, 126, 127, 128
Italy 51, 160, 162

Jordan 26

Karen and Langata District Association (KLDA) 144–45, 231, 235
Kazakhstan 19
Kenya
  absence of direct tax bargaining 138–39
  business associations 3, 141–44, 150, 152
  coffee boom and tax 123, 124, 153
  collective action by taxpayers 145–56, 158
  democratization 126, 138
  economic, race and ethnic divisions 119, 120, 151–52
  elections 124, 126, 128–30, 137, 156–57, 217, 220
  fiscal crisis 141, 155
  foreign aid 125, 126, 128, 135, 141
  indirect tax bargaining 140–57
  political economy of taxation 120–37
  political salience of tax debate 148–56, 158
  tax resistance and changes in government 131, 140–42, 156–57
  value-added tax 126–28, 129, 138, 148, 153–54, 155
Kenyan Alliance of Manufacturers 149
Kenya Alliance of Resident Associations (KARA) 145, 235
Kenya Private Sector Association (KEPSA) 144
Kenya Revenue Authority (KRA) 129, 135
Kenyatta, Jomo 121–24, 126, 140
Kibaki, Mwai 123–24, 133
kume preko protests 100, 113, 114, 125, 149, 222, 245
Kuwait 25

land reform 163–64, 167, 168
Large Taxpayers Unit (LTU) 93
Latin America 72
Levi, Margaret 39, 49, 56, 69, 75, 76, 149, 217, 226, 232, 237, 238, 245
Lien, Da-Hsiang 39, 49, 226, 227 n.
local government taxation 25, 26, 121, 145, 254, 263

Malaysia 61
Martin, Isaac 34, 72, 241, 242
Mauritius 26
Menaldo, Victor 10, 15, 45–46
mobilization
  political 25, 53–54, 56, 57, 68, 77, 80, 120, 138, 230, 234

model for tax bargaining 54–83, 213–14
  historical models of tax bargaining
    49–54
Moi, Daniel Arap 119, 123–26, 128,
  130–31, 132, 140–41, 143, 245
Moore, Mick 7, 40, 41, 49, 57, 58, 69, 74,
  77, 209, 227, 237, 238, 276
Morrison, Kevin 10, 19, 21

Nairobi Informal Sector Confederation
  (NISCOF) 143–44
National Democratic Congress (NDC) 96,
  97, 105, 109, 116
National Health Insurance Levy (NHIL)
  96, 103, 110
National Health Insurance Scheme
  (NHIS) 96, 101, 103
National Patriotic Party (NPP) 90, 91, 94,
  95, 96, 106, 107, 110–11
National Rainbow Coalition (NARC)
  133
National Reconstruction Levy (NRL) 94,
  96, 110
National Revenue Secretariat (NRS) 85,
  89, 90
National Taxpayers' Association (NTA)
  145, 222
nested-analysis, model of 36
Nigeria 19, 25, 262 n.
North Kavirondo Taxpayers Association
  120

openness, political 148, 230–31
Organization for Economic Co-operation
  and Development (OECD) 251

pastoralists, taxation of 160, 195, 196, 210
patronage 8, 21, 72, 120, 123, 131, 141
Peasant Associations (PA) 163–64
peasantry 51, 163–64, 166, 168, 171–72,
  189, 191, 198
Poland 26, 191
political economy of taxation
  Ethiopia 160–85
  Ghana 84–97
  Kenya 120–37
political goodwill 94–95, 107, 110, 136,
  153, 192
"political resource curse" 5, 10, 32, 37,
  265
political salience of taxation 31, 76–77, 81,
  224, 241–46, 252, 253–54
  Ghana 114, 116
  Kenya 120, 148–56, 158
Polity IV dataset 13, 14

"polity approach" 75
poll tax 8 n.6, 120
presumptive tax 176, 179, 180 n.39,
  187–88, 194, 219, 229
Prichard, Wilson 11, 17, 43–47
Private Enterprise Foundation 108
private sector strength 74, 202–04, 227–28
property tax 145, 236, 241, 254
Provincial National Defence Council
  (PNDC) 84–88, 90, 99, 111

Qatar 25

Rawlings, Jerry 1, 84–90, 95
repression, government 12, 30, 60, 70, 72,
  219, 221, 230–31, 243–46
  Ethiopia 177, 184, 188, 191, 200–01,
    209
  Ghana 98–99, 111, 113
  Kenya 120, 148, 153, 156
Results Based Management 133
revenue
  natural resource 8, 10–13, 19, 32, 225,
    259
  non-tax 5–17, 25, 69, 71–72, 127, 185,
    186, 197, 225
revenue pressure 4, 30, 70–73, 80, 81,
  224–26, 244, 252, 262
  Ethiopia 161, 173, 200
  Ghana 111, 115–16
  Kenya 148, 156–57
Road Funds 102
Road Maintenance Levy (RML) 130
road tolls 130, 155
Ross, Michael 9, 30, 44, 45, 59
Russia 26, 51, 173, 191

Salardi, Paola 11, 17, 43–47
sales tax 73, 85, 88, 91, 108, 122–23, 127,
  175
Saudi Arabia 25
Scandinavia 51
Scott, James 61
Segal, Paul 11, 17, 43–47
Selassie, Emperor Haile 161, 162, 187,
  188, 189
Senegal 19
Somaliland 36
South Africa 27 n.20
Southeast Asia 27 n.20, 35
Soviet Union 33 n.27, 161, 165, 169,
  197
stabilization of regime 10, 123–24
state capacity 33, 34, 35, 73, 87, 200, 239,
  265

Index

state formation 29 n.22, 33, 256
state-owned enterprises (SOEs) 167, 169, 191, 197–98, 202, 203, 228
states
 resource-dependent 5, 15 n.12, 19, 25, 32, 249
 resource-rich 10, 248, 262
structural adjustment programs
 Ethiopia 170–72
 Ghana 84, 85
 Kenya 126–29
structural factors 69–70, 78, 223–46

Tanzania 26, 240
Tax Assessment Committees, 176, 194, 195, 206, 219
tax bargaining 1–8, 31–34, 54–62, 68–77, 97–111, 212–47, 249–51
 absence of 98–99
 barriers 199–207
 contextual factors 223–46
 institutions for tax bargaining 75–76, 237–40
 sub-national level 194–96
 see also model for tax bargaining
tax compliance 140–42, 197–99
 quasi-voluntary compliance 4, 49, 55, 56, 227, 229
tax earmarking 101–04, 240, 257–58
Tax Modernization Program (TMP) 129
tax reform 140–42, 174–77, 187–88, 197–99, 228–29
tax resistance and changes in government 55–62, 73–74, 80–81, 219–22, 226–29
 Ethiopia 160–62, 197–99, 206–08
 Ghana 109–11, 115
 Kenya 131, 140–42, 156–57
tax system 228–29, 254–55

Taxpayer Identification Number (TIN) 174
taxpayer capabilities for collective action 6–7, 55–63, 68–75, 78–83, 223–24, 230–37, 262–63
 Ethiopia 161–62, 200–05
 Ghana 111–13
taxpayer expectations 236–37
taxpayer interests 148–53
Tea Act 53
Tigray People's Liberation Front (TPLF) 155, 168, 169, 170, 174, 185, 186, 187
Tilly, Charles 50, 51, 54, 55 n.2, 69, 74, 227
time horizons, political 238–39
transparency 256–58
trust 239–40

Uganda 24
United Business Association 3, 223, 231, 235
United States 54, 58, 242
 American Revolution 51, 53–54

value-added tax (VAT) 2, 218, 234
 Ethiopia 175–77, 181
 Ghana 2, 91–92, 100, 104, 106
 Kenya 126–28, 129, 138, 148, 153–54, 155
VAT Service 106
Vehicle Income Tax 105

We Can Do It campaign 145
World Bank 84, 87, 88, 90, 127, 170

Yemen 25
Youth Employment Scheme (YES) 97

Zambia 26

For EU product safety concerns, contact us at Calle de José Abascal, 56–1°,
28003 Madrid, Spain or eugpsr@cambridge.org.

www.ingramcontent.com/pod-product-compliance
Ingram Content Group UK Ltd.
Pitfield, Milton Keynes, MK11 3LW, UK
UKHW020453090825
461507UK00007B/217